Sociology in context

Printer's error

Please note that the bottom line of text on page 88 should be transposed to the bottom of page 89.

Sociology in context

Jack Nobbs BSc(Econ), **Dip. Soc.**

Formerly Senior Tutor and Head of Economics and Sociology
Department, Hewett Comprehensive School, Norwich

Macmillan Education
London and Basingstoke

First published 1983

Published by
MACMILLAN EDUCATION LIMITED
Houndmills Basingstoke Hampshire RG21 2XS
and London
Associated companies throughout the world

Printed in Hong Kong

British Library Cataloguing in Publication Data

Nobbs, Jack
  Sociology in context.
  1. Sociology
  I. Title
  301 (expanded)   HM66

  ISBN 0-333-34107-4
  ISBN 0-333-27298-6   Pbk

CONTENTS

LIST OF FIGURES

LIST OF TABLES

Preface

This book aims to provide a systematic introduction to sociology for students of both sociology as an 'A' level in colleges of further education and school sixth forms, and also for students studying sociology as a component of other courses at an equivalent level. An earnest attempt has been made to avoid the pitfalls of unnecessary use of technical language or jargon on one hand, and of a patronising 'talking down' on the other. Many sociology texts at present used in F.E. colleges and schools suffer from being written by academics who are largely without practical teaching experience in these areas.

This new sociology textbook reflects the growing emphasis placed by GCE Boards on the sociology of knowledge, i.e. the way in which knowledge is shaped according to the ideology of the student and researcher. The subject matter is therefore considered in the context of the main sociological perspectives. Consequently, from the beginning, emphasis is placed upon sociological theories and methods and the various perspectives are traced through the various subject areas.

It is intended that this book will:

(1) make for an easy transition from GCE 'O' to 'A' level;

(2) present the main sociological perspectives in a clear way and relate the various approaches to the main topics covered by the new 'A' level syllabuses;

(3) provide a readable and understandable account suitable for the 'A' level and equivalent student;

(4) supply a wide range of examples, figures and tables to expedite comprehension and learning.

Finally, the author wishes to thank all those who have contributed to his interest in sociology. No plagiarism is intended, but there are no new ideas under the sun and after years of study it is impossible to say where one's ideas come from in the first place. Gratitude is extended to many friends in the Association for the Teaching of the Social Sciences and to those who guided me whilst reading for the post-graduate diploma in sociology at the University of East Anglia – these include Michael Ashley, Rosemary Crompton, Martin Davies, John Donnelly, Gary Easthope, Roy Emmerson, Graham Fennell, Robert Groves, Jon Gubay, Bryan Heading, Gareth Jones, Philip Lawrence, Margot Russell, Mary Sykes and David Woodland. A very special note of appreciation must be extended to Robert Groves who acted as my adviser while at the university and as my mentor during the three years in which the book was being written. This book would not have been possible without the invaluable help and guidance of my editor, Penny Farrant. While acknowledging all those who guided my thoughts and writing, I hasten to add that any mistakes are my own.

Jack Nobbs

The author and publishers acknowledge, with thanks, the following photograph sources:

David Austen figure 1.5
British Museum Newspaper Library figure 4.6
Daily Mirror/Sun figure 4.7
Richard & Sally Greenhill figure 3.8
House of Holland figure 2.2 (1)
Eric Hosking figure 1.6
David Howe figure 2.9
Ron Chapman figure 6.9
Punch figure 1.1
Syndication International figure 1.2
VAG (UK) Ltd figure 2.2 (1)
Volvo figure 5.5A
Extract from the 1981 Census Form for England (OPCS) reproduced with the permission of H.M.S.O. figure 1.11

The publishers have made every effort to trace copyright holders, but if they have inadvertently overlooked any they will be pleased to make the necessary arrangement at the first opportunity.

ONE
The nature of sociology

1.1 What sociology is about

● *Is sociology just common sense?*

Sociology is frequently viewed with suspicion by people who claim that 'sociology is what everybody knows already'. There is a measure of truth in this criticism; the student of sociology can indeed take heart from the fact that he already knows some sociology. As a member of society he has inherited values, beliefs and attitudes. He has taken part in social interaction with friends and foes. His awareness of the likenesses and differences between people has given him insights into the subject.

> But they do not, of course, make him a sociologist, any more than a walk through the forest makes him a botanist, or a visit to the zoo a zoologist.
> (Bierstedt, R. *The Social Order*)

The sociologist does not merely observe the activities of people in society; he analyses, evaluates and offers explanations. For example, it has long been accepted that if 'a dog is given a bad name' he will be blamed for a large number of things. Everybody knows this, but a study of sociological labelling theory (Howard S.Becker) and of 'self-fulfilling prophecies' (Robert Merton) gives a far deeper realisation of *why* certain people continue to display social behavioural patterns generally considered as anti-social. Their behaviour is influenced by those who label them. If people are categorised as vandals or layabouts or disruptives, they are likely to live up to those labels.

> The sociologist does not look at phenomena that nobody else is aware of. But he looks at the same phenomena in a different way...
> (Berger, P. *Invitation to Sociology*)

A serious difficulty encountered by students is that sociologists often do not agree among themselves. While acknowledging that there are controversial issues in all disciplines, and that some physicists disagree about such fundamentals as the creation of the universe (supporting the big-bang or continuous creation theories), nevertheless

> ... the disagreement among sociologists probably far exceeds that which would probably be found in any of the natural sciences.
> (Inkeles, A. *What is Sociology?*)

Some students are intrigued by different sociological perspectives or viewpoints; they find such a provocative subject more enthralling than some other subjects where so much is cut and dried and where a large body of knowledge is accepted as beyond dispute. Other students are frankly puzzled by the controversies which rage within sociology. For their benefit Table 1.1 outlines some of the principal reasons for disagreement among sociologists.

Table 1.1 Reasons for disagreement among sociologists

1 Sociology is a comparatively new study and consequently changes in viewpoint are inevitable as knowledge widens.
2 The discipline has developed in different ways in different societies, because the societies themselves differ.
3 The traditional school of sociologists attempted to establish sociological laws ('grand theory'), but the modernists see little value in a rigorous scientific approach and prefer to concentrate upon social interaction ('empiricism', i.e. observed evidence).
4 Some argue that sociology should always attempt to be objective and 'value-neutral', whereas others are convinced that it is impossible for the sociologist not to become personally involved. (Can one study the deprived poor without feeling sympathy for them?)
5 Sociologists study people in society, but in analysing society they are influenced by their own backgrounds and changed by the events they are analysing. Such infinite regression means that sociological analysis proceeds with humility and reaches no final conclusions.
6 Students of society are caught up in controversial historical arguments (e.g. between types of governments, capitalism, socialism, etc.).

It is as well to have an understanding of the different outlooks, within sociology, from the beginning of our studies.

> ... there is no basic agreement among sociologists in different societies with different social structures, and even within societies, and ... they so often try to hide or play down or 'leave until later' this uncomfortable fact.
> (Coulson, M.A. and Riddell, D.S. *Approaching Society*)

It is inevitable that sociology will have its critics (Fig. 1.1). Students of sociology who become more aware of the inadequacies and problems of society are bound to be regarded as dangerous rebels by those who accept

Fig. 1.1 Sociology has its critics
(*Punch* 27 September 1978)

the status quo. Nevertheless, only a fool would claim that all is well with modern society. A reminder of the plight of a world where a third of the population suffers from malnutrition, and where people are compelled to live out their lives before a terrifying cyclorama cloth of nuclear destruction, should be sufficient proof of the worthwhileness of the study of sociology. Man possesses but a thin veneer of civilisation. If as much money and resources had been spent upon humanistic studies as upon technological advances one might be more optimistic about the future of human society. The sociologist is vitally concerned with ways by which man is taught to live in the society in which he is born, and the ways in which he is able to change that society.

- *Macro-sociology – the founding fathers*

As with many other disciplines sociology started its life as part of philosophy. Sociology thus began as a macro-study: social philosophy was concerned with searching for knowledge about all the phenomena of social life. Even after Auguste Comte (1798–1857) had launched sociology on a separate path, sociologists were still preoccupied with large issues.

Comte gave sociology its modern name and concluded that it was a *positive* human science (Positivism). He divided sociology into two broad areas.

(a) *Social Statics* was focused upon the *principal institutions of society*, e.g. family, economy, polity.

(b) *social dynamics* was concerned with *whole societies*.

Herbert Spencer (1820–1903) followed Comte in listing the main areas of sociological analysis as the family, political organisation, ecclesiastical structure, a system of restraints (social control) and industry. He stressed the importance of analysing the *whole structure* of society and the *functions* of the various parts.

Emile Durkheim (1858–1917) went further by calling sociology 'the science of societies'. He accepted Comte's emphasis that the *whole* society is greater than the individuals who comprise it. He argued that there were social facts 'out there' waiting to be discovered by sociologists. His model of man was a passive one: man accepted the values of the group or larger society and therefore his behaviour could be largely predicted. Durkheim was an advocate of *comparative sociology* whereby different societies and their institutions are compared and contrasted. He followed Comte and Spencer in stressing the need to analyse the relationships between the different large institutions which make up the structure of society. He defined sociology as 'the science of institutions' (Durkheim, E. *The Rules of Sociological Method*).

The powerful influence of Karl Marx (1818–1895) extended to economics, history and politics, as well as to sociology. His study of comparative sociology (e.g. feudal society and capitalist society) led to a determination to change things – to turn the social world upside down. Revolutionary Marxism is based upon Marx's macro-study of critical conflicts between the two main classes in society. His advocacy of radical social change was based upon his conviction that opposing social classes exist in every society. A fundamental improvement in society could only come about by the development of

> ... a science of society on the basis of which men could first understand and then deliberately change and improve the nature of social order.
> (Jordan, Z.A., ed., *Karl Marx*)

The last of the founding fathers of sociology, Max Weber (1864–1920) also regarded sociology as the science concerned with the analysis of institutions. Weber concentrated especially upon economic institutions, city communities, large bureaucratic organisations, political parties and religious bodies.

If the subject matter of sociology is delimited according to the historical work of the founding fathers, the major emphasis must be placed upon 'macro' rather than 'micro' sociology. Comte's work was undertaken at a time of great disruption of society. Durkheim and Marx were also influenced by the enormous changes in society associated with the industrial revolution including extensive use of the division of labour and the development of large towns with associated urban problems.

Macro-sociology is *positivistic*, i.e. it is characterised by the underlying belief that sociology is a positive and objective science comparable with all other sciences including the natural sciences. Until the late 1960s most sociologists would have followed the founding fathers in accepting the 'macro' positivist nature of sociology. Society was regarded as far more important than the individual. Society governed man's conduct and controlled his thinking. The idea of *society in man* was based on the belief that society was greater than man. However, during the last two decades, the emphasis has shifted to micro-sociology.

- *Micro-sociology – modern trends*

Alfred Whitehead has suggested that a sign of maturity for an academic discipline is when its exponents forget its ancestors. Physicists do not base their studies upon the findings of a few great physicists, but sociologists have been criticised for excessive preoccupation with principles laid down by Comte, Spencer, Durkheim, Marx and Weber. It is not suggested here that macro-sociology is a futile study, but with the extension of micro-sociology, the subject seems at last to be coming of age.

Micro-sociology centres upon the individual rather than upon society. It is based upon the interpretive and analytical study of inter-relationships between people: *man in society* interacts with social objects. Man, as a *social actor*, interprets social objects according to the particular meaning which he gives to them. In accordance with what George Herbert Mead (1863–1931) termed **symbolic interactionism**, a dog may be regarded by different people as a pet, an Arctic beast of burden or a house guard. Similarly, different individuals will regard a cow as a supplier of milk or a sacred object (see Table 1.2).

Table 1.2 Examples of interactionism

Object $\longrightarrow$	Meaning $\longrightarrow$	Interpretation
dog $\longrightarrow$	houseguard $\longrightarrow$	may bite
cow $\longrightarrow$	sacred $\longrightarrow$	treat as religious symbol
flag $\longrightarrow$	national emblem $\longrightarrow$	should respect

The most significant form of symbolic interactionism takes place when two people (a dyad) are involved in a *social act*.

> A common fate or enterprise, an agreement or secret between two persons, ties each of them in a very different manner than if even only three have a part in it.
> (Simmel, G. *The Dyad and the Triad*, in Thompson, K. and Tunstall, J. *Sociological Perspectives*)

Social interaction and reaction takes place. One person's behaviour towards the other, is a response to the other person's behaviour towards him. The two may go on interpreting and responding to each other's behaviour even though one may impute to the other's behaviour a meaning not intended. For example, a teacher may punish a pupil because the teacher wrongly interprets the pupil's behaviour as impertinence; the pupil may then react by intentionally behaving in an impertinent way in accordance with Merton's ideas of self-fulfilling prophecies.

> ...so in imagination, we perceive in another's mind some thought of our appearance, manners, aims, deeds, character, friends, and so on, and are variously affected by it.
> (Cooley, C.H. *Self as Sentiment and Reflection*)

The modern school of micro-sociology considers everyday explanations of social behaviour and analyses them so that their meanings are given a deeper significance. Garfinkel, H. (*Studies in Ethnomethodology*) analysed how people attempted to make sense of a variety of unusual situations. Erving Goffman has proved his genius by using a dramaturgical approach by which he shrewdly describes social encounters in theatrical terms. All the world is a stage and as social actors we play many parts. The essence of micro-sociology is to put yourself in the place of others and to see their point of view.

Mead, Cooley, Cicourel, Garfinkel and Goffman may be considered as some of the founding fathers of micro-sociology. They have provided a fresh approach to sociological research. Micro-sociologists believe that sociology is very different from the natural sciences which are concerned with studying material things (such as chemicals or rocks) in a positive manner. Micro-sociologists concentrate upon interpretive sociology and in analysing inter-relationships of individual people who make up society rather than in studying society as a whole. They realise that they themselves are restricted by pre-conceived biases and prejudices, but they endeavour to minimise their value-judgements; they appreciate that the very act of studying individuals will bring about a change in the individuals themselves, and also upon those studying them. Thus David Sudnow ('Dead on Arrival', *New Society*, 8 February 1968) avoided entering hospitals to investigate the 'dying' as he conceived them, but analysed descriptions provided by hospital staff who were involved in treating the dying. Micro-sociology takes account of the social interpretations of everyday social actors. The meaning of the simplest social events cannot be taken at their face value: all human relationships are capable of further analysis.

Table 1.3 Macro- and micro-sociology

MACRO (social structure)	MICRO (social action)
1 Concentrates upon societies and their major institutions.	1 Concentrates upon individuals' interactions
2 Positivistic: sociology is a science with its own universal laws.	2 Non-positivistic: sociology is interpretive and not comparable with physical sciences.
3 Sociology is the study of Society in Man (society is greater than the individuals who compose it). Society makes man.	3 Sociology is the study of Man in Society and centres upon social actionism. Man makes society.
4 Established by Comte and the founding fathers.	4 Stressed by G.H. Mead and by modern sociologists.
5 Objective research techniques give a scientific meaning to social facts.	5 Interprets situations in order to give meaning to those situations.

1.2 Sociological concepts

● *What are concepts?*

Concepts are abstract ideas which nevertheless relate to the real world. We are all familiar, in everyday speech, with notions of justice, honour, or sympathy. Natural scientists use concepts such as pressure and temperature; we all know what is meant by high or low temperature and degrees of heat and cold. Similarly, sociologists use concepts such as socialisation, social class, norm, culture, institutions, social role and status. Concepts are categories or classifications which provide a way of looking at the world in a more orderly way.

The information explosion of modern times has lessened the importance of learning facts for their own sake. It is preferable to learn basic concepts which will act as guidelines and lead to a fuller understanding and clarification of knowledge.

Concepts are often arbitrary and may be used by different sociologists in different ways. Changing interpretations of concepts are brought about by changing ideas in a changing world. Thus the concept of *poverty* was used in an absolute way by Booth and Rowntree who accepted the yardstick of a certain minimum level of subsistence, but a more modern conception of poverty involves the relative approach of Peter Townsend who argues that being poor is dependent upon not having things which the majority of your contemporaries enjoy.

The reason why different meanings are given to sociological concepts is because they often begin life as new words which are developed in different ways by different thinkers.

> ...few if any of the key words in the humanistic study of man and society do not begin as neologisms....
> (Nisbet, R.A. *The Sociological Tradition*)

Durkheim coined the word *anomie* to refer to an absence of standards (or norms) in people's lives, but other writers have described industrial relations, and even the whole economy, as anomic. Marx considered *alienation* in terms of a worker's separation from nature and his fellow men, whereas Robert Blauner (a modern American sociologist) sees the alienated worker as existing in a powerless and meaningless situation. Ferdinand Tonnies, the German sociologist, uses '*gemeinschaft*' to refer to a local community and '*gesellschaft*' as a national association. When the sociologist talks of an increasing tendency towards *gesellschaft* at the expense of *gemeinschaft*, other sociologists know immediately what is meant. Consider this idea yourself in the light of the counter-attack upon this trend made by Schumaker in *Small is Beautiful*.

Although the general public may be critical of the jargon of sociology,

Table 1.4 The advantages of concepts

1 A complex abstraction is expressed by a relatively simple term which is generally understood, e.g. *social class*.

2 Pairs of concepts illustrate variables, e.g. *conflict* suggests disagreement, whereas *consensus* suggests agreement. (Use sociological reference books to look up primary and secondary groups, community and society, function and dysfunction, conformity and deviance.)

3 Concepts can be 'operationalised', i.e. recognised, acknowledged and to some extent measured, e.g. it is possible to measure *social mobility*, the extent by which people move from one social class to another.

4 Concepts help us to describe society and to develop useful theories and generalisations.
   The two most general functions of theory are the facilitation of description and analysis.
   (Parsons, T. *Essays in Sociological Theory*)

the concepts are useful because they act as a system of shorthand which helps in the description of complex, abstract ideas. Every science has its jargon or technical terms. The main uses of sociological concepts are summarised in Table 1.4.

● *A biography of concepts*

Many sociology textbooks list concepts in alphabetical order. The concepts are thus easily referred to and can be learnt for purposes of revision. However, in this book, a biographical approach is used so that a few essential concepts can be introduced naturally with reference to the lifespan of an individual. It is easy to criticise any order in which concepts are introduced. Indeed, many concepts are inexorably intertwined. Nevertheless some order must be adopted and it is essential that the student gains a knowledge of basic concepts before proceeding further with his or her study of sociology. At this stage, definitions must be relatively simple, but more complex meanings will be discussed later in the book.

Socialisation refers to the process by which an individual learns to become a member of society. Socialisation is a life-long process, beginning with the *primary socialisation* of childhood and continuing as adult or *secondary socialisation*.

Primary socialisation involves the first stages of socialisation by which the infant learns from significant people ('*significant others*') around her. It is they who set the patterns for habits of eating and drinking, toiletry, sleeping and every aspect of the child's life.

We can learn a lot about socialisation by examining some of the cases of children reared by animals. They provide examples of how human individuals can be socialised in strange ways according to their environment. Famous cases which have been well documented include the wild boy of Aveyron in France, the Saharan gazelle boy and the wolf children of Midnapore. The wild boy of Aveyron was found running on all fours and surviving on nuts and berries. The boy in the Sahara was almost completely integrated in the herd, participating in animal sign language and eating the roots of dhanoun which is the survival food of the desert. The Indian wolf children were supposedly found in a wolf's lair by the Reverend J.A.C. Singh in 1920. The eldest of the two girls took three years to learn to stand and in the beginning could eat only on all fours. Even allowing for exaggeration by those who discovered the children, the examples do provide evidence of how human beings can be socialised to almost any environment. They can also be *re-socialised* to a limited degree. The French teacher, Jean-Marc Itard was able to teach 'Victor' (the wild boy of Aveyron) a few words and he died at the age of 40, a friendly and conforming character. In rare cases, it is possible for animals to learn

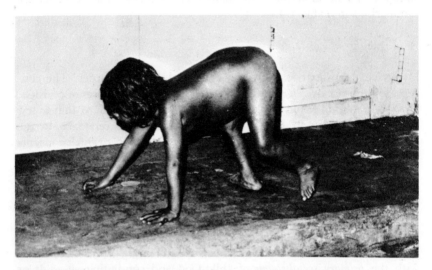

Fig. 1.2 Primary socialisation: a child brought up in the wild

things which do not come instinctively to them. Recent work with dolphins indicates that they have a very considerable learning capacity. Chimpanzees have been taught basic symbol language. Pigeons have been taught to solve certain problems in order to gain food. But despite the obvious ability of animals to learn, the socialisation of animals is strictly limited compared with that of human beings. Man can be socialised to do almost anything because his genetic code does not instinctively compel him to behave in any special way.

Social Class affects socialisation in the same way that it influences every other part of our lives. The patterns of social behaviour learnt by an infant are determined by the social groupings of the adults who influence her most. John and Elizabeth Newson's study of *Patterns of Infant Care in an Urban Community* revealed that attitudes to discipline, behaviour and training differed greatly between *working-class* and *middle-class* parents.

Social classes form a most complex part of *social stratification* and people's positions in the *class structure* are determined by such factors as occupation, income, wealth, housing and education. We shall discuss social class much more fully in the next unit.

Norms are unwritten patterns of behaviour learnt during socialisation. Those who do not conform to these shared behavioural standards may commit acts of *deviancy* and be labelled as *deviants*. If a social norm is completely integrated into a person's self he is said to have **internalised** it, i.e. it has become part of him and he has swallowed it hook, line and sinker.

> . . . the social world, with its multitude of meanings, becomes internalized in the child's own consciousness. What previously was experienced as something outside himself can now be experienced within himself as well.
> (Berger, P.L. and Berger, B. *Sociology: A Biographical Approach*)

Most people accept the norms of their society without question and become so familiar with them that they take them for granted. Changing situations within a particular society may lead to new norms, while norms differ from one society to another. Norms of other societies may appear very strange to us. For example, the Bon-pos of Tibet play musical instruments made from thigh bones of their ancestors. As it proved difficult to bury their dead in iron-hard ground, or to cremate them because of the shortage of trees and brushwood, it was customary to allow vultures to remove the flesh before the body was dismembered by relatives and friends. It seems a repulsive practice to us but it solved a problem of their society, just as the Caribou Indian and Eskimo women helped their particular society to solve the problem of starvation by voluntarily walking out on the ice to commit suicide. There is usually a basic economic and social reason underlying apparently strange norms. If cannibalism occurred in a society it may well have been due to protein deficiency. The ritual cannibalism of the Aztecs of Mexico, who killed sacrificial victims to persuade the sun to rise every morning, has been linked with diet deficiencies. Recent cases of cannibalism by survivors of isolated aircraft crashes may be explained in a similar way. Our norms may change to fit the conditions. Killing fellow-humans in peacetime is regarded as murder, but in wartime it may be regarded as the height of patriotism.

Mores are norms involving moral values which are held to be very important because they concern the way we behave towards each other. Many mores, such as marriage and the belief that we should not kill, are so greatly esteemed in most societies that they are enforced by law. *Folkways* are less important norms and there are not penalties for not complying with them. Examples of folkways, in our own society, include exchanging Christmas cards or shaking hands with friends.

Culture is made up of the norms of society, but extends to all human actions which are socially, as opposed to genetically, transmitted. Culture includes *all* the knowledge and ideas that members of a society have about their society, including all their learnt beliefs and values. Cultural patterns of social organisations are passed on from one generation to another.

The culture of a society is the way of life of its members; the collection of ideas

and habits which they learn, share and transmit from one generation to another.
(Linton, R. 'Present World Conditions in Cultural Perspective' in *The Science of Man in World Crisis*)

During the early years of our life our living and learning is, in the nature of things, most closely associated with our parents and near-relatives. As we grow older we draw more closely towards those of our own age and are inclined to adopt their standards and their cultural behaviour. The essence of culture is not only to *learn*, but also to *share*, life's experiences.

Each society has its own culture with its people having shared norms. Some sociologists would argue that the general acceptance of values is essential to the maintenance of society. Nevertheless within a particular culture there may exist sub-cultures determined by race or sex or age.

For example *peer groups* include those people of similar age and social class with whom a person associates. Peer groups are especially important to adolescents who are likely to pay less attention to their family and wish to influence, and be influenced by, those whom they meet in a close social context. It has been suggested that, in our modern Western society, there is a *youth culture* based on two interlocking ideas:

1 The generation to which one belongs is now as influential as, if not more influential than a person's social class background.

2 The generation consciousness of adolescents is sustained by the symbols and meanings of modern pop music. But although young people may seek to break away from mainstream society, it is difficult to escape from the institutions which are deeply-rooted influences upon our lives.

Institutions are established behavioural patterns which are imposed upon individuals by society. Peter and Brigitte Berger (*Sociology: A Biographical Approach*) argue that language is the first institution with which we are confronted. Language makes the world meaningful and allows it to be organised in terms of familiar objects and the relations between them. A child does not merely learn word symbols for cats or cars; she also learns that a cat may go 'on' or 'under' a car. Language can be used to replace pictures. The child objectifies reality by naming things and by describing the relationships between them. Eventually she learns to think in words, and language helps her to construct her own view of social reality as she experiences it. Before we face up to other institutions or established patterns of behaviour we must learn the language of society. Language is the institution underlying all other institutions.

Now language is learnt within the family which is itself an institution within the broader institution of kinship. At first a child is not aware of kin or family, but may later realise that behavioural patterns have been imposed upon her by those who are closely related in terms of kin. She needs language to clarify the *roles* of those around her, be they mother, father, sister or brother. Later on we shall discuss the different language patterns used by middle-class and working-class children.

The more elaborate the language used, the more complex the concepts which can be grasped. Before Aristotle, words were regarded simply as a means of communication. Aristotle used his syllogisms to relate concepts to each other. Language is thus seen as a sophisticated tool for classifying concepts (see Fig. 1.3).

Social Role is the expected behaviour associated with a person who occupies a particular *status* or social position. The concepts of role and status are frequently confused because they are very closely related.

> A role represents the dynamic aspect of a status . . . there are no roles without statuses and no statuses without roles.
> (Linton, R. *The Study of Man*)

Individuals occupy certain social positions and the activities associated with these positions make up their roles in society. People play different

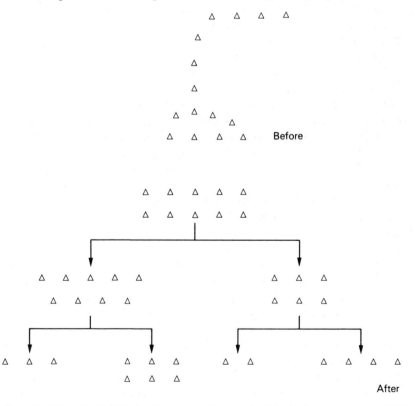

Fig. 1.3 Aristotle classified and categorised concepts in order to extract their full meaning and their relationship to each other

roles at different times. We start life in the role of children in our families of origin, but later act out the role of parents in our families of procreation. The concept of role may be used in many useful ways.

Role pairs occur because roles are rarely fulfilled by individuals acting on their own. It is necessary to refer to a person's position in a social structure. Thus a teacher must have at least one pupil. Examples of role pairs include teacher and pupil, doctor and patient, husband and wife.

The concept of *role set* is particularly associated with R.K. Merton and refers to those closely associated with an individual in helping to determine his pattern of behaviour. Thus a teacher's social behaviour will be affected by his pupils, colleagues, headmaster and other relevant or significant others, such as a school caretaker, who may exert an influence upon the teacher's role. His pupils (and their parents) expect him to teach, his colleagues expect him to keep his class in order so their own lessons are not disturbed, while the headmaster (looking through the class-room window) expects the teacher to be performing the two essential roles of instructor and disciplinarian. At varying times a role set will include different role pairs such as teacher and pupil, or teacher and headmaster. The activities of the role set involve role relationships which create tensions.

Role conflicts are tensions brought about by individuals pursuing different roles within a role set. For example a prison welfare officer is pulled in different directions by those with whom he has to work. He is responsible for the social welfare of the prisoners who may be considered as his clients. The other prison officers see the prisoners in a different light and may regard the welfare officer as being a sentimentalist, on the side of the prisoners. If he is to perform his function efficiently he must work with prisoners and prison officers. If he makes out a case on behalf of a prisoner he may well clash with the prison governor, who is preoccupied with running an efficient institution. Visits from members of the prisoner's family bring further role conflicts as he tries to satisfy complaints within the framework of the prison discipline.

Role-taking is taking or copying the role of another. It has been suggested that one reason for having children is that it provides an excuse to behave childishly, e.g. for a father to play space invaders.

The particular way in which a person defines her role will affect her *role performance*. Although other members of society may have clear-cut ideas about the *role demands* associated with a social position, an individual occupying that position may interpret it in her own peculiar way. She may modify the acting out of her role in the light of changing circumstances. A married woman's *definition of her role* will depend on role-specific attitudes. Her husband may expect a conforming wife and mother, but she may act out her own role in the light of a 'liberated woman' who is an equal partner in a symmetrical marriage. Her role performance is determined by her personal definition of the role and may be very different from the norm.

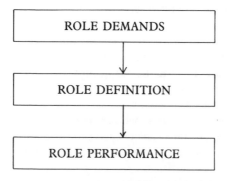

Status is used in sociology in two main ways. Firstly, status is used to signify a social position such as a child, teenager or married person. Secondly and more specifically, status is used to designate a position of esteem, prestige and social honour; thus a headmaster or college principal has a certain status and with the status goes a collection of rights and responsibilities. The headmaster has the right to perform his role because he possesses the status of headmaster.

Max Weber is the sociologist most closely associated with the concept of status. Weber saw the distribution of status as associated with social class, but whereas class is economically determined, status is more closely related to life-styles and the consumption of economic goods. Whereas class derives from the social relations of production, status is related to the consumption of goods, i.e. those with similar status share similar life-styles. Clearly those who have most property and money have the power to command most goods. They are those who have the highest status and the power which goes with that status. Two groups have most power and status in our society:

1 Those who control the economy largely by means of inherited wealth.
2 Those who control the government (including the army and police) and who have been socialised by public schools and/or the universities of Oxford and Cambridge.

Ascribed status derives from honour accorded to a person because of accident of birth, e.g. Prince Charles is accorded such a status. *Achieved status* results when an individual gains prestige by his own merit, e.g. Trevor Francis as a soccer striker. An open society, with a high level of social mobility (i.e. movement between social classes), is likely to give more importance to achieved status.

1.3 Sociology and science

- *What is a science?*

If a science is loosely defined as a disinterested search after truth then sociology or any other study would qualify. In such a context sociology may be regarded as an 'umbrella science', under which residual studies, not already claimed by other disciplines, can take shelter. Examples of such residual studies include the family and social stratification. The idea of an all-embracing discipline was accepted by Comte who referred to sociology as the 'queen of sciences'.

However, the claims of those who regard sociology as a scientific study must be examined rigorously against accepted criteria of what constitutes a science. Table 1.5 lists some generally accepted criteria of a science.

- *Are sociological methods scientific?*

There are those who would reject outright any claim that sociology should be termed a science on the grounds that the very nature of the subject

Table 1.5 The criteria of a science

1 Scientific methods are employed.
   (a) empirical evidence is gained from observation;
   (b) data is collected and collated;
   (c) facts are presented statistically;
   (d) experimentation and research are used in order to add to knowledge.

2 Theories are put forward, and hypotheses tested in an attempt to establish generalisations or laws.

3 Attempts are made to refute hypotheses; consequently scientific laws may be amended and given greater validity.

4 As scientific laws have a universal application, they form the basis of accurate predictions.

5 The subject matter is capable of clear-cut and useful classification; e.g. in botany, chemistry and geology.

6 The science becomes increasingly esoteric; it is difficult to express many of its ideas in layman's terms, so a specialised language is developed.

7 A science has its own specialised subject area and operates within a *paradigm*, i.e. explanatory models made up of a set of related concepts, theories, hypotheses, laws and methods of inquiry.

8 A science must be objective and value-free; its practitioners study things *as they exist* and are not concerned with *how they ought to be*.

makes it impossible for sociologists to be truly scientific. Recent sociological developments stress the many different interpretations of social phenomena and indicate´that the construction of social reality is based upon different interpretations of human actions. It is not possible for the sociologist to set up closely controlled experiments comparable with those conducted in the physical sciences, e.g. it is not possible to see how modern Britain would get on without the institution of the monarchy. Comparative sociology can be useful, but it can never be as revealing as experiments conducted in the natural sciences, e.g. laboratory experiments are conducted by physicists who control temperature, pressure and other conditions. The results of sociological data collection (from questionnaires, interviews, case studies and social surveys) are never exact. Cicourel (*Method and Measurement in Sociology*) makes the point that not only are survey questions posed from the standpoint of researchers, but also it is impossible to analyse meaningfully the many different interpretations placed upon the questions. For example, Turner's account of his attempts to measure the degree of ambition existing among Californian students (Turner, R. *The Social Context of Ambition*) has been severely criticised because the questions were based upon his particular view of what constitutes ambition – for example, 'A nine-room house and a new top-priced car?' Observers are influenced by the very social phenomena being examined, so that intended objectivity becomes mingled with subjectivity.

● *Are there sociological laws?*

Regularities exist in social life, but it is doubtful if there are any immutable sociological laws. Even Durkheim's well-known declaration that

> the suicide rate varies inversely with the degree of integration characteristic of any group

suffers from serious defects. Statistics may indicate that Roman Catholics, who are supposedly well-integrated into their religious groups, are less prone to commit suicide than protestants, whose freedom of individual conscience makes for lesser integration. Nevertheless, suicide statistics may be inaccurate. As suicide is regarded as a sin by catholics, it may be possible that the true figures are not revealed; attempts may be made to 'cover up' the suicide.

> ... all suicide research has been retrospective like any other post-mortem investigation. As such, it has considerable limitations because the chief source of information is no longer available.
>   (Stengel, E. *Suicide and Attempted Suicide*)

The number of attempted suicides is unknown, while medical opinion of the cause of death may be controversial. How can the degree of catholic or protestant integration be measured? Douglas, in his critique of Durkheim's work, argues that if the way in which statistics are compiled is examined, it is clear that additions of different things are being calculated; coroners attach different meanings to labelling suicides, e.g. some coroners will not accept that an act of suicide has been committed unless there is a suicide note.

It has been argued by Marxists that it is a sociological law that 'social classes exist in all societies', but it is not possible to investigate *all* societies. To be fair to Marx, he confined his claims about the universality of social classes to the history of 'all hitherto existing society' (Marx, K., Engels, F. *The Communist Manifesto*). The complexity and divergency of social phenomena make it extremely difficult to establish and apply immutable sociological laws.

● *Is sociology a study in its own right?*

On the one hand, if the subject area of sociology is the understanding of *society as a whole*, it will inevitably include facets of other subject disciplines such as biology, anthropology, economics, politics, psychology and history. On the other hand, if its subject area is merely *residual* to other studies then it can hardly claim to have its own specialised subject area. The modern trend towards a number of sociological perspectives results in sociology being less likely to be regarded as a separate scientific study. Alan Dawe's article entitled 'The Two Sociologies' (*British Journal of Sociology*, Vol. 21, 1970) has been much acclaimed by sociologists, but an article entitled 'The Two Chemistries' would be likely to be regarded with ridicule by chemists. A modern sociologist might justifiably argue that there are three, or even four sociologies depending upon different sociological perspectives.

In the short run, scholars of a physical science may not agree about a particular issue, but in the long run it may be assumed that they will reach an agreement and that a consensus view will be accepted. Kuhn (*Structure of Scientific Revolutions*) points out that it is only on rare occasions (such as those associated with Copernicus, Galileo or Einstein) that scientists discard major theories and accept a whole new body of theory. Normally, scientific problems are solved within the framework of existing theories. Thus Kepler's first law of planetary motion stated that the orbit of a planet is an ellipse with the sun at the focus; when deviations in the predicted position of Uranus showed that its orbit was not elliptical, investigations into the cause of the deviation led to the discovery of a new planet, Neptune, which was pulling Uranus off course. In the light of traditional scientific thinking, pluralistic perspectives such as those found in sociology, are difficult for laymen to comprehend. The different viewpoints cause sociology to appear a subjective, rather than an objective, study. Sociologists continue to disagree among themselves about fundamental aspects of their study.

- *Has sociology a technical language?*

Sociologists use a number of terms which are especially important to the subject. Alienation, class, deviance, mores, norms, peer group, role and status are acceptable enough; the meaning attached to them by sociologists is little different from that used in ordinary speech. Critics of sociological jargon have accused sociologists of using long words where short words would do, and invoking words from obscure lexicologies for use in an academic way, e.g. epistomology (the science of knowledge). Students should judge such criticisms for themselves. Are 'simplistic' and 'phenomena' merely long words meaning 'simple' and 'facts'?

The Shorter Oxford Dictionary defines 'phenomenon' as 'a thing that appears, or is perceived or observed; applied chiefly to a fact or occurrence', but adds a further meaning of 'an immediate object of perception (as distinguished from substance, or a thing in itself)'. The second interpretation, relating to the interpretive processes of the human mind, is that which has been used in sociology since Alfred Schutz (*Studies in Social Theory*). In commonsense parlance 'things are not always what they seem' or 'we see that which we wish to see.' 'Simplistic' denotes simplification possible to the extent of erring on the side of over-generalisation. The relevant point here is that these words are not peculiar to one particular study.

The student of sociology would do well to look up ambivalence, charismatic, divisive, empiricism, functional (and dysfunctional), pervasive and structured. She will find these words in a comprehensive dictionary: she will also find them used frequently in her study of the works of sociologists.

However, a claim can be made that there are some specialised terms peculiar to sociology. Such terms include anomie, embourgeoisement, folkways, *gemeinschaft, gesellschaft*, ideal type, reference group, routinisation and social distance (see G. Duncan Mitchell, *A Dictionary of Sociology*).

A collection of technical terms do not make a science. Soccer has its own terms: only the initiated properly understand what it means to be a striker, to be offside, to take a dive, to play in the back four, or how a goal may be scored from a set piece. A science develops its own specialised terms but every activity with its own terms is not a science. It is less important to argue the claims that sociology is a science with its own scientific terminology than to get on with the study of a subject the great popularity of which is exemplified by the enormous increase in the numbers studying it.

- *Sociology uses scientific analogies*

Sociology has used analogies from such natural sciences as biology. The sociological perspective of structural functionalism depends upon a comparison between society and a living organism where all the parts of the structure contribute to the functioning of the whole.

The study of urban growth has been compared with the processes of plant ecology. Towns have been considered as consisting of a number of transitional zones with each area attempting dominance over the rest by 'invasion', 'succession' and 'adaptation'. A system of interdependence evolves similar to the biological process by which all living organisms are linked together. The use of such analogies links sociology with the natural sciences but does not make sociology itself a science.

- *Positivism and phenomenology*

Positivists claim that sociology should rank as a positive science. They hold that it is possible to study the social world in the same way as physical scientists study the natural world. Positivists believe in a science of society based upon social facts which can be expressed quantitatively – for example, birth rates, death rates, illegitimacy rates and suicide rates. Those who believe that sociology is a science comparable with the natural sciences argue that social facts when studied scientifically make possible the formulation of scientific laws which are as valid as the laws of natural science so long as the conditions remain the same. Durkheim was the positivistic sociologist par excellence; he believed that laws relating to society could be verified by social facts. Durkheim argued that there is a body of beliefs and sentiments common to the mass of members of society.

When Durkheim studied suicide he endeavoured to proceed by stages in a scientific way.

1 Durkheim *defined* society as accurately as possible.
2 He examined suicide *statistics*. (Durkheim did not interview those who had attempted suicide because he could not be sure that they would tell the truth or even know the truth.)
3 He *classified* three types of suicide:
   (a) egoistic suicide – where individuals think of themselves rather than any social group;

(b) altruistic suicide – where individuals are so much part of a social group that they are willing to forfeit their lives (e.g. Japanese Kamikazi pilots);

(c) anomic suicide – where the individual is antagonised by the special group to which he is supposed to belong.

4 He put forward the sociological '*law*' that there would be fewer suicides when individuals were closely integrated into a social group, and more suicides if they were not so integrated.

5 He *attempted to verify* his '*law*': in modern societies suicide increases because there is more economic stress than in primitive societies.

Talcott Parsons, an American sociologist, has exerted an influence upon sociology comparable to that of Durkheim. Under Parsons's influence, sociology developed a unified theory based on the idea that society was made up of complex parts, or sub-systems with interlocking processes, e.g. the family provided workers for the economy while the economy provided food for the family.

Phenomenologists reject positivism and claim that sociology should study the social world in a qualitative rather than a quantitative way. Their ideas are based upon the belief that the social world is very different from the material world. Schutz (*Studies in Social Theory*) argued that individuals differ from physical objects because human beings are capable of reflecting about the social world and about themselves. Their actions are not merely the result of responding to biological instincts; an individual's social actions are affected by his particular conception of social reality.

Weber may be regarded as the sociologist who bridges positivism and phenomenology; although he analysed societal uniformities he believed that sociology needed to go further than causal explanations. Weber used the term *verstehen* to describe the meaning underlying social acts. Each person has a different perception of reality for nobody can really get inside the skin of another. Phenomenologists argue that each individual has his own interpretation of what the social world is like. The subject matter studied by the sociologist affects him and he affects it. Phenomenologists argue that it is too simplistic to regard sociology as a science comparable to natural sciences. They are sceptical of perceiving of sociology as an objective study with irrevocable laws. They treat sociology as a facet of the study of humanity and argue that it is less important to categorise sociology as a science, an art or a craft, than to consider what questions it poses and how it attempts to answer them.

- *Can sociology be value-free?*

One of the major considerations relating to whether sociology can be properly classified as a science centres upon the question of *objectivity*.

Positivists would wish to argue that it is possible to study objectively 'what is' rather than 'what ought to be'. They contend that sociologists should observe social facts in an independent, unbiased way. According to this argument, society can be looked upon as something 'out there' waiting to be analysed in accordance with functional prerequisites which can be objectively studied using the Parsonian model of four basic societal needs. These can be remembered by the acronym, AGIL.

1 **Adaptation** – an assessment can be made of the way a society adapts to its environment, e.g. television has forced people to adapt to changes in leisure habits and employment opportunities.

2 **Goal attainment** – it is possible to determine the principal goals which members of society are endeavouring to achieve by collective action, e.g. all the main political parties in Britain at present accept that the economy should be organised as a mixture of private firms and public corporations (mixed economy).

3 **Integration** – links, holding together the members of a society, can be distinguished, e.g. the vast majority of people marry and have families, and this involves community commitments.

4 **Latency or pattern maintenance** – a society has an accepted pattern of social order which can be objectively studied, e.g. it has traditions, rules, values and customs.

Comte believed in a science of society which in its final positive state would enable everything to be explained scientifically. Following this objective approach, Durkheim saw social facts as external to the individual and forming part of the social order in the same way that physical facts form part of the natural order.

In contrast to the thinking of the founding fathers, many modern sociologists perceive peculiar difficulties facing the sociologist in his search for objective truth. They argue that as the sociologist is an active participant in the very society he studies, it is impossible for him to discard his personal experiences. In his explanations of society he inevitably interprets and analyses it. In such an analysis the sociologist is guided by his own beliefs, attitudes, loyalties and viewpoints. He cannot be certain that he is accurately recording the meanings that social actors themselves attach to situations.

Four significant factors impinge on objectivity. Firstly, the very choice of the subject for sociological research involves value judgement. Secondly, a sociologist is bound to be influenced by the values of his own society. Thirdly, the language used is likely to include value-laden terms such as 'racist' or 'sexist'. Fourthly, the sociologist has to decide whether to publish the results of his research even though he may have doubts about betraying confidences, or that his findings may be used harmfully; for example, if research revealed apparent IQ discrepancies between blacks and whites, it might be taken out of context and used to incite racial prejudices.

Alvin Gouldner (*The Coming Crisis of Western Sociology*) has argued that as sociologists can never be completely objective it is preferable to accept this fact and state clearly that bias exists. Is it imperative that the sociologist should be value-free as long as he acts with social responsibility?

Howard Becker has gone even further (*Whose Side are We On?*), and has argued in favour of the complete rejection of attempts to be objective. Becker used empathy to establish an intuitive understanding with marijuana smokers; he purposely portrayed deviants in a sympathetic light on the grounds that they were not adequately organised to protect themselves. Becker's development of labelling theory convinced him that deviants were victims of official labelling and any sociologist who studied their situation would feel bound to come down on their side. Gouldner (*The Sociologist as Partisan*) has accused Becker of going too far in his identification with underdogs.

In brief, sociology has to tread very carefully between objectivity and subjectivity. The sociologist must strive not to identify with either underdogs or overdogs but to study both with as little bias as possible. One can be objective about rocks (geology), chemicals (chemistry) or plants and animals (biology), but not about people. If absolute objectivity is an essential hallmark of science, then it can be argued that it is better that sociology should be found wanting, on the grounds that sociologists ought to be realistic.

> ... if sociology is defined as a science, it is nevertheless a very different sort of science from physics or chemistry, and it certainly does not have a set of ready-made answers nor a method for arriving at foolproof solutions.
> (Brown, C. *Understanding Society*)

1.4 Sociological Perspectives

● *Social reality*

An individual's particular viewpoint or *perspective* of society will determine his understanding of society. We all attempt to make some sense of the social world around us. In Fig. 1.4 the man and the woman form part of the same scene, but they have different perspectives, i.e. they see things from different viewpoints.

Sociologists view society in different ways depending on the particular model of society which they adopt. As embryonic sociologists you must be shamelessly interested in society. From different perspectives you may see

Fig. 1.4 Different perspectives

different things, but it is better to see than not to bother to look. Although sociological perspectives have varying emphases, it would be wrong to consider that they are contradictory. In everyday life, it is generally accepted that different individuals interpret a piece of music, or a painting, or a passage from literature in different ways. Different sociological perspectives afford a fuller meaning of social reality. Throughout the other units of this book we shall frequently refer to three perspectives which are particularly useful to our understanding of social reality. We shall find it helpful to look at aspects of sociology (such as social stratification, family, education and work) from different angles.

The three main sociological perspectives are:
1 The structural-functionalist perspective
2 The structural-conflict perspective
3 The interactionist perspective.

- *Structural-functionalism*

One of the oldest devices used in an attempt to explain the underlying meaning of society is to compare it with a living organism. According to the structural-functionalist perspective, it is necessary to examine the *structure* of society if we are to understand the actions of individuals who make up the whole. Just as it is not possible to understand the purpose of the heart or the hands or the feet without relating them to the whole body, so it is not possible to understand the actions of individual members of society without understanding the nature of society as a whole.

The apostle Paul used the structural-functionalist perspective when he wrote to the Christians at Corinth.

> A body is not one single organ, but many. Suppose the foot should say, 'Because I am not a hand I do not belong to the body', it does belong to the body none the less. Suppose the ear were to say, 'Because I am not an eye I do not belong to the body,' it does still belong to the body. If the body were all eye, how could it hear? If the body were all ear, how could it smell?
>
> (NEB, I *Corinthians* 12: 14–17)

In Shakespeare's *Coriolanus*, Menenius Agrippa argues that the senators of Rome are like the 'belly'; the citizens cannot manage without their leaders any more than the body can manage without the belly, or indeed, without any of its various parts.

> The organic analogy was widely prevalent in pre-Comteian thought, and it is not surprising that it appeared very early in sociology's history. The most important manifestation of this pattern has been in the linked concepts of 'structure' and 'function', which already appear in Spencer, were used by Durkheim, and figured prominently in the work of the great sociologically oriented British anthropologists, Malinowski and Radcliffe-Brown. Through these and other channels this perspective came to have substantial influence in American sociology, particularly among students and followers of Talcott Parsons, and it is now generally known as the structural-functional school of sociology.
>
> (Inkeles, A. *What is Sociology?*)

London is frequently referred to as the *heart* of Britain, connected to other parts by *arterial* roads. A certain cabinet minister is said to have the *ear* of the premier. Order in our society is maintained by the *arm* of the law. The media refers to the *voice* of the people; the important fact that what 'the people' are really saying is often ambiguous, indicates one of the weaknesses of the structural-functionalist perspective. Human activities are regarded as useful when they help to maintain the social structure. Those who argue for the structural-functionalist perspective believe that human actions are largely structured by our social environment. Our values, attitudes, beliefs, norms, roles and institutions are the result of the culture of our society. It is because we share in a general agreement or *consensus* that people behave in a way to ensure that social order prevails and we are able to predict with a fair degree of certainty just how they will behave. Any deviancies from accepted norms are the result of inadequate socialisation. Each individual is structured by the society in which he lives. When sociologists talk of 'Society in Man' they mean that society is greater than us all in the same way that the body is greater than its separate parts. The parts have their distinctive purposes but they would not be able to function properly without the body.

Structural-functionalists stress the importance of certain *functional prerequisites* of society. These absolute necessities for the functioning of society may be illustrated by considering the situation of the animals in George Orwell's *Animal Farm* (see Table 1.6).

Structural-functionalism explains how society holds together and works as a united whole. Society seems to possess a force beyond man's control. Man is governed by the social order and has very little chance of changing it. Sociologists examine patterns of behaviour for regularities which help in the prediction of future social acts. Unless we can be fairly sure how the

Table 1.6 Functional prerequisites of Orwell's *Animal Farm* society

---

1 The *needs* of the animals were supplied by the farm.

2 A *political leader* emerged in the shape of Napoleon, a large fierce-looking Berkshire boar.

3 A *consensus* about the beliefs and attitudes of the animals was expressed in the seven commandments.
   1 Whatever goes upon two legs is an enemy.
   2 Whatever goes upon four legs, or has wings, is a friend.
   3 No animal shall wear clothes.
   4 No animal shall sleep in a bed.
   5 No animal shall drink alcohol.
   6 No animal shall kill any other animal.
   7 All animals are equal.

4 *Social control* was exercised: those who refused to accept the rules, such as Snowball the alleged traitor, were hounded from the society. The animals' behaviour was controlled by the dogs acting in a policing role.

5 *Different roles* were undertaken in pursuance of shared goals. The division of labour made for greater competence in specific tasks: the old carthorse, Boxer, was valued for his strength while the cunning pigs formed the ruling elite.

6 *Adaptation* proved necessary; the initial goal was to overthrow the tyranny and exploitation of Farmer Jones, but this goal was superseded by subsidiary goals such as constructing the windmill. The rules and regulations were also amended as time passed and the goals were changed.

7 *Norms and values* of the animal society were learnt as part of the process of *socialisation*. The sheep were taught to bleat 'Four legs good, two legs bad', while Squealer communicated the leader's ideas to the other animals.

majority of people will re-act in certain situations, social life becomes impossible.

Every part of the structure of society has a *function*. Robert Merton (*Social Theory and Social Structure*) divided functions into *manifest* functions and *latent* functions. Manifest functions are intended and recognised by participants, but latent functions are neither recognised nor intended. The manifest function of the coronation ceremony is to crown the monarch and it is recognised to be so by all who take part or observe. The latent function of the ceremony is to bring together important people from home and abroad, to inculcate a spirit of loyalty and to foster consensus.

When things are not functioning normally, *dysfunctions* occur. In a peculiar way, even these dysfunctions may help the functioning of society: crime has its uses because it allows society to punish those who step out of line and thus deter others who might contemplate following suit.

Herbert Spencer (1820–1903) suggested four significant comparisons between society and biological organisms (see Table 1.7).

Table 1.7 Analogies between society and biological organisms

---

1 They begin in a small way and grow much larger:
   (a) all life began with a single-celled amoeba,
   (b) primitive men lived in small tribes, but in modern society millions live in conurbations.

2 Their structures become increasingly complex as they develop.

3 Their parts become mutually dependent until the life of each part is made possible only by the existence of the rest; society consists of interrelated orderly systems (institutions) such as the family and the economy.

4 The life of the whole becomes independent of, and more prolonged than, its component parts.
   (Individuals, according to T.S. Eliot, experience 'Birth, and copulation and death', but although individuals die society continues. It existed before we were born and will continue after our death.)

Emile Durkheim extended the structural-functionalist approach by emphasising the *moral* nature of society. He examined the ways in which members of society learn to accept codes of conduct. Society not only determined our social world and our view of social reality, but society was also a moral force and a moral reality.

Radcliffe-Brown, Malinowski and other anthropologists, found the functionalist perspective useful in explaining to those at home what appeared to be the weird behaviour of primitive peoples. Why should the Trobiand Islanders give away their yams and pigs? When people, in modern societies, are able to understand the function of collective giving, then they will accept it as a useful and reasonable activity. (Collect modern examples for yourself e.g. the Marshall Plan to aid war-stricken Europe, help for peoples afflicted by earthquakes, etc.)

Table 1.8 is based on John Rex's summary of comparisons (first put forward by Radcliffe-Brown) between biological and social organisms.

Although a consensus exists at any given time, structural functionalists argue that gradual changes can still take place: societies remain in a state of equilibrium until changes occur and a new state of equilibrium is necessary. The term *homeostasis* is used to describe the natural maintenance of equilibrium. Just as the congealing or clotting of blood assists in the healing of the human body, while its temperature is continually regulated through shivering and sweating, similarly society is subject to regulated change.

Durkheim's conception of a new morality geared to modern technological changes provides an answer to those who question whether struc-

Table 1.8 Biological and social organisms

	Biological organism	Social organism
Units	Cell	Individual human beings
Structure	Relations between the cells	Relations between human beings
Activities	Observed behaviour of cells	Observed behaviour of human beings and groups
Functions	Active roles in maintaining the physical structure	Active roles in maintaining the social structure

Table 1.9 Summary of the weaknesses of structural-functionalism

1 In a complex society, it is doubtful whether there is a normative consensus with shared values.

2 There is a limit to the social control which society can exercise over the individual.

3 It is a fallacy to reify society, i.e. to regard non-living things as possessing feelings, goals and needs.

4 Structural functionalism is a rigid perspective because it is based on maintaining the status quo (existing conditions).

5 The perspective does not provide a satisfactory explanation of rapid social change.

tural-functionalism can be reconciled to change. The main significance of Durkheim's approach is that he tended to reify society (i.e. to assume that society is a real object having a life of its own). Society may be analogous to a biological organism, but it is dangerous to push the analogy too far. Society has no tangible form: it cannot see or speak. Neither can we see it or speak to it. The people who make up society move about independently and do not form a continuous mass.

There are sociological textbooks which give a one-sided view of structural-functionalism and ignore the inadequacies of the perspective. It is thought essential that, in this book, where the main perspectives are used as terms of reference, students should be aware of some of the weaknesses of the perspective before setting out on their sociological travels. When considering a sociological study from a particular perspective, weaknesses of that perspective should be borne in mind (see Table 1.9).

The preoccupation with the status quo makes the perspective far too conservative, while the so-called consensus of values within society may well break down as societies evolve and change. The perspective is challenged by those who regard conflict as inevitable.

• *Conflict-structuralism*

Conflict theorists believe that society has a structure, but rather that being a natural order of things, this structure has been determined by the way past conflicts have been resolved. Conflict-structuralists do not reify society by regarding structure as a property of a social organism, but rather they see society as constantly subject to *change*. Conflicts arise because those who wish to see change are opposed to those who resist change; those who resist change have a vested interest in trying to keep things as they are.

Karl Marx has made the most important analysis of the conflict perspective. Although the ideology of Marxism may arouse emotive hostility among millions of people in the western world, their numbers are far exceeded by those who now live in countries where Marxism has been adopted as the basis of economic and political life. Marx believed that in every society there existed a ruling class and a subject class. Perpetual conflict existed between these two classes.

> The history of all hitherto existing society is the history of class struggles.
> (*Communist Manifesto*, 1848)

The main principles of Marx's ideas, and the concepts associated with his analysis of society are listed in Tables 1.10 and 1.11.

Table 1.10 Marxist analysis of society

1 The social, economic and political world is more subject to change than to stability.

2 Certain regularities which are associated with change can be observed and analysed.

3 The most important changes are of an economic nature but these changes are pervasive, influencing all aspects of life.

4 Men are born into a certain social class determined by economic circumstances from which it is almost impossible to escape.

5 Capitalism involves the exploitation of the working class and so creates the seeds of conflict and capitalism's own inevitable destruction.

Table 1.11 Marxist concepts

Concept	Analysis
1 *Social class*	Social class depends upon people's relationship to the means of production. People are *conscious* of belonging either to the class which dominates the means of production or to the class which suffers the common plight of being exploited by the dominant class.
2 *Social change*	Social change derives from the class struggle between those who have a vested interest in maintaining the present order and those who hope to benefit by changing it.
3 *Alienation*	The alienation of man (from his fellow men, from his product and from society) derives from the existence of private property in a capitalist society.
4 *Power*	Power is derived from the economy and the world of work; power is possessed by those who dominate economic life.

Although the structural-conflict perspective leaves many loose ends and is less tidy than the structural-functionalist perspective, there are many who find it more realistic. Society has norms but they are always subject to change. As change is usually very gradual it is usually imperceptible, but nevertheless it is always taking place. Come the revolution and social changes become apparent even to the most undiscerning. In everyday life it is obvious that conflicts abound (see Table 1.12).

Table 1.12 Everyday conflicts

Sphere of life	Examples
1 Family	Husband and wife argue about household expenditure
2 School	Teacher and pupils contest a 'blackboard jungle'
3 Workplace	Boss and unions disagree on pay, so workers come out on strike
4 Leisure/media	Do you choose to view BBC or ITV? Do you choose to read the *Daily Telegraph* or the *Morning Star*?
5 Politics	Will you vote Conservative, or Labour or Liberal or SDP?
6 Religion	Are you Catholic or Protestant? Anglican or Methodist? Agnostic or atheist?
7 Education	Should parents send their children to state or private schools?
8 Youth	On which side of the generation gap are you?

As the divisions in society are numerous and diverse, conflict theorists argue that their view of society is the more realistic. The different parts of society are always in conflict with one another, overtly or covertly. Society is very different from a biological organism, because no biological organism could maintain its existence with so much division between its independent parts. It is thus argued that conflict-structuralism provides the more accurate view of our imperfect society riddled with its contradictions. Those who hold this perspective further argue that the so-called consensus is a myth invented by the ruling class in order to maintain their privileged position. Life is a struggle for power and those who exercise it exploit those without it.

Both conflict and consensus perspectives help us to understand the complexities of society (see Fig. 1.5). The two perspectives are not necessarily mutually exclusive. Both perspectives help to explain why social unity exists: consensus theorists view society as a whole with independent, co-operating groups all holding the same basic values; conflict theorists see society as composed of diverse groups but with dominant groups imposing their values on society until overthrown by conflicting groups.

I do not intend to fall victim to the mistake of many structural-functionalists and advance for the conflict model a claim to comprehensive and exclusive applicability. As far as I can see, we need for the explanation of sociological problems both the equilibrium and conflict models of society; and it may well be that, in a

Fig. 1.5 Consensus and conflict in the economic world
(*Society Today*, No. 24, 6 January 1978)

philosophical sense, society has two faces of equal reality; one of stability, harmony and consensus, and one of change, conflict and constraint.
(Dahrendorf, R. 'Out of Utopia', in Coser and Rosenberg, eds, *Sociological Theory*)

Sociologists tend to favour either one or other of the two perspectives. While we await the great reconciliation it is useful to study Ralf Dahrendorf's contrast of the consensus and conflict perspectives:

Consensus
1 Every society is a relatively persistent, stable structure of elements.
2 Every society is a well-integrated structure of elements.
3 Every element in a society has a function, i.e. renders a contribution to its maintenance as a system.
4 Every functioning social structure is based on a consensus of value among its members.

Conflict
1 Every society is at every point subject to processes of change; social change is ubiquitous.
2 Every society displays at every point dissensus and conflict; social conflict is ubiquitous.

3 Every element in a society renders a contribution to its disintegration and change.
4 Every society is based on the coercion of some of its members by others.
    (Dahrendorf, R. *Class and Class Conflict in Industrial Society*, 1959)

On the one hand, conflict-structuralists see the social order as determined by the outcome of a power struggle between the prevailing dominant group and other exploited groups. On the other hand, structural-functionalists see the social order as the result of a normative consensus i.e. an agreement over common values and beliefs.

• *Interactionism*

Max Weber was the first major sociologist to emphasise the importance of interpreting the actions and interactions of individuals. Weber was not an interactionist in the modern sense, but his social action theory may be linked with interactionist research carried out since the 1920s.

Sociology is a science which attempts the interpretive understanding of social action in order thereby to arrive at a causal explanation of its course and effects.
    (Weber, M. *The Theory of Social and Economic Organisation*)

Weber died in 1920, and it was after his death that interactionism became sociologically significant in the United States. The interactionism approach marked a change of direction in sociology. Whereas, according to the consensus and conflict perspectives society is a structured whole, interactionists interpret and analyse social interaction between individual members of society.

Interactionism is fraught with difficulties, because when we study interaction it will inevitably interact upon us and affect our judgement.

A man looks at a woman; she appreciates that he is looking and reacts accordingly; he realises that she is reacting and modifies his actions in response to her 'come hither' or 'brush-off' reaction.

In spite of its difficulties, the interactionist perspective has a special value because it does not consider people en bloc or turn them into numbers by attempting to measure them statistically. Interactionists believe that it is possible to find out more about society by analysing what those actually involved think about it than by comparing society with a biological organism (consensus theory) or by considering a structure of competing groups (conflict theory).

There are those who believe we are so conditioned that we have no real control over what we do, but most of us cherish a belief in our freedom of action. We are continually choosing how we shall dress and behave, who will be our friend or enemy, where we will go, what we will say, or what we will do. Although we may sometimes choose to do things we would rather not do, our very unwillingness suggests that we have an independence of action, albeit a resentful one on occasion.

The interactionist perspective is not as unified as are consensus and conflict perspectives. Indeed interactionism is made up of a number of related perspectives. Certain sociologists, such as Howard Becker and Erving Goffman, who are frequently labelled as interactionists, would consider that they are really doing their own thing by pursuing individualistic lines of research. It is possible, however, to identify common characteristics upon which we can base our study of the interactionist perspective. To do this it is useful to consider two models of analysing social action, one of which is known as *symbolic interactionism* and the other as *ethnomethodology*.

1 Symbolic interactionism

The origin of symbolic interactionism is associated with George Herbert Mead (1863–1931) who believed that man should be distinguished from animals because man has a *self* with two components to be identified as 'I' and 'Me'. Man not only undergoes experience but is also aware of this experience. Mead considered 'I' as the active part of the self (non-socialised self) and 'Me' as the passive element of the self (the socialised self). 'Me' results from experiences and reflects a person's interactions with others. These 'others' include:

(a) the *generalised other*, i.e. a set of ideas held by a person about the socially significant attitudes of others; it is the general social code of others with which the individual fits in and into which he integrates himself;

(b) *significant others*, i.e. those people who have the greatest influence over us; these significant others change as we pursue our *careers* through life and pass from one status to another (status passage);

(c) *others whose role we take (taking the role of another)* – we are able to cast ourselves imaginatively in the role of others and thus anticipate their actions.

Role-playing depends upon a person's *definition of the situation*, i.e. the typical meaning which people attach to a social situation; a teacher defines the situation in a classroom differently from the way in which the pupils define it. The teacher defines the situation in terms of his authority and his task of imparting knowledge. The pupil may well define the situation in terms of playing about or dodging as much schoolwork as possible. We are able to see, in this example, the dovetailing of all three main sociological perspectives. In face of interaction between teacher and pupils, either a consensus will be reached where both parties accept a compromise situation or conflict will prevail so that effective teaching is impossible. In the long run, it is rare for teachers' and pupils' definition of the situation to be so incongruent that no consensus is possible. Often pseudo-concord is reached – somewhere between consensus and conflict.

'I' and 'Me' are closely linked and cannot be sensibly viewed separately. 'I' can be considered the subject of an action, whereas 'Me' is the object acted upon. A person's identity combines how he sees himself and how others see him. 'Me' integrates a person into the social community and is closely related to the concept of 'the generalised other'.

The concept of 'the generalised other' links the identity of self with others of like mind; we are able to indulge in social interaction because of our shared perspective. Significant others are people who have the greatest influence over us. A child learns the roles of his parents, other close relatives, friends and neighbours, and is able to locate his own social role within the community of which he is a part. Later, his teachers, employers and workmates may become significant. A person's actions are influenced by opinions and attitudes he attributes to these significant others. As we perceive all actions to be meaningful, we attempt to comprehend the purposes of others and interact accordingly. People always consider themselves in relation to others. A sprinter wonders whether he will be first, or second or last. A penalty-taker in soccer has to think of ways of out-witting the goalkeeper. A student is interested in his examination performance in relation to the performance of his fellow students.

In order to understand what a person does, necessitates that we have some appreciation of his particular definition of the situation; this requires knowing those things which he takes for granted and has internalised. For example, a sociologist wishing to analyse the degree of alienation experienced by a particular worker must take into account the worker's own definition of the situation.

> ... a factor of decisive importance in determining whether or not industrial workers are likely to become increasingly integrated into their employing organisations is *their own definition* of the work situation ...
>> (Goldthorpe, J.H., Lockwood, D. *et al. The Affluent Worker in the Class Structure*)

Each new encounter will give us the opportunity to confirm or revise our ideas of the way in which others see us. Our lives constitute a series of *careers*, e.g.

> Thus our career in the educational sector may run from nursery-school toddler to doctoral candidate, in the sexual sector from eager experimenter to frustrated observer, in the occupational sector from promising young man to certified failure, and so forth.
>> (Berger, P. and Berger, B. *Sociology: A Biographical Approach*)

A person's particular self is changed by interactions throughout each 'career'. Other people's views of us may be changed even after our death. Poor old Saint Christopher has been decanonised. A famous man, not long dead, may be discredited as was Sir Cyril Burt when it was alleged that he had faked the results of IQ tests in order to advance his pet educational theories.

The term *symbolic* (interactionism) is used because symbols play a vital part in all our interactions. A cross symbolises a barbarous method of execution or a religious movement. A red light symbolises a brothel or an indication that traffic should come to a halt. If we are to understand social behaviour then we must try to comprehend the relevant use of symbols. A symbolic gesture, such as the V sign, may signify vulgarity or victory. The symbolic meaning depends upon who made the gesture, in what social context it was made and who is responding to the gesture. A soccer fan uses the V-sign in a derisory fashion, whereas Winston Churchill elevated the gesture to a symbol of national aspiration. Most important is the use of words as symbols for objects or ideas. The same word may symbolise different meanings but we must learn to respond to the appropriate meaning. The word 'sovereign' denotes a ruler or a coin, and the kind of confusion that could arise through misuse is illustrated by the following illogicality:

Queen Elizabeth II is a sovereign

A sovereign is worth about £100

Therefore Queen Elizabeth II is worth about £100.

The appropriate symbol for the particular social situation must be used if sense is to be made of social interactions. It is meet and right that we should shake hands with an Englishman but be prepared to be kissed on both cheeks by a Frenchman.

Two models are used in connection with interactionist research.

1 *The game model* is based on the idea of social actors playing a game according to agreed rules. People who refuse to abide by the rules are 'ordered off': for example, those who break the law are sent to prison, disruptive pupils are suspended from school, blackleg workers are sent to Coventry by fellow trade unionists. Social order is arrived at by agreement after actors have bargained with each other and employed various strategies.

2 *The dramaturgical model* is based upon social life being regarded as a theatrical performance.

All the world's a stage,
And all the men and women merely players;
They have their exits and their entrances.
And one man in his time plays many parts.
    (Shakespeare, W. *As You Like It*, Act 2, Scene viii)

We play our various parts before an audience, and this audience affects our performance. A soccer team, uplifted by its fans, turns on an inspiring performance. Social interaction takes place as our performance affects the audience. Unruly acts on the field may provoke hooliganism among supporters. Good teachers or barristers must be convincing actors. Their performances become realistic when they forget they are acting and really believe in the parts they are playing.

2 Ethnomethodology

Ethnomethodology analyses the *commonsense* nature of social interactions. We must not deprecate the value of common sense. Anthropologists have found that intuitive knowledge is often the basis for social actions. What the world and his wife have thought for generations is probably somewhere near the truth. The accumulated common sense of generations results in patterns of behavioural typicalities. Social order is dependent upon people behaving in a commonsense way. Ethnomethodology is the study of the methodological nature of that common sense which has resulted from numerous individual experiences and collective hunches.

The criticism has been made that 'sociologists tell people much that they know in language they often cannot understand.' But there is more to it than that. The ethnomethodologist *analyses* commonsense sociological explanations to a depth beyond that which a layman would probe. Ethnomethodologists (such as Harold Garfinkel, Aaron Cicourel and Harvey Sacks) spell out ordinary commonsense explanations held by average and competent persons, in such a way that new and deeper meanings are given to social interactions. These sociologists know what everybody knows, but they also know more about the whys and wherefores. The very words common sense imply that there are basic ideas which we hold in common; this consensus of understanding underlies the whole social order. When people do not behave in a commonsensical fashion we 'normalise' their actions by explaining them away. We say that they were preoccupied, or under the weather, or suffering from the grief of bereavement, or worried because of their overdraft or that their marriage was likely to break up. It is expected that as soon as a person, who is behaving strangely, recovers from the problems which beset him, then his behaviour will return to normality.

If a pupil is called to the headmaster's study he expects to be treated in a certain way and he will react accordingly. He is so familiar with the normal routine, that were he to swap places with the headmaster he would probably make quite a good job of assuming the headmaster's role. If, out of the blue, the headmaster acts in a strange way, such as standing on his head on his desk, then commonsense assumptions will have to be abandoned. The pupil will not know how to react. He would probably flee the room and social interaction would break down.

Nobody can understand everything. However far sociological analysis goes it could always be taken further if there were world enough and time.

A man rushes home from a football match and informs his son,
'Town won 6–0!'
His son replies in disbelief,
'Town won 6–0?'
When asked to give a more complete account the father says,
'Ipswich Town beat Manchester United 6–0, and they also missed two
penalties.'
His son pesters him with further questions:
Who scored the goals?
Did any player score a hat-trick?
Did the goalkeeper save the penalties?
It is impossible for his father to recount all the details of the ninety
minutes' play.
Consider the commonsense aversion to the practice of incest. In his
excellent book, *Kinship and Marriage*, Robin Fox spends an entire chapter
of over twenty pages examining facets of the incest taboo, such as its
disastrous effects upon family relationships and the dangers of inbreeding. He then concludes:

> The reader will no doubt be dismayed to hear, having ploughed through this
> chapter, that this is not even the half of it. I have only been able to skim the
> surface of the complexities involved. But let no one now say that there is nothing
> to explain.
>   (Fox, R. *Kinship and Marriage*)

When Garfinkel (*Studies in Ethnomethodology*) asked his students to
amplify their conversations, he found that their elaborations made for
ambiguities and necessitated further more complex explanations. During
his experiments, Garfinkel encouraged his students to write out snatches
of recent conversations and then explain the conversations in far greater
detail. An example is given below.

> If, for whatever a student wrote, I was able to persuade him that it was not yet
> accurate, distinct or clear enough, and if he remained willing to repair the
> ambiguity . . . then the writing itself developed the conversation as a branching
> texture of relevant matters.
>   (Garfinkel, H. *Studies in Ethnomethodology*)

The students found that the explanation of their conversation was far
the more difficult part of the exercise. When Garfinkel demonstrated that
each explanation was not sufficiently clear or precise, the students
eventually gave up. There becomes a point in our analysis beyond which
we cannot go. Our interpretations of social interaction are inevitably
incomplete. That does not mean that we should not analyse a social
situation as far as we can. Experiment for yourself on digging deeper into

social intercourse – but be prepared to face some antagonism! For example, one of Garfinkel's students had the following response.

Victim. How are you?
Student. How am I in regard to what? My health, my finances, my school, my work, my peace of mind.. . .
Victim (*Red in face and out of control*). Look! I was trying to be polite. Frankly I don't give a damn how you are.

Clearly, there comes a point when it is necessary to call a halt to explanations. The Jeremy Thorpe trial of 1979 went on for many weeks. There came a time when the jury had to make a decision. They came to their verdict based on a commonsense judgement of what they had heard *to that date*. There must have been much more evidence they could have heard if there had been more time. We can never be completely sure in our judgement; so we adopt a commonsense perspective based on experience. As social reality is always subject to change and ambiguity, and sociological accounts are based upon common sense, then no one sociological account can claim to be truly objective. The ethnomethodological school of interactionism presents one particular interpretation of social reality.

1.5 Sociology and related subjects

• *Biology*

Biologically, man is an animal, akin to the primates. Nevertheless, in spite of Desmond Morris's vivid description in *The Naked Ape*, man is not descended from apes. Richard Leakey's discoveries of human remains in Kenya suggest that man has existed as a separate species for about $2\frac{1}{2}$ million years. The human species has evolved to become *homo sapiens* – *thinking* men and women.

Biology studies man as a form of life, but sociology studies man as a social being. Both studies are concerned with *heredity* and *environment*. Heredity determines human chromosomatic patterns and genetic differences. The environment changes man while man changes his environment. Biology and sociology join forces in their interest in the environment. In the nineteenth century, Charles Darwin revolutionised biology with his principle of *natural selection*. Those less suited to the environment died and their weaknesses died with them. Modern man has evolved through the survival of the fittest: he has undergone adaptation and modification.

Man is a social animal, very different from all other animals. Interactionists believe that man is able to rationalise, to be introspective, and to organise his resources to cooperate with other humans and above all to develop a sophisticated language with which he communicates. Whereas other species studied by the biologist must start each lifespan from scratch, man is able to begin where the previous generation left off. It took man two thousand years to develop an elementary understanding of the number concept but a small child today can learn to count to hundreds and appreciate numerical implications. A modern young woman of eighteen may know more about nuclear physics than Rutherford, the first man to split the atom.

Man is capable of absorbing the knowledge of past generations, developing it and passing even more advanced knowledge to the next generation. We have seen that all those things which humans learn, add to and transmit, make up what the sociologist classifies as *culture*. Culture, in a sociological context, is not confined to the arts (such as literature, music, painting and architecture) but is extended to include man's entire social inheritance. Culture includes everything not biologically acquired. Concorde, credit cards and calculators are part of our culture as much as classical music. Take-away foods, continental package holidays, digital watches, the EEC, videos, contraceptive pills and Prestel are of the stuff of our culture. Their use and influence would have been unknown to past generations, but a youth of today has little trouble in coping with their intricacies.

Man's inheritance of culture makes him the species least influenced by biological factors. There is very little physical difference between human beings at birth, but society imposes its culture upon us. We are affected by unequal opportunities in such spheres as family backgrounds, housing, education and employment. We internalise behavioural standards, ideals, codes of conduct and modes of thought. We are affected by society's goals and lifestyles.

Biology studies the resemblances which human beings bear towards one another. Sociology studies human beings who have been made different by virtue of the culture of their particular society.

Biology is sufficiently occupied studying the numerous different forms of life that it cannot be expected to concentrate upon man's social structures. It is sociology which concerns itself with man's social institutions and social interactions.

Sociologists, looking at society from a functionalist perspective, have borrowed from biology useful analogies which have contributed to man's understanding of human society. Firstly, societies may be considered as passing through processes of evolution similar to the biological evolution of living creatures expounded by Darwin. Secondly, society may be regarded as analogous to living organisms with each part fulfilling a function which is essential to the whole. These are only analogies and must not be pressed too far. Heredity and environment provide biology and sociology with much common ground, but man's existence as a social being is quite distinctive. Man is not biologically or genetically pro-grammed to behave in any special way.

Biologists have found that salmon leave the river where they are born and swim hundreds of miles out to sea, only to return after five years to the same river, in order to fertilise their eggs and die; it must be instinctive behaviour as they are unable to observe the similar life cycle of their predecessors. Every autumn millions of Greater Shearwater seabirds gather on the coastlines of Europe and unerringly fly to the Tristan da Cunha islands in the south Atlantic; on the way they start courtship, for it is the only place where they nest and rear their families. But man, as the least biologically influenced species, has no genetic code which instructs him to behave in such an instinctive way (see Fig. 1.6).

● *Social Anthropology*

Social anthropology and sociology are closely related studies. If sociology is thought of as the study of *all* human societies, then social anthropology

Fig. 1.6 Migrating birds obey a genetic code

may be considered as a branch of that study. Anthropology concentrates upon social organisations and social customs of primitive, often pre-literate peoples. Some social anthropologists would dispute the term 'primitive society' preferring to use the term 'small-scale society'. Sociology tends to concentrate upon contemporary, industrial and post-industrial societies: social anthropology provides invaluable comparisons with other societies. Social anthropology is a very worthwhile study for a sociologist because it casts scepticism upon conventional wisdom.

Sociology is nothing if it is not comparative; social anthropology assists sociology by providing examples of varieties of culture. Studies of other cultures provide evidence of refreshingly novel ways of facing problems of social life and may well give an insight into the shortcomings of our own society.

> Isolated on small Pacific islands, in dense African jungles or Asiatic wastes, it is still possible to find untouched societies which have chosen solutions of life's problems different from our own which can give us precious evidence on the malleability of human nature.
> (Mead, M. *Growing up in New Guinea*)

People in any one society often regard the social behaviour practised by those around them as normal, acceptable and as a matter of commonsense. A social custom accepted as the norm in a primitive society, may be looked upon as bizarre by members of a modern society. Yet an analysis of exotic customs may reveal that they are grounded in a common sense which is lost on superficial observers who make snap judgements.

Interactionists claim that judgements of what is 'normal' are relative:

> What a man sees depends upon what he looks at, and also upon what his previous visual conceptual experience has taught him to see.
> (Kuhn, T.S. *The Structure of Scientific Revolutions*)

So an experienced anthropologist gets closer to the meaning which primitive peoples put upon their own actions. He is involved in what Max Weber termed social action; he interprets the meaning of those he studies. They in their turn will estimate what the social anthropologist thinks of them and this indeed may affect their behaviour and make it more difficult to interpret. Social customs which were relevant to life centuries ago may exert an influence upon our life today.

Bronislaw Malinowski's anthropological studies of the peoples of the Trobriand archipelago and other islands to the east of New Guinea revealed what appeared initially to be a random exchange of virtually useless goods. For many centuries these Papuo-Melanesian peoples have been operating a social system centred upon gifts and counter-gifts. The circulating exchange of goods, over a vast geographical area, is known as the Kula ring. A priori, this inter-island trade appears nonsensical to people living in a modern society dominated by the profit motive and powerful multi-national companies. Yet those living in materialist societies can learn from the social value of the Kula ring. For the Kula involves trust and commercial honour, with liberality being the greatest virtue and meanness the greatest shame. J.P. Singh Uberoi (*Politics of the Kula Ring*) has argued that the ultimate social importance of the Kula ring is that the individual giver is symbolic of a whole chain of partnerships. Reciprocity expresses and achieves friendship in symmetrical social relationships. A semblance of such relationship is exemplified in our exchange of Christmas gifts and cards. Sahlins (*Stone Age Economics*) contends that the economic basis of Trobriand tribal politics is chiefly generosity. Marcel Mauss (*The Gift*) believes that civilised man has lost much by instituting economic systems involving large-scale exchange of goods and services undertaken purely for financial profit, in place of non-economic giving where transactions are of great moral value as an aid to social relations. Mutual giving enhances social relations. The gift may be made without thought of reciprocation, but the act of giving is likely to bring future returns to the giver. The size of the gift represents the status in which the giver is held.

> The human condition appears as one of general indebtedness.
> (Burridge, K. *New Heaven, New Earth*)

Social anthropologists' study of gifts throws light upon modern examples of social generosity, e.g. blood donors give their blood without payment. Such giving has unique attributes:

1 It is an impersonal gift because the recipient is not known to the donor.
2 The act of giving involves pain.
3 There are no penalties imposed on those who do not give.
4 There are no obligations upon recipients of blood.
5 No corresponding gift is expected by donors.

> ... it is only in the last twenty years or so that every country's need for blood on a large and rapidly increasing scale has raised in a new and impersonal guise these fundamental questions of social relations; of giving, receiving and paying.
> (Titmuss, R. *The Gift Relationship*)

As sociologists, we all benefit from social anthropological studies of cultures other than our own, because they record an infinite variety of human customs. That these studies are kept up is regarded as outstandingly important by those who adopt the conflict perspective; they stress the *dynamic* (constantly changing) character of cultures and argue that the social framework and details of organisations should be recorded before any are lost to posterity. Primitive peoples have social values worthy of study. As human beings are very similar biologically it is important to endeavour to trace reasons for the enormous cultural variety in the world. Sir James Frazer, author of *The Golden Bough*, and the first to hold a professorial chair in Social Anthropology in 1907, believed that there were three main progressive stages by which human beings developed from the savage to the sophisticated. The extent of development depended on whether the structure of society was based upon (1) the *magical*, (2) the *religious* or (3) the *scientific*. Frazer's tripartite evolutionary scheme may be useful but it is now considered to be too simplistic to accept that social life is determined by the evolutionary stage reached by a particular society. Geography plays its part; Montesquieu pointed to a relationship between climate and society.

Social anthropology and sociology share many investigatory methods. The social anthropologist attempts to eliminate preconceptions and to be as objective as possible. There are no taboo subjects for the anthropologist. He studies the customs of primitive societies as he finds them, be they incest, or the strangest, bloodthirstiest religious rite. As an interactionist would point out, however, observation of primitive rituals may also be qualitative and interpretive; the anthropologist attends a religious ceremony to 'get the feeling' of the occasion, and impressions of those involved such as priests, other participants and passive onlookers; he notes their excitements, agitations and other emotions. The social anthropologist is also able to understand primitive peoples by *participant observation*: he learns their language and lives among them; within limitations imposed by modern prejudices, he puts himself in the place of primitive peoples. The social anthropologist must try to see as they see; act as they act; feel as they feel; think as they think.

Modern social anthropology owes much to Radcliffe-Brown and Malinowski, the two most eminent social anthropologists-cum-sociologists. Radcliffe-Brown's work among the tribes and aborigines of Australasia advanced sociological understanding of kinship and marriage while his appreciation of the importance of structure and function helped to establish a distinct school of sociological thought – structural functionalism. Sociology also owes a debt to Malinowski for attempting to expose what he regarded as fundamental errors which have been used as arguments to vindicate modern industrial societies. Firstly, Malinowski's photographic evidence of surfeits of yams and pigs, indicated that it is erroneous to regard primitive man as so preoccupied with eking out an existence that he only had utilitarian articles and did not store wealth for its own sake. Secondly, Malinowski argued that it was misleading to apply over-simplified evolutionary theories of successive stages of development in a world context; societies are so different that communal ownership among so-called 'communism of savages' is not necessarily a justification for supporting modern communistic theories and the materialistic perspective of history.

Some modern sociologists have based their own work upon systematic studies in social anthropology. W. Lloyd Warner, for example, carried out an anthropological study of Australian aborigines as a preparation for his urban studies of American society. A further link between sociology and social anthropology has been the attempt to establish a rural-urban continuum between primitive and modern societies (see Fig. 1.7). Although such a continuum provides a useful bridge between sociology and social anthropology, it should only be used as a model and not as evidence of a grand evolutionary scheme for all societies.

- *Psychology*

Psychology is the study of mind, of mental processes, and of behaviour. Sociology is concerned with human behaviour in the context of social relationships. Max Weber believed strongly than an understanding of psychology is necessary in order that sociologists should gain a more meaningful comprehension of social actions. It is most important that

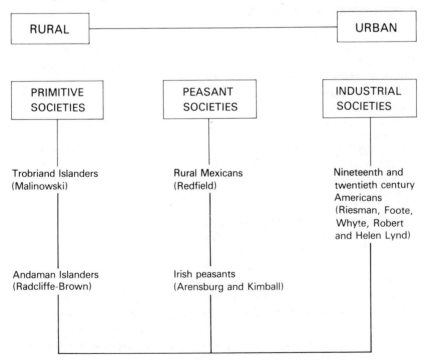

Fig. 1.7 The rural-urban continuum

sociologists should examine the motivation behind human behaviour. The sociology of a fish tank can only be studied from observations of the fishes' behaviour but, according to interactionists, the sociology of human society can be analysed far more profoundly because sociologists possess subjective insight into the behaviour of other human beings. Only humans are introspective: they can reflect upon themselves and evaluate their own behaviour.

The psychologist's study of human sentiments, emotions, conditioning, understanding, perception, learning, memory and other cognitive processes are closely linked with the sociologist's study of the inter-relationship between the individual and society. Sociology studies how society influences human behaviour, and ways in which human behaviour determines the nature of society.

Psychology and sociology draw close together in the specialised field of *social psychology* which studies the ways in which behaviour is influenced by social environment. A human baby is born helpless with the potentialities to develop into a mature human being, but this evolution depends upon the presence of other humans and the socialising effect they have upon the baby. Socialisation begins within the family and then extends to a variety of group relationships.

> Throughout the world it is normal for the process of socialization to be initiated by the parents: it is from their behaviour towards him that the child first learns to label his own actions as 'good' or 'bad'. The network of social relationships through which the process continues is gradually extended, earlier or later in the child's life according to the family and community structures of the individual culture.
>
> (Newson, J. and E. *Four Years Old in an Urban Community*)

Social psychology studies the various consequences of interactions among the members of a group. The effects of socialisation must be borne in mind when studying male and female behaviour; biological differences between the sexes are not very significant at birth.

> One is not born, but rather becomes, a woman.
> (Beauvoir, S. de *The Second Sex*)

Social psychology is especially concerned with ways in which individuals relate to a group. An individual develops as a member of a human group. A man left alone on a desert island might well revert to savage instincts. A small isolated group is likely to forget quickly the influence of a larger group of which it has been part. William Golding describes such an experience in *Lord of the Flies* when one of the boys (Jack) reveals inherent traits of sadism and cruelty with calamitous results for the rest of the group marooned on the island. The psychologist Carl Jung analysed the *collective subconscious* which integrates members of a human group; the more integrated the group, the more developed the collective subconscious. Collective behaviour is less obvious in a non-integrated group, such as a theatre audience, where there is little or no communication between individual members. Social psychology concentrates upon the integrated group where the social self is developed through socialisation.

Social psychologists study the ways by which an individual's personality is formed and developed. Personality is emergent, rather than instinctive. A child of parents with dominant personalities may develop an indecisive and submissive personality because all vital decisions are made for her. The sociologist studies how authority within a society may be affected by the leader's personality. A leader who displays a strong personality exercises charismatic authority and gathers to himself a superior presence as exemplified by Christ or Hitler.

A strong case can be argued in favour of a closer association between social psychology and sociology. A closer link between the two studies does not imply that they cover the same fields: the two studies complement each other by affording different perspectives of human behaviour.

● *Economics*

Economics shares with sociology the dubious distinction of being treated with initial scepticism. Modern economics has found a measure of respectability by adopting specialised techniques and establishing a body of theory peculiar to the subject. As economics has become more abstract and hypothetical, it has received added recognition in academic circles even though it can be argued that econometrics and other quantitative aspects of economics have taken the subject further from the real world.

Economics and sociology both owe a great deal to their founding fathers. The British classical economists, (Adam Smith, Thomas Malthus, David Ricardo and John Stuart Mill) established political economy as a separate discipline. The classical economists may have been presumptuous in their attempt to postulate irrevocable, immutable laws comparable to the laws of the natural sciences, but they were guided by their belief that political economy provided an approach to the solution of socio-economic problems. Early economists were inclined to accept a structural-functionalist perspective. On the other hand, Karl Marx propounded a conflict view of economics.

There has always been a close link between economics and sociology. We have seen that the classical economists turned their attention to social problems. Modern economists and sociologists both study the works of Malthus and Marx. All branches of learning, including economics and sociology, can trace their roots to Plato, Aristotle and other philosophers of Ancient Greece, but whereas sociology is still greatly influenced by its founding fathers, modern economics owes less to the classical economists. Present-day economists are more concerned with Keynesian theory or the likely effects of monetarism as propounded by Milton Friedman. Indeed in recent years economics has adopted two main perspectives, i.e. the view of the Keynesians or the view of the monetarists.

Economic problems of resource distribution are closely linked with sociology: the way a society allocates its scarce resources is of major sociological significance. In a market economy the allocation of goods will be determined by the interplay of the forces of supply and demand: the wealthy enjoy the largest share of available goods. In a command economy, distribution is determined by the collectivist authority: if the state acts on behalf of the people, as a whole, the distribution will be more equitable than in a market economy. In Britain a mixed economy provides the best (or worst) of both worlds. Some productive units (the nationalised industries) are owned by the state, while others are owned by private individuals and institutions (joint stock companies).

A sociological view of the economy has been put forward by Karl Polanyi. He has challenged the formal meaning given to the economy as a choice induced by an insufficiency of means. In this belief he is joined by J.K. Galbraith, regarded as a maverick by economists who disagree with the sociological slant he brings to problems of economics. Galbraith has challenged the economist's pre-occupation with scarcity.

> These ideas were the product of a world in which poverty had always been man's lot, and any other state was in degree unimaginable.
> (Galbraith, J.K. *The Affluent Society*)

Polanyi has argued that:

> Only the substantive meaning of 'economic' is capable of yielding the concepts that are required by the social sciences.
> (Polanyi, K. *The Great Transformation*)

Polanyi considers that the substantive meaning of the concept 'economic' derives from man's dependence for his living upon nature and his fellows. The conception of economic science as based upon markets and prices is inadequate for sociologists. Polanyi finds it best to consider the economy as an instituted process acquiring cohesion by a combination of reciprocity, redistribution and exchange. Such a conception is not limited to market forces, scarcity and price determination but is extended to all the factors necessary for social life such as air, water and love, but which economists classify as non-economic goods since they do not command a price in the market. No man should be regarded as an 'economic man' devoted solely to his own gain.

The revival of the term 'political economy' has been advocated by Edward Nell (in Blackburn, R. *Ideology in Social Science*). The title of 'political economy' was changed to 'economics' in the nineteenth century to bring the subject in line with recognised sciences such as physics. Nell believes that economics must return to its origins in order to grapple with such problems as poverty, unemployment, mal-distribution of income between social classes and the power of multi-nationals. Economics has for too long concentrated upon suspect high theory such as perfect competition, the theory of the firm, marginal productivity and consumer sovereignty. Sociologists are more interested in ways of improving the social environment in which economic behaviour takes place.

There are so many twin considerations of economics and sociology that an all round view of human life necessitates a knowledge of both disciplines. Economics and sociology frequently study the same areas but they have their different perspectives. The economist studies the work force as a means of production, while the sociologist studies satisfaction gained from work or man's alienation from work. The economist's interest in division of labour centres upon the advantages and disadvantages of its use as a productive method while the sociologist is concerned with occupational differentiation as a basis of the social class structure. The economist studies economic systems in the light of production and allocation of goods, but the sociologist analyses the social relations of production including the possession of power and authority according to the mode of production (capitalistic or communistic). The economist studies trade unions and employers' organisations as two sides in a collective bargaining process, whereas the sociologist is interested in trade unions as instruments of social change; the economist sees strikes as a hindrance to production, but the sociologist sees them as facets of the conflict which exists in society.

Economics and sociology are linked in being closely bound with political life. In the social sciences, theory is of little value without action; the application of knowledge in both economics and sociology requires an insight into the workings of the political system.

• *Politics*

Political science encompasses the philosophical, organisational and procedural aspects of government.
1 *Philosophical* – a study of the *meaning* of government, including political theory and concepts.
2 *Organisational* – a study of the *organisation* of central and local government, comparative government and international relations.
3 *Procedural* – a study of the *procedures* of government such as the passage

of legislation, the power of the executive and the independence of the judiciary (the separation of powers).

Sociology concentrates less upon the formal functions of political organisations and more upon social aspects of politics such as decision-making processes, the formation of public opinion, popular attitudes about political issues, party membership and pressure groups. The sociologist is especially interested in power and its manipulation by elite groups, or lobbying by those with power or propaganda methods. Political sociology studies all political phenomena.

Political power is analysed by sociologists according to opposing paradigms of consensus (pluralist) or conflict views of society. Pluralists adopt a liberal perspective accepting that although there are bound to be a great variety of political opinions, a consensus is reached whereby a framework of basic shared values enables government to further the general good of society.

> The interests of all groups and people in a nation are ultimately the same.
> (Mrs Margaret Thatcher, Conservative Local Government Conference, 3 March 1979)

Conflict-political sociologists believe that society is inevitably divided into two diametrically opposed groups made up of rulers and ruled, exploiters and exploited, oppressors and oppressed, those with political power and those without: those in the dominant group ensure that the country is governed in their interest and thus political institutions, such as the legislature, the executive, the judiciary and the civil service, will draw their members from the dominant group and work for its benefit.

> The power elite is composed of men whose positions enable them to transcend the ordinary environments of ordinary men and women; they are in positions to make decisions having major consequences.... For they are in command of the major hierarchies and organizations of modern society.
> (Mills, C. Wright *The Power Elite*)

Consensus theorists believe that political power is legitimised by a mandate based upon a democratic majority and that social changes should only take place gradually. Conflict theorists believe that political power is manipulated by a conspiracy of political socialising agencies, such as families, schools and the media, intent upon convincing the masses that national unity is a reality whereas it is nothing but a meaningless myth created by those with political power.

> Institutions which enable a tiny class, amounting to less than 2 per cent of the population of Great Britain, to take year by year nearly one quarter of the nation's annual output of wealth, may appeal to the emotions of wonder, reverence and awe.
> (Tawney, R.H. *Equality*; preface to the third edition)

Sociologists have specialised in studies of psephology, i.e. in analyses of electoral voting, and have found that the majority of people vote according to the way in which they were socialised to vote. It is naive to accept that the majority of people shrewdly assess current issues and vote logically according to independent freedom of choice.

> ... humans must learn their political behaviour early and well and persist in it. Otherwise there would be no regularity – perhaps even chaos.
> (Hyman, H.H. *Political Socialization*)

The most influential factor affecting patterns of voting behaviour has been .proved to be social class. The study of class or social stratification is the special province of the sociologist. Family antecedents, housing, schooling and occupations are all important derivatives of social class. Voting behaviour, which is the very stuff of politics in a democratic community, cannot be understood in any worthwhile sense without the sociologist's analysis of social class. The claim that affluence brings about a significant change in political loyalties (*embourgeoisement* thesis) has been challenged by J.H. Goldthorpe *et al.* (*The Affluent Worker: Political Attitudes and Behaviour*).

No modern student of political science can ignore the persuasive power of large bureaucratic organisations. Political sociology has long studied the social implications of formal political organisations in general and bureaucracy in particular. Max Weber made an important sociological assessment of the political power of bureaucracy upon political life. He argued that bureaucratic institutions are liable to become far more powerful, while politics will become decreasingly unimportant. Anthony Giddens has analysed Weber's political thought in terms of the subservience of modern political institutions to bureaucratic organisations.

> In Weber's view, both conservatives and socialists share in common the misconceived belief that it is possible for modern man to 'escape from the cage'.
> (Giddens, A. *Politics and Sociology in the Thought of Max Weber*)

One of the major problems of modern political sociology is to ensure that bureaucratic social institutions provide welfare for the community while at the same time individual freedom is preserved.

Finally, sociologists have pointed to the ambivalence of the term 'public opinion': at best it is a body of articulated views of which politicians take note primarily at election times; at worst public opinion is so fickle and uninformed that politicians can ignore it with impunity. However, almost all members of the community are involved in political activity, even though for many it may be little more than casting their vote every five years or so.

Millions are, moreover, members of organizations, such as trade unions,

professional associations or trade associations which are, from time to time, involved in politics. Depending upon their traditions, they may react vigorously against the government or they may prefer to use quieter methods and behind-the-scenes pressure to obtain better consideration of their claims by ministers. But they all have to engage in politics to some extent.
(Blondel, J. *Voters, Parties and Leaders*)

• History

History concentrates upon a study of the past, whereas sociology is more concerned with contemporary society. Sociology relies upon history for accounts of major social acts which occurred in the past. The sociologist often acts as historian in the collection of data regarded by historians as beyond their traditional province. In every age

> the sociologist, but for the grace of his academic title, is the man who must listen to gossip despite himself, who is tempted to look through keyholes, to read other people's mail, to open closed cabinets.
> (Berger, P. *Invitation to Sociology*)

The study of history is a social necessity. The earliest human societies found the need to recount their history through narrators of past encounters. In everyday life, a man who suffers from amnesia finds it impossible to orientate himself to social interactions. Similarly, a society without history would have difficulty in establishing its identity. History and sociology are thus related to the need of individuals 'to find their bearings' in the world.

Sociology began its life when traumatic changes were taking place throughout the world. Comte wrote the first major sociological work at a time when science and technology were being applied on a massive scale: human society was subjected to greater changes than had been known before. Comte, Durkheim and Marx were aware of this turning point in history although each viewed the radical changes in the organisation of society from a different perspective. Each saw the need to relate their thinking to history – to survey the past, evaluate the present and make predictions for the future. Later Weber, who had been trained as an historian, emphasised that history, like all studies of mankind, could not be value-free. Englishmen and Germans write about the same events in history from different perspectives depending on their preconceptions and value-judgements. Weber believed that an historian had a moral duty to judge men and events – indeed he could do no other.

Although historians study unique events in the past, they also aim to establish a sequence of events. Braudel, an eminent modern historian, has written that:

Resounding events are often only momentary outbursts, surface manifestations of these larger movements and explicable only in terms of them.
(Braudel, F. *The Mediterranean*; preface to third edition)

It may be true that history never repeats itself exactly: events have already occurred and the same circumstances will never be reproduced in every detail. Nevertheless it is possible to examine a particular sequence of events and then to formulate generalisations. Traditional sociology began from such generalisations. Sociology attempts to formulate theories which help to explain a large number of particular events. A sociologist might study the world wars of the twentieth century with the intention of developing a theory capable of explaining the causes of war in general terms. He uses history as a source of information and as a testing bed for sociological theories.

History and sociology are closely linked with psychology. The historian Sir Hugh Trevor-Roper (*Historical Essays*) sees history as the interplay of human personality and massive social forces. The sociologist is concerned, at the micro level, with personality, and at the macro level with social forces.

Sociology is indebted to history for the conception of historical periods, while sociology has aided history in the classification of societies. Comte argued that all human civilisation moved through three stages.
1 *Theological* – man believes that all phenomena are produced by supernatural forces.
2 *Metaphysical* – man believes that all phenomena are produced by abstract, rather than supernatural, forces.
3 *Positive* – man's mind is occupied by reasoning and observation as the means of knowledge.
According to the Marxist perspective of history, a revolution of the proletariat is inevitable in the evolutionary process from capitalism to socialism. Capitalists own the means of production which establishes them as the ruling class until overthrown by a great class struggle. The revolution awaits economic crises of capitalism and the efficient organisation of the proletariat. Such crises have arisen many times in the Third World in the last decade. In Africa, South East Asia and the Caribbean the conditions have been ripe for the working of Marx's 'inevitability of History'. But Marxists still have to answer the question, whether the working class is still a revolutionary force in the West – and if not, why not?

Most modern thinkers have abandoned the ideal of a grand revolutionary scheme of history propounded by Plato, Hegel and other philosophers. Historians and sociologists find it more useful to examine stages in human development and 'trends' common to all societies. History was once preoccupied with bloody wars and the sordid personal lives of rulers, but modern historians have a bias towards social and economic history. The social significance of white rule in Africa and the doctrine of apartheid are now seen as of greater historical importance than the feats of Rhodes, the death of Gordon at Khartoum, or the relief of Mafeking.

The interpretation of modern trends form the subject matter of both sociology and history. Max Weber, from the stance of the sociologist, noted that when conditions of human industriousness and frugality (the Protestant ethic), accompanied *laissez-faire* economic philosophy (capitalism), then there would be a trend for entrepreneurs to aim at profit maximisation. R.H. Tawney, from the viewpoint of an historian, also analysed the relationship between protestantism and capitalism (*Religion and the Rise of Capitalism*) pointing out that whereas Christianity once regarded the charging of interest as a sin, the modern trend is to accept the legitimisation of unearned income. A 'trend' is less dogmatic, but more realistic, than any so-called historical law. An attempt to postulate a law such as 'there is a high propensity for dictators to be assassinated' may fit the circumstances in a number of cases but it does not fulfil the conditions of a scientific law because exemptions exist. Abraham Lincoln and John Kennedy were assassinated rulers although not dictators, whereas many dictators have died peacefully in their beds.

Henry Ford said 'History is bunk'. There are many who say the same of sociology. Yet both history and sociology show how our lives are conditioned both by our contemporaries and by those who lived in years long past. Peter Berger has pointed out how history influences the coming together in marriage of a modern young couple who are convinced that they are making a choice for themselves.

> ... 'they' who are dead have long ago written the script for almost every move that is made. The notion that sexual attraction can be translated into romantic emotion was cooked up by misty-voiced minstrels titillating the imagination of aristocratic ladies about the twelfth century or thereabouts....
>
> Just as all these hoary ancients have decided the basic framework within which the passions of our exemplary couple will develop, so each step in their courtship has been pre-defined, prefabricated – if you like, 'fixed'. It is not only that they are supposed to fall in love and to enter into a monogamous marriage in which she gives up her name and he his solvency, that this love must be manufactured at all cost or the marriage will seem insincere to all concerned, and that state and church will watch over the menage with anxious attention once it is established – all of which are fundamental assumptions concocted centuries before the protagonists were born.
>
> (Berger, P. *Invitation to Sociology*)

History and sociology are continually moving together. They both study social conditions, social forces and social processes. The social importance of history is exemplified in everyday conversations of ordinary people. Judgements about whether or not society is more permissive and promiscuous must be based upon comparisons with previous standards of morality. Sociologists appreciate that it is impossible for people living in modern society to escape the influence of history.

1.6 Sociological methods

● *Observation*

One of the easiest ways to find out about a social activity is to assume the role of an observer. Raymond Gold (*Roles in Sociological Field Observation*) suggests a continuum depending upon degrees of interaction and participation. At one end of the continuum (see Fig. 1.8) is the researcher who has no interaction with those observed; the non-participant observer does not become involved, and so is unlikely to gain a deep insight into the

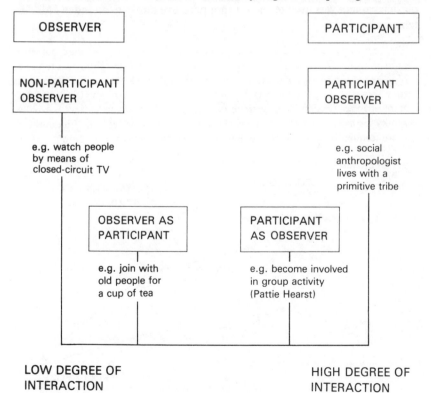

Fig. 1.8 Continuum of observation and participation

social phenomenon being investigated. At the other end of the continuum, the participant observer experiences a social activity personally; he is able to gain a deep insight into a social activity because he becomes part of it.

1 **Non-participant observation** A sociologist might mix with a crowd of soccer supporters in the Liverpool Kop without them being aware of his intentions. His observations would be largely impressional and qualitative. He watches the crowd's behaviour, listens to their chants and notes their general attitudes. Any quantitative findings are bound to be rough and ready; generalisations may be made about the age and sex structures of the group.

A non-participant observer may be physically present, but remains unobtrusive and uninvolved. One-way mirrors and closed circuit television allow people to be observed without their knowledge. A film of a group of children playing could form the basis of a sociogram. A sociogram is based upon observing the attraction or rejection between members of a social group (see Fig. 1.9). Vance Packard describes how a hidden camera was used to record shoppers' eye blinks as an index of inner tension.

> The best way to detect what was going on inside the shopper was a galvanometer or lie detector. That obviously was impractical. The next best thing was to use a hidden motion-picture camera and record the eye-blink rate of the women as they shopped. How fast a person blinks his eyes is a pretty good index of his state of inner tension. The average person, according to Mr Vicary, normally blinks his eyes about thirty-two times a minute. If he is tense he blinks them more frequently, under extreme tension up to fifty or sixty times a minute. If he

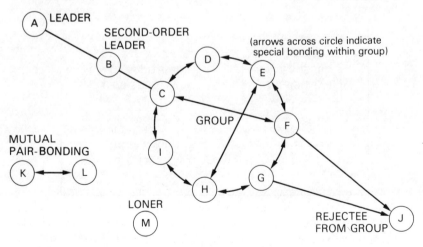

Fig. 1.9 A sociogram

is notably relaxed on the other hand his eye-blink rate may drop to a subnormal twenty or less.

Mr Vicary set up his cameras and started following the ladies as they entered the store. The results were startling, even to him. Their eye-blink rate, instead of going up to indicate mounting tension, went down and down, to a very subnormal fourteen blinks a minute. The ladies fell into what Mr Vicary calls a hypnoidal trance, a light kind of trance that, he explains, is the first stage of hypnosis. Mr Vicary has decided that the main cause of the trance is that the supermarket is packed with products that in former years would have been items that only kings and queens could afford, and here in this fairyland they were available.

(Packard, V. *The Hidden Persuaders*)

Something should be known about the purpose of the social activity being observed. Consider the following account.

It is a hot day during a period of drought. Eleven men dressed in white clothes run on to a field. They position themselves carefully and throw a spherical object at each other. Presently two men dressed in white enter the field and stand about twenty yards apart. They carry large, wide sticks. Finally two men clothed in long white coats walk slowly towards the middle of the field. Suddenly it pours with rain and all the men run for shelter.

People in England would recognise that a cricket match had been arranged but rain had stopped play. An observer from another society might assume that a successful rain ceremony had taken place. Similarly an observer from a different culture would find it most difficult to make sense of a communion service performed by Christians.

Even when the purpose of social actions are comprehended, observers may provide vastly different accounts of the same activity. Two non-participant observers, in at the kill of a fox hunt, would provide descriptive accounts at great variance if one believed foxes to be dangerous vermin while the other abhorred blood sports. It is always difficult to avoid personal bias.

The trained sociologist may consider it desirable to explain the purpose of the observation. Workers observed at the Hawthorne plant (see section 5.3) reacted to the presence of observers; production increased mainly because the workers realised they were being watched. Social researchers must allow for group reactions when using the methodological tool of observation.

2 **Observer as participant** An observer may find it necessary to indulge in limited participation. If a large number of old people are interviewed in the course of a widespread social survey, it may be expedient to win their confidence by joining them for a cup of tea. Participation is kept to the minimum necessary to secure the highest possible response rate. Limited

participation mitigates subjective involvement but the observer risks accusations of superficiality.

3 **Participant as observer** The participant as observer maintains a low profile so that those observed will react in a normal way, i.e. as if they were not being observed. He exerts a **control effect** to prevent both participants and observers from changing attitudes or actions. The researcher may use the ploy of close relationships with a key individual, who facilitates his acceptance by the group. Thus W.F. Whyte's investigation of an Italian-American slum gang was aided by his friendship with 'Doc', the gang leader.

> As I wrote, I showed the various parts to Doc and went over them with him in detail. His criticisms were invaluable in my revision. At times, when I was dealing with him and his gang, he would smile and say, 'This will embarrass me, but this is the way it was, so go ahead with it.'
> (Whyte, W.F. *Street Corner Society*)

In 1976 Pattie Hearst, daughter of an American millionaire, was kidnapped by Symbionese urban guerillas. They resocialised this middle-class girl until she became a willing participant in armed bank robbery. Her role pretence was negligible but her observations were of little value because she over-identified with the group.

4 **Participant observer** Participant observation is a key tool of social anthropology. A great deal of time is spent in gaining acceptance into the established framework of social relationships. Participant observers must

> become an unobtrusive part of the scene, people whom the participants take for granted and consider to be non-threatening.
> (Bogdan, R. and Taylor, J.S. *Introduction to Qualitative Research Methods*)

The maximum involvement and high interaction enjoyed by a participant observer poses' difficulties of objectivity; his close proximity to those observed may lead him to side with underdogs.

> In such a situation the researcher carries a heavy responsibility. He would like his book to be of some help to the people in the district.
> (Whyte, W.F. *Street Corner Society*)

● *Interviews and the use of questionnaires*

Social research requires more than mere observation. It necessitates asking questions and collating data. This involves the employment of interview techniques which can be conveniently classified as a continuum (see Fig. 1.10).

1 *Structured interviews* are customarily accompanied by the use of pre-set

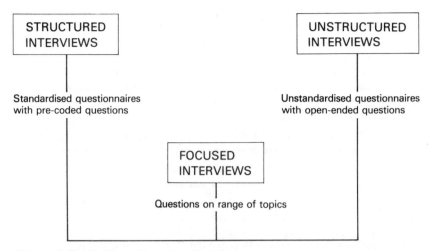

Fig. 1.10 Continuum of interview techniques

or pre-coded questionnaires. For example, enumerators are employed by the Registrar General's Department to assist citizens to complete census forms accurately (see Fig. 1.11). Such interviewers require minimal training for they are merely mechanical aids for collecting answers. Professional interviewers were used as early as the 1841 census and the early factory inspection system employed tabular forms. Research by questionnaires is an objective exercise and tendencies towards bias are minimised; information gathered can be analysed by a computer. The compilation of the schedule or questionnaire is very important; the results of structured interviews are only as good as the questions asked. It is important that the 'right' questions are asked in accordance with the objectives of the research, and that questions are framed in language familiar to the person interviewed (*the respondent*). Questions should be framed in simple, unequivocal language, but woolly generalisations must be avoided. Questions are usually asked in a uniform manner and in a pre-determined sequence. Most people are familiar with mail question-naires which are economical, convenient, speedy, objective and can be dispersed over a wide area.

2 *Focused interviews* A number of topics are selected as relevant to the research and the interviewer is given discretion in the questioning process. He can choose certain topics to cover in detail if the respondent appears to be willing to provide useful answers; supplementary questions may also be asked. Focused interviews probe deeper than structured interviews but are more prone to bias. Even if the questions are impersonal, the interviewers may become personal.

3 *Unstructured interviews* allow respondents greater freedom in expressing

opinions, and may result in detailed recollections and accounts which give a more realistic picture than the statistics collated from pre-coded questionnaires. Young and Willmott (*Family and Kinship in East London*) found that structured interviews led to a vast amount of quantitative data, but unstructured interviews provided a more useful revelation of the real feelings of the respondents. Open-ended questions encourage respondents to answer freely and fully. If interviewers are able to create a sincerely informal atmosphere, they may be able to extract answers which reveal more accurately the beliefs of respondents. Such depth interviews are likely to err on the side of subjectivity rather than objectivity, and results obtained are difficult both to classify and apply.

• *Studies*

1 *Case studies* The case studies carried out by interactionists are an example of micro-sociological research. By such studies a particular person (a drug addict), or an organisation (a firm or a school) or an event (a strike) is studied in detail. A perceptive case study of the anatomy of a strike at the Ford Halewood factory in 1971 is provided by Richard Hyman in *Strikes*. Case studies are useful in probation and social work where the inquirer is concerned with people as individuals. Such studies provide a useful counter to unrealistic stereotypes. On the one hand, Weber's notion of the ideal type is a useful classificatory technique but, on the other hand, case studies indicate the infinite variety displayed by individuals. Case studies inevitably involve high interaction between researcher and subject with subsequent disadvantages of low reliability and the collection of trivia which proves difficult to analyse. However, Gouldner contends that interaction can be a positive advantage in the search for reality. For example, Isaacs's vivid accounts of geriatrics' living conditions, in *Survival of the Unfittest*, is more indicative of the plight of old, sick people than masses of bare statistics relating to their lives.

2 *Cross-sectional studies* are limited to short periods of time and have been likened to photographic 'snapshots'. In the face of exaggerated accounts of sexual promiscuity, Michael Schofield attempted to obtain the real facts about sexual attitudes and behaviour during the 1960s. His results were based upon about two thousand interviews held with young people between the ages of thirteen and eighteen. Schofield's study carried out under the auspices of the Central Council for Health Education concluded that, for the time of his study:

> ... promiscuity, though it exists, is not a prominent feature of teenage sexual behaviour. Consequently the risks of venereal disease are not very great.
> (Schofield, M. *The Sexual Behaviour of Young People*)

3 *Longitudinal studies* extend over a long period of time. The researchers study a selected sample of people at intervals and note significant patterns of change. Longitudinal studies indicate cause and effect relationships over time. The longer the study continues the less reliable the comparability between the initial and final group: the whereabouts of some participants is lost whereas others lose interest.

> However, at least one survey in Britain has lasted more than twenty years and maintained interest and participation of 90 per cent of the original large representative sample of 5,000.
> (Krausz, E. and Miller, S.H. *Social Research Design*)

Examples of well-documented longitudinal studies include the following.
(a) J.W.B. Douglas's *The Home and the School* was a follow-up of initial investigation carried out in 1946, based upon interviews with every woman in Britain who had borne a child during a particular week in March 1946 (*Maternity in Great Britain*). The first study had been concerned with ante-natal services, whereas J.W.B. Douglas's study paid particular attention to the primary schooling of the same group of children.
(b) John and Elizabeth Newson's *Infant Care in an Urban Community* studied 700 Nottingham children in infancy and analysed aspects of child rearing such as attitudes to breast feeding, father's participatory role and disciplinary methods. The second study (*Four Years Old in an Urban Community*) examined the children as they reached their fourth birthdays and concerned

> the social and material context of their lives: the streets and street friendships, backyards and neighbours, homes and families, which make up the kaleidoscope of their everyday environments.

The Newsons compared family sizes, sibling play, rights and privileges, language codes, the control of aggression, eating habits and many other aspects of child rearing. The two studies revealed a persistence of different attitudes in child-rearing in particular relationship to the social class of the mother.
(c) *The National Children's Bureau* studied a birth cohort of 17 000 children born in the week ending 9 March 1958. This group has been studied at three distinct intervals. The findings of the first survey was entitled *From Birth to Seven*. The third follow-up, *Britain's Sixteen-Year-Olds* (ed. Ken Fogelmar, 1976), confirmed the differences in educational attainment between middle- and working-class children.
(4) *Comparative statistical studies* provide before-and-after comparisons which test the results of social changes. A good example of such a study is Triesman's examination of comparative Department of Health statistics

which gave credence to the theory that destruction of working-class areas in inner cities causes an increase in the rate of mental illness (Triesman, D. in Armistead, N., ed., *Reconstructing Social Psychology*).

• *Statistics*

The use of statistics by structural-functionalists such as Durkheim coincided with the scientific spirit which permeated nineteenth-century thought, combined with the desire of officials to collect an ever-increasing number of facts about citizens of emergent nation states. Social statisticians consider that data about people and things has advantages over subjective ideas. Such figures enable records to be collected of crimes, taxes, births, etc. One of the first officials to collect and use social statistics was Doctor William Farr, the Registrar General's medical statistician who created a national register of deaths and their causes. Farr believed that as preventative medicine was preferable to curative medicine the first stage in the prevention of disease was to discover its causes and relate them to age, sex, region and social class. Durkheim also made statistical attempts to relate social phenomena to each other, in his study of *Suicide*.

A large proportion of statistics available for sociological use are *official statistics* produced by government departments and other official bodies. There are some state organisations (such as the Office of Population Censuses and Surveys, the Central Statistical Office and the Registrar General's Department) whose principal purpose is to produce data, but most official statistics are merely subsidiary to the work of organisations established for purposes other than merely providing statistics. Official statistics are suspect in many ways, as Table 1.13 indicates.

Although statistics present serious problems as a method of inquiry, this does not mean that they do not have a distinct value provided they are collected and produced as accurately as possible. Several of the dangers listed in Table 1.13 may apply to other methods of research. Sociological statistics do not represent *new discoveries* about the social world; they are merely attempts to express information in a convenient way.

Even sociologists who have collected statistics in the course of their own research have found their efforts hindered by factors such as language, class barriers, racial prejudice and sex discrimination. Hyman, H. (*Interviewing in Social Research*) found that 40 per cent of a sample of women interviewed by women, considered that sexual offenders should be flogged publicly, but the percentage rose to 61 when the female respondents were interviewed by men. The social interaction between the different sexes clearly affected the results.

The most useful source book of statistics for sociologists is the annual edition of *Social Trends*. This Central Statistical Office publication pre-

Table 1.13 Dangers of using official statistics for sociological purposes

1 Statistical classification may be arbitrary: e.g. there is controversy about what types of death should be categorised as suicide.

2 Classifications may cut across sociological concepts such as social class.

3 It is virtually impossible to assess quantitatively the complex social world of numerous individuals and groups.

4 Statistics are based on preconceived notions: because crime statistics are based on past criminal activities it is dangerous to use the data as a basis for explaining crime.

5 Statistics are rarely definitive: suicides and crimes may be hidden, undetected or unreported.

6 Statisticians can never be sure that their questions are clearly understood, especially as language frequently obscures and distorts.

7 Statistics may reveal less about those questioned than about statisticians who compile the questions.

8 The processes involved in the collection and presentation of the statistics will affect the final results.

sents a mass of statistical information which, when expertly analysed, provides a synoptic picture of social life, given the limitations of statistical evidence. Examples of information of sociological interest in *Social Trends* include:

(a) earnings according to socio-economic grouping;
(b) details in the increase of the divorce rate;
(c) the number of people admitted to mental hospitals;
(d) the percentage of secondary pupils in comprehensive schools;
(e) how many students went to university.

The 1979 edition (*Social Trends* 10) included a special social commentary examining how life has changed in Britain. Like all statistics, those used as a basis for this commentary are inconclusive, but nevertheless a picture emerges of improved living conditions. Between 1951 and 1978 owner-occupancy rose from less than 30 per cent to over 50 per cent of householders. The extension of the welfare state is reflected in the figure relating to payments of cash benefits taking up 23 per cent of public spending in 1977 compared with 12 per cent in 1951. In 1961 most manual workers were allowed only a fortnight's paid holiday a year. By 1977 almost all had three weeks and a third were entitled to four weeks or more. The sociologist treats statistics with deserved scepticism; *Social Trends* indicate changes but offers no view on whether the changes have brought a higher quality of life. Statistics indicative of social progress must be

Where boxes are provided please tick the appropriate box (Please use ink or ballpoint pen)

	1st person	2nd person
1-3 Include on your census form:	Name and surname	Name and surname

1-3 Include on your census form:

- all the persons who spend Census night 5-6 April 1981 in this household (including anyone visiting overnight and anyone who arrives here on the Monday and who has not been included as present on another census form).
- any persons who usually live with your household but who are absent on census night.
  For example, on holiday, in hospital, at school or college. Include them even if you know they are being put on another census form elsewhere.

Write the names in the top row, starting with the head or a joint head of household (BLOCK CAPITALS please)

Include any newly born baby even if still in hospital. If not yet given a name write 'BABY' and the surname.

1st person
Name and surname

Sex
☐ Male   ☐ Female

Date of birth
Day   Month   Year

2nd person
Name and surname

Sex
☐ Male   ☐ Female

Date of birth
Day   Month   Year

---

4   Marital status
Please tick the box showing the present marital status.

If separated but not divorced please tick 'Married (1st marriage)' or 'Re-married' as appropriate.

Marital status
1 ☐ Single
2 ☐ Married (1st marriage)
3 ☐ Re-married
4 ☐ Divorced
5 ☐ Widowed

Marital status
1 ☐ Single
2 ☐ Married (1st marriage)
3 ☐ Re-married
4 ☐ Divorced
5 ☐ Widowed

---

5   Relationship in household
Please tick the box which indicates the relationship of each person to the person entered in the first column.

Please write in relationship of 'Other relative' – for example, father, daughter-in-law, brother-in-law, niece, uncle, cousin, grandchild.

Please write in position in household of 'Unrelated person' – for example, boarder, housekeeper, friend, flatmate, foster child.

Relationship to 1st person
01 ☐ Husband or wife
02 ☐ Son or daughter
☐ Other relative, please specify
....
☐ Unrelated, please specify
....

---

6   Whereabouts on night of 5-6 April 1981
Please tick the appropriate box to indicate where the person was on the night of 5-6 April 1981.

1 ☐ At this address, out on night work or travelling to this address
2 ☐ Elsewhere in England, Wales or Scotland
3 ☐ Outside Great Britain

1 ☐ At this address, out on night work or travelling to this address
2 ☐ Elsewhere in England, Wales or Scotland
3 ☐ Outside Great Britain

---

7   Usual address
If the person usually lives here please tick 'This address'. If not, tick 'Elsewhere' and write in the person's usual address.

The home address should be taken as the usual address for a head of household who lives away from home for part of the week.

For students and children away from home during term time, the home address should be taken as the usual address.

Boarders should be asked what they consider to be their usual address.

☐ This address
☐ Elsewhere – write the person's usual address and postcode
Address (BLOCK CAPITALS please)
....
....
including Postcode [ ][ ][ ][ ]

☐ This address
☐ Elsewhere – write the person's usual address and postcode
Address (BLOCK CAPITALS please)
....
....
including Postcode [ ][ ][ ][ ]

---

8   Usual address one year ago
If the person's usual address one year ago, on 5 April 1980, was the same as that given in answer to question 7 please tick 'Same'. If not, please tick 'Different' and write in the usual address.

If everyone on the form has moved from the same address, please write the address in full for the first person and indicate with an arrow that this applies to the other people on the form.

For a child born since 5 April 1980 write 'UNDER ONE'.

☐ Same as at Question 7
☐ Different – write the person's address and postcode on 5 April 1980
Address (BLOCK CAPITALS please)
....
....
including Postcode [ ][ ][ ][ ]

☐ Same as at Question 7
☐ Different – write the person's address and postcode on 5 April 1980
Address (BLOCK CAPITALS please)
....
....
including Postcode [ ][ ][ ][ ]

---

9   Country of birth
Please tick the appropriate box.

If box 6 is ticked please write in the present name of the country in which the birthplace is now situated.

Country of birth
1 ☐ England
2 ☐ Wales
3 ☐ Scotland
4 ☐ Northern Ireland
5 ☐ Irish Republic
6 ☐ Elsewhere. Please write the present name of the country.
....

Country of birth
1 ☐ England
2 ☐ Wales
3 ☐ Scotland
4 ☐ Northern Ireland
5 ☐ Irish Republic
6 ☐ Elsewhere. Please write the present name of the country.
....

Fig. 1.11 1981 census form

studied alongside statistics of the 25 million tranquillisers prescribed in 1977 compared with 16 million in 1967.

● *Social Surveys*

From the structural-functionalist perspective, perhaps the most important tool of sociological research is the social survey. The survey has been left to near the end of this topic largely because it may include all the research methods considered so far – including observation, participation, interviews, questionnaires and statistics.

The most exhaustive social survey in the UK is the census which is undertaken every decade (see Fig. 1.11). Censuses have been carried out in Britain since 1801 and gradually they have been extended in scope. No longer are they confined to a mere counting of heads but include details of housing, education, health, urban growth, public utilities, transport, migration and employment. The Registrar General's department conducts the census to assist the government in planning such requirements as infant schooling, university places, hospital beds, public transport and services for the elderly. Surveys on a much smaller scale are organised to study specific problems. Hancock, in *Survey*, considered the problem of ascertaining the required number of Second World War medals. It was known that approximately seven million people were entitled to a total of about twenty million medals, but not all would claim their entitlement. The Social Survey (set up during the Second World War to organise surveys for government departments) investigated a carefully selected sample and found that about 35 per cent would be likely to claim their medals. The government struck the number of medals estimated to be necessary. Thirty-four per cent actually claimed their medals and the accuracy of Social Survey's investigation saved the state about £150 million. Similar surveys have been carried out to assess public opinion about 'Meals on Wheels', changing attitudes to the police and suggested alterations in Bank Holiday dates.

Surveys, like statistics, must be treated with caution. If the sample selected is representative and forms a representative cross-section, then merely a few thousand people will provide the information required with only a small margin of error. The main methods of sampling are briefly outlined in Table 1.14.

A social survey should be preceded by a pre-test. This *pilot survey* is undertaken for the purpose of:

1 indicating the time and cost likely to be involved in the main survey;
2 locating any faults in the design of research techniques;
3 testing respondents' understanding of the language used in questionnaires;

Table 1.14 Methods of sampling

Type	Selection	Example
1 Random sampling	By chance, in haphazard manner	An investigator questions people in the street.
2 Systematic sampling	By taking possibly every tenth person from a *sample frame* such as the Electoral Roll	Peter Townsend (*Family Life of Old People*) picked one doctor in three in Bethnal Green and then every tenth patient on the doctor's list.
3 Stratified sampling	By dividing people into strata on a particular basis such as social class, age, sex or income	Registrar General indicates that 4 per cent of people are professional workers so 4 per cent of the sample should be chosen accordingly.

4 revealing the likely response rate and subsequently enabling researchers to calculate the number of respondents necessary to achieve the target sample.

Much sociology can be learnt by studying research methods used in some of the well-documented social surveys. Michael Young and Peter Willmott spent three years undertaking field work in Bethnal Green and a new housing estate to compile *Family and Kinship in East London*; they examined the wide social network of the extended family during a period of extensive rehousing. Margaret Stacey's study of Banbury (*Tradition and Change*) provides a perceptive account of status group patterns in an urban community; the original field work was done in 1948–51, and followed up fifteen years later by a second three-year survey (*Power, Persistence and Change: a second-study of Banbury*).

● *Secondary sources*

Secondary sources include all informative material, not primarily of a sociological nature, but which nevertheless give an insight into societal life. Secondary sources of data are used for purposes not originally intended by those who supplied them. Thus, personal letters, diaries, family records, photographs and tape recordings may be useful secondary sources of sociological inquiry.

Documents and other records of government agencies provide statistical information for researchers. Statistics themselves may be considered as a secondary source of empirical information, i.e. data based on observed evidence of actual events rather than speculative accounts. Newspapers and journals, films and TV plays, are not produced with the prime intention of fulfilling a sociological need, but may be of value so long as certain limitations are borne in mind. For example, the TV play *Life for Christine* (November 1980) portrayed a horrific account of a problem child who was sentenced to life imprisonment for setting fire to some curtains. It suggested that the present system of dealing with juvenile delinquents although based on the principle that 'punishment must be in the best interest of the child' may lead to harsh justice. (See section 7.6 on juvenile delinquency.) It is important to realise, however, that the story was based on the child's own account of her unfortunate life.

The novels of Charles Dickens provide a vivid verbal impression of family life, schools and debtors' prisons in Victorian society, but as Dickens wrote with a reforming zeal, a sociological inquirer must constantly question how much is based upon fact and how much on fiction.

It would be naive to assume that information is disseminated to give a completely honest picture. Contrary to conventional wisdom, 'facts' do not necessarily speak for themselves: they have to be expertly analysed and interpreted. The sociological inquirer needs to be selective in the use of secondary sources. Information emanating from government departments, political parties and commercial undertakings may be deliberately misleading and biased. Documentary films are likely to be more accurate than popular movies although it much depends upon the purpose behind the production. Likewise quality newspapers may be more reliable and less sensational than the popular press but the human interest stories of the tabloids may sometimes give a clearer picture of social reality. The Paston letters, or the diaries of Pepys, Evelyn and Parson Woodforde, provide middle-class accounts of social life while the great mass of humanity were then, as now, of humble disposition. The secondary sources listed in Table 1.15 must all be treated with circumspection.

● *Experiments*

Experimentation is not a common tool of sociological inquiry. The close, controlled conditions of a laboratory are not available to the sociologists although pseudo-social laboratories may be created by the establishment of *total institutions*. The interactionist Erving Goffman (*Asylums*) grouped these institutions into five categories (see Table 1.16).

Table 1.15 Sources of secondary information

1 Personal	Diaries, photographs, letters and other contemporary records
2 Family	Family Bibles, marriage certificates, genealogical tables
3 Demographic	Registration of births and deaths, Census returns
4 Governmental	HMSO publications, e.g. *Britain: an Official Handbook*
5 Political	Electoral registers, Hansard
6 Media	Newspapers, journals, periodicals, magazines, TV and radio programmes
7 Literature	Novels, short stories, poems, essays; narrative, descriptive and factual accounts
8 Reference	*Keesing's Contemporary Archives, The Statesman's Year Book, Whitaker's Almanac.*
9 Historical	Manuscripts, plans and other documents
10 Geographical	Maps, charts and climatic records

Table 1.16 Goffman's total institutions

Purpose	Examples
1 To care for the incapable and harmless	Homes for the blind, aged, orphaned and indigent
2 To care for the incapable who pose a threat to the community	TB sanitaria, mental hospitals and leprosaria
3 To protect the community from those who aim to harm it	POW camps, borstals, detention centres and prisons
4 To pursue workmanlike tasks which are justifiable on instrumental grounds	Barracks, warships and boarding schools
5 To allow retreat from the world	Abbeys, monasteries and convents

In the artificially-created conditions of total institutions there is a breakdown of the barriers which normally separate basic spheres of life such as sleep, work and play. Goffman examined disculturation whereby the props of everyday life are removed. Institutions strip their inmates of the supports they bring from the outside world so that there is a complete break with past roles and role-dispossession occurs. Total institutions are forcing houses aimed at changing people; each provides an example of an experiment of how a person's 'self' can be transformed. This is their special sociological interest.

Some adventurous modern sociologists have experimented with withdrawing themselves from social interaction in an attempt to knock down the props which give cohesion to society and enable it to hold together. Harold Garfinkel's experiments include encouraging his students to act in unnatural ways such as behaving as strangers in their own home. It would not appear to be anti-social to act as a polite stranger, but Garfinkel's students found those around them extremely disturbed by the experiment. People come to expect a certain structure of social life and are alarmed if other social actors do not behave as expected. The results of such experiments indicate that life would be extremely difficult if the behaviour of social actors was unpredictable.

An interesting experiment was carried out by Peter Collett and Gregory O'Shea when they asked the way to fictitious hotels in England and Iran. In England they affected foreign accents (*European Journal of Psychology*, Vol. 6, No. 4). Among other points of sociological interest, this experiment revealed that:

1 women in Iran were likely to ignore the questioners, this attitude of withdrawal being indicative of the more inhibited lives of females in that country;

2 lower-class males in Iran were likely to give elaborate directions to places they knew did not exist, which indicated that they wished to appear helpful or knowledgeable. Similar 'invented directions' were not given by people in London who were questioned by the experimenters.

Although the experimental method is rarely used in sociology, cross-cultural experiments of this type are of sociological interest.

In psychology, experimentation is far more common. One of the most well-known experiments was carried out by a Russian, I.P. Pavlov. A bell was rung by Pavlov just prior to giving food (stimulus) to a dog; the dog salivated (response) to the noise indicating that the bell had become a conditioned stimulus. Pavlov's experiments supported the claims of behaviourists that behaviour can be explained in terms of stimulus response analysis, and that human beings can be conditioned. (See Aldous Huxley's *Brave New World* and George Orwell's *1984*.)

In 1919, J.B. Watson and R. Rayner found that a nine-month-old baby, called Albert, did not show any fear response when subjected to the stimuli of a white rat, a rabbit, a dog, a monkey, masks, cotton wool and burning newspapers. However, a fear response was elicited by striking a steel bar with a hammer. Although the 'little Albert' experiment is recognised as a classic piece of social research, the original report has been neglected and substituted by standard textbook accounts which include over twenty errors, the most misleading being that Watson deconditioned Albert and removed his fear response. The valid presentation of research material is as important as the research methods employed.

Further Reading

Abraham, J.H. *The Origins and Growth of Sociology* (Penguin)

Abrams, P. *Origins of British Sociology* (University Chicago Press)

Aron, R. *Main Currents in Sociological Thought* Vols I and II (Penguin)

Banks, J.A. *Studies in British Society* (Routledge & Kegan Paul)

Berger, P.L. *Invitation to Sociology* (Penguin)

Berger, P.L. & Berger, B. *Sociology: A Biographical Approach* (Penguin)

Berry, D. *Central Ideas in Sociology* (Constable)

Bogdan, R. & Taylor, J.S. *Introduction to Qualitative Research Methods* (John Wiley)

Brown, C.H. *Understanding Society* (John Murray)

Butterworth, E. & Weir, D. (eds.) *The Sociology of Modern Britain* (Fontana)

Cohen, P.S. *Modern Social Theory* (Heinemann)

Coser, L.A. & Rosenberg, B. (eds.) *Sociological Theory* (Collier-Macmillan)

Coulson, M.A. & Riddell, D.S. *Approaching Society* (Routledge & Kegan Paul)

Cuff, E.C. & Payne, G.C.F. (eds.) *Perspectives in Sociology* (George Allen & Unwin)

Easthope, G. *History of Social Research Methods* (Longman)

Firth, R. *Human Types* (Abacus)

Giner, S. *Sociology* (Robertson)

Halsey, A.H. *Trends in British Society Since 1900* (Macmillan)

Hindess, B. *The Use of Official Statistics in Sociology* (Macmillan)

Inkeles, A. *What is Sociology?* (Prentice-Hall)

Krausz, E. & Miller, S.H. *Social Research Design* (Longman)

Lenski, G. *Human Societies* (McGraw Hill)

McNeill, P. & Townley, C. (eds.) *Fundamentals of Sociology* (Hutchinson)

Meighan, R., Shelton, I. & Marks, T. (eds.) *Perspectives on Society* (Nelson)

Mills, C. Wright *The Sociological Imagination* (Penguin)

Mitchell, G. Duncan *A Dictionary of Sociology* (Routledge & Kegan Paul)

Nisbet, R.A. *The Sociological Tradition* (Heinemann)

Rex, J. *Key Problems of Modern Sociological Theory* (Routledge & Kegan Paul)

Ryder, J. & Silver, H. *Modern English Society* (Methuen)

Shipman, M.D. *The Limitations of Social Research* (Longman)

Sprott, W.J.H. *Sociology* (Hutchinson)

Stacey, M. *Methods of Social Research* (Pergamon)

Thompson, K. & Tunstall, J. *Sociological Perspectives* (Longman)
Whyte, W.F. *Street Corner Society* (University of Chicago Press)
Worsley, P. (ed.) *Modern Sociology* (Penguin)

TWO
Inequality

2.1 Social stratification

● *Systems of social stratification*

There is little evidence to support the idea that there has ever been, or ever will be, a society which is not divided socially into strata or layers. In the same way that the geologist studies strata found in different rock formations, so the sociologist studies the strata found in different societies. Each stratum will have its own peculiar 'thickness' depending on its composition and age. Just as geological formations are piled one upon the other, so people in society are grouped in layers with some people at the top of the pile exerting pressure upon those unlucky enough to find themselves at the bottom.

The study of social stratification systems depends upon the criteria selected. Sociologists group people together in a variety of ways; there are many types of social stratification systems depending upon the criteria of operation. However, fundamental sociological differences commonly used as a basis of social stratification include:
1 *economic factors* such as wealth and income;
2 *prestige* in the form of esteem, honour, respect and status;
3 *power* and authority exerted in the community.

Many have paid lip-service to ideals of social equality: the French revolution was based upon principles of 'liberty, equality and fraternity'; the American constitution states that 'all men are created equal'; Christians believe that 'all men are equal before God'. But studies of the most primitive societies reveal stratified group characteristics closely linked with modern sociological concepts of social class and status.

Plato discussed in the *Republic* what he regarded as necessary conditions for the establishment of a genuine egalitarian society. He decided that the family was the main cause of inequality and subsequent social stratification. The family secures privileges for its members: it gives them their all-important initial start, socialises them in ways favourable (or unfavourable) to social progress, and leaves them with an inheritance which will accentuate inequality in succeeding generations. According to Plato, the most important step towards social equality would be to take children away from their families. There are few people who would support this idea. After the Russian revolution in 1917, one Commissar of Education wrote of children being brought up by 'pedagogical and medical personnel'; it was assumed that such terms as 'my parents' and 'our children' would eventually disappear. But by the 1930s, the Soviet Union was extolling the virtues of family life.

There are those who consider that social stratification depends upon socio-biological differences and that there are fundamental natural inequalities between people. Thus Sir Francis Galton (*Inquiries into Human Faculty and Its Development*) argued that some people possessed superior abilities; their achievements would be bound to be greater than inferior beings and they would rise naturally to the top of the social pile. Such arguments could only be proved conclusively if comparisons could be made between people who started life from an equal position. But inequality begins from the womb. Recent research has shown that on average a child whose mother smokes during pregnancy will be approximately one centimetre shorter than average at the age of seven and roughly four months behind his contemporaries in reading ability.

As we study historical examples of social stratification systems, we need to bear in mind the extent to which the system is open or closed, in the sense that people are able to move from one stratum to another. For example the caste system of India is a very closed system where one is born into a certain caste and invariably stays there for life. The social class system of modern western industrial countries exhibits a greater degree of openness; a peanut farmer or a movie star can become president of the USA.

● *Slavery*

One of the earliest examples of horizontal stratification of society was the system of *slavery* which existed in the ancient world. The study of slavery as a social stratification system provides an example of institutionalisation. Slavery was institutionalised by being accepted as a traditional custom of the city states of Rome and Greece. This custom was even given the force of the law; it was legal for a privileged group to own people from the enslaved group who were forced to work for their masters.

One of the earliest cases of class conflict occurred in Greece where the landed aristocracy were opposed by the peasantry who were heavily in debt to the aristocracy under a system where the law held that indebtedness led to slavery. In Ancient Rome, developments followed a similar pattern when plebians opposed the patricians; slavery in Rome followed an ethnic pattern, where one race imposed its dominance upon another. Ethnic considerations of stratification have always been important, never more so than in present-day Western society where the blacks find themselves, for life, in lower social strata than the whites.

- *The caste system*

One of the most clear-cut examples of stratification is the Indian *caste system* which has its roots deep in history. Although many changes are taking place in the caste system with the advent of industrialisation, social stratification by caste still dominates the lives of 300 million Hindus. Five layers of social hierarchy starting from the top are shown in Table 2.1.

Table 2.1 The five castes of India

Caste	Main occupation
1 Brahmins	priesthood
2 Kshatriyas	military service
3 Vaishyas	traders or merchants
4 Shudras	servants or labourers
5 Untouchables	extremely menial tasks

This five-fold categorisation is very much over-simplified; the basic unit of the caste system is the sub-caste called jati which is an endogamous group practising a traditional occupation. A man is born into a jati and this is the only way of acquiring membership; he has structured expectations, i.e. he fatalistically regards the social order which determines his life, as just and legitimate. The Hindu doctrine of Karma teaches a little Hindu that he is born into a particular sub-caste because that is where he deserves to be born. His life is governed by principles of pollution which rigidly enforce the separation of the castes; contact of any kind (such as dining and having sex) between any of the other castes would result in those of higher caste becoming polluted. For example, if a Brahmin ate food cooked by an Untouchable, the resulting pollution would be thought to be so great that the Brahmin would be excommunicated by the caste court. As in so many societies women are regarded as forming the bottom of any given stratum.

As in the social class system of modern societies, occupation is the basic separator of the social strata. Each caste is traditionally associated with a distinctive occupation. Any occupation connected with the destruction of sentient life is thought to be defiling and would be prohibited to higher castes; such occupations include butchery, fishing and even the selling of eggs. A further consequence of the social stratification embodied in the caste system is the tendency for each level of sub-castes among the myriad of jatis to inhabit the same village area which has its own social world. Caste membership is linked to status: not only houses, but clothes, customs and manners become symbols of status for those who share a common culture. Every caste tends to imitate the customs of the caste directly above and jatis occupying lower rungs try to raise their status by taking over the rituals of those above them. Under the influence of industrialisation social mobility is taking place between the jatis; the association of castes with traditional occupations is disintegrating and helping to spread a uniform culture throughout Indian society. Nevertheless, if a study of caste is to be useful in sociological analysis, it must be based on the structural criterion of occupational differentiation and not upon Hindu philosophy. The caste system of social stratification is worthy of study as a complex system of statuses with clearly delimited positions into one or another of which all members of the community are placed.

Castes have provided the pattern for social relations outside the caste system. It is interesting to note that the caste system has proved a self-equilibrating social force and succeeded in absorbing or repelling people or groups who attempted to change it.

> Caste, which was so successful in absorbing autonomous groups everywhere, also provided the pattern for relations with non-Hindu groups. Christians and Muslims were regarded as castes, too, and they accepted such a status. Even revolutionary movements which had aimed at the overthrow of the caste system ended by either becoming castes themselves or reproduced the caste system within themselves. The main body of Hindus regarded these sects as castes and not as sects. Thus the caste system effectively neutralized all attempts to change it.
>
> (Srinivas, M.N. 'The Caste System in India', in A. Beteille, ed., *Inequality*)

- ## *The hydraulic system (or Asiatic mode of production)*

The social stratification system which arose out of the hydraulic system, whereby the top strata of society exercised absolute power by virtue of its control over the vital large-scale irrigation system, is of special interest because of its exhaustive sociological analysis by Marx. He linked each historical era and was convinced that the main criteria for the determination of social stratification was a person's relationship to the means of production. In the hydraulic system, the people who held power controlled the methods of irrigation upon which the economy depended. It was they who exploited those who worked the methods of production. Thus, the hydraulic system was based upon an agricultural economy resulting in a two-fold social stratification. At the top of the social hierarchy was a bureaucratic ruling class with officials enjoying enormous power and prestige. Below them, were the masses who performed a range of tasks geared towards the operation of an effective system of irrigation involving the collection, conservation and control of water.

In the course of history extensive areas of land have been cultivated in accordance with this so-called Asiatic mode of production. Countries involved included China, India, Arabia, Persia, Egypt, Mesopotamia and Turkey. In every case a centralised state was the judicial proprietor of the soil and the peasants, who worked the land, were obliged to pay taxes in kind to those who controlled the irrigation system. The main ideas of the Asiatic mode of production (following Marxist analysis) are given in Table 2.2.

Table 2.2 The hydraulic or Asiatic mode of production

1 There was a lack of private property in the form of land.
2 All producers were subordinate to the state.
3 The basic social structure was stable and self-sufficient.
4 The 'surplus product' (i.e. production above the needs of subsistence) was appropriated by the state in the form of rent.
5 The state was the supreme landlord; rents and taxes therefore coincided.
6 The government was centralised and despotic.
7 The exploited masses passively submitted.
8 The government undertook large public works of irrigation in order to maintain its receipts from rent/taxes.

B. Hindes and P. Hirst, in *Pre-Capitalistic Modes of Production* have argued that the Asiatic mode of production may be more theoretical than real, but even if it is largely a theoretical conception, it still provides a useful tool of sociological analysis. It enables us to examine a social system involving the following characteristics, all of which make towards some degree of social equality. These characteristics include:
1 no wealth-owning ruling class, power being vested in the bureaucracy;
2 the abolition of private property;
3 the appropriation of surplus labour by the state for the sake of the community;
4 production by non-property-owning, independent workers or by communal labour;
5 the state-financed public works from the taxes and rent which are inseparable.

● *The estate system of feudal Europe*

The type of social differentiation known as feudalism is especially connected with Europe but it has been experienced in other parts of the world including Japan, Russia and China. Social strata were again based upon the means of production, in this case, the ownership of land itself. Feudalism is usually considered to have lasted from about the tenth to the fourteenth century but there were variations. In essence, the system depended upon four basic conditions.

1 The ownership of land by the king, nobility and church.

2 A large body of serfs to work the land.

3 The appropriation of the serfs' surplus product by the king, nobility and church.

4 A supply of loyal fighting men to protect people and to defend territory both nationally and locally.

In order that the basic conditions of feudalism could be maintained the two medieval institutions of the vassal and the fief were evolved. The vassal owed allegiance to his superior lord. After the breakdown of the tribal system, the weak felt the need to be protected by someone more powerful. The fief was originally a form of remuneration in return for special services, but later the term was used to refer to the grant of land to a vassal (subordinate), in return for military service. Feudalism depended upon personal relations: those below the lord in the social stratification system owed all kinds of loyalties to the lord who commanded their allegiance by virtue of the reciprocities which he offered. The king owned the land and his tenants provided his fighting men.

The lowest stratum consisted of serfs. Serfdom involved a complex range of obligations. Tenant serfs had rights over their strips on the open field but had an economic obligation to work on their lord's land. Other serfs worked entirely for their lord who provisioned them. Serfs had to pay all sorts of taxes (e.g. at times of marriage and harvest) and had to pay the lord for the use of his mill, bull, woodland, wine-press, etc.

All groups in the community were permanently tied to the land. There was a comparable relationship between the tenant and the land on economic terms, to the relationship between lord and serf on social terms, while the personal relationship between lord and serf was sanctified by traditional rites and ceremonies.

The church was an integral part of the feudal system. As the largest landowner it controlled a third of the property in feudal Europe. Apart from taking tithes, the church monopolised knowledge and preached against self-seeking. R.H. Tawney (*Religion and the Rise of Capitalism*) has stressed the important influence of the church in teaching that economic interests in this world ought to be subordinated to salvation in the next.

world. Economic motives were controlled by the church and feudalism as a system of social stratification which lasted for over four centuries only broke up when social relationships in society were altered by the gradual movement of serfs to the towns where they exchanged their feudal obligations for wage-payments.

- ● *The class system of industrial societies*

Modern industrial societies are stratified in accordance with a social class system. The term class is ridden with ambiguities and we shall postpone our discussion of this ambivalent aspect of sociology until we treat the matter in detail in Topic 2.3. However, before we discuss social stratification from the three main sociological perspectives, we must briefly refer to the economic determination of social class in modern societies. Although social classes are not purely economic groupings, nevertheless economic relationships determine most social relationships. The study of the class system gives an insight into our own personal social relationships and into the way modern society is organised. Therefore a study of social stratification systems is vital if one wishes to know how society is organised. The division of modern society according to a social class structure affects our family life, the educational system, the economy, and political structures. Anybody who is not worried about social inequalities arising from the social class system has little comprehension of what is really going on.

2.2 Social stratification perspectives

- ● *The functionalist perspective of social stratification*

Functionalists believe that social inequality is necessary and useful for society. They consider the relationship between the different social strata as one of interdependence and cooperation.

Following Radcliffe-Brown's description of the way in which a large number of different cells assist in the functioning of an animal organism, so the different strata of a society are essential to the adequate functioning of that society.

To turn from organic life to social life, if we examine such a community as an African or Australian tribe we can recognise the existence of a social structure.... The continuity of structure is maintained by the process of social life, which consists of the activities and interactions of the individual human beings and of the organised groups into which they are united.

(Radcliffe-Brown, A. *Structure and Function in Primitive Society*)

Emile Durkheim vehemently believed in a consensus which prevails throughout society and brings all the strands (strata) together to serve the whole and work for the stability of society. This consensus perspective is based upon the view that there is a prevailing agreement in society relating to the fact that some people occupy higher positions than others and that social differentiations are acceptable to the majority. Social stratification is thus deemed to be right and proper by both top and bottom people and by those in between. It serves a positive function for society. Arrangement into strata is a normal characteristic feature of society. Structural-functionalists argue that because social stratification is there, and is found to be useful, it must be justifiable.

The more complex the society, the less likely is it that any one group will be self-sufficient. In a modern industrial society different groups specialise in certain jobs and exchange their labour for goods and services produced by others. Society depends upon reciprocal relationships: each group needs every other group.

Talcott Parsons also believed that the social position which people occupy in society is based upon a value consensus or general agreement among the members of different strata. In any society the system of social stratification will be a reflection of society as a whole; evaluation of a person's position is inevitable – everybody rates everybody else. Every social system will have an accepted pattern of differentiation and this pattern is necessary for a society to function adequately. Parsons divided the social system into sub-systems. The sub-system which any particular society ranks highest will gain the greatest material rewards. For US society, it could be argued that the rewards to various sub-systems is roughly in accordance with the following order:

1 economy
2 education
3 religion
4 politics.

The rewards to those engaged in politics are relatively low because the USA lacks an overall systems goal.

Although Durkheim and Parsons based their ideas largely upon the consensus model, they both realised that conflicts could arise out of malintegration of the system. Durkheim pointed to abnormal forms of the division of labour: the *anomic division of labour* arose when alienated workers were doing apparently meaningless jobs and could not see the end in view; *forced division of labour* occurred when a mediocre offspring inherited a top job. Parsons recognised that 'difficulties' within the social system could lead to temporary conflicts. For example:

1 a family may be able to bestow status which is not in accordance with the real worth of its individual members;

2 in any society, there are 'winners' and 'losers' with subsequent resentment by the losers;

3 it is not possible to evaluate people's worth with absolute objectivity, so it is inevitable that some groups will feel unfairly treated (this is one of the main reasons why it is so difficult to set up an acceptable incomes policy);

4 complex organisational structures lead to conflicts especially if disciplinary measures are imposed (consider for example the series of strikes which have stricken British Leyland).

But both Durkheim and Parsons believed that sources of conflict could be overcome by a better integration of the system. In the long run, the common value system justified the unequal distribution of rewards to the different social strata. Conflicts could be removed by a fine tuning of the system. Social stratification remains essential and works for the integration of different groups. There must be those with power and influence capable of controlling the system and exercising the fine tuning which mitigates conflicts.

A famous example of the application of the structural-functionalist perspective to social change is Neil Smelser's detailed study of the Lancashire cotton industry from 1770 to 1840 (*Social Change in the Industrial Revolution*). Smelser examined the series of adjustments which were made in the industry until, by fine tuning, new equilibrium was successfully achieved.

The most discussed attempted justification of the functionalist perspective of social stratification is that of Kingsley Davis and Wilbert E. Moore. In their original paper, in 1945, Davis and Moore put forward three basic principles applicable to social stratification.

1 Social stratification is functionally necessary and is therefore a universal and permanent feature of society.

2 Every society requires a mechanism to induce people to occupy those important social positions which necessitate the sacrifices which accompany lengthy training.

3 This mechanism ensures that the most important positions are conscientiously filled by the most qualified people.

It is true, as Davis and Moore contend, that every society does require a mechanism relating to role-selection and role-performance. If such a mechanism is to be effective three important things are necessary:

1 A system of allocation geared to ensure that all roles are occupied by those best able to cope with the task.

2 Stringent training of those selected for specific roles.

3 Commensurate rewards to ensure that tasks are carried out conscientiously and effectively.

According to Davis and Moore, certain positions in society are functionally more important than others and the social stratification system should ensure that the most able people fill the top jobs. This can be achieved by offering high rewards, status and other incentives to those prepared to undertake long periods of arduous training to secure high qualifications. The degree of functional importance of a role may be measured by its specificness. Some roles are highly specific and very few people are able to perform them. This helps to explain why brain surgeons receive greater rewards than roadsweepers. The difference in remuneration can also be explained by the esteem in which jobs are held; there is a fairly general agreement, especially in industrial societies, relating to the evaluation of the functional importance of different roles. The interdependence of roles is also a criterion of functional importance. Those groups who are at the lower end of the stratification league table tend to be supportive of the role of others. Roadsweepers carry out their work under the control of the county surveyor or other officials delegated by him. A dentist could do the job of his receptionist, but the receptionist would not be trusted by society to carry out the work of a dental surgeon.

Davis and Moore justify social stratification because it solves the universal societal problem of placing and motivating people. However, there are many criticisms of their case. While it may be true that the uneven distribution of prestige and rewards is functionally necessary with *achieved status*, it would not appear to hold true for *ascribed status*. Motivational mechanisms of reward are unnecessary in societies where important social positions are filled by ascription. For example, in the feudal system a man was born to be a lord or a serf and neither reward nor lack of reward made him any more proficient at his task. Davis and Moore set out a very conservative view. Those belonging to the dominant value system applaud their findings. It can be argued that Davis and Moore perpetuate inequality by attempting to justify a social stratification system which is dysfunctional: the son of well-born parents gets the opportunities – and the discovery of new talents from the next generation is truncated. The more rigidly stratified the society, the more difficult it is to locate those who have most talent.

The most important critic of Moore and Davis is Melvin M. Tumin who argues that there is no logical justification in assuming that those positions which are the most highly rewarded are the most important functionally. It is a criticism of any functional explanation of social stratification that the effect is treated as a cause. A circular argument develops because the desired end is used to prove the means. Tumin contends that many occupations which receive little reward or prestige are vital to society. Witness the work of a nurse or a fireman or an ambulanceman. Davis and Moore ignore the influence of the power of certain groups; for example coalminers have been able to secure relatively high rewards in recent years because of their increasing 'muscle' in the world of industrial relations.

Tumin also questions Davis and Moore's pessimistic view relating to the supposed scarcity of talent. There is no effective way of measuring latent talent, but all the indications from the field of educational sociology point to a vast pool of talent available from the children of the so-called lower social classes. Finally, it is not a sound argument that training is costly or that the elite undertake enormous sacrifices. Nowadays the cost is mainly borne by the state and the great rewards following lengthy training more than compensate for the sacrifice. Davis and Moore pay little attention to intrinsic rewards that go with the job; some people just enjoy being in responsible jobs and revel in the social prestige. How much would Margaret Thatcher be willing to pay to be Prime Minister or Ronald Reagan to be President? One has to have doubts about any social stratification evaluation which fails to explain the real motives of those who hold the very top jobs.

Nevertheless the functionalist perspective does tally with empirical facts that in terms of power and social prestige, social stratification is inevitable. Eva Rosenfeld (*Social Stratification in a 'Classless' Society*) found that the leaders of 240 Israeli *kibbutzim* (settlements) held positions of such great authority that they could be regarded as a distinctive stratum in a society based upon principles of social equality. An examination of the power struggles in the USSR and China suggest that the functional pre-requisites of any society lead to a social stratification system.

● *The conflict perspective of social stratification*

Those who take a conflict perspective of social stratification believe that the structure of society is based upon two opposing camps. At the top of the social stratification league table is the dominant class of elite people who exert their supposed superiority by controlling the economic system, and subsequently the political system, the educational system and the media. Opposed to them, in the nature of things, is the subordinate class or stratum against whom the die is cast. It is they who hold up the pyramidal pile; their surplus value is appropriated depending upon the system of social stratification. In our own society the forces of capitalism control the dominant value system.

Supporters of the conflict perspective believe that conflict between social groups is therefore inevitable: the higher strata struggle to maintain their social position, power and privileges; the lower social strata fight for a new structure in which a radical value system would emerge opposed to all social inequalities. The conflict perspective is less tidy than the functionalist perspective because instead of the different groups in society accepting their position in the social pyramid, they are seen to be continually in conflict with one another. The conflict structure is a dynamic one, rather than a docile acceptance of so-called normative values. The conflict theorists would say that there is no consensus, no agreement about who should occupy the important positions and who should be subservient. Whereas the functionalist perspective is one of conservation and preservation of the status quo, the conflict perspective is one of inevitable change.

Many writers suggest that the conflict perspective and the Marxist perspective are synonymous. Others have argued that the Marxist perspective is not strictly a conflict perspective because a society based on Marxist principles would not experience structural conflict, i.e. conflict arising in a society so structured that the dominant class and the subordinate class continually war against each other. Marxists would wish to argue that conflict is not an inevitable or necessary condition of all societies. A classless society would obviate conflict.

Nevertheless, when sociologists discuss the conflict perspective, it is mainly the Marxist perspective with which they are concerned. In spite of claims to the contrary the Marxist perspective is usually considered to be the main conflict perspective.

Marx's conflict theory of social stratification is based upon the following criteria.

1 The structure of society results in two main classes made up of groups of individuals placed in an opposing relationship to the means of production.

2 Social stratification is basically a two-fold division between the owners of the means of production (the bourgeoisie) and the non-owners (the proletariat).

3 The two classes are always in conflict as their interests are diametrically opposed.

4 The conflict between the two classes depends on people's own personal awareness of the class to which they belong, i.e. *class consciousness*.

It is only when individuals become aware of their class position that conflict takes place, because it is only then that the subordinate classes, who have little share in the dominant value culture, are activated into political conflict as organised groups. Class consciousness is not inevitable. One of the reasons why the working class is not a revolutionary force in Britain is because the Labour Party and the trade unions are institutionalised under capitalism, i.e. they are accepted as legal institutions within the capitalist system. Their policies and actions suggest that they have no desire to change the system radically. The Marxist perspective believes in a 'revolutionary reconstitution' of society at large. It does not believe in peripheral changes which nibble at the edges of capitalism, but rather at a fundamental change which will destroy the social stratification system set up under capitalism.

Marx may have seen the capitalist system as functional. After all, slavery is functional in the sense that it works. But it was the dysfunctions of capitalism (whereby there was an almost closed social stratification system) which he believed would bring the revolutionary struggle and the end of capitalism. For capitalism had within it the seeds of its own destruction, and the two opposing groups or strata would fight it out to the end. In the USSR this has been seen to be true. Whether or not it will come true eventually in the west depends upon the validity or invalidity of the convergence thesis which we will discuss in Topic 2.5, i.e. that affluent workers have been absorbed into the institutional structure of capitalism and have not sufficient class awareness to wage conflict against the dominant group in society. Students should ask themselves whether it is inevitable that we accept the present stratification system based on social classes and the maintenance of institutionalised inequality.

To sum up the Marxist conflict perspective of social stratification, class is a social group whose members share the same relations to the means of production. In the hydraulic system, those who controlled the irrigation methods were the ruling class and those who worked the irrigation methods were the subjugated peasant class. In the feudal system, lords owned the land and landless serfs worked their land. In the capitalist system, the capitalists need labourers to work their machines and the labourers need the capitalists to pay wages. But the relationship is not simply one of mutual dependence, but rather of exploiter and exploited. The political power of the ruling class depends upon its economic power. The dominance of the ruling class in the economic infrastructure results in their dominance in the superstructure of society (its major institutions, culture, attitudes and beliefs). The working class is socialised into accepting the concepts of capitalism such as the 'free market', 'free press' and the 'free world'. But these are all illusory to those who hold the Marxist conflict perspective. A 'false consciousness' is produced whereby the working class accepts ruling class ideology. Unbeknown to themselves, and probably to many of the ruling class who present this false picture of reality, the conflict between oppressor and oppressed goes on. Social stratification is seen as a cohesive force in society by those who hold the functionalist perspective, whereas conflict theorists consider stratification as divisive.

- *The interactionist perspective of social stratification*

The interactionist is concerned with micro-sociology and therefore his study of social stratification centres upon an individual's view of his own position in any stratification system. The interactionist sees class as what people say it is – how each individual feels about himself in relation to others and how he sees himself within a stratification system. To the interactionist, social stratification is less concerned with social structures and people's positions within those structures, than with a continually fluctuating stream of subjective experience. Arthur Marwick (*Class: Image and Reality in Britain, France and the USA since 1930*) has suggested that there is little evidence that an individual pays more than perfunctory attention to the question of social class as such. If any person were asked his view of his own social class position he would probably set himself one step further up the ladder than would the Registrar General or any sociologist putting forward his own taxonomy of social strata. As any social stratification system is somewhat arbitrary it can be argued that one man's subjective view of class is as good as another's. David Butler and Donald Stokes (*Political Change in Britain*) found 'one cheerful eccentric, a very fat publican, who said he belonged to the "sporting class".' None of the historical patterns which we have so far examined in this unit are patently false.

American farmworkers consider themselves as middle-class; it is common in the USA for the term 'working class' to be avoided and 'common man' substituted. Some French sociologists see intellectuals as constituting a separate class and this does suggest that classes need not necessarily be rooted in production, as functionalists and Marxists would tend to argue. People who are engaged in the same industry may regard themselves as linked together, but from the sociologist's point of view there is a fundamental weakness in this position. For if we were to include in one social group all those engaged in education, we would have to link the university professor and the school caretaker; this would cut vertically through the population whereas the concept of social stratification involves horizontal positions or layers. Professors and school caretakers may share the same occupational interests of looking after students, but they would generally regard themselves as belonging to different classes. From a scientific point of view it would be useful if each stratum in a stratification system could be perfectly determined. Sombart conceived of a social class as a group which is delimited by its way of thinking, its ideology, attitudes, beliefs and aspirations.

However, rigid class delimitations rarely work out in practice. Those who are probably most aware of their class position are traditional workers of the proletarian type. Jeremy Tunstall found that a trawlerman sees himself as a member of a class drawn together by an occupation so that 'he has indelibly printed on him certain habits, reflexes, patterns of spending, attitudes to life. . . .' (Tunstall, J. *The Fisherman*)

Another individual who sees and feels himself to be a member of the old traditional working class is the coalminer; Dennis, Henriques and Slaughter (*Coal is our Life*) found the miner sharing occupational hazards with those with whom he drinks at the pub during his leisure time. On the other hand the schoolteacher who spends much of his time in the classroom, separated from his colleagues, is less aware of his class position. His attitudes are likely to remain individualistic and insular because of the absence of 'significant others'. Both deep-sea fishermen and miners are much more aware of a feeling of class-consciousness. David Lockwood (*Sources of Variation in Working Class Images of Society*) delineates three types of workers all of whom see their class position differently. Apart from the traditional proletarian workers displaying their fraternity and working-class solidarity, Lockwood distinguished another type of traditional worker who defers to those whom he regards as superiors and takes a functionalist view of society as a status hierarchy; thirdly, Lockwood classifies the privatised worker wrapped up with the pecuniary model of society and feeling no 'class consciousness' or 'status-consciousness', being aware of divisions in society only in terms of material possessions (i.e. 'commodity-consciousness').

Explanations of class differences in patterns of behaviour, social attitudes, aspirations, lifestyles and ideology, remain the least developed area of social stratification theory. David Lockwood (*The Blackcoated Worker*) has examined how 'the matrix of social relations' between employees, supervisors and managers interacting in the workplace determines feelings of class conflict. Melvin L. Kohn (*Class and Conformity*) and John and Elizabeth Newson (*Patterns of Infant Care*) examined the different attitudes of the middle and working classes to child-rearing practices.

The most important feeling of class consciousness in the future is likely to be experienced among the underprivileged people of the third world. Peter Lloyd (*Power and Independence: Urban Africans' Perception of Social Inequality*) studied town immigrants in Nigeria and contrary to general expectation found that the inhabitants themselves regard their shanty towns as 'slums of hope'. They are not concerned with objective approaches to social stratification which explore a respondent's placement in class terms rather than how he wishes to describe his own place in society. Phenomenological sociology is not concerned with functional and conflict perspectives but with individual awareness of class position. Those seen as downtrodden by the two traditional perspectives may indeed see themselves as being part of a culture which has its own values and a value in itself. This is true of Oscar Lewis's analysis of the culture of poverty where the Mexican peasants have their own values and determinedly pass them on from one generation to another. Basil Bernstein has criticised the label 'culturally deprived' because it suggests that those who share working-class culture consider themselves as less worthy than the middle classes.

If children are labelled 'culturally deprived', then it follows that the parents are inadequate; the spontaneous realisations of their culture, its images and symbolic representations are of reduced value and significance.

(Bernstein, B. 'Education Cannot Compensate for Society', *New Society*, 26 February 1970)

Brian Jackson (*Working-Class Community*) argues that the working class do not consider themselves as problem mutations of middle-class norms but rather as proud possessors of their own class culture possessing a special richness and vitality. Richard Hoggart (*The Uses of Literacy*) and E.P. Thompson (*The Making of the English Working Class*) give support to the view that the working class have an optimistic, introspective view of their class position.

2.3   Social class

● *Early analyses of social class: Marx and Weber*

It is usually assumed that analyses of social class began with Karl Marx in the nineteenth century. However, the real origins of systematic social class analysis stem from the work of John Millar and Adam Ferguson writing in Scotland in the late eighteenth century. They considered class to be strata ranked hierarchically on the basis of wealth alone. Although social class is no longer viewed according to this basis, there is little doubt that the unequal possession of wealth plays a key part in the division of the structure of society into social classes. Community actions such as factory sit-ins, rent-strikes or squatting suggest that private property rights are still effectively divisive and that possession or non-possession of wealth remains an important factor in class analysis.

Marx did not confine his analysis of class to 'vulgar commonsense' explanations which tended to view the position of social strata as being caused by 'differences in the size of one's purse'. We have seen (section 2.1) that Marx considered social classes as arising from the system of production. Marx believed that social classes originated when productive forces reached an advanced enough state to provide people with more than Weberians, the boundaries between the classes are less clear than to the

Table 2.3   Marx's review of the historical relations of production

Society	Social relations of production
1 Ancient	Master/slave
2 Feudal	Lord/serf
3 Capitalist	Bourgeoisie/proletariat.

sufficient for a subsistence standard of life; it was then possible for the labourers' surplus value to be appropriated by those who enjoyed the private ownership of the means of production and were consequently able to accumulate surplus wealth. Marx divided the history of production into three epochs each of which had its own particular social relations of production (see Table 2.3).

Conflict was inevitable between the two opposing social classes in each of the historic phases. Productive forces and the general economic structure of society determine the social life of a society. Conflict between the two main classes merely reflects incompatibilities within a particular mode of production. As a result of a class struggle, the oppressed will eventually throw off the yoke of the oppressor and society will be reorganised. This has been the case with ancient and feudal societies and will eventually be the case with capitalist society. Marx saw capitalist society as the last of the antagonistic forms of production: with increasing technical innovations there will be less work for the proletariat, less demand for the goods produced and less profit for the bourgeoisie. Unemployment is endemic. Capitalism has within it the seeds of its own destruction.

There are those who believe that the class divisions have become less pronounced, as the proletariat is more affluent and has been absorbed into the very structure of capitalism. We shall consider this convergence thesis of embourgeoisement in section 2.5.

Max Weber qualified Marx's conception of social classes arising out of the means of production. According to Weber, an individual's class situation is determined by his market situation. We all have lifechances which give us the opportunity to acquire material and non-material goods. Property and lack of property are basic distinctions, and within these two categories Weber distinguished four main groupings in capitalist society:
1 the dominant ownership and commercial class
2 the propertyless white-collar workers and intelligentsia
3 the petty bourgeoisie such as small shopkeepers
4 the manual working class.
Central to Weber's concept of class are groups of people who share a communality of lifechances which may occur in *any* economic order or system. Weber's conception of class is not restricted to the social relations arising from productive forces, but extends from production to include distribution and exchange. Class depends upon market situations and market capacities which vary because different lifechances arise from inequalities of distribution. Property and lack of property are therefore basic distinctions related to Weberian ideas about class. An individual's market situation also depends upon the skills and services which he can contribute to the process of production, distribution and exchange. To

Marxists. Class conflict is not inevitable but it is nevertheless possible. Class conflicts are only likely to be acute when there are very great inequalities of material possessions and the underprivileged appreciate that these inequalities exist. Large firms are particularly conducive to class conflict because they make class differences especially obvious and enable conflicting ideas to be quickly disseminated throughout the workforce. According to Weber, class consciousness may also arise from increases in lifechances; this helps us to understand the position of white-collar workers who have exhibited increased unity in modern society. Whereas Marx saw stratification as a simple dichotomy of social classes largely economically determined, Weber conceived of class as three-dimensional; the three types of division in society are (1) class, (2) status and (3) party. Class depended on access to the scarce goods and services found in a market economy. Status referred to the unequal distribution of social honour. Parties were groups which pursued power through action. The three divisions of class, status and party are closely related. Weber thought it simplistic to consider class separately from status and party. Consequently, the neo-Weberian approach gives us a more all-round conception of the divisions within society.

● *Objective assessments of social class*

We have seen that the simplest classifications of class are two-fold divisions. The common workaday division in modern society is based upon occupational differences:
1 non-manual workers – middle-class
2 manual workers – working-class.
The so-called upper class is usually considered to consist of less than one per cent of the population depending upon the classification criteria used and, because of their statistical insignificance, are normally included with the middle class. The greater the simplicity of classification, the greater the generality. Whatever the classification system used there will always be controversy and an arbitrary nature to the class divisions used (see Fig. 2.1). Most sociologists, and the Registrar General, use *occupation* as the main criterion of stratification by social classes. Occupation reflects so many other facets of life: an individual's occupation depends upon his family background, his education, his qualifications and his way of speech. His occupation will also largely determine his housing, his leisure activities and his income. The receipt of income is perhaps the least satisfactory guide to social class divisions. Apart from the fact that a football pools winner may suddenly receive a million pounds (and spend, spend, spend it almost as quickly!) it is quite possible nowadays for manual workers to earn more than non-manual workers. Skilled printers

Fig. 2.1 Categorising social classes presents ambiguities

will earn more than most schoolteachers. The possession of wealth, especially large-scale inherited wealth, is entirely another matter which we will consider in detail in section 2.4.

The Registrar General uses a five-fold social class stratification but divides class 3 into manual and non-manual workers (see Table 2.4). The Registrar General's original five-point scale was compiled in 1911 and there have been changes in occupational status since then. Some occupations have been moved up or down a class depending on the degree of skill involved. Do you think that postmen, for example, should be placed in Class 3 (skilled) or Class 4 (semi-skilled) categories? Although there have been peripheral changes, Table 2.4 indicates that the percentages for each of the five social classes have remained fairly constant since 1951, the only marked change being an elevation of some unskilled workers to semi-skilled categories.

Advertisers also use five categories (A,B,C,D, and E) largely based upon income and market potentiality:

Class A Members of families in which the chief wage-earner is a doctor, professor, clergyman, lawyer, architect; owner, director, senior executive of a large commercial or industrial organisation; senior civil servant; or a high-ranking industrial technician such as a scientist or consulting engineer. This group covers about 5 per cent of the population.

Table 2.4 Registrar General's five-fold classification

Class	Type of occupations	Percentages		
		1951	1961	1971
1	*Professional and higher administrative* e.g. lawyers, architects, doctors, managers, university teachers	3	4	4
2	*Intermediate professionals and administrative* e.g. shopkeepers, farmers, actors, musicians, teachers	18	15	18
3	*Skilled* (a) Non-manual (1971:21.1%) e.g. draughtsmen, shop assistants, clerks (b) Manual (1971:28.4%) e.g. electricians, coalminers	50	51	49
4	*Semi-skilled* e.g. milk roundsmen, bus conductors, telephone operators, fishermen, farm workers	17	21	21
5	*Unskilled* e.g. nightwatchmen, porters, refuse collectors, cleaners, labourers	12	9	8

Class B Members of families in which the chief wage-earner is a bank clerk, senior office worker, teacher, small employer; manager or shop-keeper of larger shops; supervisor in a factory; professional worker not coming into class A. Class B covers about 25 per cent of the population.
Class C, D and E The remaining 70 per cent of the population.

Advertisers also note carefully the following social class categorisation used in the national readership survey.

Class A Upper middle class. The head of household's occupation (or former occupation) is higher managerial, administrative or professional.
Class B Middle class. The head of household's occupation (or former occupation) is intermediate managerial, administrative or professional.
Class CI Lower middle class. The head of household's occupation (or former occupation) is supervisory or clerical, or is junior managerial, administrative or professional.
Class C2 Skilled working class. Skilled manual workers.
Class D Working class. Semi-skilled and unskilled manual workers.
This classification allows newspapers or magazines to aim their advertising

towards the type of people who generally purchase their publications (see Fig. 2.2) in which (a) is aimed at AB and (b) at CD.

In the early 1950s, John Hall and D. Carog Jones developed a seven-point scale based upon occupations.

Table 2.5 Hall-Jones seven-fold classification

Class	Type of occupation	Example
1	Professional and high administrative	Company director of large firm
2	Managerial and executive	Civil servant
3	Inspectional, supervisory and other non-manual, higher grade	Teacher
4	Inspectional, supervisory and other non-manual, lower grade	Insurance agent
5	Skilled manual and routine grades of non-manual	Clerk
6	Semi-skilled manual	Agricultural worker
7	Unskilled manual	Barman

On the one hand, the more complex the classification, the more scope for fine adjustments: seven groupings clearly offer more refinements than five. On the other hand, a more complex classification creates its own difficulties. In industrial countries there is generally relatively common agreement about who is middle-class and who is working-class, but it may be more difficult to decide whether a person should be placed in Class 1 or 2 according to the Hall-Jones scale. Some sociologists consider that the Hall-Jones scale is biased in favour of non-manual workers. If you test any occupation for yourself you will appreciate that some part of an individual's work is skilled and some is unskilled; even more obvious is the fact that some parts consist of manual work while other parts require brainwork. Heart surgeons perform a great deal of manual labour in the course of a ten-hour operation. Many sociologists have used adaptations of the Hall-Jones scale or have compiled their own categorisation.

Dr John H. Goldthorpe (*Social Mobility and Class Structure*, 1980) compiled a seven-class social class model of British society in the twentieth century, for the purposes of his research into social mobility.

Another recent classification has been put forward by A. Halsey *et al.* (*Origins and Destinations*, 1980). It follows the general pattern of Goldthorpe's scheme which differentiates by occupational function and employment status. Halsey uses eight occupational groups within three main

Fig. 2.2 Advertisements aimed at different classes of readers

categories of intermediate, service and working classes. These three broad groupings include incumbents who typically share in similar *market* and *work* situations following David Lockwood's emphasis in *The Blackcoated Worker*. The categories 'service class', 'intermediate class' and 'working

Table 2.6 Goldthorpe's seven-fold classification

Class	Type of occupation
1	higher-grade professionals, administrators and managers
2	lower-grade professionals, managers, administrators, technicians and officials
3	routine non-manual workers, mainly clerical
4	small proprietors, including farmers and self-employed artisans
5	lower-grade technicians and supervisors of manual workers
6	skilled manual workers
7	semi-skilled and unskilled manual workers

Table 2.7 Halsey *et al.*'s eight-fold classification

Eight groupings	%	Three groupings	%
1 Higher-grade professionals, administrators, managers and proprietors.	7.7	Service	13.7
2 Lower-grade professionals, administrators and managers. Supervisors and higher-grade technicians.	6.0		
3 Clerical, sales and rank-and-file service workers.	7.4	Intermediate	31.4
4 Small proprietors and self-employed artisans. The 'petty bourgeoisie'.	12.6		
5 Lower-grade technicians and foremen. The 'aristocracy' of labour.	11.3		
6 Skilled manual workers in industry	27.2	Working	54.9
7 Semi-and unskilled workers in industry	22.6		
8 Agricultural workers and smallholders	5.2		
All	100		100

class' are in keeping with recent trends in a society which gives emphasis to a distinctive service class.

Halsey *et al*.'s eight-fold classification was criticised by Donald MacRae who, among other things, disliked especially the middle and professional grouping and argued that:

> This new usage involves a double ambiguity for the self-evident reason that the connotation and the denotation of 'service' point in opposite directions.
> (MacRae, D. 'Bad taxonomy leads to bad sociology', *Times Educational Supplement*, 18 January 1980)

A far less ambiguous social class categorisation was provided by a series of five *New Society* articles in 1976. These articles have given rise to the title 'the new classes'.

● *The new classes*

Norman St John Stevas has said,

> We talk a lot about class, but its significance, socially, is very small.

It may seem surprising to the student who has read this book so far to find that any intelligent man could still hold this conviction. Yet deeper thought will reveal that people of the upper middle class, who are in the nature of things above class, cannot hope to understand what it is all about. There are those who criticise social stratification studies believing that such studies exacerbate class conflicts, whereas they only reveal class differences which already exist. To teach working-class children about their inferior social position enables them to be aware of the barriers they have to surmount. A realistic picture of social class patterns may enable them to fight social injustice and bring about a greater measure of equality. Any idea that the significance of class is socially small would be dismissed by a serious study of the five *New Society* articles on:

1 the rich;
2 the salariat;
3 the new intelligentsia;
4 the working class;
5 the rough.

This five-fold classification may well be regarded as a far more realistic and empirical grouping than the categories of the Registrar General, Hall-Jones, Goldthorpe and Halsey *et al*. The 'new class' groupings may be less objective and more subjective, but from the interactionist perspective they are more realistic. The rich really 'feel' rich, while the roughs really 'feel' rough and have empathy with others in a like condition.

1 *The rich*

Anthony Giddens argues that the very rich are still with us, but rather than exhibit what Thorstein Veblen called *conspicuous consumption*, the rich in modern society keep a low profile. Giddens examines a press account of the prospective marriage of the 21-year-old Duke of Roxburghe and Lady Jane Grosvenor in 1976:

> The bride-to-be is the younger daughter of the Duke of Westminster who owns 300 acres in Mayfair and Belgravia in London and considerable estates in Cheshire and Scotland as part of his father's estate, estimated at £2½ million.
> (Giddens, A. 'The rich', *New Society*, 14 October 1976)

These enormous riches are held by the same elite families over generations. The two wealthiest families over the past 150 years are probably the Rothschilds and the Wills family of tobacco magnates: twenty-one members of each family have died leaving over half a million pounds each. The Duke of Buccleuch owns 220 000 acres in Scotland, while the Duke of Bedford's London estate of only 30 acres is worth roughly £30 million. Kinship ties help the rich to perpetuate their riches. The top 1 per cent of the adult population own about a quarter of the total personal wealth of the nation. The landed gentry are still powerful, but far less powerful than the rich who control the City of London. Giddens distinguishes three overlapping life styles by which the rich maintain their network of contacts.
(a) The entrepreneurs of big business.
(b) The jet-set of show business.
(c) Country gentlemen from past and present generations.

2 *The salariat*

In the salariat, Kristan Kumar includes over three million solidly middle-class professional and managerial people who are still comfortably well-off. It is very difficult to define the salaried class because their relationship to the means of production is ambivalent and they have little class-consciousness. Nevertheless, from a neo-Weberian stance they can be distinguished because they enjoy similar, favourable life chances and market opportunities. They are often managers rather than owners of industry, but nevertheless share the same ideology and life style as profit-reaping owners. They are favoured by handsome fringe benefits while at work, tax concessions on mortgage interest and their pensions are index-linked to protect them against inflation. The salariat takes a disproportionate share from the Welfare State: they can speak on equal terms with their doctors, while their offspring are more likely to benefit from grants and payment of fees related to higher educational qualifications. Thus the possible redistributive effects of social services within the framework of the Welfare State is open to question. Social inequalities are sustained.

3 *The new intelligentsia*

Geoffrey Hawthorne argues the new intelligentsia is 'the product of a new kind of evenness'. The nine new universities opened in the sixties, combined with the expansion of redbrick city universities and polytechnics, have given rise to a large increase in the number of graduates. The progressive ideas of the New Left, the struggle by the National Union of Students for higher educational grants and Women's Liberation have resulted in the emergence of a well-educated radical class ready to exploit their privileges. Many of them have since been caught up with the three million unemployed of the eighties and have become disillusioned, cynical, despairing and angry. The majority of post-war graduates share working-class antecedents and inbred hostility to the traditional middle class.

4 *The working class*

The working class still maintains a high degree of class consciousness, but their hostility to those in higher strata has become diluted. Their conflict has become institutionalised and according to Michael Mann, it 'takes ritualistic forms that are not politically dangerous.' Marx would have been disgusted with the British working class who show little signs of displaying revolutionary tendencies.

Until struck by the high unemployment of the eighties the average member of the working class enjoyed relatively cheap housing in an urban environment, combined with steadily improving standards of living. In Harold Macmillan's famous phrase he had 'never had it so good.' Increasing prosperity came about largely through increased production which accompanied technological changes; but greater affluence for the population as a whole did not mean increased social equality. The Nuffield Social Mobility Survey (directed by A.H. Halsey and J.H. Goldthorpe) collected information from interviews in 1972 with more than 10 000 men aged between 20 and 64, and found that although there had been considerable *absolute* upward social mobility in Britain in the past 60 years with more people reaching the top through general economic progress, nevertheless there had been no real change in the relative chances of reaching the top by those born into different social classes. The working classes have little chance of advancement.

The modern working class experiences urban industrial life. Apart from the top 10–20 per cent of skilled craftsmen who enjoy job security and autonomy in the work situation, most of the remainder work in factories using various degrees of mechanisation.

They are dependent solely upon wages and social security benefits and have only a one-in-four chance of securing a non-manual job. Their income is greatest at about the age of thirty and their wives are expected to go out to work even during child-bearing years. Their property consists mainly of household goods but there is a current tendency for about forty per cent to be purchasing a house and/or car.

From the interactionist perspective, the modern working class is very aware of its class position. There is an in-built hesitation to break through class barriers and mix socially with the middle classes. An individual's accent remains one of the most potent indicators of social class. The move from rural to urban life has been one of the main factors making for increased class barriers. People who live in urban working-class areas are proud of their working-class antecedents.

Although they are likely to belong to a trade union and vote Labour, the working class has limited political objectives. Their unions and their political party have become institutionalised and the working class are guaranteed security within the capitalist system as long as they stick to the rules the capitalist has laid down. Mann believes that the main way in which the working class fight back is by working less hard. This is their defence against long hours, low wages and the time clock. It is a non-revolutionary protest against the exploitation of the capitalist system.

5 *The rough*

Margaret Stacey (*Tradition and Change: A study of Banbury*) found that a large proportion of the population of Banbury divided people into three social groups which they thought of as 'respectable' 'ordinary' and 'rough'. Respectable people tend to be withdrawn and unwilling to become socially intimate, whereas ordinary people mix freely and form a network of social relationships. The roughs are a class apart. They are ostracised both by respectable and by ordinary people.

> The persistence of poverty, large-scale housing deprivation, health and educational inequalities, and currently the growth of unemployment, have fuelled the debate on whether a fraction of the working class are rough mainly because they are poor, and what proportion of the poor are poor because they are rough. The latter group would represent the so-called 'culture of poverty'.
> (Marsden, D. 'The Roughs', *New Society*, 11 November 1976)

Many of the roughs come from problem families and are accustomed to being dubbed as 'workshy' and 'social-security scroungers'. These labelling devices lead to self-fulfilled prophecies and values regarded as debasing by the rest of society; they are passed down through each succeeding generation of the rough. As a result of feeling inferior, their existential behaviour appears anti-social to respectable and ordinary people. Some of the roughest of the rough become social isolates, criminals and deviants such as prostitutes or drug addicts. But the

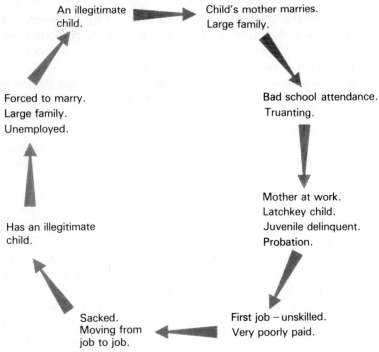

Fig. 2.3 The cycle of disadvantage

majority are merely social misfits caught up in a cycle of disadvantage (see Fig. 2.3).

- *Class in advanced societies*

The social class system of advanced society is influenced by four key elements.
1 The historical inheritance of inequality which can be traced through ancient, feudal and capitalist societies.
2 The international nature of social inequality which can be empirically observed in all advanced societies whether post-industrial, post-capitalist or state-capitalist.
3 The increase in the functional division of labour which has highly complex structures of inequality related to differentiated occupations.
4 The polarisation of society into two classes which has been accentuated by an increasing gap between those who have technological and expert knowledge and those who are deprived of it.
    The key sociological ideas associated with *post-industrial* society have been put forward by Daniel Bell (*The Coming of Post-Industrial Society*).

Bell believes that we are moving towards a technocratic society where the powerful will be the people who have the all-important knowledge necessary to run society, while the powerless are those without this knowledge. Services, rather than goods, predominate. Changes in occupational structures result in social class changes. The world in which manual labour power is important is replaced by a world of cybernetics, automation, ergonomics, robots, micro-electronics and silicon chips. White-collar workers are in control and they have already replaced manufacturing workers as the largest proportion of the workforce. Bell goes on to emphasise the dominance of intellectual technology, theoretical knowledge (e.g. of managers and economists) and increased professionalisation.

Alain Touraine (*The Post-Industrial Society*) puts forward similar ideas about this 'programmed society' in which the most essential characteristic is the systematic application of technical knowledge to predetermined social and economic ends. The powerful elite can continually innovate and sustain economic growth with the development of computerised systems of information-processing.

Knowledge rules OK? As the answer to this question is in the affirmative, the university becomes the key institution in the post-industrial society. Touraine believes that the 'technocrats' are the new dominant class. Similar conclusions have been reached by other thinkers such as Habermas (*Towards a Rational Society*), Ellul (*The Technological Society*) and Galbraith (*The New Industrial State*).

> It is known that retirement, death and replacement, however important for the individual involved, have not the slightest effect on General Motors or Continental Can. Power, it is implicity recognised, has passed to the technostructure....
> (Galbraith, J.K. *The New Industrial State*)

A powerful critique of technocratic theories of classes in contemporary society is provided by Anthony Giddens (*The Class Structure of Advanced Societies*). Giddens believes that Bell puts too much emphasis upon the United States as providing the model for the emergent new society. The United States may well be the most advanced post-industrial society and techniques pioneered there will be introduced into other countries,

> But this is altogether different from the proposition that the United States, in terms of broad aspects of its social and political structure, represents the prototype of a new type of society emergent in the modern world. As in the instance of the Soviet Union among the state socialist societies, a good case can be made for the view that the United States has been, is, and will continue to be, quite distinct in its socio-political organisation from most of the other capitalist societies.
> (Giddens, A. *The Class Structure of Advanced Societies*)

It does seem rather simplistic to argue that in post-industrial society possession of knowledge confers power and privilege in a similar way that ownership of the means of production did in the nineteenth century and the first half of the twentieth century. Giddens attempts to advance a class analysis applicable to all advanced societies, industrial and post-industrial. He believes that social class theories and the interpretations of them have been fudged by oversimplified comparisons between traditional and modern societies, as expressed in such typologies as feudalism versus capitalism. Giddens argues that rather than thinking of the 'existence' or 'non-existence' of classes, we should consider types of *class structuration*.

> Capitalism . . . is intrinsically a class society, and this is true of the United States as it is of other societies; but this does not invalidate the fact that levels of class structuration in the latter country have been, and are likely to continue to be in the foreseeable future, more weakly defined than in most other capitalist countries.
>
> (Giddens, A. *The Class Structure of Advanced Societies*)

The idea that capitalist and state socialist societies are converging or becoming less different is also criticised by Giddens. This idea is considered misleading because it is based upon naive comparisons between the United States and the Soviet Union. Both these societies are dominated by knowledge, planning, technology and large-scale organisations but the basis of social class differs between the two countries because of the different approach to the appropriation of surplus value.

Giddens believes that Marx was wrong to identify the heyday of capitalist society with early nineteenth-century Britain. The apex of British capitalism came in the mid-twentieth century and is typified by a shift in emphasis by large corporations which aim at growth rather than merely profit-making. Even this switch to a 'soulful' corporation does not indicate a wide transformation in the character of capitalism. In modern capitalist societies owners and managers share the same ideology. The majority of business managers, whether propertied or propertyless, are drawn from a narrow background of economic privilege and share an overall homogeneity of values and social solidarity. Following neo-Weberian thinking, Giddens believes that in advanced societies a class is a group with similar lifechances in the market. Broadly speaking, advanced societies have three major or basic classes brought about by class structuration:

1 *upper class* – owners and controllers of property
2 *middle class* – possessors of technical and educational skills
3 *lower class* – manual workers.

The term *underclass* is used by Giddens to distinguish those disqualified from market capacity for ethnic reasons, or because of unemployment. They approximate to Marsden's interactionist view of the 'roughs'.

2.4 Social differences

● *Occupational differentiation*

We saw in section 2.3 that the Registrar General used occupational differentiation as the main criterion of his five-point scale of social class stratification. The occupational order is the backbone of the class structure, so a study of social differences brought about by occupations is vital to a study of social inequality.

It is at the workplace that social class differences are most marked. Generally, the middle class undertake non-manual occupations where they enjoy relatively high pay, job security, autonomy, responsibility and interesting work. The working class undertake manual occupations where they are likely to suffer less pay, insecurity, close supervision and boring, repetitive work. The middle class enjoy fringe benefits, longer holidays and good working conditions. The working class have few 'perks' (apart from illegal ones), shorter holidays and working conditions which are frequently noisy and dirty.

Dorothy Wedderburn conducted an inquiry into the varying employment situations of male workers in manufacturing industry (*Society Today*, 14 January 1977). The survey, undertaken with the collaboration and help of the Department of Employment, showed an enormous gulf between manual and non-manual workers (see Table 2.8).

In every respect Wedderburn found that non-manual workers were at an advantage compared with their manual counterparts, i.e. the occupations of those in social classes 1 and 2 and 3(a) gave them considerable advantages over those in social classes 3(b), 4 and 5. Examples of differences included the following:

1 *Pension schemes* – one quarter of the establishments who took part in the survey, had no pension schemes for their manual workers whereas the non-manual grades were almost completely covered by pension schemes.

2 *Sick pay* – 43 per cent of the establishments in Wedderburn's survey made no provision at all for supplementing the national insurance sickness benefit of their manual workers, but only a very small proportion of the non-manual workers were without some such provision.

3 *Inequalities* of earnings over the life cycle was greater than would be expected by examining levels of earnings at any point of time, largely because non-manual workers' earnings are more likely to be sustained during their working life, whereas earnings of manual workers reach a peak and then drop steeply as they get older.

4 *Opportunities of promotion* – in 80 to 90 per cent of the firms all the non-manual workers had the possibility of an annual pay increment but this only applied to a fifth of manual workers.

Table 2.8 Selected differences in terms and conditions of employment

	per cent of establishments in which the condition applies					
	opera- tives	fore- men	clerical workers	tech- nicians	middle managers	senior managers
holiday: 15 days+	38	72	74	77	84	88
choice of holiday time	35	54	76	76	84	88
normal working 40+ hours per week	97	94	9	23	27	22
sick pay – employers' scheme	57	94	98	97	98	98
pension – employers' scheme	67	94	90	94	96	96
time off with pay for personal reasons	29	84	83	86	91	93
pay deductions for any lateness	90	20	8	11	1	0
warning followed by dismissal for persistent lateness	84	66	78	71	48	41
no clocking-in or booking-in	2	46	48	45	81	94

5 *Hours of work* – both manual operatives and foremen worked the longest hours of those employed and they were also more likely to have to perform shift work and unsocial hours.

6 *Holidays* – non-manual workers not only enjoyed longer holidays but were more likely to be allowed to choose holiday dates.

7 *Time off* – although most firms allow time off on compassionate grounds only 29 per cent of manual workers would be paid for such time off, compared with 80 to 90 per cent of non-manual workers.

8 *Clocking-on* – 95 per cent of the firms made manual workers clock-on or book-in, and 90 per cent made deductions for lateness. In cases of persistent lateness, 84 per cent of the establishments would give manual workers one warning and then dismiss them. Non-manual workers were far more favourably treated; for the management grades persistent lateness

would do little more than damage their promotion prospects.

The necessity for skilled, semi-skilled and unskilled manual workers, in social class 3(a), 4 and 5, to clock-in is indicative of the 'feeling' of being a member of an inferior class in an occupational environment. The worker comes to hate the clock and rejoices when his time at the workplace is over.

An interactionist perspective of the feeling of class while at work is seen in the social relations of work. Wedderburn found that the physical organisation of production was geared to minimal contact between workers of different social classes. Segregation between manual and non-manual workers was often extended to such spheres as canteens/restaurants, recreational facilities and to predictability and regularity of earnings.

Non-manual workers are likely to receive their pay by monthly cheques or bank credit transfers, whereas 98 per cent of manual workers are paid in cash usually in a manilla envelope, on Friday afternoons. The data which Wedderburn collected suggest that employers assume that non-manual workers share with them the same class ideology and value system. The manual worker, on the other hand, is looked upon as a person who has to be watched, made to clock-in and be subjected to formal rules and prescriptions.

Inequalities which derive from differences in occupations have many implications in non-work life. Differences in holiday times, holiday choices, working hours, pension provisions, flexibility of time-keeping, regularity of earnings and methods of payment are important to a worker's lifestyle and in the organisation of his entire social life, especially in the ways in which he spends his leisure. The non-manual worker who is subjected to restraints, rules and regulations is likely to join a trade union in the fond hope that union activities will lessen the social inequalities with which he is forced to contend.

'What does he do?' remains the most illuminating question to ask about someone met for the first time. It is illuminating precisely because a man's or a woman's work, or the fact that they do not need to work or cannot work, is indicative of so much else about their social situations and their likely life experiences.

(Brown, R. in Abrams, P., ed., *Work, Urbanism and Inequality*)

A sociologist is able to use social class categories based upon occupational differentiations as a basis for predicting many other things about an individual. It is possible to make a shrewd guess about the TV programmes he watches, the type of schools his children attend, how he spends his holidays, the diseases he may contract and a host of other things which affect his lifestyle.

According to Peter Berger (*Invitation to Sociology*) the other basic index of class and subsequent sociological predictions, is the income an individual receives.

● *Income distribution*

By far the most exhaustive recent survey on both income and wealth has been carried out by the Royal Commission on the Distribution of Income and Wealth (The Diamond Commission, 1974–79). The Diamond Commission inquired into, and reported on, matters concerning the distribution of personal incomes both earned and unearned. The commission investigated the distribution of the personal income of all UK citizens in 1976–7. Of the total of £93 billion before tax, earnings from employment and self-employment made up four-fifths, while the rest came from state pensions, income from investments and property, etc. Figure 2.4 shows changes in income distribution over the last thirty years. The share of the bottom half has not changed since 1949. Figure 2.5 shows that income tax makes for a slight step towards greater equality of incomes, but the overall effect is minimal. You will see that decreases in the share received by the top tenth have been largely retained in the top half of the income spread. Note that the share of the bottom half has not changed since 1949.

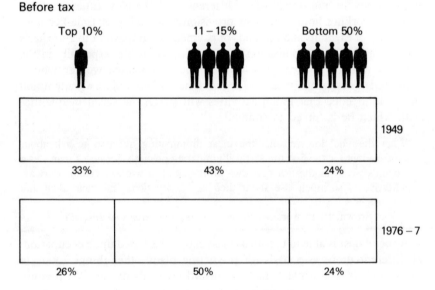

Fig. 2.4 Changes over 30 years of income distribution
(*An A to Z of Income and Wealth*, HMSO)

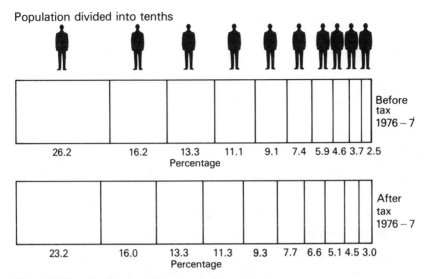

Fig. 2.5 The distribution of income before and after tax
(*An A to Z of Income and Wealth*, HMSO)

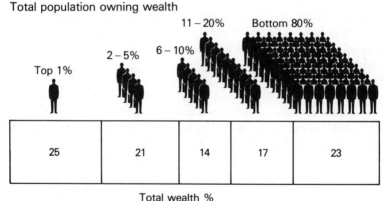

Fig. 2.6 The distribution of wealth in the UK
(*An A to Z of Income and Wealth*, HMSO)

Table 2.9 also indicates that changes in income distribution have not been very pronounced.

Marked differences still exist in the distribution of incomes. Those in social class 1 (professional and higher administrative workers) are likely to receive 3.5 times the earnings of those in social class 5 (unskilled workers). The higher incomes of many professions are the result of deliberate manipulation; supply is limited by practitioners in order to maintain a

Table 2.9 Trends in the distribution of personal income

Share owned by	1949	1959	1964	1967	1972–3
	%	%	%	%	%
Top 1 per cent	6.4	5.3	5.3	4.9	4.4
2–5 per cent	11.3	10.5	10.7	9.9	9.8
6–10 per cent	9.4	9.4	9.9	9.5	9.4
11–20 per cent	14.5	15.7	16.1	15.2	15.8
21–50 per cent	31.9	34.0	32.8	33.7	33.9

(Ivor Morgan, *The Social Science Teacher*, November 1976 and *Royal Commission on the Distribution of Income and Wealth*, HMSO, 1976)

relatively high income for members of their profession. This can be done in a variety of ways,

> ... one of the most popular being to raise the level and broaden the range of subjects in which would-be entrants must demonstrate their competence far beyond the point genuinely required for the successful performance of their work roles.
> (Kelsall, R.K. and H.M. *Stratification*)

Randall Collins collected examples of educational requirements being artificially inflated with no corresponding improvement in work performance (Collins, R. *Functional and Conflict Theories of Educational Stratification*).

It can be argued that how much a person earns depends on breeding rather than brains. In *Who Gets Ahead?*, Christopher Jencks found that 15 to 35 per cent of variance in men's earnings in the United States depended upon family background. Family background factors (social class, parental income, race and family size) have a crucial effect upon qualifications likely to be gained in later life, such as degrees or professional certification.

The middle classes are able to secure greater pay rises largely because they have a higher occupational status; rightly or wrongly, their work is more highly valued by society. Also, as they are fewer in number, increased incomes for middle-class groups pass less noticed than increased incomes for members of the working class. A similar argument applies to shareholders who receive increased income through higher dividends.

> But the average member of the middle class strikes his own individual wage bargain with his employer, or if he is involved in collective bargaining (as is increasingly the case) the group is normally a small one. Salaries count for less than half as much as wages in the nation's distribution. This means that the middle classes can get pay rises which, averaged out over each individual recipient, are pretty substantial, but whose effect on the national economy is

nevertheless quite small. This gives the middle classes a considerable if often unappreciated advantage in dividing the national cake. The same problem arises over the relation of wages to dividends. Union leaders frequently justify claims for wage increases by pointing to increases in the amount of dividend distributed to shareholders. Employers almost always reply, quite correctly, that the total value of the dividend is small compared to the value of the total wage bill. The share of wages and salaries in the national income comes to nearly six times as much as rent, interest, and dividends combined. If one is thinking in terms of social morality, the unions clearly have a case; if dividends can go up, why not wages? The average shareholder is a good deal better off, it is safe to assume, than the average wage-earner. The economic argument leads in a different direction. A large proportionate rise in dividend may be less inflationary – because it involves a much smaller total sum of money – than a quite modest round of wage increases.

(Shanks, M. *The Stagnant Society*)

The distribution of income from property is far more unequal than the distribution of income from earnings. It has been estimated that 92 per cent of property income goes to the top five per cent of the adult population (Meade, J.E. *Efficiency, Equality and the Ownership of Property*).

There are two aspects of income distribution, and changes in income distribution, which are of particular sociological significance.
1 Progressive taxation and welfare state benefits have not had the egalitarian effect that was thought likely to be the case.
2 The Marxist prophecy of an ever-increasing gulf between the social classes has not taken place; the working classes, in western capitalist countries, are therefore not inclined to support revolutionary aims.

● *Distribution of wealth*

The distribution of wealth in the UK is far more unequal than the distribution of income. Using marketable wealth (i.e. assets that can be bought and sold) as their definition of wealth, the Diamond Commission found that the top one per cent of the population owns a quarter of all the wealth. The bottom 80 per cent of the population owns less than a quarter (see Fig. 2.6 on p. 107).

During the last two decades the distribution of wealth has become a little less unequal; this has largely been caused by relatively low share prices of public companies and rising house prices – in 1982, about 56 per cent of housing stock was held by individual owner occupiers. Land prices have increased steadily, however, and this especially applies to farming land (see Fig. 2.7) which is in the hands of a relatively small number of people (see Table 2.10). Apart from the significance of shares as valuable financial assets, even more important is the fact that the ownership of

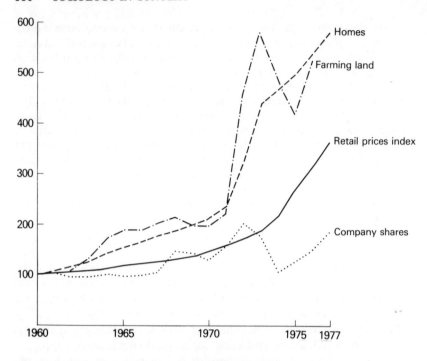

Fig. 2.7 Increased prices of different types of wealth
(*An A to Z of Income and Wealth*, HMSO)

ordinary share capital carries with it the control of large companies, including the commercial banks and other major financial institutions. The Diamond Commission found that the top $3\frac{1}{2}$ per cent of the population owned nearly 90 per cent of all share capital. The same tiny group owned 96 per cent of the land (see Table 2.10).

So wealth in the UK is highly concentrated and the proportion held by those at the top has declined only marginally. Most of the wealth tends to

Table 2.10 Percentage shares of different types of wealth in the UK

	Percentage share of top $1\frac{1}{4}$ per cent	Percentage share of top $3\frac{1}{2}$ per cent
Listed ordinary shares	65.5	87.2
Other company securities	73.0	93.8
Land	78.9	95.9
Dwellings	11.4	30.5
Building society deposits	14.0	40.4
National savings	6.4	19.7
Life policies	7.7	25.7

remain in the hands of the same few aristocratic families. Although a distinction may be drawn between the landed gentry and the wealthy business entrepreneurs, the City of London (as the financial centre of the nation) links traditional banking families with country-based aristocratic families.

> Fluctuations in wealth-holding over time do not affect the really rich: they are confined to the outer category of the well-off. Thus, a recent study shows that about three-quarters of those leaving estates of £100 000 or more had inherited at least £10 000 from their fathers, and about half had inherited £50 000 or more. Very few of the rich, judged by the criterion of those leaving £100 000 or more, are completely self-made men in the sense of having started with nothing.
> (Giddens, A. 'The Rich', *Society Today*, 2 December 1977)

The Queen is extremely wealthy in her own right and her private fortune has been estimated at exceeding £60 million. The Crown is the second largest landowner with nearly 300 000 acres including properties in the most exclusive parts of London. Roy Perrott, in *The Aristocrats*, has analysed how patterns of land-ownership persist especially among the hereditary aristocracy. The Swintons, Ardews and Berkeley families still farm some of their land and are able to trace their descent back to the Norman Conquest. But many members of the landed aristocracy are not interested in farming as such, but play the role of absentee landlords; their interest in the land is as a source of rent although they may employ an agent to supervise a farm on their behalf, largely because farming is currently profitable and there are also subsequent tax advantages.

Even the newer aristocracy are usually recruited from the wealthy and powerful. The principal source of wealth is in the financial world of the City which has been described as 'the most lawless square mile in the country' (Irving, C. *True Brit*). Giddens has pointed out that it is 'lawless' only in the sense that it is impervious to outside control. By this he means that this almost independent nation-state has legitimised modern rackets and operates under what is superficially a gentlemanly code of conduct.

The maldistribution of wealth in the UK has led to a position where real power is in the hands of the wealthy few. The economy is controlled by those who have inherited wealth; the merchant banking families are dominated by a traditional aristocratic elite. The government is controlled overwhelmingly by the sons of the rich who have been socialised by public schools and Oxbridge. It may appear surprising that poorer people do not more keenly resent large inherited wealth, but this is mainly because the implications of the privileges that wealth brings are usually obscured from public view especially by the government, the civil service, the traditional educational establishments and the media, all of whom have a considerable vested interest in maintaining the status quo.

An excellent account of the sociological significance of inequalities of wealth as a key to social class divisions is provided by John Westergaard and Henrietta Resler in *Class in a Capitalist Society* (see their chapter 7, *Capital: the ownership of property.*)

> Private ownership of capital is the key to class division in Britain as in other capitalist countries. Taxation and public welfare provision have done little to alter the broad pattern of material inequality between classes, because the objectives and effects of public policy are limited – though they are not rigidly fixed – by the needs and influence of business in an economy where private enterprise continues to play the predominant role.... Possession of property – of capital in the means of production in particular – remains the crucial source of wealth, and the most potent cause of inequality of income.
>
> (Westergaard, J. and Resler, H. *Class in a Capitalist Society*)

Table 2.11 Reasons for continuation of inequalities of income and wealth

1 *Inheritance* is the main reason for the continuation of private wealth in the hands of a small proportion of the people.

2 *Savings*, according to the Diamond Commission, make for a distribution of wealth that is much more unequal than is the distribution of income; this is especially the case when savings are in the form of property and land (see Fig. 2.7).

3 *Tax evasion*, which is largely the prerogative of the middle class, was estimated at £3500 million per year by Sir Lawrence Airey, the Inland Revenue chairman, in 1980.

4 *The wealthy gain more from welfare services* by making greater use of the NHS and having their children educated for longer periods.

5 *Self-employment* is far more profitable than working for a private firm or for the state; the Diamond Commission found that three-quarters of highest income earners worked for themselves.

6 *Lack of take-up of social security benefits* by the poor is brought about largely because of a bureaucratic social security system; in 1977 it was estimated that 850 000 people out of 4 million who were entitled to social security benefits, did not receive them.

7 *Fringe benefits* are enjoyed more by the wealthy and may even exceed high salaries gained from work.

8 *Pension schemes* are more generous and prolific for the better-off; they are also often index-linked in accordance with the inflation rate.

9 *The cycle of deprivation* ensures that poverty passes from one generation to another.

10 *Multi-directorship of companies* helps the very rich, e.g. in 1978 Sir John Davies was reported to be a director of 28 companies.

Westergaard and Resler make the point that the ownership of property which yields no taxable income (houses, cars, consumer durables, etc.) is spread widely, although still unevenly. But the most outstanding fact is the very limited degree in which private wealth has been diffused. They also refute two widely-held beliefs. Firstly, the contention that the concentration of property ownership is little more than the natural accumulation of wealth by middle-aged and elderly men; but in fact, the concentration of private wealth is almost as marked for age as it is overall, and women own about 40 per cent of wealth. Secondly, the argument that inequality of wealth contributes little to overall inequality is not in fact supported by any empirical evidence.

Table 2.12 Some attempted methods to redistribute wealth and income

---

1 *Increased capital taxes:*
  (a) corporation tax upon company profits.
  (b) capital gains tax upon profits received from the sale of shares or property.
  (c) capital transfer tax upon gifts made by the rich to their offspring.
  (In the early 1970s, the Labour Government suggested a Wealth Tax to be imposed upon those owning wealth valued at over £100 000 – Green Paper, Wealth Tax, Cmnd 5704.)

2 *Progressive taxation* of income so that the greatest burden falls upon the rich; but income tax was made less progressive by Sir Geoffrey Howe's Conservative Budget of 1979.

3 *Subsidies for the less well-to-do* including cheap housing, food and medicines.

4 *Improved welfare services and social security benefits* combined with a policy of compassion to ensure maximum eligibility and assistance for beneficiaries.

- *Class differences of life-chances*

Apart from class differences in family background, education and other major areas which we shall consider in detail in subsequent units, there are other social differences which we must touch upon. Space only permits consideration of a few.

1 *Health*

It is well-documented that the lower social classes suffer worse health than the middle classes; the lower class have higher rates of infant mortality, high rates of chronic sickness and they die earlier. The middle class not only gain more from the health service, but they can also afford to buy private health care and rush the queue for treatment. Social class differences relating to health have changed very little over the last 20 years, in spite of our comprehensive National Health Service. The Report of the Committee on Child Health Services 1976 (The Court Report), indicated that the death rate of children of workers in social class 5 was more than twice as high as for children of parents in social class 1.

Table 2.13 Child death rates per 100 000 per year 1959–1963, England and Wales

Social class	Type of occupation	Age		
		1–4 years	5–9 years	10–14 years
I	Professional	69	32.8	29.6
II	Managerial	73.4	35.1	28.8
III	Skilled	88.7	41.1	31.3
IV	Semi-skilled	93.3	41.4	30.3
V	Unskilled	154.0	66.6	41.4

Table 2.13 shows that with few exceptions death rates amongst children under 15 years of age were highest among those whose parents were unskilled or semi-skilled. Although these figures relate to over twenty years ago, it is unlikely that social class differences have changed much. In 1973, for example, perinatal mortality rates (i.e. still births plus deaths of babies under one week, as a rate per 1000 live births) for babies of unskilled workers (26.8) were about double those of professional workers (13.9).

Class distinctions of disease are maintained from the womb to the tomb. Table 2.14 show how semi-skilled and unskilled manual workers suffer most from sickness throughout their lives.

Table 2.14 Class distribution of disease

Cause of Death	Unskilled	Semi-skilled	Skilled	Managerial	Professional
All causes	+43	+3	AVERAGE	−19	−24
Tuberculosis	+85	+8	−4	−46	−60
Stomach cancer	+63	+14	+1	−37	−51
Lung cancer	+48	+4	+7	−28	−37
Coronary disease	+12	−4	+6	−5	−2
Bronchitis	+94	+16	−3	−50	−72
Duodenal ulcer	+73	+7	−4	−25	−52

(Registrar General, Office of Population Census and Surveys)

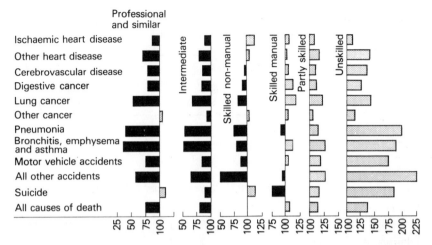

Fig. 2.8 Deaths of men: by major cause and social class, England and Wales, 1970–72 (Standard mortality ratios, i.e. actual deaths against expected numbers randomly distributed)
(*Social Trends*, HMSO, 1979)

Figure 2.8 offers further proof of the disadvantages, in the mortality stakes, of being an unskilled worker, compared with being a professional worker. Only in the case of suicide and obscure cancers, such as leukaemia, are professional workers shown to bear a risk slightly above the average.

Barbara Preston has produced evidence, using the Registrar General decennial supplement, that the higher mortality rate of the lower classes has become more pronounced over time. Table 2.15 indicates increased or decreased risk in percentage terms, of a man from each of the five social classes dying from certain major causes.

Although most of the statistics given are for men, similar social-class differences relating to disease apply to the wives of men in these categories. This indicates that the particular work which a man does is not the principal contributory factor relating to diseases. General lifestyles, including diet and housing, are also major influences.

2 *Diet*

Better-off families consume more nutritious foods, such as fruit and meat, than do poorer families. The poor are forced, by financial circumstances, to consume more of the cheaper 'filling' foods which are higher in carbohydrates and lower in such important nutrients as protein and calcium (see Table 2.17).

3 *Housing*

There is a strong correlation between occupation and home ownership as shown in Table 2.18.

Table 2.15 Chronic sickness: by socio-economic group, age, and sex, 1974 and 1975 (in Great Britain; rates per thousand)

	Males aged					Females aged				
	0–14	15–44	45–64	65 or over	All ages	0–14	15–44	45–64	65 or over	All ages
Persons reporting limiting long-standing illness:										
Professional	36	66	161	239	88	28	79	134	286	84
Employers & managers	50	74	162	336	122	26	72	161	412	119
Intermediate and junior non-manual	40	83	274	363	148	20	66	200	417	148
Skilled manual and own account non-professional	45	85	237	397	138	35	93	202	419	132
Semi-skilled manual and personal service	47	84	265	373	155	25	95	260	437	197
Unskilled manual	56	112	390	377	226	44	115	264	419	246
All persons	46	83	234	366	140	29	84	209	424	155

(*Social Trends*, 1979)

Table 2.16 Standardised mortality rates of social classes 1930–63: adult males under 65

period	Registrar General's social classes				
	I	II	III	IV	V
1930–32	90	94	97	102	111
1949–53	86	92	101	104	118
1959–63	76	81	100	103	143

(Preston, B. *Sociological Review*, Vol. 22, No. 1)

Table 2.17 Food consumption per head per week in 1974

		'A' families (i.e. the top 6.4%)	'D' and 'E2' families (i.e. the bottom 12.6%)
Liquid milk	(pints)	4.86	4.48
Cheese	(ounces)	4.11	2.66
Carcase meat	"	17.25	11.50
Poultry	"	5.41	3.28
Fish	"	4.18	3.73
Butter	"	5.53	4.64
Fresh green vegetables	"	9.87	7.64
Frozen vegetables	"	3.66	1.07
Fresh fruit	"	22.60	7.49
White bread	"	18.23	31.02
Margarine	"	2.15	3.28
Potatoes	"	33.41	35.83

(*Household Food Consumption and Expenditure, 1974*)

Table 2.18 Tenure of households: by socio-economic group (Great Britain; by percentages)

Socio-economic group	Owner-occupiers		Tenants			All tenures	
	Outright owners	Mortgagors	Local authority	Unfurnished private	Furnished private	Total (percentages)	Total sample (numbers) (=100%)
1 *Economically active heads:*							
Professional & managerial	19	63	7	9	2	100	1762
Intermediate & junior non-manual	15	46	22	12	4	100	1574
Skilled manual, etc.	12	39	38	9	2	100	2832
Semi-skilled manual, etc.	14	23	49	12	2	100	1209
Unskilled	12	14	61	12	2	100	338
2 *Economically inactive heads:*							
men	43	5	38	11	2	100	1806
women	36	3	46	14	2	100	1950

(*Social Trends*, 1980)

More than 80 per cent of professional and managerial workers are owner-occupiers compared with 26 per cent of unskilled workers. Nevertheless, the increase in owner-occupation of homes has brought about greater equality of wealth. At the 1911 census only about 10 per cent of householders owned their own homes. George Polanyi and J.B. Wood (*How Much Inequality?*) cite the case of increased home ownership as a general leveller; in their debate with Professor A.B. Atkinson (*Unequal Shares*) Polanyi and Wood contend that the Inland Revenue underestimates the value of private property. It must also be borne in mind that mass house ownership offers the additional benefits of greater security and freedom of action. The majority of home-owners are the first generation of their families to join the new propertied class. Whether or not that makes them members of the middle class, and subject to the process of embourgeoisement, we shall touch upon in the next topic. The highest proportion of council tenants are manual workers who pay rent for most of their lives without ever accumulating wealth by means of house purchase. The Conservative Government policy of decreasing public spending has brought about a steep decline in council housebuilding and has caused much suffering to the lower social classes. There has been an increase in home ownership, but the benefits of that are felt less among unskilled and semi-skilled manual workers who are unable to afford the deposit, the legal fees, or the repayments which have included very high interest rates in recent years.

Millions of people in the lower social classes live in substandard conditions. A survey carried out in 1976 found that 790 000 dwellings (4.6 per cent) were unfit for habitation and a further 920 000 (5.4 per cent) lacked such basic amenities as an internal WC, fixed bath, wash basin, sink and cold water. Although some people are without a home at all, it has been estimated by Shelton that about 700 000 families have two homes. Such are the inequality and social differences in our modern society.

2.5 Social trends

- *Social mobility*

Social mobility concerns movements between social groups and is more possible with an open society. In closed societies, such as caste and feudal societies, there is unlikely to be any significant upward or downward social mobility. This mobility is a process, recurring over time whereby individuals and their family units move from one social class to another.

Social mobility is but one type of a range of mobilities. It is most closely related to occupational mobility but it may also be associated with geographical mobility; movement from rural to urban areas, between different parts of the country, or from one country to another, may bring a change in occupation. But for real social mobility to take place the change in occupation must involve not merely a change of job or a change of employer, but a change in economic and consequently social status.

All societies have some social mobility but no societies have complete social mobility. Modern industrial societies are often classified as 'open societies' or 'class societies' because they afford some freedom of movement between social strata. It is usually recognised that the United States is a more open society than European societies. If perfect mobility existed, the number recruited to any class would be proportionate to their numbers in the population, e.g. as working-class members of British society form the largest proportion of the population, recruits with working-class antecedents would make up the majority in the professional occupations. But perfect mobility can never exist because of important variables such as educational opportunity and career possibilities: educational opportunity is affected by differential access to schooling, parental encouragement, home conditions, etc., while career possibilities are influenced by the occupational structure (e.g. how easy is it to move from a job on the assembly line to a managerial position?). Other factors affecting social mobility include family size, motivation, marriage, etc. (see Fig. 2.9). Differential fertility is also important, e.g. if those in middle-class occupations do not produce enough children to fill those occupations there will be more opportunities for the working class to experience upward social mobility.

The principal cause of social mobility is a change in the occupational structure of society. We saw in our study of the Hindu caste society that there was little interchange between strata; an individual's position in society is ascribed rather than achieved – one is born into a caste, traditionally associated with an occupation, and one normally dies as a member of that caste. However, industrial and post-industrial societies are characterised by change. In recent years, there has been the creation of an increasing number of highly-skilled occupations, especially with the advent of the service economy. The development of a large number of high-level jobs is a most important determinant of social mobility.

Social mobility is multi-dimensional and could be measured in a number of ways, such as by changes in wealth, income, power, status and skills. However, measurement of social mobility is mainly concerned with changes in economic and occupational prestige. It would be simple to measure mobility between manual and non-manual groups, but this is so simplistic and general that it might be misleading. Three types of vertical social mobility may be distinguished.

Fig. 2.9 Who is experiencing upward social mobility and who is experiencing downward social mobility?

1 *Intergenerational* – measuring an individual's movement to a higher or lower social class or status from that of his father.

2 *Intragenerational* – measuring an individual's movement classwise during his lifetime.

3 *Stratum mobility* – measuring the movement of an occupational stratum from a higher or lower position in the stratification structure, e.g. David Lockwood's analysis of the blackcoated worker.

There are important questions posed in attempting to measure social mobility.

1 What social categorisation system is taken as the starting point, when considering upward or downward movements?

2 What is the rate of movement out of a stratum? This is the most customary measurement of social mobility, but it is erroneous to think that it is the only one.

3 Is the mobility upwards or downwards? Many people assume that upward mobility is the norm, but S. Miller found that in some societies 20 per cent or more of sons of non-manual fathers finish up in manual occupations.

4 How far has an individual moved from his class of origin? Has he moved up or down just one social class, or has a working-class child risen right to the top?

5 Do those who experience upward or downward mobility remain in their new position, or is there a change back in the next generation?

One of the most significant studies of social mobility in Britain was undertaken by D.V. Glass *et al.* in 1949. Using a classification based on occupational prestige, Glass discovered a relatively high level of inter-generational mobility. In Table 2.19, the percentages in the horizontal rows (in the top-right hand corner of each square) show the extent to which sons have the same occupational status as their fathers. For example, the series of squares in the top row (1) show that among the sons whose fathers were in occupational status category 1, 14.6 per cent are in category 2, 20.2 per cent are in category 3, and so on through to category 7 where only 1.5 per cent of those born into category 1 are located. Of sons who were in category 7, none rose to category 1. The figures in bold type, going diagonally across the table, indicate the extent to which occupational status has remained constant as between fathers and sons. For example, 38.8 per cent whose fathers were in category 1 are themselves in the same category in 1949.

The percentages in the vertical columns, in the bottom left-hand corner of each square, refer to the parental status of the men found in each category in 1949. For example, of all men in occupational status category 1 in 1949, 48.5 per cent had fathers of the same occupational status. This is an indication of the degree of self-recruitment to a status category. The tendency for upward mobility was found to be most marked among men whose fathers were in the lower occupational status categories, but the distance traversed when changes occurred was not very great; where men have an occupational status different from their fathers, they still tend to cluster around the parental category. Typically the movement is one or two status categories. The higher the parental status, the further the fall below it; this may be thought to be a truism as there are a greater number of categories through which to fall.

The main points which emerged from Glass's study included:

Table 2.19 Social mobility – distribution of the male sample according to subjects' and subjects' fathers' status and category

subjects' present status category

		1	2	3	4	5	6	7	total
father's status category	1	38.8 / 48.5	14.6 / 11.9	20.2 / 7.9	6.2 / 1.7	14.0 / 1.3	4.7 / 1.0	1.5 / 0.5.	100.0 (129)
	2	10.7 / 15.5	26.7 / 25.2	22.7 / 10.3	12.0 / 3.9	20.6 / 2.2	5.3 / 1.4	2.0 / 0.7	100.0 (150)
	3	3.5 / 11.7	10.1 / 22.0	18.8 / 19.7	19.1 / 14.4	35.7 / 8.6	6.7 / 3.9	6.1 / 5.0	100.0 (345)
	4	2.1 / 10.7	3.9 / 12.6	11.2 / 17.6	21.2 / 24.0	43.0 / 15.6	12.4 / 10.8	6.2 / 7.5	100.0 (518)
	5	0.9 / 13.6	2.4 / 22.6	7.5 / 34.5	12.3 / 40.3	47.3 / 50.0	17.1 / 43.5	12.5 / 44.6	100.0 (1510)
	6	0.0 / 0.0	1.3 / 3.8	4.1 / 5.8	8.8 / 8.7	39.1 / 12.5	31.2 / 24.1	15.5 / 16.7	100.0 (458)
	7	0.0 / 0.0	0.8 / 1.9	3.6 / 4.2	8.3 / 7.0	36.4 / 9.8	23.5 / 15.3	27.4 / 25.0	100.0 (387)
	total	100.0 (103)	100.0 (159)	100.0 (330)	100.0 (459)	100.0 (1429)	100.0 (593)	100.0 (424)	(3497)

(Glass, D.V. *et al. Social Mobility in Britain*)

1 Self-recruitment was highest amongst professional and higher administrative occupational status categories.
2 Most social mobility was short-range between adjacent occupational
groups.
3 The proportion of sons with the same occupational status as the fathers
was approximately one-third.
4 Very limited long-range movement takes place between the top groups
and the bottom groups.

In the 1980s the results of the most exhausting social mobility survey
ever carried out in Britain during the twentieth century was published.
The Nuffield Social Mobility Survey under the direction of Professor
A.H. Halsey and Dr John Goldthorpe was based on data collected from
interviews in 1972 with more than 10 000 men aged between 20 and 64. Its
main finding was that while there has been considerable social mobility in
Britain in the past sixty years with more individuals reaching the top
because of the general economic progress and changes in occupational
structure, there has been no change at all in the relative chances of

reaching the top by those born into the lower social classes.

J.H. Goldthorpe found that those in classes VI and VII (see Table 2.20) remained more than three times less likely, and those born into classes III, IV and V more than twice as unlikely to finish up in classes I and II as those born in the top two classes. A.H. Halsey's analysis of the educational data collected in the survey showed that while overall there was more widespread access to secondary and higher education for all classes, relative inequalities persisted and even widened in some cases. Goldthorpe identifies the 'service class' as the most privileged group in society after the landed gentry. The service class consists of people in well-paid, secure jobs in the professions, government, administration and management; the class now includes one in four of employed males. Downward mobility from this class is virtually non-existent, as service workers invariably maintain or improve their position and transmit social advantage to their offspring. Some impression of equality is given by the limited recruitment to this group from among working-class children. On the whole, however, the prospect of a working-class boy reaching the top is as unlikely as ever. We have seen in the eighties how the service class has taken up defensive postures at a time when cuts in its number have been advocated; the class has been in a privileged position for it has been responsible for the pruning of the labour force. It is more prone to prune at the bottom than to prune its own members. With an economic recession, Goldthorpe concludes,

a decline in openness would seem to be a particularly high probability.
(Goldthorpe, J.H. *Social Mobility and Class Structure in Modern Britain*)

Goldthorpe's and Halsey's findings make depressing reading for those who had put their faith in the Welfare State and improved educational access to make for that increased social mobility which would lead to greater social equality. However, it can be argued that egalitarian policies pursued by successive governments since the war have stopped things being more unequal than they otherwise would have been.

The general nature of the class structure is to move towards greater inequality. Social policy has probably prevented a tendency towards even greater inequality than we have shown to exist.
(Goldthorpe, J.H. *Social Mobility and Class Structure*)

The Oxford mobility study was based on social class rather than Glass's status ranking. Table 2.20 summarises the main findings of the Oxford survey on intergenerational mobility.

Two important sociologically significant points arise from recent studies of social mobility.
1 Our society is now more open although a large degree of elite self-recruitment still prevails.

Table 2.20 Findings of Oxford Survey on intergenerational mobility, 1980

Sons' class in 1972

		1	2	3	4	5	6	7	total
	1	**45.7** 25.3	19.1 12.4	11.6 9.6	6.8 6.7	4.9 3.2	5.4 2.0	6.5 2.4	100.0 (680)
	2	29.4 13.1	**23.3** 12.2	12.1 8.0	6.0 4.8	9.7 5.2	10.8 3.1	8.6 2.5	100.0 (547)
	3	18.6 10.4	15.9 10.4	**13.0** 10.8	7.4 7.4	13.0 8.7	15.7 5.7	16.4 6.0	100.0 (687)
Father's class	4	14.0 10.1	14.4 12.2	9.1 9.8	**21.1** 27.2	9.9 8.6	15.1 7.1	16.3 7.7	100.0 (886)
	5	14.4 12.5	13.7 14.0	10.2 13.2	7.7 12.1	**15.9** 16.6	21.4 12.2	16.8 9.6	100.0 (1072)
	6	7.8 16.4	8.8 21.7	8.4 26.1	6.4 24.0	12.4 31.1	**30.6** 41.8	25.6 35.2	100.0 (2577)
	7	7.1 12.1	8.5 17.1	8.8 22.6	5.7 17.8	12.9 26.7	24.8 28.0	**32.2** 36.6	100.0 (2126)
	Total	100.0 (1230)	100.0 (1050)	100.0 (827)	100.0 (687)	100.0 (1026)	100.0 (1883)	100.0 (1872)	(8575)

Classes

1 Higher professionals, higher-grade administrators, managers in large industrial concerns and large proprietors
2 Lower professionals, higher-grade technicians, lower-grade administrators, managers in small businesses and supervisors of non-manual employees
3 Routine non-manual – mainly clerical and sales personnel
4 Small proprietors and self-employed artisans
5 Lower-grade technicans and supervisors of manual workers
6 Skilled manual workers
7 Semi-skilled and unskilled manual workers
(Adapted from Goldthorpe, J.H. *Social Mobility and Class Structure*, Tables 2.1 and 2.2)

2 There is increased long-range mobility out of the lower social classes; this has been made possible by the increase in the number of top jobs available, and by differential fertility whereby middle-class families do not produce enough children to fill the elite occupations.

Social mobility has generally increased with the economic development of industrial societies, but the increase has been due very largely to changes in the occupational structure....

(Bottomore, T.B. *Classes in Modern Society*)

It has been argued that our more open society with its higher degree of social mobility militates against the creation of solidaristic class groups. S.M. Miller has pointed out that even if social mobility were the principal determinant of class consciousness it would be difficult to appraise its effects. It would be possible to have fifty per cent upward social mobility of the sons of the working class and retain class consciousness.

> For example, if a society were divided 50 per cent into lower-class groups and 50 per cent into upper-class groups and if there were high mobility in that every individual has an equal chance of being in either class section, then 50 per cent of the sons of lower-class fathers would move into upper-class positions and 50 per cent would remain in the lower class. The upper class would have a similar breakdown, and the lower class would, therefore, be made up of 50 per cent of sons of lower-class fathers and 50 per cent of sons of upper-class fathers. In this highly mobile situation would there be any chance of class consciousness in the lower strata? The answer is likely to be yes, because 50 per cent of the lower-class groups would have a lower-class family background (assumed to be conducive to class consciousness), and 50 per cent of the lower class group would have fallen in the class structure (also assumed to be conducive to revolutionary class activity). Thus, with high rates of mobility, class consciousness would not necessarily decline.
>
> (Miller, S.M. 'The Concept and Measurement of Social Mobility' in Coxon, A.P.M., ed., *Social Mobility*)

It could, however, be the case that class consciousness among the working class decreases because sons originating from the working class have more chance of reaching middle-class occupational status groups where they embrace middle-class ideology and values. This brings us to what has been called the embourgeoisement thesis which holds that class differences are fading as the more affluent members of the working class adopt middle-class lifestyles.

- *Are we all middle-class now?*

It has been claimed that with the emergence of post-capitalist society, embourgeoisement takes place as the working class adopts the lifestyles, aspirations and social perspectives of the middle class. Major proponents of this theory include Clark Kerr et al. (*Industrialism and Industrial Man*) and F. Zweig (*The Worker in An Affluent Society*). Clark Kerr put forward the concept of the 'logic of industrialism' which is associated with the universality of urban life and work, shared by both working and middle classes. Zweig focused on the cultural changes of the working class with its increase in acquisitive instincts, a rise in security-mindedness, combined with a desire to better one's self by higher earnings. In the 1950s and early 1960s the thesis of incipient embourgeoisement gained some acceptance. In Britain, the Labour Party blamed embourgeoisement for its 1959 election defeat and Harold Wilson urged his party to discard its cloth-cap image.

The embourgeoisement argument that more and more of the working class are becoming middle class is based upon the following social, economic and political changes.

1 Since the 1950s workers in capitalist countries have become part of what J.K. Galbraith has called *The Affluent Society*, as living standards have advanced to include the purchase of houses, cars, numerous consumer durables and other items of mass consumption.

2 Laissez-faire capitalist society has been replaced by the mixed economy where many workers are employed not by big business but by nationalised concerns, the civil service, quangos and local government enterprises.

3 The state is less of a coercive force in society associated mainly with law and order, but nowadays has also assumed a caring role especially in the realms of social welfare, health, education and consumer protection.

4 Capitalism has been modified in the face of challenges from such bodies as the Monopolies Commission, the Restrictive Practices Court, the Office of Fair Trading, the Prices Commission, Consumers' Councils and the National Consumer Council.

5 Class conflict as predicted by Marx has waned as conflict is now institutionalised; it is argued by some that Labour and Conservative Governments can alternate without any radical change of social policies (Laski, H. *The Grammar of Politics*).

6 The purposes of capitalistic organisations have changed as the ownership and control of public companies have become separated; it is argued that large companies are now run by managers, rather than the owners of private capital (shareholders) and are consequently more benign as they are no longer motivated solely by profit maximisation.

7 It is suggested that acute poverty has been conquered by the welfare state and adequate social security benefits.

8 The membership of the Labour Party has declined, especially in more prosperous areas, and in 1981 a breakaway group formed the Social Democratic Party.

9 The pluralist theory of power sees power dispersed over a large number of groups in society, and not concentrated in the hands of an elitist group such as the owners of the means of production.

10 The growth of the service economy has led to large increases in the number of white-collar workers who have been institutionalised into the structure of capitalism.

11 The distribution of wealth and income has become less unequal and consequently social differentiation in economic terms has been reduced.

12 Increased educational access, brought about by comprehensive schools and the increase in higher education places, has meant that qualifications

rather than the kinship network enable individuals to attain to occupational positions of high reward. This is the theme of Michael Young's *The Rise of the Meritocracy*, which involves a lighthearted projection into the next century, where upward social mobility is brought about by merit alone.

Some sociologists, especially in the USA and in Britain, have argued that all these things constitute sufficient evidence for embourgeoisement, and that this means that the Marxist analysis of the polarisation of the classes is no longer tenable. Manual workers are much better-off, less exploited and afforded protection by the Welfare State. More workers have joined the ranks of the non-manual categories and the distinctions between social classes are now blurred as many workers approach the material standards of the middle classes who themselves suffer high progressive taxes.

However, it is comparatively easy to contest some of the current trends which have been used to support the thesis of embourgeoisement. We have seen that inequalities of wealth and income still help to produce a power elite. Peter Townsend's studies have shown that abject poverty still exists and this has become more pronounced in the eighties with more than 14 per cent of the working population unemployed and with a whittling away of welfare benefits. The separation of the ownership and control of public companies is more apparent than real with owners and managers embracing similar values and attitudes. Limitations placed upon capitalism by government agencies have had only a peripheral effect upon the actions of large business empires, while the mixed economy is only 'mixed' on an 80 per cent 'private' and 20 per cent 'public' ownership basis. It can never be proved conclusively that workers have embraced the values and ideology of capitalism.

The best-known challenge to the embourgeoisement thesis is in the work of John H. Goldthorpe, David Lockwood *et al*. Their three volumes in *The Affluent Worker* studies were based upon empirical research. Goldthorpe and Lockwood state that the main objective of their study was to test the widely-accepted thesis of working-class embourgeoisement: the thesis that affluent manual workers have become progressively assimilated into middle-class society. In planning their field investigations their first concern was to find a locality which would be suitable for the validation of the embourgeoisement thesis. Their eventual choice was Luton, for the following reasons:

1 Luton was a prosperous and growing industrial town in an area which had experienced economic expansion.

2 The labour force included a high proportion of geographically mobile workers who might well have come to Luton motivated by hopes of improved living standards.

3 A high proportion of the population lived in new housing areas which included a relatively large amount of private development.

4 Luton was isolated from older industrial regions and therefore not dominated by traditional industrial relations.

5 Luton included a number of industrial firms noted for high wages, advanced personnel and welfare policies and with a background of industrial harmony.

Having decided upon Luton, Goldthorpe and Lockwood drew up a sample of workers to be studied through an interviewing programme. It was decided that the best basis for doing this was to select workers from the following three firms which accounted for about 30 per cent of the total labour force of the town and its surroundings:

1 Vauxhall Motors Ltd, a subsidiary of General Motors.

2 Skefko Ball Bearing Company Ltd, a member of the international SKF Organisation.

3 Laporte Chemicals, a member of the Laporte Group.

They then confined their attention to male employees working in shop-floor jobs who fulfilled the following conditions:

1 Aged between 21 and 46

2 Married and living with their wives

3 Regularly earning £17 per week gross (1962)

4 Resident in Luton or adjoining areas

Assembly-line workers were studied at Vauxhall, machine operators at Skefko and process workers at Laporte. Table 2.21 gives the distribution of the final sample of 229 male manual workers who consented, together with their wives, to further interviews.

Table 2.21 Distribution of final sample by firm and type of work – used in *The Affluent Worker* studies

Firm	Type of work	No. of workers interviewed
Vauxhall	Assembly	86
Skefko	Machining	41
	Machine-setting	23
	Maintenance, etc. (craftsmen)	45
Laporte	Process work	23
	Process maintenance (craftsmen)	11
	Total	229

(Goldthorpe, J.H. *et al.*, *The Affluent Worker: industrial attitudes and behaviour*)

In addition to the main sample, for comparative purposes, fifty-four white-collar workers were interviewed. Interviews were the main research method used; a one-hour interview took place at the workplace followed, some weeks later, by a three-hour interview of husband and wife together in their home. Among the many questions posed, all the respondents were asked to compare their present job with:

1 other jobs they had previously had with the same firm;
2 other jobs which might be regarded as potentially open to them in their present employment.

After exhaustive inquiries extending over many years from 1959, Goldthorpe *et al.* found that the thesis of embourgeoisement was not proven. Some of the most important reasons for their conclusions are given below under three headings.

A *Economic aspect (working life)*
1 Most of the manual workers considered their work to be little more than mere manual labour which offered no reward in itself but was motivated primarily by the intrinsic reward of relatively high wages; a sizeable proportion of the workers in the sample were attached to their employment by a mainly pecuniary kind of attachment.
2 Many manual workers had abandoned jobs which afforded a greater degree of immediate satisfaction in order to take jobs offering more money and security which in the long run made for income maximisation; the white collar workers liked their work and were not preoccupied with levels of pay.

B *Relational aspect (community life)*
1 The working-class people in the sample did not adopt middle-class social lifestyles, e.g. they did not entertain as did the white-collar workers, or participate to the same extent in formal organisations of a religious, charitable or sporting nature.
2 Rather than being assimilated into middle-class life based upon residential stability and social homogeneity, manual workers experienced status segregation and a privatised mode of living centred upon home, family and the maintenance of close kinship relations.

C *Normative aspect (political orientation)*
1 There was no real evidence of any appreciable switch in political allegiance towards the right, as most affluent manual workers were members of trade unions, remaining loyal to the Labour Party and regarding working-class Conservative voters as deviant.
2 They still saw their position in class terms and voted for Labour as their class party, largely because increases in living standards had not altered the differences in social relationships which divided them from the middle class.

Goldthorpe and Lockwood conducted painstaking research and their findings still carry great weight, but nevertheless their efforts have been subject to some criticism.

1 Their initial sceptical attitude towards embourgeoisement meant that they merely verified what they set out to prove in the first place, i.e. that embourgeoisement has not taken place.

2 Most of their findings were of a negative nature.

3 The research was carried out over a long period of increasing affluence and the opinions of the respondents could well have changed during that period.

4 The firms chosen were not typically British; Skefko was Swedish-owned while Vauxhall was a subsidiary of General Motors.

5 Luton did not comply in every respect to the researchers' criteria although it was reasonably suitable.

6 The sample included a high proportion of semi-skilled workers whereas it is the skilled workers who are more likely to move in the direction of 'middle-classness'.

7 The sample was also unrepresentative as a fair proportion of the sample had middle-class family connections but had undergone downward social mobility and consequently were instrumental in outlook.

8 Some of the interviews were unstructured and the resultant open-ended questions were impossible to quantify systematically.

9 Some of their suppositions were indefinite, e.g.

> the workers we have studied, if not highly typical of the present, may well prove to be in many ways typical of the future.
> (Goldthorpe, J.H. *et al.*, *The Affluent Worker: Industrial attitudes and behaviour*)

Although we should be sceptical of the embourgeoisement thesis, nevertheless it does appear that the working and middle classes are converging as the convergence thesis says they will. This is a less sweeping claim than that of embourgeoisement. Goldthorpe and Lockwood accepted that rapid and far-reaching changes were probably occurring in the pattern of working-class life. These changes do not entail the merging of manual workers and their families into the social world of the middle class, but a coming together of the outlooks and attitudes of some working- and middle-class groups.

Two aspects of the convergence thesis should be noted:

1 *Social mobility* has increased, with the high degree of openness of advanced industrial societies; consequently, achieved status is becoming more important than ascribed status.

2 *Differentiation* has been reduced in social, economic and political dimensions.

Further Reading

Atkinson, A.B. *Unequal Shares* (Penguin)

Beteille, A. (ed.) *Inequality* (Penguin)

Bottomore, T. *Classes in Modern Society* (George Allen & Unwin)

Coxon, A.P.M. (ed.) *Social Mobility* (Penguin)

Dahrendorf, R. *Class and Class Conflict in Industrial Society* (OUP)

Davies, I. *Social Mobility and Political Change* (Macmillan)

Giddens, A. *The Class Structure of Advanced Societies* (Hutchinson)

Goldthorpe, J.H. *et al. The Affluent Worker in the Class Structure* (Cambridge University Press)

Goldthorpe, J.H. *et al. Social Mobility and Class Structure in Modern Britain* (OUP)

Halsey, A. *et al. Origins and Destinations* (OUP)

Jackson, B. *Working-Class Community* (Penguin)

Jencks, C. *Inequality* (Penguin)

Kelsall, R.K. & H.M. *Stratification* (Longman)

Kincaid, J.C. *Poverty and Equality in Britain* (Penguin)

Parkin, P. *Class, Inequality and Political Order* (Paladin)

Raynor, J. *The Middle Class* (Longman)

Thompson, E.P. *The Making of the English Working Class* (Penguin)

Titmuss, R.M. *Income Distribution and Social Change* (George Allen & Unwin)

Veblen, T. *The Theory of the Leisure Class* (George Allen & Unwin)

Westergaard, J. and Resler, H. *Class in a Capitalist Society* (Penguin)

Willmott, P. & Young, M. *Family and Class in a London Suburb* (Mentor)

Young, M. *The Rise of the Meritocracy* (Penguin)

THREE
The family and population

3.1 Structure of the family

● *What is the family?*

At first sight you may say that everybody knows what a family is. But the more you examine it, the more you will realise that 'the family' is an ambivalent term. It could be taken to mean:
1 you and your mother, father, sisters and brothers;
2 you and all those related to you by blood or marriage;
3 a mother, father and children, either their own or adopted – must a family include children?

Usually, sociologists consider children an essential part of a family unit; a married couple will say, 'We are starting a family.'

Some anthropologists tend to avoid the word 'family' because of the many difficulties of interpretation. Instead they use the term 'kinship'. Webs of kinship relations can be traced through the male line (patrilineal) or through the female line (matrilineal). There are two main types of kin.
1 *Consanguinal kin* are of the same blood, genetically related. All of us have many hundreds of blood kin whom we do not know. Man is different from other animals, because he can look back to his ancestry. But how far back can you look? Do you know even the names of your great-great grandparents, and how many descendants do you know of your four pairs of great grandparents? Usually, people do not marry their consanguinal kin.
2 *Affinal kin* are relatives by marriage. Affines are people who are married to our consanguines. Our social relations with affines, such as a step-father or a mother-in-law, are likely to be less close than with genetic relations, but it would be wrong to generalise.

There are two principles of distinguishing kinship.
1 Descent is either unilineal or cognatic.
   (a) *unilineal*, i.e. from father's or mother's line.
   (b) *cognatic*, i.e. from both lines.

2 The kinship system is either:
  (a) *ego-focused*, i.e. where each person would give a different group of people as his or her kin, or
  (b) *ancestor-focused*, i.e. either patrilineal or matrilineal.
  In Britain kinship is cognatic (from both lines) and ego-focused (different for each person).
  A study of a few basic ideas about kinship will help us to understand about the family. All societies make provision for the transfer of property and status upon death and the transfer is normally to one of the same kin. Robin Fox (*Kinship and Marriage*) has argued that although some regard ours as a 'kinshipless' society, sentiments of kinship still linger; blood is thicker than water and many would feel an obligation to a long-lost cousin who had fallen on hard times, or consider that we have some claim on uncles and aunts simply by virtue of kinship.

> ... no society has managed to dispense with an irreducible minimum of kinship-based social relationships.
>   (Fox, R. *Kinship and Marriage*)

A somewhat opposing viewpoint is taken by Michael Gordon in *Industrialisation and the Family* where he argues that kinship ties are functionally irrelevant in the case of relationships with more distant kin such as cousins, aunts and uncles. It is probably true of most of us that we recognise cousins but do not feel any special responsibility towards them.
  The family is still the most important social group to which we belong. The most common type of family structure today is the *nuclear family*. This is a single household unit comprised of husband, wife and children. Most of us belong to two nuclear families during our lifetime. We start as children in our *family of origin*, and later go on to form our own *family of procreation*. We do not have any choice about our family of origin; it would be most unusual to knock on somebody else's door and say, 'Can I join your family?' But looked at from the social status of parents, we do have choices about our family of procreation.
  The structure of a family can be shown by using symbols: the male is symbolised by a phallic triangle while the female is a circle. An equals sign denotes sexual union. Thus a nuclear family is depicted simply in Fig. 3.1. This family group follows the normal western pattern of father, mother and two children. As brothers and sisters are referred to as *siblings*, each child in our example has one sibling. Families are in a state of flux because individuals who occupy statuses of father, mother, brother and sister grow older; brothers and sisters leave home to start new families for themselves. Fig. 3.2 shows a typical *family life-cycle*. The nuclear family is a single economic unit, as opposed to the tribal system which is based upon the cooperation of people of different kin. However, the nuclear family does

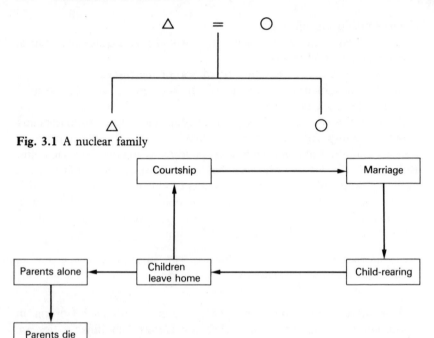

Fig. 3.1 A nuclear family

Fig. 3.2 The family life cycle

not function in isolation, but associates with wider kin, friends and neighbours.

Perhaps the most outstanding single characteristic of contemporary families is their general similarity: the average family size is four, including two children, and typical goals are a house, a car, annual holidays and a good start in life for the offspring. Compared with family structures in previous centuries, the differences between family patterns of present social class groups is far less apparent. However, there is some historical evidence indicating that the nuclear family was the prevailing residential unit in certain areas of England even before the industrial revolution. According to Peter Laslett (*The World We Have Lost*), the family in England ten or fifteen generations ago, was of the nuclear type, and not very different from the family today. It is generally accepted, however, that the prevalence of the nuclear family is closely associated with the advent of industrialisation. The modern family is no longer self-sufficient. Before the industrial revolution the family was a productive unit growing its own food and making its own clothes. Today the family is a unit of consumption. The family joins together in spending money upon economic goods and services, rather than upon producing things for itself.

Economic goods are produced in factories and workshops and the older members of the family, including the women, find opportunities for employment outside the home. The standard of living of the family has increased with the development of advanced productive techniques. These changes in family life are linked with the emancipation of women economically, socially, sexually and politically. The Welfare State has also transformed family life by replacing or supplementing the traditional functions of the family.

In the 1950s, the Institute of Community Studies conducted surveys which indicated that the extended family is still important, especially in many working-class areas. The extended family (see Fig. 3.3) is

> any persistent kinship-grouping of persons related by descent, marriage or adoption, which is wider than the (nuclear) family, in that it characteristically spans three generations from grandparents to grandchildren.
>
> (Rosser, C. and Harris, C. *The Family and Social Change*)

In medieval times, the extended family was common throughout Britain. When there was a scarcity of houses, transport and job opportunities away from home, it was customary for father, mother, children and grandparents to live together under one roof. In Saxon times the family was extended to include cousins, aunts, uncles, nephews and nieces. The Dyaks of Sarawak still maintain extended family living arrangements; sometimes twenty families belonging to the same kinship group crowd into their long houses. Children in Samoa are brought up with many older relatives to care for them.

The close relationship between parent and child, which has such decisive influence upon so many in our civilisation that submission to the parent or

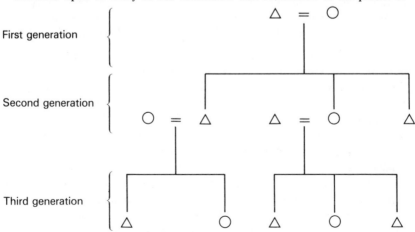

Fig. 3.3 An example of an extended family stretching over three generations

defiance of the parent may become the dominating pattern of a lifetime, is not found in Samoa. Children reared in households where there are half a dozen adult women to care for them and dry their tears, and a half-dozen adult males, all of whom represent constituted authority, do not distinguish their parents as sharply as our children do.

(Mead, M. *Coming of Age in Samoa*)

Peter Townsend (*Family Life of Old People*) found that the extended family still flourished in Bethnal Green, a typical working-class area of London. The extended families of Bethnal Green did not live under one roof, but they did offer close-knit social relationships and security to both young and old. In their study of the same London suburb, Michael Young and Peter Willmott (*Family and Kinship in East London*) found that the traditional working-class extended family remained as a vigorous social structure. Members of the extended family lived close to one another so that relatives were in close touch and willing to give a helping hand.

> Because they have lived in it for so long, most Bethnal Greeners are surrounded by scores of people they know very well, people who are one minute relations and another minute neighbours, another minute friends, another minute counsellors. The emphasis is not so much on the individual home, prized as this is, as on the informal collective life outside it in the extended family, the street, the pub and the open air market.
>
> In a place like Bethnal Green you can find several generations of families and their relatives. They may live, work and spend their leisure together....
>
> In Bethnal Green many families continue to act together as a single unit. The young people look after their parents when they are old. Newlyweds often live with the wife's parents; the daughter goes out to work or to shop, leaving the children with mother. When advice is needed, 'Mum' is at hand. The tie between mother and daughter is very strong: here the old proverb is very true: 'My son's a son until he gets him a wife, my daughter's a daughter all her life.'
>
> (Young, M. and Willmott, P. *Family and Kinship in East London*)

The key figure in this mutual support system was the wife's mother ('Mum') who maintained close relationships with her married daughters. The lives of husband and wife and their children centred upon what was going on at Mum's place. The husband's family played a far less significant part. Young and Willmott found that 'Mum' helped her married daughter, possibly by speaking to the rent-collector for a house, or by looking after the children, or by doing her daughter's shopping. The husband was seen mainly as the breadwinner and it was not customary for him to look after the children or help with domestic chores. This separation of the marital role of husband and wife is termed the *segregated conjugal role*. We shall see later that family structures are changing so that *joint conjugal roles* are now more the norm, with husband and wife sharing the family tasks.

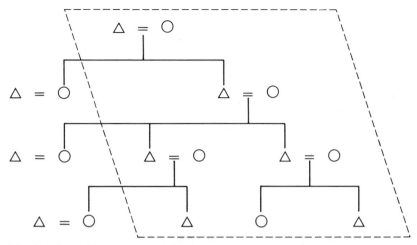

Fig. 3.4 A patrilineal extended family

Rosser and Harris (*The Family and Social Change*) also found an extended family network existing in Swansea. The area surveyed consisted of a social mix of working-class and middle-class families. The extended family, centred around 'Mum', existed mostly among the working classes, but the middle classes were not isolated from their kin – they were involved in extended family relationships which gave them social identification and practical support in times of need. Rosser and Harris's studies suggest that urbanisation does not necessarily cause family disruption, and where the extended family pattern is disrupted, the disruption may be only temporary. A modified form of extended family is also emerging; families are making use of cars, telephones and generally improved communications to adjust to greater distances between them.

The extended family includes within it many nuclear family patterns. See Fig. 3.4, where the extended family is patrilineal, i.e. descent is through the male line. For census purposes, the husband is regarded as head of the household in Britain, but as with most western societies British extended families are bilineal, with descent and inheritance determined equally by both male and female lines.

● *Is the family dying?*

From time to time different writers have criticised the family and argued that if it is not actually dying, it is nevertheless very, very ill. In his series of 1967 Reith lectures, the anthropologist Sir Edmund Leach contended that 'the family with its narrow privacy and tawdry secrets is the source of all our discontents.' This smacks of the cynicism of George Bernard Shaw who once said that our parents ruin the first half of our lives, while our children ruin the second half. People talk about the need to preserve the family in the same way that they talk about preserving the whale and other endangered species.

If the family is endangered, this is a very modern social trend. From age immemorial the family has been considered to be the cornerstone of all societies. George Peter Murdock (*Social Structure*) examined 250 societies and found that a form of family organisation existed in all of them. He concluded that the institution of the family is universal. Murdock's three criteria of a family included:

1 common residence;
2 economic cooperation;
3 sexual reproduction.

Each criterion might be challenged. In Israeli *kibbutzim* (settlements) there is no common residence; about four per cent of Israelis live in 240 *kibbutzim* where children are separated from their parents. The children inhabit communal dormitories and their parents have their own bedroom. The main purpose of the experiment was to allow male and female adults to share in the economic tasks which faced people trying to build a new nation. Women were freed from the mother role. The economic role was embedded in the welfare of the communal settlement; everybody worked for the community as a whole and not for the family in particular.

The family is usually considered as necessary for sexual reproduction, but even in this instance it is not essential for the father to be in constant association with the mother-child unit. The vital elementary social grouping is the mother and her children. The family as an institution becomes important when it is found to be necessary for providing protection for the mother-child unit; the presence of the male is usually regarded as essential if the family is to be successfully defended, fed and brought to maturity. This can be seen most clearly where the environment is harsh. Eskimo men and women work together to survive. The man builds the igloo, the sledge and the kayak, and is responsible for keeping the family supplied with food. The woman makes the clothes and bears the children. Similar sexual role division of labour is the norm in many societies. However, Ann Oakley (*Housewife*) has pointed out that sexual role division is not universal. The Mbuti pygmies of the Congo have a minimal division of labour: generally the men hunt while the women gather roots and vegetables, but the roles are interchangeable without loss of social esteem.

For most people, the family is the most significant social group to which they belong during their lifetimes. The family gives ordinary people a role and an identity. We cannot all rise to positions of prestige and high social status, but most of us gain personal satisfaction by being a good husband, a good wife, a good father or a good mother. A father and mother have specific roles and this gives them an identity. Children too are given roles and identity by the family which gives them their name.

In Britain, the family is still esteemed by society. At Christmas time, people make cribs and speak in awe of the Holy Family. The Royal Family receives widespread admiration by a doting public who expect them to set a good example of family life. Politicians pay lip-service to the family. When he was Prime Minister, James Callaghan declared that, 'the overriding social concern is to preserve and enhance the influence of the family as a whole: an influence which is beneficial in every way.'

In the 1980s Patrick Jenkin, as Secretary of State for Social Services, warned of the dangers involved in the Welfare State's encroachment on the time-honoured social tasks of the family. Some of the less essential functions may well have been stripped away from the family. Modern states such as the Soviet Union and Nazi Germany attempted to disband the family, but later found it necessary to reverse their policies, and offer state encouragement and protection to the institution of the family. R.M. MacIver and C.H. Page (*Society*) have pointed out that the state controls the family and exercises over it a more stringent supervision than over any other partnership or association. MacIver believes that the reason for this rigorous state control of the family results from the realisation of the family's vital function of perpetuating the race.

> The function of procreating and rearing children involves responsibilities utterly unlike, and more significant socially than those of any other voluntary relationship. Therefore the marriage contract, though the most intimate of all contracts, is not simply the personal concern of all the contracting parties. The state, as the agent of society, is also deeply interested. The relation of marriage to procreation is sufficient, and, as we shall see, alone sufficient to justify a peculiar control of the state over the family.
>
> (MacIver, R.M. and Page, C.H. *Society*)

Rumney and Maier (*The Science of Society*) contend that the functions of the modern family are few; the economic, educational, religious and protective functions have largely been transferred to the state. But the function of procreating can never be taken over by the state. The family thus remains essential to perpetuating the race. It is indeed possible to procreate outside the family structure, but it is of utmost significance that all states, from ancient times to the present day, have accepted the family as an essential institution.

Alternatives to the family have been tried. Experiences of the Israeli *kibbutz* suggest that the family still plays a part in rearing children. In the early days of the experiment, the children were taken to Children's Houses in infancy and brought up together by metaplets (trained nurses) and teachers. The children returned to their homes for only a few hours in the evening and their mothers were free to pursue their careers sharing equal work opportunities with their husbands. However, in recent times, children return from the *kibbutzim* to spend the night at their parents' dwelling. Similarly, the communes of the People's Republic of China supplement the family by supplying creches and nurseries, but although this frees mothers to work alongside their husbands in the communes, it has not meant the end of the family.

Indeed, Ronald Fletcher (*The Family and Marriage in Britain*) believes that the family has increased its functions rather than diminished them. Fletcher examines the contentions that the family is disintegrating. He quotes W.J.H. Sprott (*Sociology*) that 'the family under Western cultural conditions, has shrunk functionally,' and W. Goodsell (*Problems of The Family*) that,

> within the last two generations ... the social and economic forces silently at work for more than a century undermining the unity of the family have affected transformations in the home dramatic in their rapidity and extent ...

Fletcher also considers the viewpoints of Carle Zimmerman (*Family and Civilisation*) that there is a rapid trend towards a climactic breakup of the family, and Bertrand Russell (*Marriage and Morals*) that the decay of the family in recent times is attributable to the industrial revolution and the increasing intervention of the state between parents and children. After an exhaustive review of the critics of the family, Fletcher puts forward his own conviction that these indictments of the family are naive, insufficiently considered and in large measure false. The criticisms suggest that the family has deteriorated from a better state where it had possessed more functions and fulfilled them more adequately. Fletcher denies all this and considers the family is just as important as ever.

> Indeed I shall argue that, on the contrary, the family is now responsible for the fulfilment of more functions than hitherto, and that it is more tightly and more responsibly woven into the wider structure of society than was the case before the onset of industrialisation.
>
> (Fletcher, R. *The Family and Marriage in Britain*)

● *Functions of the family*

We shall discuss the way in which different sociologists see the functions of the family and then summarise them in accordance with the position of the family in modern life. Fletcher considers functions from two perspectives: firstly, that the family satisfies human needs and purposes, and, secondly, in the sense of functional interconnections which the family has with the wider network of institutions in the whole social system. In both these senses the family retains vital distinctive functions. On the one hand the family today satisfies in a qualified way more needs than it did in previous generations, while on the other hand it is more intimately connected with the social institutions organised by the modern state.

R.M. MacIver (*Society*) considered that the family had three essential functions:

1 *Procreation and child-rearing*

The family provides a legitimate basis for procreation and child-rearing. About ninety per cent of births take place within the structure of the family. Social statistics of previous centuries are grossly inaccurate, but evidence points to a reduction in the proportion of illegitimate births; procreation is even more exclusively a family task today, than in most other historical periods. Nowadays far more love, care, skill and knowledge are devoted to child-rearing. This can be objectively assessed by studying statistics relating to infant mortality and infantile diseases. It may be argued that these improved results could not have been obtained without the aid of external specialised agencies, but it is also true that these agencies could not operate without the cooperation and support of parents. The practice of contraception reduces procreation, but it provides a beneficial form of human control which improves both the lot of mothers and the care of children.

2 *Regulating sexual behaviour*

Birth control has introduced a distinction between the reproductive and sexual functions of the family. The use of modern contraceptive methods has largely removed the fear of pregnancy as a result of sexual intercourse and allowed husband and wife more freedom in the satisfaction of the sex urge. The degree in which marriage satisfies this need is highly variable depending on personality differences. Sexual satisfaction within the family varies from mere satisfaction of physical appetite to a feeling of coming together in mutual union. In either event the marriage is cemented and the family satisfies the need.

3 *Provision of a home*

In all societies, men and women exhibit the need for a home which provides enduring relationships and a base for their activities. In pre-industrial times the home was also the workplace as the family strove to exist as a productive unit. In modern times the home is more of 'a home' in a pleasurable sense; it is the centre where the family is able to pursue its social, recreational and leisure activities. The main economic tasks of the world of work are pursued outside the home.

If the home has lost some of its former unity because other agencies compete with it, it has also gained in that it has become more liberated from conditions, both of drudgery and of male dominance, which prevented it from being, in a finer sense, a home.

(MacIver, R.M. and Page, C.H. *Society*)

MacIver suggests six non-essential family functions which have been partially transferred to specialised agencies. Agencies facilitating non-essential functions include:

1 governmental agencies of the state
2 religious agencies of the church
3 educational agencies such as nurseries, schools and colleges
4 economic agencies concentrating upon work and the workplace
5 health agencies such as clinics and hospitals
6 recreational agencies such as multifunctional clubs and societies.

Talcott Parsons thought that the functions of the modern American family had transcended procreation, sex-needs and the home, and were concentrated upon two basic and irreducible functions.

1 *The primary socialisation of children*

The two basic processes involved in the early socialisation of children are the internalisation of the culture of their particular society and the formation of the child's personality. The wife is the marriage partner mainly concerned with socialisation of the children. According to Parsons, as there is more affinity between womenfolk, primary socialisation in the family tends to result in 'good girls' and 'bad boys'. This is obviously a generalisation, but the greater influence of the mother is borne out by J.W.B. Douglas's study *The Home and The School*.

We cannot afford to ignore the backgrounds of the mothers when looking at the educational progress of their children; they make an equal contribution with the fathers to inherited ability and possibly a greater one to attitudes to learning. In ambitious working-class households it is not unusual to find that the mother comes from a middle-class family and supplies the drive and incentive for her children to do well at school.

(Douglas, J.W.B. *The Home and The School*)

Parsons sees the family as the only institution which is capable of providing the necessary love, care and mutual support to allow the optimum development of the human personality. He sees families as 'factories' for producing human personalities.

2 *The stabilisation of adult personalities*

Primary socialisation starts the formation of an individual's personality, and it is then within the framework of the family that the personality is stabilised. Youth culture has developed to tide people over from being dependent children to the establishment of their own family of procreation. In modern societies youth culture is a *rite de passage* or a universal occurrence which enables individuals to pass from one status to another. During this transitional period roles within the family are often reversed and adult norms and values are repudiated. The modern well-adjusted family is not likely to be shocked if its teenagers are irresponsible or promiscuous. Indeed the family will often go along with reconciling ideas such as 'wild oats must be sown' and 'this is the best time of your life.'

But Parsons was more concerned with emotional stability between the married partners of the family. Men become separated from their wives because of intensive male job-specialisation, while women especially feel the isolation from kin that is experienced by the nuclear family in Western industrial societies. The married couple look to each other for emotional support as their children grow up, and especially in old age which men find more traumatic than women; for women the pattern of life continues much as before whereas men lose their status and have to adjust to new roles. Emotional adjustments and reconciliations are more likely to be achieved within a stable family.

George Peter Murdock (*Social Structure*) argues that the family performs four basic functions.

1 *Sexual desires* are regulated, restrained and satisfied. The sexual desire is a powerful impulse and cannot be left without the control which the nuclear family provides. The sexual division of labour is also a characteristic of the nuclear family.

2 *Reproduction* is essential for human survival and is best controlled through the institution of the family.

3 *Economic cooperation* is necessary. Although in the nuclear family, the man is the main breadwinner for most of his adult life, the family needs the woman to prepare the food and generally supervise the home. This is less true in the modern symmetrical family where roles are shared.

4 *Education*, including socialisation, assumes that children fit into society and acquire values, beliefs, expectations and accumulated knowledge which constitute culture. Education and socialisation may be seen as satisfying two conditions:

> One that children develop psychologically in such a way as to make it possible for them to constitute members of a society, and the other that they should be made members of that *particular* society by virtue of their having acquired the values, beliefs, expectations and accumulated knowledge which constitute its culture.
>
> (Harris, C.C. *The Family*)

Kingsley Davis (*Human Society*) suggests four main functions of the family: reproduction, maintenance, socialisation and placement. The first three functions of reproduction, maintenance and socialisation are essential for the fulfilment of the conditions for the perpetuation of society.

The last two functions fulfil the conditions of transmission between generation of culture and social position.

The various functions of the family could be performed separately, but only the family provides the setting for the performance of all the tasks we have considered. Any summary is open to criticism, but students should find Table 3.1 a useful basis for discussion.

Table 3.1 Functions of the modern family

A PRIMARY FUNCTIONS

1 *Procreation* – sexual reproduction, essential for the preservation of the human race, is legitimised in the family.

2 *Sex-need* – control and satisfaction of sexual behaviour is best achieved within the family.

3 *Provision of a home* – the home provides security and a place where members of the family establish their identity.

4 *Socialisation of children* – children are reared and taught the social norms and mores of their society.

5 *Stabilisation of personality* – members of the family give each other emotional support and share in stable relationships.

B SECONDARY FUNCTIONS

6 *Economic unit* – the modern family concentrates upon consumption and spending patterns.

7 *Health and welfare* – the family looks after its members who are sick, disabled or old.

8 *Recreation* – parents play with their children, while the family join together in holidays and other leisure pursuits.

9 *Education* – father no longer teaches his son a trade, but parents still provide a wide educational background.

10 *Religious* – traditional religion plays a small part, but the family is still expected to lay down standards of conduct.

● *Changes in the family*

One of the main changes in the family has been the widespread adoption of the nuclear form of family in industrial societies. Some sociologists argue that the modern family has adopted this particular form because no other form would 'fit' the economic institutions with which it is associated. The family has changed because it must fit the sets of expectations which govern the performance of economic activities.

Talcott Parsons argued that the isolated nuclear family has emerged as the norm in modern industrial societies. Economic life today necessitates geographical and occupational mobility. People are able to move about freely in pursuance of economic activities largely because they do not form part of an extended kinship pattern.

Children are an economic burden in the modern industrial world, whereas they were an economic asset in Victorian times and indeed remain so in the Third World today. It is the adult members of the family who act as providers in industrial countries. Therefore it is necessary for each conjugal unit to be structurally separate and isolated, so that the adults can move about within a modern economy.

Family sizes have decreased as parents ask themselves the question, 'Can we afford to have another child?' Often a better house, a new car, and a continental holiday, are put first, and this helps to account for a decreasing population. The family of procreation tends to be given priority and obligations to the family of origin are less inclined to be accepted, especially after marriage.

However, Talcott Parsons's claim that industrialisation is the main force bringing about a change towards the isolated nuclear family is open to question. There is evidence of the existence of nuclear families in non-industrial societies while studies (such as those by Townsend, Young and Willmott) have shown that the extended family does still remain in industrialised Britain. Parsons's examination of the reasons for changes in family structures may well have been more applicable to the United States where it was essential to facilitate intensive mobility following waves of immigration and government policy of 'Go west, young man.'

W.J. Goode (*World Revolution and Family Patterns*) approaches the problem of the fit between family structures and other social institutions by examining the effects of industrialisation upon different economic categories. In a capitalistic industrial society, the new economic institutions tend to be under the control of those who owned property and wealth in the period before the advent of industrialisation. Consequently, parents in the upper economic categories are able to exert far more influence over their children because their offspring desire to inherit property. Parents in the lower social classes have little to offer their children in terms of property or status jobs.

Elizabeth Bott (*Urban Families: Conjugal Roles and Social Networks*) studied changes and variations in the ways that husbands and wives perform their conjugal roles. She contrasted the two extremes of a family basing her study upon considerable segregation between husband and wife in their role relationship and the family where the conjugal role relationship was as joint as possible.

A joint conjugal role-relationship is one in which husband and wife carry out many activities together, with a minimum of task differentiation and separation of interests; in such cases husband and wife not only plan the affairs of the family together, but also exchange many household tasks and spend much of their leisure time together. A segregated conjugal role-relationship is one in which husband and wife have a clear differentiation of tasks and a considerable number of separate interests and activities; in such cases, husband and wife have a clearly-defined division of labour into male tasks and female tasks; they expect to have different leisure pursuits; the husband has his friends outside the home and the wife has hers. It should be stressed, however, that these are only differences of degree. All families must have some division of labour between husband and wife; all families must have some joint activities.'

(Bott, E. *Urban Families: Conjugal Roles and Social Networks*)

It is over a quarter of a century since Bott described the joint conjugal role-relationship within the family structure, but few families have arrived at this stage. Division of labour within the family remains the general rule with the husband doing the 'man's' work of gardening, decorating, cleaning the car, etc. while his wife takes on the prime responsibility for looking after the children and doing the housework. Nevertheless the direction of family change in this respect is towards joint conjugal roles. This fact has been demonstrated by Michael Young and Peter Willmott in *The Symmetrical Family*. Slowly emerging is a new type of family to which different names have been given. Terms such as companionate, partnership, egalitarian and home-centred, all give some indication of the move towards symmetry between husband and wife on the one hand, and between parents and children on the other.

Young and Willmott examine three stages in the growth of the symmetrical family.

1 *The unit of production* was synonymous with the pre-industrial family where there was a rigid, crucial and necessary division of labour between all the members of the family.

2 *The spread of disruption* took place in the early days of industrialism when the family ceased to be a business partnership; home and work-place became separate entities.

3 *The move towards family symmetry* has been motivated by a financial partnership between husband and wife and the new feminism accompanied by birth control which gives women the power to control their own fertility.

Young and Willmott concede that the symmetrical family would not have developed without the aid of advanced technology: there has been a marked increase in the number of consumer goods especially in the form of time-saving gadgets, combined with improved housing facilities. Young and Willmott draw attention to the idea that the past and future are embodied in the present and that in accordance with their 'Principle' many social changes start at the top and work downwards. The 'Principle' may be criticised as a universal truism. In fact this so-called Principle of Stratified Diffusion is Young and Willmott's account of Daniel Bell's account of de Tocqueville's account of a fact of experience, viz. that the luxury of yesterday becomes commonplace to the upper classes today and the necessity of the working class tomorrow. We have already examined this aspect of embourgeoisement which contends that class differences are disappearing in Britain as better-off working-class families adopt middle-class life-styles (see section 2.5). Such changes are likely to work downwards, because it is the top classes who can afford material innovations before cheap mass-production makes them available for the lower classes.

The final stage in the change towards the symmetrical family is reached when the home-based family is transformed by a reversal of roles. The idea of husbands doing the cleaning while their wives drive the car or do the gardening, is a mere extension of Bott's thesis relating to urban families. What is new is the idea that the logical conclusion of this role re-polarisation is that both spouses will have vital work and interests inside and outside the home, so there will be 'two demanding jobs for the wife and two for the husband. The symmetry will be complete; instead of two jobs there will be four.'

3.2 Perspectives of the family

● *Structural-functionalist perspective of the family*

The structural-functionalist perspective is the most common approach adopted by sociologists writing about the family. We have seen that it is customary to look upon the family as the cornerstone of society and a beneficial influence upon its members. The family is generally regarded as the most important single social institution to which we belong. It has been accorded universal acceptance and approbation. The family is regarded as necessary for procreation, regulation of the sex urge, offering a home to members of society, socialising each new generation and affording emotional support to its members. It has many secondary functions concerned with providing sustenance, looking after those in need, giving moral guidance, and as a base for our leisure-time activities. Although the functions of the family have changed, are changing, and will change yet again, the family remains paramount as a vital force and influence.

As the family has lost certain functions it has gained others. These new functions are basically concerned with the private needs, expectations and fulfilments of the individual. In a way which would have been quite surprising even to our grandparents, the family today is widely expected to provide fundamental personal fulfilment and satisfaction to all its members. Morally this has meant a great shift in emphasis from duties and responsibilities to rights and gratifications in the area of family life.

(Berger, P. and B. *Sociology: A Biographical Approach*)

Numerous sociologists have described many varied family patterns. They have considered the emphasis placed upon the different functions of the family. The emphases change, but the family remains (see Table 3.2).

If you look back at section 1.4, you will see that structural-functionalists stress the importance of certain societal functional prerequisites. Society is regarded as a social system, surviving its original members and replacing them through biological reproduction. We have seen that the family plays

Table 3.2 Examples of research into different family patterns

Author(s)	Title	Description
Bell, C.	*Middle-Class Families*	Structure and relationships of families in Swansea
Billingsley, A.	*Black Families in White America*	Black family life in America
Firth, R. *et al.*	*Families and Their Relatives*	Middle-class families in Highgate
Kerr, M.	*The People of Ship Street*	Traditional family life in working-class England
Lewis, O.	*The Children of Sanchez*	Family life among the poor of Mexico.
Pahl, J.M. & R.E.	*Managers and Their Wives*	Middle-class career and family relationships
Rapoport, R. & R.	*Dual-Career Families*	Families where husband and wife pursue different roles
Schlesinger, B.	*Family Life in the Kibbutz of Israel*	Collective rearing of children
Willmott, P. and Young, M.	*Family and Class in a London Suburb*	Middle-class family life in Woodford
Willmott, P. and Young, M.	*Family and Kinship in East London*	Extended family life with matriarchal influence

a vital functional part in this social system which has four main defining properties.

1 *Differentiation* – members of the family perform differentiated roles and occupy differentiated statuses.

2 *Organisation* – the family affords a pattern of organisation which governs the relationship of its members, sets out their rights and obligations, and inculcates shared cultural values.

3 *Boundary maintenance* – families provide relatively clear boundaries within social systems.

4 *Equilibrium* – in spite of changes in family patterns, there exists a built-in mechanism tending to conserve the stability of family life.

Although structural-functionalism takes a status quo approach to the family, it recognises that there are likely to be changes in role differentiation within the family. However, in spite of the trend towards the symmetrical family, the husband-father is still primarily concerned with the *instrumental* activities associated with his role as the main breadwinner, while the mother-wife performs the *expressive* tasks of integrating and stabilising family life.

Structural-functionalists believe that every part of the structure of society has a function. The family performs the basic functions that enable society to survive. Each individual family is a social sub-system within the larger social system.

The family has vital functional interchanges with the other social sub-systems such as:

1 *the economy* (adaptation) – the family provides labour and consumes goods and services;

2 *politics* (goal-gratification) – the family instils loyalty and recognises the authority of society's leaders;

3 *the community* (integration) – the family encourages coordination and participation by institutionalising its members to conform;

4 *value system* (pattern-maintenance) – the family has (a) an enculturisation function by which common cultural objectives are transmitted to children, and (b) a stabilisation function which facilitates the emotional adjustment of adult members.

Three facets of the structural-functionalist family perspective are well worth considering.

1 The functions of the family for society.

2 The functions of the sub-systems within a family for the family and for each other.

3 The functions of the family for its individual members including the primary socialisation of the young and the growth of the mature personalities of adult members.

Structural-functionalists see the nuclear family as the norm. The belief that the nuclear family is a universal social institution is based upon the fact that a child is produced by one man and one woman; even though societies undoubtedly differ, there must inevitably be a very special link between people related in this way. Talcott Parsons argued that the justification of the nuclear family centred around intimate relationships between a mother and her child and the fact that the father established the legitimacy of the child's status.

Structural-functionalists would argue that the family has essential social functions and that it is a necessary institution for the existence of all other institutions in society. The family takes its special form because it 'fits' in with other institutions in society. If there were other ways of performing the functions for which the family is responsible, then there would be plausible functional alternatives. Structural-functionalists would contend that the fact that this is not the case explains adequately the universality of the family.

> The 'functional theory' of the family seeks to explain the existence of the family by showing that it has certain SOCIAL FUNCTIONS. To say that an institution has a social function is to say that the performance of the activities (governed by that set of expectations concerning the way people should behave to one another, to which we refer when we speak of the institution concerned) has certain effects on the other social institutions which go to make up the society. However, it says more than this. When we speak of the social functions of an institution, we are not concerned with any effects the activities which it governs may have. We are concerned with those effects without which a society could not exist.
>
> (Harris, C.C. *The Family and Industrial Society*)

- *Conflict-structuralist perspective of the family*

One of the joys of sociology to the student with an inquiring mind is to find that different sociological approaches are challenging because they bring new outlooks to bear upon familiar subjects. You may have already felt uneasy about some of the arguments put forward to support the structural-functionalist perspective of the family. For example, if it is so easy to explain and justify the existence of the family in a cut and dried way, why do we read so much in the media about family breakdowns, divorce, separation, illegitimacy and the generation gap? Why are experiments tried to find alternatives to the family such as the *kibbutzim* in Israel or the communes of the People's Republic of China? Why has David Cooper written such a hypercritical book entitled *The Death of The Family*?

> The power of the family resides in its social mediating function. It reinforces the effective power of the ruling class in any exploitative society by providing a

highly controllable paradigmatic form for every social institution. So we find the family form replicated through the social structures of the factory, the union branch, the school (primary and secondary), the university, the business corporation, the church, political parties and governmental apparatus, the armed forces, general and mental hospitals, and so on. . . . The Family is expert at the self-terrified and self-terrorizing inculcation of the non-necessity of entertaining doubts. . . . The family, since it cannot bear doubt about itself and its capacity to engender 'mental health' and 'correct attitudes', destroys doubt as a possibility in each of its members.

(Cooper, D. *The Death of The Family*)

We all of us belong to families and therefore may find it disturbing to question a social institution to which we owe so much. Criticism of the family smacks of disloyalty to our parents, our heritage and to so many things we have been taught to hold dear. The operative word is 'taught'. It is this very fact that we have been socialised into so many preconceived ideas concerning family unity that makes it difficult for us to take a reflective look at the institution which has done so much to make us what we are. Yet it is this detached outlook which is so essential if we are to attempt to be socially scientific. Hence the conflict-structuralist perspective lays emphasis upon all the obvious contradictions exemplified in family conflicts. Marxists would argue that it is wrong to conceive of the family as the only possible social institution capable of providing a legitimate basis for procreation, child-rearing, primary socialisation, regulation of sexual behaviour and stabilisation of mature emotions. They would further argue that there must be many new and varied patterns of social organisation which could replace the family.

One of the best accounts of the conflict-perspective of the family is Sydney Peiris's 'The Family: A Marxist View' (in Meighan, R. *et al.*, eds, *Perspectives on Society*) which provides an historical account of the evolution of the family; it is argued that the coming of capitalist industrial society brought about the degradation of women so that they became confined to the home and domesticity. Private property made it essential to establish the paternity of the children who would inherit a man's possessions. So women became subjugated both sexually and socially. It is only since the end of the Second World War that a small minority of families have begun to move towards Bott's conception of joint conjugal role-relationships and further towards Young and Willmott's idea of family symmetry. The work of the housewife is still generally regarded as valueless work not worthy of a monetary wage. Further, the family in capitalist societies is the main agent of primary socialisation and successfully transmits all the conservative political norms of the dominant class. Thus the family, and its accompanying political and economic ideology, is self-perpetuating. The majority of people accept the political philosophy they are taught and tend to vote the same way as their parents. At a later stage, the school combines with the family to augment the status quo socialisation process. The instruments of the mass media add the final touches and come down heavily on the side of family conformity as we know it.

Conflict theorists recognise that the family is an important institution but would argue that it is not necessarily the type of organisation suitable for all members of society. Instead of the family serving as a unique and universal social unit, conflict theorists would look for a wide range of institutions geared to serve the varied needs of men and women.

Alvin Toffler has suggested that future family patterns may well take many innovative forms:

> We may expect many among the people of the future to carry the streamlining process a step further by remaining childless, cutting the family down to its most elemental components, a man and woman. Two people, perhaps with matched careers, will prove more efficient at navigating through educational and social shoals, through job changes and geographic relocations, than the ordinary child-centred family.
>
> A compromise may be the postponement of children, rather than childlessness. Men and women today are often torn in conflict between a commitment to career and a commitment to children. In the future, many couples will sidestep this problem by deferring the entire task of raising children until after retirement. This may strike people of the present as odd. Yet once child-bearing is broken away from its biological base, nothing more than tradition suggests having children at an early age. Thus childlessness is likely to spread among young and middle-aged couples; sexagenarians who raise infants may be far more common. The post-retirement family could become a recognised social institution.
>
> We might also see the gradual relaxation of bars against polygamy. Polygamous families exist now, more widely than is generally believed, in the midst of 'normal' society. Writer Ben Merson, after visiting several such families in Utah, where polygamy is still regarded as essential by certain Mormon fundamentalists, estimated that there are some 30 000 people living in underground family units of this type in the United States.
>
> Childless marriage, professional parenthood, post-retirement child-rearing, corporate families, polygamy – these are a few of the family forms and practices with which innovative minorities will experiment in the future.

  (Toffler, A. *Future Shock*)

• *Interactionist perspective of the family*

Although we have considered the family in broad terms, it is the micro-family unit which is the primary interest of the individual. In the same way that, as individuals, we are at heart more concerned with our own money than with the money supply and with our own income rather than the national income, so as members of a family we are most concerned with our own particular family and our interactions within it. Symbolic interactionism is closely related to social psychology and is particularly concerned with the processes of primary socialisation, social behaviour,the development of the personality, parent-child relationships, mating selection and courtship, husband-wife relations and marital adjustments.

The structural-functionalist studies the functions of the family and attempts to justify its existence: he considers that the family must be necessary or it would not be such a commonplace form of social organisation. The conflict-structuralist recognises the existence of the family but because of all the frictions and contentions which family organisations provoke, conflict theorists are interested in other forms of social organisation which might well perform the same tasks more smooothly and efficiently. The interactionist does not just accept the family or alternative forms of social organisations but believes that the best way to find out about the family is to study what those actually involved think about it. This is no mean task because we are all conditioned by the family from the outset. It is the parents, grandparents and other older members of the family who define for the child the meaning of events, attitudes, beliefs, values and norms. The family is responsible for our socially significant ideas (generalised other); those people who have most influence upon us, in our formative years, are the older members of our family (significant others).

Symbolic interactionists stress the importance of our symbolic environment. We have seen that language, the most important symbol we use, is learned and developed by interaction with other members of the family. Human beings are actors and reactors: socialisation and social action are two-way processes. As children we have situations defined for us and as parents we define situations for our children.

By the time we come to the age of marriage, we have been influenced for many years by interacting with those around us. As David Coleman has pointed out in 'Assortative Mating in Britain', in Chester, R. and Peel, J. (eds) *Equalities and Inequalities in Family Life*, there is a strong tendency for *assortative* mating, i.e. we are most likely to marry people who share a similar class, social (housing) environment, status, leisure pursuits and religious beliefs. Surveys carried out in Britain have indicated that the number of boy or girl friends prior to marriage is likely to be very limited:

If the choice is indeed rather small, then the way in which young people meet, move about and organise their social lives may have considerable bearing on the

likely origins of their future spouse, and on the breadth of choice they will enjoy.
(Coleman, D. 'A Territorial Approach to Marriage' in Meighan, R. *et al.*,
eds, *Perspectives on Society*)

The number of marriage-choices open to a man or woman is likely to be
very limited. As Coleman sums up, 'An average person living in the
average town will still marry someone from the same place as their parents
did.' So the effects of family interaction continue from birth to marriage –
from family of origin to family of procreation.

• Liberationist perspective of the family

We have seen in our study of the conflict-structuralist family perspective
that from time immemorial woman's place within the family framework
has been one of savage subjugation. Those who view the family from a
liberationist approach look for the complete freedom of women within or
without the family context. Many would argue that such a liberation of
women is not possible because of the child-bearing role that they alone can
perform. They have a function from which they cannot escape if the
human race is to survive. Even the dual-career family, where the wife's
career is seen as just as important as the husband's, is a statistically minor
variant.

> Marriage and housewifery are basic impediments to occupational sex-equality.
> The female professional worker is likely to differ in one important respect from
> the male professional worker: she is between three and four times more likely to
> be unmarried.
> (Oakley, A. *Housewife*)

Sociologists most associated with the liberationist perspective are women
such as Ann Oakley and Juliet Mitchell. Nevertheless a number of men
support the Women's Liberation Movement; we have moved a long way
from the ultra male chauvinist who regarded the woman's place as in the
marital bed unless she was bringing in the coal. Liberationists are
experimenting with new ways by which a man, a woman and their
children can live together.

Liberationists face tremendous in-built opposition from the state,
church and society at large. It is generally regarded as the norm for a
woman to get married and have a family. So the liberationist is looked
upon as a deviant and a failure. Labelling devices such as 'frigid woman'
or an 'old maid' are used to deride those who reject the traditional
feminine role of wife and mother. A bachelor is commonly considered to
be a man who has not yet popped the question, whereas a spinster is
regarded as one who has not yet been fortunate enough to have received a
proposal of marriage. The term 'bachelor-girl' has been adopted by some

unmarried females to indicate equality with bachelor males and to make it clear that they have chosen this particular role for themselves. Liberation-ists object to the fact that at marriage the woman is 'given away' by one man (usually her father) to another man (her husband), that in many cases she still promises to 'honour and obey' her new master, while the marriage service ends with the declaration 'man and wife' rather than 'husband and wife'.

In the face of all the opposition to those who rebel against marriage and family life, the liberationists are very much in the minority. The state still regards the female as the only partner in law who can be regarded as undertaking the role of housewife. This makes it very difficult for a man to stay at home to do the housework and look after the children so that his female partner can be liberated to pursue her chosen career. This was borne out by the verdict in the Mills case of 1970. Vera Mills had been working and bringing the money into the home for five years: Albert Mills looked after the home, but Vera's claim for the dependent's wife benefit for her husband under the 1965 National Insurance Act was rejected.

The 'new feminism' did not really begin until 1968 when reports seeped through to the British media that women in Atlantic City, New Jersey, were burning their bras. What really happened was that a number of women belonging to the 'new consciousness-raising groups' protested at the Miss America pageant. From a liberationist perspective this event degraded women and forced them to push their bodies into alien shapes just for the pleasure of the male sex. In response to this degradation, liberated women dumped their bras and girdles into a 'freedom trash basket'. 'Bra-burning' became an international catchphrase. The women's liberation movement was born.

One may ask why the feminine liberation movement was delayed so long. It may seem strange that, after women gained the vote, they did not struggle on for further liberation. However, the suffragettes were mainly middle-class women with a limited aim. After the success of the suffrage campaign, the movement collapsed. A new generation of women had to discover for themselves that there was still a fight to be won. Many people still had not realised the essential difference between *sex* and *gender*: that sex refers to biological differences between male and female particularly in visible differences in genitalia, whereas gender is a matter of culture referring to social classification of 'masculine' and 'feminine' – that sex is something you are born with, while gender is something acquired by socialisation.

the present-day women's liberation movement does, on the other hand, have certain characteristics which separate it from the feminism of the two earlier periods. Today's liberationists point out that both men and women are caught in the web of conventional sex-role definition, and that both sexes may suffer from a restriction of personal freedom as a result – not just women. This is a new idea, due perhaps to the perception that conventional ideas about the roles of the sexes persist despite the removal of institutional restrictions on the freedom of women to behave 'like men'. This perception, together with the increasingly crucial economic importance of women, should lead us to look again, as dispassionately as we can, at the extent of the differences – and the similarities – between male and female'.

(Oakley, A. *Sex, Gender and Society*)

The American sociologist Betty Friedan was the first to identify the discontent of women striving for full liberation in *The Feminine Mystique*. Friedan spoke for women who were discontented with their role as isolated home-makers. The radical politics of the sixties provided an excellent breeding-ground for the new women's liberation movement. From the interactionist perspective, women were involved in 'consciousness-raising'. They detested being seen by men as mere 'sex objects'. In 1970, Germaine Greer's *The Female Eunuch* became the most popular primer of women's liberationists. Greer argued that women should go out and do their own thing – or rather go out and beat men at their own things such as job-advancement and sexual conquests.

The Liberation Movement is now well entrenched, but as Juliet Mitchell warns in *Woman's Estate*, women must beware of being at the centre of an ideological contradiction. In their pursuit of liberation women must be wary of merely aping men and adopting the worst characteristics of male behaviour.

The Women's Liberation Movement has demanded, alongside the youth movement, the validation of certain qualities and, at the same time, because these qualities have been oppressed in their previous forms, they have been counter-acted. Thus, on the one hand, we build up feminine virtues to have a status in a male supremacist world – we are kindly, soft-spoken, inward-looking – believing these to be women's contributions to 'human nature' – but where these same values have been abused we will overcome them, so we will learn self-defence and aggression. There is nothing wrong with this instinct – except that that is all it is. Similarly, in trying to organize around our own values, we try not to imitate the structure of male-dominated radical groups.'

(Mitchell, J. *Woman's Estate*)

Although in a minority, conflict-structuralists and liberationists offer a balance to the staid structural-functionalist view that all is well with society and that the family must inevitably play its part as a well-adjusted and contented social institution. You should read R.D. Laing's *The Politics of the Family* for an unusual rejection of the happy families myth. Laing's studies of schizophrenics led him to believe that the difference between so-called normal and abnormal families is small. If schizophrenia only makes sense within the terms of family relationships, then liberation from the family seems a worthy end. But many would consider Laing's findings as both simplistic and pessimistic.

3.3 Marriage and family breakdown

● *Marriage*

We normally think of marriage as a legal relationship between a man and a woman. Society recognises the marriage following a wedding ceremony. It has been suggested that a marriage could take place between any group of two people (i.e. a dyad) regardless of sex, but society considers that a biological sex difference is of paramount importance in any marriage. Ann Oakley (*Housewife*) quotes a press report illustrating this fact.

> Detectives today prepared a report for the Director of Public Prosecutions on the couple who went through a form of marriage at Southend register office knowing they were both women.... The couple are Terry Floyd, 24, and blonde 23-year-old Carole Mary Lloyd.... Floyd said, 'I am technically female. But I feel and I always have felt like a man.' Carole said, 'I have known all along that my husband is a woman ... but it does not make the slightest difference to us'.
>
> (*Evening Standard*, 24 August 1970)

The Church of England Prayer Book, first published in 1561, gives three traditional (one might almost say structural-functionalist) reasons for the existence and continuance of marriage. Marriage exists:
1 for the procreation of children;
2 to avoid fornication;
3 for the mutual help and comfort of the marriage partners.

More than three-quarters of the people of the world live in communities where custom, law or religion decree that a man or woman has only one marriage partner. This particular marriage structure is known as *monogamy*. However, marriage does not always take place simply between one man and one woman (see Table 3.3). Where more than two people of different sexes enter into marriage this is known as *polygamy*. People of the Masai tribe practise a form of polygamy known as *polygyny* where one man has several wives simultaneously. This form of social organisation has great advantages considering the economic environment of that part of Africa in which the Masai live. After marriage, herds of cattle are combined and placed under the supervision of the children of both wives. A man thus acquires not only wives, but also workers, property and

Table 3.3 Forms of marriage

Type	Description		Examples
MONOGAMY	One man + One woman	Husband + Wife	Great Britain; Europe; USA, most western societies
POLYGYNY	One man + Several wives (simultaneously)	Husband + Wives	The Masai of East Africa; the Sisala of Northern Ghana; Moslem societies e.g. Egypt allows a man four wives
POLYANDRY	One woman + Several husbands This is less usual than POLYGYNY	Wife + Husbands	Marquesan Islands; Tibet; the Sinhalese of Cerflou; some Himalayan tribes
POLYGAMY	This is a category which embraces POLYGYNY and POLYANDRY. It is sometimes used as a general term to replace these.		As in second and third categories above

status. The first wife has seniority over the other wives and her eldest son inherits the herds and becomes head of the family. The hierarchy of statuses which result provides social advantages and appears to work successfully for the Masai people. As it is the custom for a Masai man to obey his mother, the eldest son will respect his mother's wishes. Any family frictions arising between the wives are taken up by the menfolk, who finally accept the ruling of the head of the family. The Melpa people of New Guinea are accustomed to a man having about three wives. Faced with a surplus of women, the early Mormon communities accepted polygyny as an answer to a particular social problem. Many Muslims also practise polygyny. Older wives exercise seniority in the household management while the younger wives satisfy the husband's sexual needs. Eskimos are likely to practise polyandry whereby a woman has more than one husband. They live in a dangerous environment and if one husband is killed the other looks after the wife and children.

In Moslem and some other societies, the *arranged marriage* still prevails. The parents of the couple vet the proposed marriage which only takes place if the parents agree that a satisfactory match would result. The parents are likely to look for compatible social class grouping and to pay due regard to property, occupational qualifications of the male, age difference and family connections. There is little evidence to indicate that this is a less satisfactory basis for marriage than some of the hit-and-miss relationships of our own society. We should be careful not to be hypercritical of arranged marriages merely because they form part of a different type of social organisation than that practised in our own society. Many sociologists are very sceptical of the idea that nowadays couples marry because they think that they have 'fallen in love'. Is the modern ideal of romantic marriage a reality of a myth? The seeds of romantic love may be sown by writers in popular magazines for girls such as *Favourite Story*, *Love Affair* and *Loving*; similar romantic ideals are perpetuated by popular periodicals such as *Woman*, *Woman's Mirror* and *Woman's Realm*. So-called 'love marriages' may mean the hasty choice of an unsuitable partner despite the protestations of parents whose experience tells them that the marriage is unlikely to last. A woman may be socialised into the assumption that there is a natural progression from 'falling in love' to engagement and finally to marriage itself.

> I always knew as a child that I was going to grow up and go to college and then get married and that's as far as a girl has to think.
> (Friedan, B. *The Feminine Mystique*)

Marriage has been traditionally the structural keystone of the kinship systems in western society. However, parents nowadays have little say in who their children will marry, but the conception of romantic love or 'being in love' helps to sustain people as they move from their families of origin to their families of procreation.

Marriage is becoming slightly less popular in Britain. At 356 954, the total number of marriages (in England and Wales) in 1977 was fewer than in 1976. For every 1000 single men, 61 were married in 1977; this was four per cent lower than in the previous year, and was the lowest proportion since the early 1930s. For every 1000 single women, 76 got married, which was three per cent lower than 1976 and the lowest figure since the early 1950s. Figure 3.5 indicates that a steep decline has taken place since the early 1970s in the rate of first marriages. The marriage rate peaked in 1970 when the Family Law Reform Act reduced the age of marriage without parental consent from 21 to 18. Although Fig. 3.5 relates to England and Wales, most other western countries have experienced a similar rise and fall of marriages over the last two decades. The fall in the marriage rate is mainly caused by men and women marrying later. Reasons likely to have contributed to a later age for first marriages include the raising of the compulsory school-leaving age from 15 to 16 in 1972–3

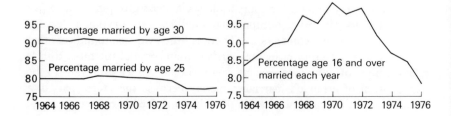

Fig. 3.5 First marriage of women (England and Wales) 1974–6
(*New Society*, 8 March 1979)

and the widespread availability of efficient contraceptive methods, making for the sexual emancipation of women, combined with the legalisation of abortion under certain circumstances. Consequently, the median age of first marriage has risen for men from 23.1 in 1969 to 23.7 in 1976, and for women from 21.2 in 1967 to 21.5 in 1976.

There has been a significant fall in the number of 'shotgun' weddings. Between 1964 and 1976, the number of pregnant brides under 20 fell from 37 per cent of brides to 23 per cent. Considering all brides under the age of 45, 22 per cent were pregnant in 1964 compared with 12 per cent in 1976.

Economic factors are related to the marriage rate. In nineteenth-century Britain, the marriage rate was thought to be closely tied to improving economic conditions and was termed the barometer of economic prosperity. The Victorian family, averaging seven children, corresponded with the days of British industrial advance and colonial expansion. However, attempts at statistical correlation between the marriage rate and prosperity must be treated with caution.

A modern complication is the increase in the number of men and women living together outside the framework of legalised marriage; the actual figures for Britain are not known, but the term 'shacking-up' is now part of the language and it is generally agreed that it is a social arrangement which has increased considerably. In Britain, a 1976 survey found that of women in the sample marrying under the age of 20, 82 per cent had had premarital sex with their husbands compared with only 34 per cent of this age group in 1951. Research carried out in Sweden indicates that more men and women in their late teens and early twenties are living together, than those who have chosen to have their unions legitimised by marriage. In 1977, a French sample survey found that about one-third of young marrieds had cohabited with their partner for an average period of six months before taking part in a marriage service. Thus marriage is delayed but in many cases the couple eventually agree to legitimisation for such reasons as financial convenience (including mortgage and taxation arrangements) and for rearing children. Marriage is still popular and this is illustrated by the increase in the number of remarriages; more than one-third of divorced people remarry within one year.

● *Divorce*

The ultimate form of family breakdown is when divorce is legally granted by the state. Divorce has increased from an average of two divorces a year in 1857 to over 100 000 divorces a year since 1971 (see Fig. 3.6). Before 1857 divorce in Britain was too expensive for all except the very wealthy upper classes. Each divorce required an Act of Parliament and cost hundreds of pounds. After 1857, it was possible to obtain a divorce through the courts, but it was still far too expensive a procedure for the lower middle classes and working classes. Women's appeals for divorce were less favourably considered: men had only to prove adultery, whereas women had to prove cruelty as well. The 1937 Matrimonial Causes Act extended the grounds for divorce, but opportunities for the working classes to obtain divorce relatively easily came only with the legal aid scheme introduced for the armed forces during the Second World War and for the whole population by the 1949 Legal Aid and Advice Act. The number of divorces increased considerably during the 1970s, with the 'irretrievable breakdown of marriage' being the sole basis of divorce (1969 Divorce Reform Act). The reasons for the increase in the divorce rate are many and various but Table 3.4 offers a guide. It is clearly too simplistic but provides a basis for discussion. Each marriage is different and may be terminated for a variety of reasons.

Although the number of divorces in Britain has increased greatly, especially in the last decade, the figures are not indicative of such a decadent state of marriage as may at first appear. The following press report from *The Sunday Times* (9 October 1977) presents a more balanced picture than is often given.

Are we really that bad at marriage?
Britain's divorce rate is not nearly as bad as it was depicted by Sir George Baker, a High Court judge whose remarks sparked a remarkable burst of agonised headlines yesterday.

'One break-up for every two marriages,' said the *Daily Express*. 'Britain is even ahead of California,' said the *Daily Mail*, which described the trend as 'the great dash for divorce.'

Baker, President of the Family Division of the High Court, was reported as saying on Friday that divorce statistics had deteriorated from the mid-sixties – when one marriage in seven or eight ended in divorce – to today, when it appeared the figures were more like one in two. But careful analysis shows that

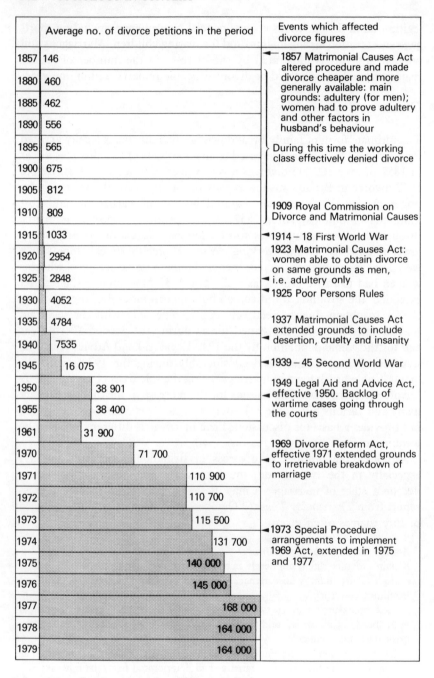

	Average no. of divorce petitions in the period	Events which affected divorce figures
1857	146	◄ 1857 Matrimonial Causes Act altered procedure and made divorce cheaper and more generally available: main grounds: adultery (for men); women had to prove adultery and other factors in husband's behaviour
1880	460	
1885	462	
1890	556	
1895	565	During this time the working class effectively denied divorce
1900	675	
1905	812	
1910	809	1909 Royal Commission on Divorce and Matrimonial Causes
1915	1033	◄ 1914 – 18 First World War
1920	2954	1923 Matrimonial Causes Act: women able to obtain divorce on same grounds as men, ◄ i.e. adultery only
1925	2848	
1930	4052	◄ 1925 Poor Persons Rules
1935	4784	1937 Matrimonial Causes Act extended grounds to include ◄ desertion, cruelty and insanity
1940	7535	
1945	16 075	◄ 1939 – 45 Second World War
1950	38 901	1949 Legal Aid and Advice Act, ◄ effective 1950. Backlog of wartime cases going through the courts
1955	38 400	
1961	31 900	
1970	71 700	1969 Divorce Reform Act, effective 1971 extended grounds ◄ to irretrievable breakdown of marriage
1971	110 900	
1972	110 700	
1973	115 500	
1974	131 700	◄ 1973 Special Procedure arrangements to implement 1969 Act, extended in 1975 and 1977
1975	140 000	
1976	145 000	
1977	168 000	
1978	164 000	
1979	164 000	

Fig. 3.6 Divorce legislation and its effects on the divorce rate

Table 3.4 Some reasons for the increase in divorce

1 The trend towards women's liberation, combined with a democratic spirit within marriage, provides the potential for a more open airing of family frictions, e.g. there is often an amicable acceptance of divorce by husband and wife who both appreciate that the marriage is better ended.

2 The symmetrical or dual-career family means marriage partners are economically independent of each other, e.g. they may decide to terminate the marriage and provide for themselves separately.

3 Society has adopted more liberal attitudes, and divorce is no longer stigmatised.

4 The nuclear privatised family is more isolated and independent than the extended family, e.g. there is often little kinship pressure to prevent the breakdown of marriage.

5 Changes in the law have broadened the grounds for divorce, e.g. from adultery (1857) to the irretrievable breakdown of marriage (1971).

6 Some churches recognise re-marriage and will conduct a wedding service for divorcees from previous marriages, e.g. the Methodist Church.

7 There has been a decline in the influence of organised religion, and a secular society pays little heed to the church's teachings against divorce.

8 For most of this century (until 1977) there was a tendency for couples to marry younger; earlier marriages are more likely to end in divorce. The divorce rate for women who marry under the age of 20 is more than twice that of women who marry between the ages of 20 and 24.

9 There has been a decline in the average size of the family and consequently a decline in the responsibility which parents feel towards their children. Over 30 per cent of divorces are to childless couples.

10 It is cheaper nowadays to obtain a divorce. There is, for example, the Legal Aid and Advice Act (1949).

11 The growth of urban communities has resulted in a wider network of social relationships. Married people have greater opportunities to meet others outside their marriage and this may lead them to realise that they made the wrong choice of marriage partner initially.

12 Greater mobility, occupationally and geographically, may help to cause the breakdown of marriage, e.g. a couple may grow away from each other.

13 Society is a more heterogeneous social mix. Great stress may result if people marry somebody outside their own social class or from another race.

14 Longer expectation of life means that unsuitable marriages, which would have been terminated previously by the death of one of the partners, now end by divorce: when life was shorter an unhappy marriage only had to be endured for twenty years.

15 Divorce is more likely to occur if the wife was pregnant at marriage. This is more likely to occur if the wife is under the age of 20.

16 The increased intensity of modern marriage relationships tends to make them more vulnerable to breakdown.

SOCIOLOGY IN CONTEXT

Britain's moral fibre is crumbling rather more slowly than Baker implies. Baker said that last year 356 000 couples married in England and Wales, and 146 000 got divorced. (As it happens, the true figures are slightly different: 359 000 weddings, and 127 000 divorces.) On the surface this does indeed suggest a frightening divorce rate.

However, a totally different view can be obtained from the same set of official statistics (published quarterly in *Population Trends*). These show that England and Wales has 12.5 million married couples. Each year, only one in 100 get divorced.

(*The Sunday Times*, 9 October 1977)

There are several reasons for statistical confusion. Firstly, there are a number of different ways in which divorce is recorded. The figure quoted by Sir George Baker was the number of divorce petitions, although a divorce does not legally take place until the decree is made absolute. O.R. McGregor (*Divorce in England*) believes that it is more useful to examine the numbers of divorce petitions because these do not reflect differences in court procedure over time. However, the figure for divorce petitions is always higher and not all petitions are granted. Secondly, there are dangers in comparing the number of weddings and divorces within a single year. Those getting married and those seeking divorce are two very separate groups with different marriage patterns. We have already seen that the age of first marriage is being postponed, but in the late 1960s, because of the post-war baby bulge, there was an above-average number of girls in their twenties, which is the most popular age for first marriage. The increased number of early marriages in the late sixties was always likely to lead to an increase in divorces in the seventies seeing that the most common time to seek divorce is between four and nine years after marriage. The 1969 Divorce Reform Act provided greater opportunities for divorce; there was bound to be a large increase from 1976 because of the completion of the five-year separations (with the consent of one party only) which began in 1971 when the new Act became effective.

The 1969 Act is unlikely to make much difference to the divorce rate in the long run. Figure 3.7 indicates that by the 1980s, the curves representing the actual divorce trend and the estimated trend (based on pre-1971 grounds) would have merged. All western societies are experiencing the same trend of increases in the divorce rate. In fact, the divorce rate is higher in the United States, Sweden and Denmark than it is in Britain. It seems logical to conclude that the broadening of the law and the removal of religious restraints are not the main reasons for the higher level of divorce (see Table 3.4). The increasing number of marriage breakdowns is more likely to be the result of people's changing expectations of marriage. They are less likely to put up with an unsatisfactory marital state: men and women expect to participate in joint conjugal role relationships and are no

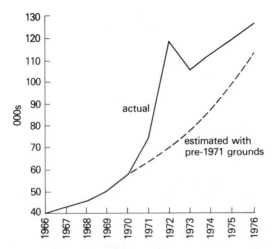

Fig. 3.7 Divorce in England and Wales, 1966–76
(*New Society*, 8 March 1979)

longer content to accept a simple dichotomy between 'breadwinners' or 'housewives'. Women especially are not so ready to tolerate a marriage which they find unsatisfactory. Since 1923 women have always filed the majority of divorce petitions but in 1976 the proportion increased dramatically to 70 per cent of the petitions. Nevertheless many will seek happiness in a second marriage. They are not so much disillusioned with the institution of marriage as with continuing a marriage which they regard as irrevocably ended.

Marital breakdown is rarely taken lightly by the spouses and usually brings in its train a great deal of personal distress. There is a loss of self-esteem resulting from feelings of shame and guilt in failing to live up to the normative pattern of marriage as recognised by society; the working class are likely to feel shame, whereas the middle class are more prone to feelings of guilt. Usually one of the spouses suffers more than the other; the spouse who is more emotionally involved may feel that life without a spouse is not worth living. In extreme cases suicide may be contemplated.

> Some spouses feel that the end of marriage is the end of everything and commit suicide or attempt to. Thus a marriage ended by separation is often felt more sharply than loss by death because the loss is accentuated by feelings of guilt and responsibility.
>
> (Dominian, J. *Marital Breakdown*)

The consequences of marital breakdown do not affect only the married couples. More than 60 per cent of divorcees have children under the age of 16. Many of the children of divorced couples may well be better off than they would have been if the unhappy marriage had continued. American sociologists have found that unhappily married husbands and wives tend to be emotionally unstable, over-critical and domineering; living in an atmosphere created by such people is likely to be harmful to children of the marriage. Much of the research in this area is concerned, in the nature of things, with the adverse effects that marital discord has upon the members of the family. Statistics indicate a close correlation between the increase in divorce and the increase in juvenile delinquency, but there are so many factors involved other than marital status; apart from the increase in detection of juvenile crimes, there has also been a marked increase in the number of juvenile delinquents whose parents are not divorced.

Divorce has naturally brought a large increase in the number of single-parent families (see Fig. 3.8). If there is a dispute about the children, the courts usually give custody to the mother. Matters of finance, housing and family relationships must be borne in mind. If children are to cope satisfactorily with their changed circumstances, it is preferable that they should have regular contact with both parents and that satisfactory relationships should be maintained. Children become disturbed, the more disturbed the relationships between their parents.

Parents provide role-models for their children so it is vital that post-divorce emotional relationships should be as stable as possible. The departing parent should be seen in the best possible light without any

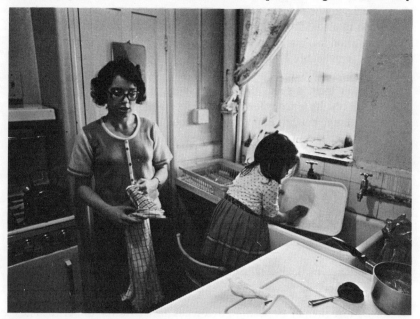

Fig. 3.8 A single-parent family

idealistic or distorted fantasy picture emerging. If the children are able to overcome the psychological reconstruction period which follows the marital breakdown, there is a better chance that they will grow up normally. However, there is evidence to suggest that rates of crime amongst young people, and alcoholism amongst the middle-aged, are likely to be higher among those from broken homes. There is also a natural sequence resulting in people from broken homes entering themselves into marriages which will themselves break up. There is no easy answer to these problems. Many divorcees attempt to escape from their problems by allowing themselves to be pressurised into another marriage which is no more likely to be successful than was the previous one. Such vulnerable people may marry and re-marry, thus artificially boosting divorce rates and practising what has been termed sequential polygamy. A Home Office working party on marriage suggested that a minister should be appointed to be responsible for marital problems. This seems an attractive proposal, faced with over £5 million a week being paid out in supplementary benefits to about 250 000 families unsupported following divorce and separation. However it is unlikely that a Cabinet minister could do much to decrease the human misery brought about by the breakdown of marriage.

3.4 Population

● *Importance of demography*

The study of population is a social science in its own right, known as demography. The examination of population statistics has led to numerous social investigations.

(a) Between 1781 and 1841, the population of Ireland almost doubled from about 4 million to 8 million and later dropped back to about 3 million. These demographic changes, combined with the impact of Irish emigrants to America, help us to understand more about social structure and social change.

(b) From 1951 to 1981 the population of Mexico City approximately doubled, leading to intense urbanisation, slum-dwelling and dramatic occupational changes.

(c) About 15 per cent of the population of Switzerland are immigrants, resulting in a relatively low-paid immigrant population with precarious occupational rights. In all, the industrial European countries depend for their production upon over 20 million immigrants, including 2 million women who perform mainly menial work in factories or domestic service. John Berger and Jean Mohr (*A Seventh Man*) have described the immigrants' plight in a pictorial account which is beyond words.

(d) In the United Kingdom, we are still feeling the effects of the post-Second World War baby-bulge which resulted in an increased demand for housing, school places, teachers, social services and medical care. The secondary effects of the bulge have affected university intakes in the 1960s, divorce statistics, the increase in juvenile delinquency, etc.

(e) The increase in world population confronts us with the immediate problem of feeding and generally sustaining those who are part of the population explosion, while at the same time seeking long-term answers to control population growth by widespread contraception, sterilisation, abortion and other methods. How practicable is a world population plan? Dr Luc Hoffman has said,

> If it proves impossible to control population increase, the human race is doomed to extinction.

Carlo Cipolla (*The Economic History of World Population*) stressed that world population problems can only be solved if they are studied in historical perspective. Figure 3.9 shows the world population growth from 1750 with a projection to 2150 AD; in the last few years there has been evidence to suggest that population projections for the next century have been subject to over-estimation.

Two main demographic considerations are of major interest to the sociologist:

1 *Structures* (proportions) e.g. how many men are there in the population compared with the number of women? What proportion of the population lives in urban areas? What is the proportion of young to old people?

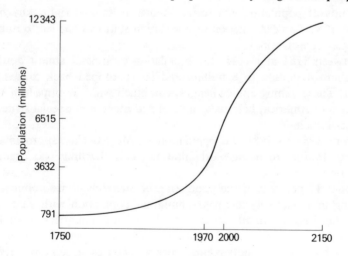

Fig. 3.9 World population growth from 1750 to 2150 AD

2 *Processes* There are three key rates of change relating to birth, death and migration.

The main tools for analysing population are provided by the regular flow of statistical information based on compulsory registration of births, marriages, deaths, migration and family structure, plus data from census returns, usually rendered in the form of statistical tables. Every ten years from 1801 to 1981 (except for 1941, during the Second World War) the government has gathered information about the inhabitants of Britain. The census is conducted by the Registrar General's department which appoints thousands of enumerators to whom are assigned a number of households. In the two weeks before 5 April 1981, enumerators from the Census Office (Office of Population Census and Surveys) delivered census forms to each household and collected them soon after 6 April 1981. Translations of the census questions were available in Bengali, Cantonese, Greek, Gujarati, Hindi, Italian, Punjabi, Turkish and Urdu. All house-holders are legally bound to provide details of everyone staying in their house during the night of the census. The 1981 census form sought information about:

1 Household accommodation including the number of rooms
2 Tenure (e.g owner-occupied or rented)
3 Amenities (e.g. baths, toilets, etc.)
4 Private transport (cars and vans)
5 Marital status
6 Country of birth
7 Employment
8 Professional qualifications.

The census is strictly confidential. It is taken solely to provide figures about the nation as a whole or some part of it, such as numbers of students, numbers of owner-occupiers, numbers of council tenants, numbers of people in each locality; it does not give information about any named person, family or household. Names and addresses are needed to take the census accurately, but they are not fed into the computer. After the census, the forms are locked away and not released to anyone outside the Census Office for 100 years. The answers given on the census form are treated in strict confidence. No one outside the Census Office sees the completed form. Everyone working on the census is sworn to secrecy and could be prosecuted if he or she improperly revealed information.

The most modern computers are used to process the vast amount of demographic information collected, but it still takes many years for all the data to be analysed in detail.

Study carefully Fig. 3.10 which sets out in pyramidal form the population of England and Wales by age, sex and marital condition in 1975. What general conclusions can you draw?

Table 3.5 Some social uses of the census

1 *Housing* – to work out future needs, the government wants to know details of how people are housed at present, and the sizes and ages of their families.

2 *Hospitals, schools and other local government services* – the size of annual grants made by the government to local authorities depends on the number and needs of the people in the area.

3 *Social security benefits* – to calculate future public spending, facts are required about people's ages, proportions of men and women, whether they are single, married or divorced, and the size of the family.

4 *Planning* – the census shows how many people have moved from one area to another and how the local workforce is changing. This information is made use of for planning public transport, factories, offices, shops and recreational facilities.

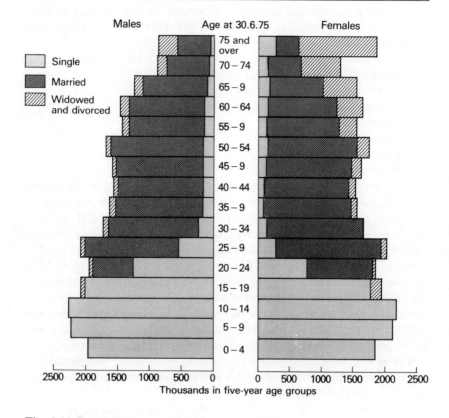

Fig. 3.10 Population structure: by age, sex and marital status, 1975 (*Social Trends*, HMSO, 1977)

These are some of the major ones which you should have determined:
(a) *More males are born than females* (sex ratio); there are about six per cent more male than female births every year.
(b) *There are more elderly females than elderly males*; there is a higher mortality rate for males at all ages, and from the age of about 45 years the number of women exceed the number of men. Considering the population as a whole, there are more than 105 females to every 100 males and the imbalance between the sexes increases with age (see Fig. 3.11).
(c) *Females marry earlier than males*: the proportion of single people in the population aged 15 years or over fell from 33.3 per cent to 23.4 per cent from 1939 to 1977, while the proportion who were or had been married rose from 52 to 60 per cent in the same period.
(d) *More females than males are widowed*; at birth the expectation of life for a man is just over 69 years while for a woman it is nearly 76 years.

What else have you determined from your own analysis of the pyramid depicting population structure? Some other points of demographic importance are more easily ascertained from a statistical table. Examine Table 3.6 which gives similar information to that supplied in Fig. 3.10. What new points arise?

You should see at a glance that there are more females in the population than males. This could be caused by birth-rate differences, or death-rate

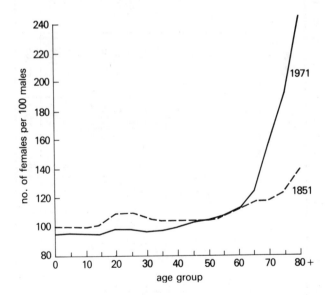

Fig. 3.11 Sex ratio: the number of females per hundred males in 1851 and 1971 by age group
(*New Society*, 28 March 1974)

Table 3.6 Population of England and Wales by age, sex and marital condition (1961)

Age	Males					Females				
	Total	Single	Married	Widowed	Divorced	Total	Single	Married	Widowed	Divorced
0–4	1 846 141					1 750 880				
5–9	1 670 620					1 591 666				
10–14	1 907 303					1 817 861				
15–19	1 621 962	1 604 910	17 040	10	2	1 578 698	1 475 077	103 536	65	20
20–24	1 434 391	989 661	443 938	247	545	1 443 898	606 938	833 643	1 336	1 921
25–29	1 445 983	425 643	1 015 145	1 135	4 060	1 400 178	219 676	1 168 696	3 800	8 006
30–34	1 501 640	262 656	1 227 625	2 744	8 615	1 482 675	162 238	1 297 725	8 781	13 931
35–39	1 616 192	213 826	1 383 178	6 164	13 024	1 625 692	159 138	1 422 720	21 243	22 591
40–44	1 493 821	160 092	1 309 133	10 481	14 115	1 542 765	149 326	1 325 147	42 118	26 174
45–49	1 583 800	151 219	1 397 117	19 633	15 831	1 644 953	173 032	1 361 828	82 470	27 573
50–54	1 575 399	139 916	1 386 171	34 345	14 967	1 645 693	201 525	1 280 261	138 909	24 998
55–59	1 407 842	120 481	1 224 788	51 694	10 879	1 519 920	210 249	1 073 590	217 072	19 009
60–64	1 096 306	86 933	931 128	71 721	6 524	1 361 772	195 535	830 230	323 030	12 977
65–69	818 924	60 040	664 645	91 022	3 217	1 159 854	176 605	571 499	404 452	7 298
70–74	599 580	45 618	440 073	112 268	1 621	942 092	145 773	345 433	447 196	3 690
75+	683 929	54 188	372 961	256 729	1 051	1 292 118	206 392	246 159	837 336	2 221
TOTAL	22 303 833	9 738 247	11 812 942	658 193	94 451	23 800 715	9 242 001	11 860 467	2 527 838	170 409

differences or migration. It is not due to births because there are more males born each year. It is not due to migration because statistics indicate that migrants have little effect on the sex ratio. It is likely to be due to the fact that there are more male deaths than female deaths. Further investigation would reveal that:

(a) at all ages, males are more likely to die than females;

(b) at older ages, women are in the majority;

(c) increasing age results in the attrition of the male advantage at birth.

Now examine marital situations. You will see that twice as many women than men marry between the ages of 15 and 25. In the older age groups, more men marry than women; women marry at a younger age, but men begin to catch up after the age of 45. Married women are more likely to leave the category 'married' than are men. There are various reasons for this: men are more likely to die earlier and as men tend to be older than their wives, women set themselves up for a long period of widowhood. It is difficult for women to find a second husband; the table shows that there were 446 000 unmarried women between the age of 55 to 59, but only 180 000 men. The table also shows clearly that more women than men seek divorce at all ages.

There are sociologically significant factors which can never be seen from graphs and tables. For example, we know that there is a larger proportion of old people in society today. We can look for the causes of this phenomenon in the mass of statistics at our disposal. Older people are likely to stay alive longer, but strangely the major cause is not the increase in life-expectancy. The life-expectancy of those over 45 has not changed markedly since 1841. Once you have reached 65, life-expectancy has hardly changed in the last 130 years, remaining at about 76 (*Trends in Mortality*, HMSO). We must look at the young end of the age range. Firstly, there has been a decline in infant mortality. The first year of life is a most dangerous time so that the more children who survive beyond the age of one, the greater the proportion of old people in the population. Secondly, there has been a decline in fertility; there has been a smaller proportion of young people and consequently a smaller proportion of old people. So the figures can help to explain causes, but they are less satisfactory in helping us to solve problems. For example, how can we give back social esteem to old people in a society which so frequently displays little regard for kinship? In societies where kinship remains a social institution, the old often enjoy a great deal of prestige and power. They are not dependent on the state and are not treated as unwanted outcasts. Whether or not there is a plight of the elderly depends upon how old people are regarded in the community – whether they are afforded esteem or treated with a lack of esteem (see section 7.3).

• *Fertility*

Of all the demographic variables the most important is *fertility*. Nearly all classical theories relating to fertility have assumed that *fecundity* is relatively constant. In simple terms, fertility is concerned with reproductive performance while fecundity is about reproductive potential or the maximum biological capacity for reproduction. The basic question in fertility studies is how many women have how many children in any given period of time. The emancipation of women combined with economic circumstances in the modern world, mean that women far from realise their reproductive potential. Fertility is measured in terms of the annual number of births for every thousand women in a specific age group.

The two main classical theories relating to fertility were:

1 the Malthusian theory and
2 the standard of living theory.

1 *Malthusian theory*

Malthus believed that the sexual passion between the sexes would continue unabated, but that there were possible checks upon the increase in the population. Population would press upon food supply and therefore famine, disease and war were inevitable. There were many people in the lottery of life who had drawn a blank. He argued that whereas the food supply increased in an arithmetical progression (1, 2, 3, 4 ...) population increased in a geometrical progression (2,4,8,16 ...). Such an exact mathematical correlation has been rightly described as a misleading mathematical jungle, but nevertheless the plight of millions of starving children in the Third World today suggests that Malthusian tendencies still operate and that the ghost of Malthus still lurks.

> Through the animal and vegetable kingdoms, nature has scattered the seeds of life abroad with the most profuse and liberal hand. She has been comparatively sparing in the room and the nourishment necessary to rear them.
>   (Malthus, T. *Essay on Population*)

In revisions of his book, Malthus concentrated more upon his observations that, in early industrial England, couples were curbing their fertility in order to improve their standard of living. He advocated moral restraint and towards the end of his life predicted that the lower classes would use methods of birth control to improve their nutritional standards.

2 *Standard of living theory*

There is a close link between Malthus's later arguments about people controlling the population growth to satisfy desires for material goods and Alfred Marshall's arguments, expressed at the end of the nineteenth century, that each population attempts to secure an optional relationship with its environment. He contended that the average age at marriage depends upon the ease with which young people can establish themselves. Marshall's arguments regarding fertility are more convincing than those of Malthus. Sociologists must examine social norms (see Fig. 3.12) and relate them to people's actual behaviour, but it does seem logical to assume that people will breed at a rate consistent with improving, or at the very least maintaining, their standard of living.

Two important factors influencing fertility are fecundability (i.e. the probability of conception within one menstrual cycle) and foetal mortality. The proportion of sterile women in the population is also important: female sterility increases with age, whereas there is little evidence that male sterility changes over the years. Coition is naturally highest immediately after marriage, but declines with age. Factors associated with potential fertility are listed in Table 3.7.

On the one hand suggestions have been put forward in an attempt to substantiate a supposed decline in fecundity: there is no real evidence to support the claim that fecundity decreased in the nineteenth century because of the stresses of urban industrial life or when ladies started bicycling! On the other hand, it has been claimed that fecundity has increased owing to improvements in nutrition and health. J.M. Tanner (*The Trend Towards Early Physical Maturation*) records progressive earlier maturation regarding height, weight and the first menstruation among girls. It is probable, however, that fecundity has changed little, but

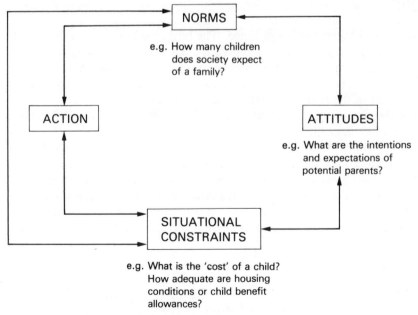

Fig. 3.12 Model affecting fertility and the birth rate

Table 3.7 Associated factors affecting fertility

---

1 Age of entry into sexual unions and the average age of marriage.

2 Coital frequency, i.e. number of times sexual intercourse takes place in a month.

3 Contraception – the pill is generally more reliable than the condom: birth control has always been more prevalent among higher social classes.

4 Sterility – effective fecundability (probability of producing a live birth) is less for older women; most women stop child-bearing after the age of 40.

5 Celibacy – more women than men never participate in sexual inter-course.

6 Voluntary abstinence – the wife pretends to have a headache.

7 Involuntary abstinence – e.g. impotence or illness.

8 Reproductive periods lost because of marital breakdown or the death of a spouse; unstable unions tend to produce fewer children.

9 Foetal death.

10 Abortion: the 1967 Abortion Act made abortion possible in the UK, where continuing pregnacy
   (a) risks the life of the pregnant woman;
   (b) might cause her injury, physically or mentally;
   (c) might injure the physical or mental health of any children.

---

nevertheless fertility has declined. The birth rate today is less than a half what it was in 1880 (34.2 per thousand), but the actual number of births is about the same. The average number of children per family has more than halved, but an increase in the number of family units producing children has led to the overall growth of the UK population.

The use of the term birth-rate needs qualification. Table 3.8 defines some key demographic terms.

The crude birth rate is frequently quoted but it is not very useful when comparing fertility levels. It gives an indication of the rate at which the population is reproducing itself, but comparisons of crude birth rates can be very misleading; in Alaska the crude birth rate is exceptionally low because of the large proportion of males in the population. The *general fertility rate* is a better index because it includes all women between the ages of 15 to 44.

$$\frac{\text{Number of births}}{\text{Number of women 'at risk'}} \times 1000$$

Table 3.8 Useful demographic definitions

1 *Crude birth rate* Number of live births per year per 1000 people. A key determinant of overall population but not a very good index for comparing *fertility levels* as it is affected by the composition of the population in regard to age, sex and marital status.

2 *Age-specific birth rate* Number of live births per year to 1000 women of a given age group (six five-year age groups are commonly used: 15–19, 20–24, 25–29, 30–34, 35–39, 40–44.) A good basis for making comparisons as it is not affected by the *age-distribution* of the population.

3 *General fertility rate* Number of live births per year per 1000 women aged 15–44 years; strongly affected by the age distribution of women in the 15–44 age span.

4 *Total fertility rate* The average number of children a woman will have if she experiences a given set of age-specific fertility rates throughout her lifetime. A good index to measure *fertility changes*, as it is independent of age and sex distribution.

5 *Gross reproduction rate* The average number of daughters a woman will bear if she experiences a given set of age-specific fertility rates throughout the reproductive ages, with no allowance for mortality over this period. A good index for measuring changes in *future fertility* potential.

6 *Net reproduction rate* Same as the gross reproduction rate but adjusted for mortality of women over their reproductive years.

7 *Infant mortality rate* Annual deaths of infants aged under one year per 1000 live births during the same year. A good index of *mortality* at a critical age level.

8 *Crude death rate* Number of deaths per year per 1000 people. Another key determinant of population growth but not a very good index for comparing *mortality levels* as it is affected by the age and sex composition of the population.

9 *Life-expectancy* Average number of years remaining to be lived after attaining a given age.

10 *Dependency ratio* Number of people of 16 years or under, plus 65 or over, divided by the population aged 16–64 years. A measure of the balance between *non-producing and producing* members of society.

11 *Rate of natural increase* Difference between crude birth and crude death rate – usually expressed as a percentage.

12 *Rate of population growth* Rate of natural increase adjusted for (net) immigration or emigration.

A much better basis for fertility comparisons is the *age-specific birth rate*. This index is confined to women and is unaffected by the age distribution of the population (see Fig. 3.13).

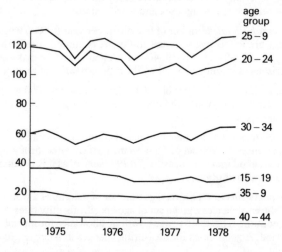

$$\frac{\text{Number of births to women aged 30 to 34}}{\text{Number of women aged 30 to 34}} \times 1000$$

Fig. 3.13 Births per 1000 women 1975–8 – age-specific birth rates
(*New Society*, 22 March 1979)

Table 3.9 Some reasons for the decrease in the birth rate

1 We have moved through a natural progressive demographic cycle from
 (a) high birth rate and high death rate in the eighteenth century to
 (b) low birth rate and low death rate in the twentieth century (see
  Fig. 3.14).

2 Improved medical standards have resulted in a decrease in infant mortality
 from 150 per 1000 in the early part of the nineteenth century to 14 per
 1000 today.

3 There appears to be a close association between greater family prosperity
 and the number of offspring.

4 Improved old age pensions, old people's homes, sheltered housing, and
 social security benefits, mean that old people are not forced to rely upon
 the earnings of a large number of children.

5 Improved methods of contraception combined with the emancipation of
 women and the democratisation of the family.

6 The increasing desire for women to go out to work and pursue their own
 careers; many women return to work permanently after the birth of their
 second child.

This measurement makes it possible to find the peak child-bearing age for a community. It is also possible to compare other factors such as the birth rate of married women and the birth rate of unmarried women who have illegitimate children. Reasons for the decrease in the birth rate are suggested in Table 3.9.

• *Mortality*

In recent years, there has been controversy about different medical definitions of death. There are sociological implications relating to the cause of death. For example, what is the actual cause of death of a man admitted to hospital following a car crash who discharges himself and later dies?

Is it: (a) the car accident;
        (b) the fact that he discharged himself from hospital;
        (c) the failure of the hospital to prevent his unwise departure;
        (d) the man's possible desire to get back to his family?

The whole matter of causes of mortality has been complicated by life-support machines which may have to be switched off by somebody after a certain period of time. There are frequently multiple causes of death. Consider the case of the coalminer or schoolteacher who dies very shortly after retirement. But the death rate among farmers may be higher than that of coalminers and schoolteachers, because farmers often do not retire – they die as farmers!

As with birth rates, death rates vary.

Crude death rate:

$$\frac{\text{Number of deaths}}{\text{Number of the population}} \times 1000$$

Specific death rate:

$$\frac{\text{Number who died in a certain sex or age group}}{\text{Number of people in that sex or age group}} \times 1000$$

The crude death rate of about 12 per thousand in Britain has stayed comparatively stable for very many years. The life-expectancy for males has improved little since 1960, but over the last 150 years there has been a steady decline in the death rate and in the life-expectancy of boys and girls. Significantly there has been a rapid decline in the mortality rate of children since the 1940s. The National Health Service, improved nutritional standards, and greater prosperity have clearly contributed to this advance.

The crude death rate varies greatly in different countries according to life-expectancy and the structure of the population. The expectation of life at birth is 75 years in Sweden, but only 37 years in Nigeria. However, some useful generalisations can be made:

1 Age-specific death rate is higher in the older age groups.

2 At all ages mortality rate for males is higher than that for females.

3 Those in the lower social classes (IV and V) will die earlier than those in social classes I and II (see section 2.4).

(a) the infant mortality rate for social class V is over twice as high as class I.

(b) the foetal mortality rate is one and a half times greater for social class V than for class I.

Before 1946 malaria was the principal cause of death throughout the world. It was thought to have been wiped out by the application of DDT and other insecticides, but in recent years mosquitos carrying the disease

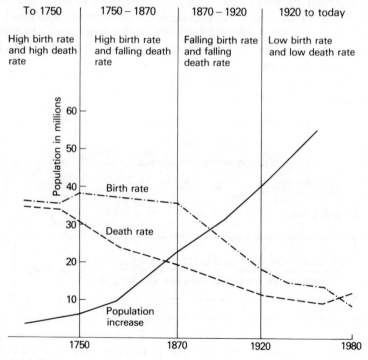

Fig. 3.14 Four stages in the demographic cycle

have become immune and malaria is again increasing rapidly. Smallpox and tuberculosis, which were once great killer-diseases, have been almost eradicated by immunisation and vaccination. The worst killer diseases in the Third World today include leprosy, yaws and syphilis. Improved nutrition could do much to eradicate diseases such as scurvy which causes a large number of deaths, especially among children. In the Third World, mortality follows the fate of the harvest. The World Health Organisation often keeps people alive longer than the World Agriculture Organisation can feed them.

The growth of large urban areas has been accompanied by the spread of certain diseases and consequently increased mortality. Urban living conditions need expensive and efficient sewage projects otherwise cholera and other excreta diseases will be prevalent. Nearly 2000 million people today live in cities and by the end of the century the number will have exceeded 3000 million.

The most probable reasons for the decrease in the death rate in Britain are similar to those appertaining to the birth rate and are given in Table 3.10.

Table 3.10 Some reasons for the decrease in the death rate

1 The demographic cycle involving a change, in the last two centuries, from a high death rate (35 per 1000) to a comparatively low death rate (12 per 1000) (see Fig. 3.14).

2 Economic prosperity allowing better housing and social services.

3 Scientific advances leading to mass use of new drugs such as penicillin and antibiotics, plus improved hospital and surgical techniques, under the National Health Service.

4 Healthier attitudes to hygiene, especially among young children.

5 A better start for the young in terms of ante-natal and post-natal care, dental treatment, medical inspections, free school milk and well-balanced school meals; unfortunately the nutritional value of school meals has deteriorated with the Conservative Government cuts in the 1980s.

6 Increased foreign trade, making for a far greater variety of foodstuffs, large-scale importation of new drugs and medical equipment, etc.

7 Death rates among manual workers have always been higher than those of the professional classes so the increased proportion of white-collar workers in the population may have contributed to the decline in mortality.

8 Ways of life have also changed, involving fewer dangerous and dirty jobs, shorter hours, more relaxation, and a decline in smoking amongst males. (But there are also changes which are likely to have increased mortality, e.g. motor accidents, alcoholism, drug abuse, etc.)

● *Migration*

Several important sociological dimensions of migration warrant investigation.

1 How great a distance have the migrants travelled?

2 Is the migration temporary or permanent? Many people see themselves originally as temporary migrants but later decide to stay permanently.

3 Are they voluntary or compulsory migrants?

   (a) Voluntary migration was exemplified in the Brain Drain of doctors, scientists and technologists from the UK to America in the 1960s.

   (b) Compulsory migration is the lot of refugees.

4 Is the migration national or international? If migrants cross national boundaries, then they are likely to be subjected to very limited rights relating to their life situations.

5 Is the migration from rural to urban areas, or vice versa? There is a modern tendency for the rural population in less developed countries to migrate to industrial areas. Such migration is especially attractive to young people.

Forced migration does not involve making decisions, but migration often does take place because people have made a definite decision to move, in the hopes of making a better living, to cement family ties or because of a feeling of restlessness and dissatisfaction with their own society. Any decision to migrate is constrained by objective opportunities such as adequate finance, convenient transport, satisfactory occupational possibilities in the host country and socially approved aspirations.

A case study of the emigration of three million Irish, from 1845–70, is of special interest to sociologists. Many complex factors played a part and the severe potato famines do not adequately explain the migratory process. Factors which played an important part included:

1 Irish land holdings took the form of very small farms which were divided on the death of the holder.

2 Absentee landlords deprived Irish farmers of capital investment and made them economically vulnerable.

3 Early migrants facilitated later migration by providing funds to help their kin to follow in their footsteps.

4 The abolition of the Corn Laws in 1846 deprived Irish corn-growers of the protected English market; in later years it was found impossible to compete against relatively cheap American corn.

5 Irish industry could not compete against English industry.

Shortage of time prevents a full discussion of the contributory factors to the Irish immigrant epic. It is sufficient to say that they all help to throw light upon the social structural complexity of migration.

The situation of migrants in the host country is of sociological interest.

Migrants will enjoy social adhesion if they can adapt speedily and harmoniously to the host society, but one must remember that the migrant has to face entry into a society already full of conflicts. Some of the problems migrants face include:

1 a lack of job opportunities, e.g. in the UK it is difficult for young blacks to find employment and where work is found it is frequently in relatively unpleasant jobs;
2 employers in the host country will be expecting to get migrant labour on the cheap; e.g. in Western Germany, migrants from Turkey and Yugoslavia are used as regulators of the work force and are sent home during a depression;
3 differences in sex and age structures, e.g. in France, there are three times as many Algerian male immigrants than Algerian female immigrants;
4 the availability of educational provision, housing, welfare and social services in the host country.

There are also sociological consequences for the host countries. It is true that the indigenous population often discriminates racially because of prejudice; but prejudices may be rationalisations based on good reasons such as migrants taking up jobs normally available to nationals. Migrants who face social problems in the host country have two useful ways of working for improvements:

1 *unitary action* by all immigrants;
2 *sectional actions* to gain access to certain resources.

It is easier for sectional action to be taken than for all the immigrants to be organised in unison. Migration can work in favour of the nationals of the host country; many Swiss occupy well-paid, professional-type work, while leaving migrants to perform menial tasks.

Migration presents consequences for the country of origin. Entire villages may be left with a serious shortage of able-bodied young men. Even when the migrants return, they often remain unskilled, being employed in low-grade jobs whilst away. On the whole, the earnings of the migrants do not contribute to the financial benefit of the country of origin, although there are a few recorded cases of migrants' remittances helping to improve the balance of payments of their country of origin: more often than not such remittances facilitate further migration or are spent on technical goods from the host country to the advantage of that already rich country. In this way migration represents massive foreign aid to the host country which can utilise cheap labout for its own advantage.

In spite of all the loaded, pejorative statements about the supposed adverse effect of migration upon Britain, the fact is that this country has been one of the major exporters of people over the last 175 years. From 1881 to 1921, Britain experienced a net loss of population through

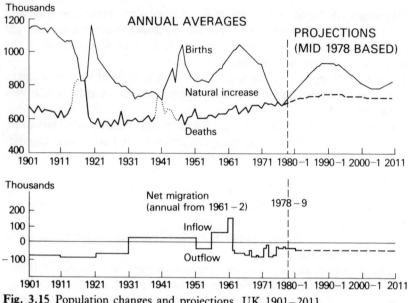

Fig. 3.15 Population changes and projections, UK 1901–2011
(*Social Trends*, HMSO, 1980)

migration of between two and three per cent a year. Many Britons sought a new life in North America, Australasia and elsewhere. From 1911 to 1921, the total loss by emigration amounted to 919 000. In terms of net migration during the twentieth century, Britain has been a net exporter, except during two periods (see Fig. 3.15):

1 1931–51 – there was a net import of 462 000 people, most of them refugees from Europe.

2 1955–62 – about a half million immigrants came from India, Pakistan and the Caribbean.

The large net inflow in 1961–62 was caused by Commonwealth immigrants beating the deadline of the first stringent Immigration Act (see section 7.4). Another net inflow of migrants took place in 1972–73, when Uganda expelled thousands of Asians who were holding British passports. It is well worth noting that a great deal of false, extremist and prejudiced comments have been made about coloured immigrants to Britain. From 1967 to 1975, when racial controversy was a matter of serious political contention, and when Enoch Powell was making his most inflammatory speeches, there was a net migratory outflow of over 400 000 from the UK.

● *Population trends and projections*

You will see from Fig. 3.16 that 1977 was a significant demographic year for Britain. It was the year when the crude birth rate fell below the crude death rate: the year of zero population growth; the year when the population did not reproduce itself. Between mid-1978 and mid-1979 the population of UK fell by 17 000. In England and Wales there were 11.6 births per 1000 of the population, while the crude death rate remained relatively stable at about 12 per 1000. However, this seems to have been but a hiccup in the birth rate curve. Since 1978, the birth rate has been rising steadily again, but demographic projections relating to future population figures are fraught with difficulties and dangers. After thirteen years of continuous decline in the birth rate, with the fall particularly steep after 1971, there was a hint in 1978 that babies were coming back into fashion (see Fig. 3.16).

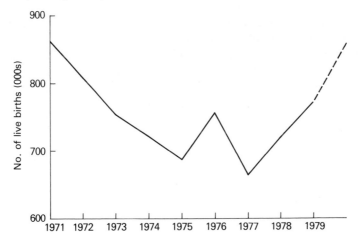

Fig. 3.16 Live births, 1971–8
(*New Society*, 22 March 1979)

Demographic projections indicate that the small increase in the birth rate is likely to remain, but there are all sorts of qualifications and these are early days in which to attempt to make confident predictions. Some increase in the birth rate had been forecast because of the one per cent annual increase in the number of women of childbearing age. When making population projections one important statistic of which we can be pretty certain is the number of females who will be capable of giving birth during a certain period. Those females who will give birth in sixteen years time or more, are already born. When the birth rate began to rise again in 1978 it may have been an indication that people had *not* made a *permanent* decision to have smaller families; it may rather have been the result of couples merely postponing having a family. It does seem, however, that the birth rate is likely to continue to be restored to its customary position, i.e. higher than the death rate. In the first quarter of 1979, the 156 000 births in England and Wales represented a nearly 10 per cent increase over the corresponding quarter in 1978. The fertility rate (the number of births per 1000 women aged 15 to 44) is also increasing; in 1978 it was three per cent higher than in 1977.

The task of the demographers would be easier if populations increased by regular, unvarying amounts. Unfortunately, for those who attempt demographic projections, this is not so. If projections were more accurate government population policies and plans would be more feasible. But there are peaks and troughs in the annual number of births. Just as factors combine to produce an unexpectedly rapid decline in births, so they could combine to produce a rapid increase. Factors such as methods of contraception, housing, abortion law, trends towards early or postponed marriage, deferment of childbearing and attitudes towards starting a family, all play their part. Explaining past behaviour is difficult enough: forecasting future trends is subject to a host of inaccuracies. As British death rates and migration rates are comparatively static, changes in the birth rate are most influential in establishing future population growth. Figure 3.17 shows how difficult it is to forecast the number of live births in Great Britain.

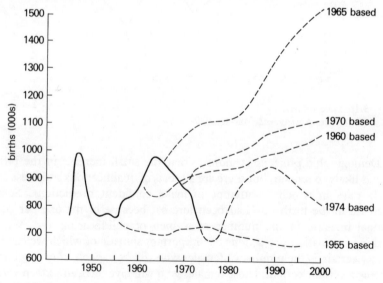

Fig. 3.17 Actual and projected live births in Great Britain, 1950–2000 AD (*New Society*, 16 February 1978)

Further Reading

Anderson, M. (ed.) *Sociology of the Family* (Penguin)

Bott, E. *Family and Social Network* (Tavistock)

Cooper, D. *The Death of the Family* (Penguin)

Coote, A. & Gill, T. *Women's Rights* (Penguin)

Douglas, J.W.B. *The Home and the School* (Panther)

Erikson, E.H. *Childhood and Society* (Penguin)

Fletcher, R. *The Family and Marriage in Britain* (Penguin)

Fox, R. *Kinship and Marriage* (Penguin)

Friedan, B. *The Feminine Mystique* (Penguin)

Gavron, H. *The Captive Wife* (Penguin)

Harris, C.C. *The Family* (George Allen & Unwin)

Heer, D.M. *Society and Population* (Prentice-Hall)

Kelsall, R.K. *Population* (Longman)

Mair, L. *Marriage* (Penguin)

Mead, M. *Growing up in New Guinea* (Penguin)

Mead, M. *Coming of Age in Samoa* (Penguin)

Mitchell, J. *Woman's Estate* (Penguin)

Newson, J. & E. *Patterns of Infant Care in an Urban Community* (Penguin)

Newson, J. & E. *Four Years Old in an Urban Community* (Penguin)

Oakley, A. *Housewife* (Penguin)

Oakley, A. *Sex, Gender and Society* (Temple-Smith)

Park, C.W. *The Population Explosion* (Heinemann)

Pressat, R. *Population* (Penguin)

Ramelson, M. *Petticoat Rebellion* (Lawrence & Wishart)

Rosser, C. & Harris, C. *The Family and Social Change* (Routledge & Kegan Paul)

Sharpe, S. *Just Like a Girl* (Penguin)

Townsend, P. *Family Life of Old People* (Penguin)

Turner, C. *Family and Kinship in Modern Britain* (Routledge & Kegan Paul)

Winnicott, D.W. *The Child, The Family and the Outside World* (Penguin)

Wrong, D.H. *Population and Society* (Random House)

Young, M. & Willmott, P. *Family and Kinship in East London* (Penguin)

Young, M. & Willmott, P. *The Symmetrical Family* (Penguin)

FOUR
Education and mass media

4.1 Educational perspectives

• *Structural-functionalist perspective of education*

Education is part of the social structure: it influences the social structure and in its turn is influenced by the social structure. Education involves a set of institutions (schools, colleges, polytechnics, universities, etc.) which have evolved to meet the requirements of modern industrial society. Functionalists would argue that social structure is a static concept, involving regular patterns of human behaviour; the education system is responsible for maintaining the status quo and performing certain definite functions (see Table 4.1).

Table 4.1 Some of the main functions of education

---

1 Socialises the young by the transmission of the culture of society and the acceptance of traditional values, norms, beliefs and attitudes.
  (Socialisation cannot be left solely to the family; schools cooperate with the family in the socialisation process.)

2 Teaches knowledge, language, skills and methods of evaluation and judgement.

3 Selects pupils for different tasks and helps to allocate to them eventual social roles as adults in society.

4 Acts as a crucial mechanism of social control: e.g. religious instruction is mandatory in British schools while Marxist philosophy is taught to young people in communist countries.

5 Facilitates the development of an individual's personality; in a Utopian society education would enable each individual to develop to the peak of his or her potential.

6 Affords social mobility so that children attain improved occupational status and the prestige which goes with it.

The organic model of society (as propounded by Spencer, Radcliffe-Brown and Malinowski) maintains that the social structure becomes increasingly complex while the sub-sections become increasingly inter-dependent. Thus the educational system has become more intricate and more closely interlinked with the economic system and the political system. Each sustains the other. Talcott Parsons used a systems theory which is closer to a mechanical analogy stressing the nature of understanding the different parts of the social system. The organic and mechanical approaches emphasise different aspects of social reality. Emile Durkheim was more concerned with moral reality; he believed that society's survival depended upon education reinforcing the homogeneity which exists between members of society by 'fixing in the children from the beginning the essential similarities which collective life demands'. In an industrial society based on organic solidarity (see section 5.1), social control may move from treating people all the same to a basis of individualistic achievement.

Two ideal-typical normative patterns of upward mobility have been put forward by Ralph H. Turner ('Sponsored and Contest Mobility in The School System'). On the one hand, *contest mobility* is compared with a sporting event in which the players start equal and compete for a few recognised prizes. Victory goes to those who are able to use the system to their advantage and triumph by means of enterprise, initiative, perseverance and craft. Victory by a person of moderate intelligence, using his common sense and wits, is more to be applauded than success by the most intelligent and the best educated. On the other hand, *sponsored mobility* favours a controlled selection process whereby an elite group is favoured. The elite are selected at an early age, as in the English public school system, and trained for their elitist responsibilities. Turner would contend that the US educational system functions by encouraging contest mobility, whereas the British educational system is based on sponsored mobility. Although only about four per cent of British children attend the privileged public schools, all the posts except two in Mrs Thatcher's Cabinet of the early 1980s were occupied by ex-public school pupils; similarly seventeen Cabinet ministers had an Oxbridge background. How is social control maintained in the light of such conditions of gross inequality?

> The most conspicuous control problem is that of ensuring loyalty in the disadvantaged classes towards a system in which their members receive less than a proportional share of society's goods. In a system of contest mobility this is accomplished by a combination of futuristic orientation, the norm of ambition, and a general sense of fellowship with the elite. Each individual is encouraged to think of himself as competing for an elite position so that loyalty to the system and conventional attitudes are cultivated in the process of preparation for this possibility. It is essential that this futuristic orientation be kept alive by delaying

a sense of final irreparable failure to reach elite status until attitudes are well established.

> (Turner, R.H.'Sponsored and Contest Mobility in The School System' in Hopper, E., ed., *Readings in The Theory of Educational Systems*)

Frank Parkin (*Class Inequality and Political Order*) contends that the British educational system functions in such a way that it deliberately lowers the aspirations of the majority of schoolchildren although still providing a controlled mechanism which ensures that a limited but adequate number of skilled workers are provided for in the economic system. Even under conditions of sponsored mobility it is still possible for a non-graduate of humble origins, such as James Callaghan, to reach the top job of Prime Minister.

Ironically, it was the aspiring Labour Prime Minister who in 1976 pointed to the dysfunction of the educational system in not supplying sufficient numbers of recruits to the labour force of industry and commerce.

> I am concerned on my journeys to find complaints from industry that new recruits from the schools sometimes do not have the basic tools to do the job that is required.
>
> (Callaghan, J., speech at Ruskin College, Oxford, October, 1976)

In other words he saw education as falling down on its vocational function. It is often seen as a functional requisite that educational institutions should supply a workforce more qualified than would have been necessary in an ascriptive pre-industrial society.

R. Collins ('Functional and Conflict Theories of Educational Stratification', in Cosin, B.R., ed., *Education: Structure and Society*), discusses the technical-function theory of education. Technical-functionalists believe that educational requirements in a modern industrial society are based upon three propositions.

1 Skill requirements of jobs constantly increase because of technological change. Two processes are involved:

   (a) the proportion of jobs requiring low skill decreases and the proportion requiring high skill increases;
   (b) the same jobs are upgraded in skill requirements.

2 Formal education provides the training, either in specific skills or in general capacities, necessary for the more highly skilled jobs.

3 Therefore, educational requirements for employment constantly rise, and increasingly larger proportions of the population are required to spend longer and longer periods in school.

The technical-functional theory of education fits in with the general functional-stratification approach of Davis and Moore (see section 2.2) that occupational positions require particular kinds of skilled performance and that positions must be filled with persons who have undergone the training and acquired the necessary qualifications to perform a specific occupational role. Collins is critical of the technical-function theory of education. The over-production of education personnel in countries whose level of economic development cannot absorb them (see Doré, R. *The Diploma Disease*) suggests that the demand of education does not come directly from the economy and indeed may run counter to economic needs.

> The technical-function theory of education, then, does not give an adequate account of the evidence. Economic evidence indicates no clear contributions of education to economic development beyond the provisions of mass literacy.... The quality of schools themselves, and the nature of dominant student cultures suggest that schooling is very inefficient as a means of training for work skills.
> (Collins, R. 'Functional and Conflict Theories of Educational Stratification', in Cosin, B.R., ed., *Education: Structure and Society*)

If we now turn to the conflict perspective, we may get a balanced understanding of the educational process in a modern industrial society.

• Conflict perspective of education

Max Weber believed that the basic units of society are status groups which share a common culture, such as background, language, opinions, values, conversational topics and leisure pursuits. Status groups compete against each other and distinguish themselves in terms of categories of moral evaluation such as breeding, taste, propriety, respectability, prestige, etc. Weber outlined three derivations of status groups: differences in lifestyle based on economic position (social class); differences in life situation based on power; and differences in life situation dependent upon cultural differences. There is a continual struggle for advantage within society in the realms of wealth, power and prestige. This struggle is carried out mostly through organisations and nowhere is this more true than in educational organisations. The principal activity of the school, according to conflict theorists, is to teach particular status cultures. A particular status group controls the educational system and teaches the values, language, manners and aesthetic tastes of the dominant group.

The educational system acts as an agent of social stratification and this is especially applicable to public schools. The headmaster is a member of The Headmasters' Conference, and the relationships with other public schools are close and unifying, while the connections with Oxbridge clinch the dominant role of the public school within the educational system. The public school is an organisational form of community but does not form part of the local community. It is one of Goffman's total institutions where like-situated individuals share a place of residence cut off from wider society, and live a formally administered, enclosed life. It is in these isolated surroundings that 'The Cloistered Elite' (Wakeford, J.) live out their lives in 'The Hothouse Society' (Lambert, R.) of stresses. Parents are kept at a distance, a system of hierarchies (headmaster, housemasters, prefects) is created, and new pupils are put through a traditional ritual. Goffman would argue that they are purposely degraded in order to remove their old self-identity. Preparatory schools and public schools offer continuity to the system, but divisiveness arises over who mixes with whom; day pupils are likely to be more alienated than boarders who must conform more rigidly to the rules and discipline imposed. There is an inherent conflict between the upper middle classes in public schools and the working classes in state schools.

From the early days of working-class education in Britain, it was the intention of the dominant middle class to make workers more docile and willing to accept the emerging structure of industrial society. S. Sharpin and B. Barnes ('Science, nature and control: interpreting Mechanics Institutes', in Dale, R., ed., *Schooling and Capitalism*) have argued that in the early nineteenth century, the founders of the British Mechanics' Institutes considered that a scientific education would facilitate the social control of artisans. The middle-class leaders of the MI movement thought that studying the scientific laws of nature would improve working-class morals and lead workers away from the sins of the flesh towards a knowledge of God. The study of nature was recommended to mechanics as it revealed the wisdom of God in creating things as they were, viz.

> God bless the squire and his relations,
> And keep us in our proper stations.

This movement, which by 1840 had established institutes in every sizeable British town, was more concerned with teaching the working class to accept status quo capitalism than with educating the masses. Science could be taught to a working-class elite, but not to all the working class. The study of science was considered good for the working-class élite, because it was objective and value-neutral; political economy was banned from the curriculum of most institutes because it was controversial and thought to be a threat to social order. Pure science was factual and drained of moral content. Teaching science and mathematics fitted in with the new industrialism without threatening the existing social structure.

Marxists also see the educational system as a conservative force perpetuating the existing class structure with its inequalities of wealth, income, privilege and power.

The ideas of the ruling class are, in every age, the ruling ideas; i.e. the class which is the dominant material force in society is at the same time its dominant intellectual force. The class which has the means of material production at its disposal, has control at the same time over the means of mental production. (Marx, K. *The German Ideology*)

Marx saw compulsory mass education as serving to reproduce workers with the skills and attitudes required by their capitalist masters. Cultural reproduction and class relationships were maintained by the educational system.

Louis Althusser, a structural Marxist, sees education as reflecting the social relations of production. He contends that the machinery of government includes two sets of apparatuses, i.e. repressive state apparatuses (RSAs) and ideological state apparatuses (ISAs). RSAs include police, magistrates, judges, courts, penal institutions and the armed forces. ISAs include education, families, law, religion, and politics. If the ISAs are very effective in promoting social control, then RSAs become less necessary. Education is currently the most important ideological state apparatus, responsible for reproducing values, attitudes, beliefs and morals. The middle class ensures that the ideology reproduced by the educational system works towards the stability of the modern state. Those of lesser ability are taught basic skills and ejected into the economy to perform manual tasks. Those of greater ability are provided with opportunities to go on to further and higher education so that they can be used later as agents of capitalist exploitation. Althusser believes that ideological control is far more effective, in the long run, than control by coercion.

S. Bowles and H. Gintis (*Schooling in Capitalist America*) have also argued that education is used to reproduce ideology, skills and consciousness which maintain the social relations of capitalism and the social class structure. Schools are organised as a hierarchy: teachers give the orders and determine what is taught, while pupils obey the orders and have no influence over the curriculum.

> The social relations of schooling are best seen as reproducing the social relations of capitalist production and thus the sort of personality attuned to working contentedly under that mode of production.
> (Bowles, S. and Gintis, H. *Schooling in Capitalist America*)

Basil Bernstein sees the context in which children learn as dominated by the middle class. Teachers are mainly middle-class by virtue of educational status and they have middle-class norms which separate them from working-class pupils. Teacher and pupils talk past one another. There is a conflict between the middle-class formal code of language used by the teachers, and the restricted code of public language used by working-class pupils; the elaborated code is a middle-class speech pattern capable of conveying complicated generalisations unfamiliar to the working classes. Conflicts arise because the middle-class teachers label working-class children as linguistically and culturally deprived with consequent lower educational expectations. Finally, there is conflict between the working-class child as a member of his family and community, and as a member of a school. Bernstein considers that these conflicts could be mitigated if children and parents were encouraged to retain their social identity. The working class have their own culture which is worth preserving. So-called compensatory education merely aims to make working-class children ape the middle classes. This in itself brings conflict:

> The concept 'compensatory education' serves to direct attention away from the internal organisation and the educational context of the school, and focus our attention on the families and children. 'Compensatory education' implies that something is lacking in the family, and so in the child. As a result, the children are unable to benefit from schools.
>
>   (Bernstein, B. 'Education Cannot Compensate for Society', *New Society*, 26 February 1970)

• *Interactionist perspective of education*

The interactionist concentrates upon face-to-face interaction within the classroom where it is possible by observation and participation to experience what is actually taking place (social reality). The interactionist approach does not aim to produce educational theories or to measure or test educational achievement, but rather to share and evaluate the life of the participants. R. Sharp and A. Green (*Education and Social Control*) have argued that a new perspective of educational sociology is emerging by the application of phenomenological sociology and symbolic interactionism (see section 1.4). Other sociologists associated with the interactionist perspective include:

N. Keddie 'Classroom Knowledge', in M.F.D. Young, ed., *Knowledge and Control*;

M. Hammersley 'The Organisation of Pupil Participation', *Sociological Review*, Vol. 22, No. 3, 1974;

B. Geer 'Teaching' in *School and Society*, ed. B. Cosin;

G. Esland 'Teaching and Learning as the Organisation of Knowledge' in M.F.D. Young, ed., *Knowledge and Control*;

D. Hargreaves *Interpersonal Relations and Education*, chapter 6.

The interactionist perspective is concerned with the problem of subjective meaning as a basis for an understanding of the world of the classroom. This perspective is often more illuminating than the paradigmatic crisis arising from sharp distinctions between structural-functionalists who accept the present traditional role of education as a means of social control, and Marxists who emphasise the inherent conflict within the educational system without suggesting ways of achieving a worthwhile consensus. A sympathetic interactionist approach is helpful if we are to understand the meaning of classroom events as comprehended by the pupil. Keddie observes that some educational aims are formulated by teachers acting as educationalists, but in the face óf commitments which arise during their day-to-day work, they act in a conventional manner and compromise their educational philosophies. Esland believes that we are witnessing a profound change in our understanding of consciousness and owe much to P. Berger and T. Luckmann (*The Social Construction of Reality*).

There are two main views of classroom reality: the teacher's view and the pupil's view. Most writers, until the 1960s, had emphasised the teacher's definition of reality; interactionists are aware that we require to understand the pupil's definition of reality if we are to attempt to put together a complete picture. The teacher perceives and evaluates his pupils according to the ways in which they respond to his basic roles of disciplinarian and instructor. He rewards pupils who are good and clever. The teacher creates a 'classroom climate' and uses labelling devices (such as 'thick' or 'disruptive') which act as self-fulfilling prophecies. If a teacher thinks a pupil will improve, then he probably will. B. Geer ('Teaching', in Cosin, B., ed., *School and Society*) points out that the authority of the teacher is legitimised by the classroom being his own ground, by other teachers acting as allies, by continuous grading of pupils, by superior knowledge and qualifications and by encouraging pupils to compete against each other: E. Hoyle (*The Role of The Teacher*) found a 'them and us' culture conflict: middle-class teachers are preoccupied with their pupils 'getting on', but this involves working-class children 'getting out' of their families. The teacher's definition of the situation encourages him to use many devices to impose his will upon the pupils: these devices include dramatic stratagems (see Goffman, E. *The Presentation of Self in Everyday Life*) and the attachment of exaggerated importance to what goes on at school in an attempt to overawe the pupils. The teacher places a social-role distance between him and his pupils.

However, the teacher is usually compelled to enter into negotiation with his pupils. Children are accustomed to having the situation defined for them by parents, so in the majority of interactions with adults, children acquiesce in the situation. If pupils define the classroom situation differently from their teacher, he will attempt to persuade them to change their notions, e.g. by sanctions, or by invoking the support of the headmaster and other colleagues or, as a last resort, the children's parents. Most children accept the situation as defined for them: D. Hargreaves (*Social Relations in a Secondary School*) found that 74 per cent of boys in the final year liked school as a whole. Only exceptionally boring and unhelpful teachers come to grief at the pupils' expense.

An excellent example of the clash of cultures which can take place in the schoolroom is found in Dumont and Wax's account of Indian children resisting the teacher's attempt to impose his white alien culture upon them (Dumount, R. and Wax, M. 'Cherokee School Society', in *School and Society*, ed. Cosin, B.). The children refused to discuss certain categories of knowledge which they considered to be unnecessary, e.g. the name of the President of the United States. One pupil may act as mediator and define the situation for the rest; in this way the pupils may be able to construct their own social reality of the classroom.

Readers of Evan Hunter's *The Blackboard Jungle* will realise that some pupils' dissatisfaction with what goes on in the classroom is inevitable. Ninety-five per cent of the time is spent in listening and the amount of participation in the average classroom in secondary schools is negligible. David Hargreaves has suggested three kinds of outcome in the teachers' and pupils' attempts to reach a consensus.

1 Concord – where teachers and pupils are compatible and define the situation identically.

2 Discord – where they are incompatible.

3 Pseudo-concord – where teachers and pupils are not completely compatible, but where they decide to sink their differences for most of their time together.

Pseudo-concord is most common. Very difficult children are in the minority; on the whole, teachers and children like each other. Pseudo-concord consists of four main elements:

1 *Consensus* – aspects of definitions of the situation are accepted by teacher and pupils.

2 *Compromise* – conflicts arise, but teacher and pupils negotiate a settlement.

3 *Imposition* – the teacher imposes his own definition of the situation.

4 *Counter-imposition* – the pupils' definition of the situation prevails; pupils are in the ascendancy – the teacher is forced to yield, but may try to make it look as if he is granting privileges.

It is very rare for pupils' and teachers' definition of classroom reality to be so incongruent that no consensus is possible. The teacher has to impose a definition of the situation which is acceptable to the headmaster and other members of staff. In practice, he compromises and moderates his demands upon the children so that the most important ones are met. The pupils realise that they are not in a strong bargaining position and are content with the working consensus which is reached. Pupil power is growing, however. Fortunately for teachers, most pupils underestimate the power of the group; a teacher would be very vulnerable against a united opposition. Headmaster and teachers fear unions of school students; like the early trade-union martyrs, pupils who refuse to comply go underground. The teacher who is able to single out a troublemaker can divide and rule.

Interactionists would argue that we require to understand the pupils' definition of the situation if we are to understand their perspective of life. This view of education is seen from the interior in contrast to the exterior view yielded by more objective perspectives. Child-centred theorists have come closest to the interactionist approach, largely because of their aim to treat schoolchildren as persons rather than as objects in the traditional scientific manner. Interactionists try to see things from the viewpoint of the majority who are involved in the educational process, i.e. the students. Many interactionists believe that children would be better out of the school environment; such deschoolers are regarded as romantics by traditional educational researchers. Modernists worth reading include John Holt (*The Underachieving School*), Sara Delamont (*Interaction in The Classroom*), Everett Reimer (*School is Dead*), and Ivan Illich (*Deschooling Society*).

4.2   The organisation of the school

• *The role of the teacher*

A well-organised, large-scale teaching profession exists only in advanced societies. In pre-industrial societies the father usually educated his son, although isolated teachers were employed to teach the classics to the sons of the aristocracy and to give them a cultured style. The teacher was mainly a transmitter of high culture and a distinctive set of values to an elite group. He acted as a conservative agent and concentrated upon traditional knowledge.

The role of the headteacher is of utmost importance and is more complex in modern society as schools become larger and the curriculum more exhaustive. Aspects of the headmaster's role include:

1 *Leadership* – a school is what its headmaster makes of it.

2 *Bureaucratic* – the headmaster is the chief executive at the top of a hierarchical pyramid.

3 *Managerial* – the headmaster increasingly performs an entrepreneurial function especially where his salary is linked to the number and age of the pupils.

4 *Ritualistic* – he is responsible for behaviour, cultural values and social control.

5 *Charismatic* – personal qualities are probably becoming less important –

especially in large schools where the head assumes a less paternalistic role and delegates responsibilities to staff who concentrate upon pastoral care.

The general public has never awarded to teachers the same high status it awards to doctors or lawyers. The teacher's role is not so dramatic and he receives less remuneration and status. Some of the reasons why the teaching profession has never been afforded high status include:

1 the supply of would-be teachers has always exceeded the demand for teachers;

2 teachers are not very conscious of a sense of unified professional ethic (see section 5.7);

3 more regard is given to those who put things right, than to those who keep things right;

4 teachers are not so much trained as certified (or certificated);

5 about two-thirds of the profession are women at a time when women generally still receive lower remuneration and prestige than men;

6 the teacher's role is very diffusive and subject to role-conflict.

Role-conflicts often relate to problems of authority and a lack of consensus. The teacher has to face the diverse expectations of his role set (see section 1.2): headmaster, colleagues, parents and pupils expect different things from him. Academic and pastoral boundaries are not clearly drawn, and those with a marginal role within the general school organisation (e.g. teachers of physical education, woodwork, music, cookery, etc.) frequently feel a sense of insecurity which may contribute towards an inadequate role-performance. Most teachers feel little control over the organisation of the school; conflict arises as the school increases in size and the organisation becomes more impersonal. There must be continuity if a teacher is to fulfil his role competently, but frequently role-commitments are in opposition to career ambitions. The teacher may feel an inducement to make a good impression on the 'right people'. But who are the 'right people'? It is arguable that for the best teacher they should be the pupils. Male teachers are likely to suffer more from role-conflicts than females do, since women teachers are financially less career-orientated and may not be so deeply involved in the purpose and organisation of the school.

E. Hoyle (*The Role of The Teacher*) considers that the teacher has three main roles in modern society.

1 *Instruction* – since the 1944 Education Act, instruction accords with criteria of the age, ability and aptitude (the 3 As).

2 *Socialisation* – values are not so much 'taught' but 'caught' by teacher-pupil interaction.

3 *Evaluation* – the teacher acts as a 'judge': because of his judgements, self-fulfilling prophecies come into play: the bright become brighter and the dull become duller.

The teacher's role has a value-context: traditionally, in the USA, teaching has placed high value upon equality and achievement (contest mobility), while in the UK teaching has been determined by middle-class elitism (sponsored mobility). Educational achievement can itself create conflict, because the achievement of some may lead to the lack of achievement of others with subsequent inequality. Comprehensive education in Britain since the 1960s has tended to move the organisation of the secondary school from ascriptive elitism to achievement egalitarianism, but some teachers' attitudes have hindered this social change; teachers generally retain middle-class values and this is especially applicable to ex-grammar school teachers inadequately dealing with less-able children in comprehensive schools. The 1944 Education Act offered equality of opportunity (see section 4.3) in theory, but in practice the three different types of secondary school (modern, technical and grammar) merely re-inforced the class structure and the educational ladder was replaced by a greasy pole. In an industrial society, the teacher's role should be seen in both social and academic terms. A school's organisation must be judged by the extent to which it fosters equality and academic excellence. Some would question whether it is possible to increase equality and excellence at the same time. Comprehensives have brought problems: the social mix of pupils makes for heterogeneity, but this poses the teacher with new complexities in the organisation of instruction and in the motivation of those who have been culturally deprived.

Within the classroom the teacher enjoys a high degree of autonomy over what he teaches and how he shall teach it. A classroom teacher is called upon to perform a number of sub-roles (see Table 4.2). The emphasis must be on role flexibility.

Table 4.2 Some sub-roles of a teacher in the classroom

---

1 *Parent-surrogate* – an object of affection for younger children.

2 *Society's representative* – guardian of moral values and arbiter of behavioural goals.

3 *Resource supplier* – qualified possessor of knowledge.

4 *Judge* – selects, rewards and punishes.

5 *Mediator* – a detective and referee.

6 *Object of identification* – children imitate traits and take the role of others (see Topic 1.2).

7 *Target for hostilities* – pupils must have a release for conflicts.

8 *Helper* – friend, confidante, limiter of anxiety, and ego-supporter.

Neville Bennett (*Teaching Styles and Pupil Progress*) researched the effects of different approaches to teaching upon pupils in primary schools. When his work was first published in 1976, it was considered to be of great educational significance because Bennett discovered, contrary to general expectation, that formal teaching styles produced better results in English and mathematics than did informal methods. Consequently it was argued that progressive schools were less efficient than traditional schools. Bennett's work was followed by condemnation of open-plan primary school methods so enthusiastically endorsed by the Plowden Committee. Similar conclusions were reached by B. Friedlander (*American Educational Research Journal*, Vol. 12, No. 4, 1975) who argued that it was a gross oversight of available knowledge to assume that a looser structure in the environment of the classroom is of benefit to all children. After re-working his earlier research results, in 1981, Bennett revised some of the most important conclusions of his earlier work (*British Journal of Educational Psychology*, June 1981). He found that the data failed to confirm differences between formal and informal teaching. Several teachers had been reassigned between formal, informal and mixed teaching environments, and the differences were not statistically significant. The differences between teachers in each category could be 20 points or more, whereas differences between the groups were no more than three points.

> Professor Bennett said this indicated the lack of importance of formal and informal as descriptions of teachers' styles. There were more important differences between good teachers and the not so good.
> (Reported in the *Times Educational Supplement*, 10 April 1981)

This leads us to beware of being seduced by old and new wives' tales. Myth and reality are frequently not clearly differentiated. It is common-sensical (ethnomethodological!) and predictable that children with a low toleration for ambiguity find open-plan teaching threatening and insecure; such children need the environment to be defined for them in certain, clear-cut terms. There has been too much innovation in education without adequate research – too many fads and hunches. Children respond differently to different forms of school and classroom organisation.

● *The curriculum*

In 1981 the Department of Education and Science published *The School Curriculum*. This document did not include earlier suggestions made by the Government that schools should be organised so that a required amount of time should be spent on English, mathematics, science and a foreign language. Instead, the DES's advice simply asked schools to stop pupils dropping vital subjects at the end of the third year of secondary schooling. *The School Curriculum* stated that schools should offer a broad and largely common curriculum up to the age of sixteen. Earlier suggestions, in *The Framework for the School Curriculum*, that not less than 10 per cent of the timetable should be devoted to English, mathematics and science, were dropped. Schools retain their autonomy in settling details of the curriculum though they are expected to take into account national needs and the expectations of others such as LEAs, school governors, parents, and prospective employers. Although schools decide the details of what every child should learn, the government has a duty to see that all schools provide an adequate grounding in literacy, numeracy and other essential skills required in a technological society. Local authorities are also expected to have curriculum policies to ensure that schools are so organised to provide sufficient content and quality of education for their pupils. The background to *The School Curriculum* report is shown in Table 4.3.

Table 4.3 Steps towards curriculum reform

1 October 1976: Labour Prime Minister James Callaghan makes Ruskin College speech to launch Great Debate on the curriculum.

2 November 1977: government asks local authorities for their curriculum policies.

3 November 1979: report on local curriculum policies says government will seek a consensus for a national curriculum framework.

4 February 1980: government's *Framework for the Curriculum* proposes minimum times for maths, English, science and languages.

5 March 1981: in *The School Curriculum*, minimum periods are dropped, but schools are given guidance on a broad curriculum and asked to stop pupils dropping vital subjects.

6 April 1981: the Schools Council publishes *The Practical Curriculum* giving its own suggestions for curriculum review.

The School Curriculum argues that:

The school curriculum needs to be rooted in educational aims which are accepted within and outside the education service.

School organisation should aim to satisfy the following 'widely accepted' educational aims.
1 to help pupils to develop lively, inquiring minds, the ability to question and argue rationally and to apply themselves to tasks and physical skills;
2 to help pupils to acquire knowledge and skills relevant to adult life and employment in a fast-changing world;

3 to help pupils to use language and numbers effectively;
4 to instil respect for religious and moral values and tolerance of other races, religions and ways of life;
5 to help pupils to understand the world in which they live, and the interdependence of individuals, groups and nations;
6 to help pupils to appreciate human achievements and aspirations.

What is taught and the way it is taught must reflect fundamental values in our society.

Three issues are highlighted:
1 the multicultural society and the diverse range of personal values;
2 the more flexible and self-reliant workforce demanded by new technology;
3 the equal treatment of men and women.

Moral education, health education, sex education and preparation for parenthood and family life were also essential constituents of the broad curriculum.

The School Council's working paper on *The Practical Curriculum* suggested six central issues in working out the curriculum.
1 To find a rationale for each school and for the country as a whole.
2 To identify the irreducible minimum to which every pupil should have a right of access.
3 To decide what mix of subject disciplines and kinds of experience a school should provide.
4 To take account of the implications of having externally examined outcomes for most pupils.
5 To negotiate a match between the desired curriculum and the staff, accommodation, equipment and materials available.
6 To think out ways of discovering whether the planned curriculum achieves what is hoped of it.

The Practical Curriculum is likely to be useful to schools seeking guidance on realistic ways of reforming their curriculum. It identifies fourteen aims for primary schools including getting pupils to read fluently, write legibly, speak clearly, master basic scientific ideas and apply computational skills with speed and accuracy. A common curriculum is suggested for 14 and 15 year-olds (see Table 4.4).

The most important sociological contribution to a discussion of the curriculum has been provided by Basil Bernstein ('On the Classification and Framing of Educational Knowledge', in Young, M.F.D., ed., *Knowledge and Control*). School life is organised into periods of varying time during which certain 'content' is taught. Bernstein examines the content taught according to two criteria.
1 The relationships between contents in terms of the amount of time

Table 4.4 The Schools Council version of the fourth- and fifth-year curriculum

Time (%)	Subject
20	Science
20	Two from: art, craft, design technology, home economics, second language or third science
10	Politics, economics, RE, music and careers
10	Physical education, games or outdoor education
10	History or geography or social science
10	Maths
10	Foreign language
10	English

(*The Times Educational Supplement*, 10 April 1981)

accorded to a given content: more time is devoted to some contents at the expense of others.

2 Some of the contents may, from the point of view of the pupils, be compulsory or optional.

It is important to consider whether the boundary between one content and another is clear-cut or blurred at the edges. If the various contents are well-insulated from each other, then Bernstein refers to the contents as standing in a closed relationship; if there is reduced insulation then the contents stand in an open relationship. The term classification is used to refer to relationships between the contents and the degree of boundary maintenance between contents. Classification focuses attention upon boundary strength between content (or school subjects) as the critical distinguishing feature of educational knowledge and gives the basic structure of the curriculum. Bernstein uses the concept of 'frame' to determine the structure of the message system or pedagogy, i.e. the valid transmission of knowledge. Frame thus refers to the pedagogical relationship between teacher and taught: the degree of control which teacher and pupil possess over the selection, organisation and pacing of the knowledge transmitted and received. The strength of classification and frames may vary independently of each other. For example, in the case of programmed learning, there may be weak classification (with blurred boundaries between educational boundaries) and strong framing (with little control by the pupil over what is learned). Bernstein uses the distinction between collection and integrated curricula to formulate a typography of educational codes.

Any organisation of educational knowledge which involves strong classification gives rise to what is here called a collection code. Any organisation of educational knowledge which involves a marked attempt to reduce the strength of classification is here called an integrated code. Collection codes may give rise to a series of sub-types, each varying in the relative strength of their classification and frames. Integrated codes can also vary in terms of the strength of frames, as these refer to the teacher/pupil/student control over the knowledge that is transmitted.

(Bernstein, B. *Classification and Framing of Educational Knowledge*)

Collection codes develop subject loyalty to a greater extent than do integrated codes. With specialisation of knowledge, teachers transmit a loyalty to their subject and inculcate pupils to become increasingly different from those who do not specialise in their subject. This is why, in large comprehensives, Heads of Department often express a keen desire to teach their discipline to younger pupils. Specialisation reveals differences from rather than communality with, and creates clear-cut educational identities. In England, there is a traditional dislike of mixed categories and blurred identities. Specialisation is the rule and may be considered in the light of pure and impure varieties (see Fig. 4.1). The pure variety exists where pupils opt for closely-related subjects such as pure mathematics, applied mathematics and physics, whereas the impure variety exists where school subjects are drawn from less-related disciplines such as sociology, physics and geography. In England, it is customary for pupils to be socialised in subjects with clear-cut boundaries and mixed categories; subjects such as bio-chemistry and social studies are only allowed to

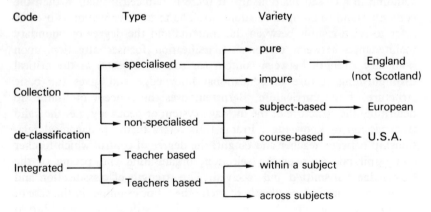

Fig. 4.1 Bernstein's typology of collection and integrated educational codes
(Bernstein, B. *Classification and Framing of Educational Knowledge*)

develop after a long period of traditional subject loyalty. Comprehensive schools have provided the stimulus for much curriculum reform. The traditional model of the curriculum based on separate subjects was the principal inhibitor of curriculum development until the 1960s. In recent years there has been more dialogue between teachers across the curriculum. Timetables have been derived, with integrated courses underpinning the work of subject departments.

New subject loyalties can only evolve if old subject loyalties are weakened. If a student has a degree in economics and wishes to read for a post-graduate diploma in sociology he has to enter into social relationships with sociologists and learn to think like a sociologist rather than like an economist. He has to be re-socialised into accepting a new subject loyalty. An attempt to change or weaken classification strength may well be considered to be a threat to one's previous identity; this idea of the pollution of already acquired knowledge is a source of resistance to change in educational codes.

Although collection codes are largely accepted in European countries, integrated codes are becoming more established in England. In the most extreme form, classification is weak because teachers and pupils have more control over the teaching/learning process. Evidence for the evolution of integrated codes is found in progressive theme-teaching in primary

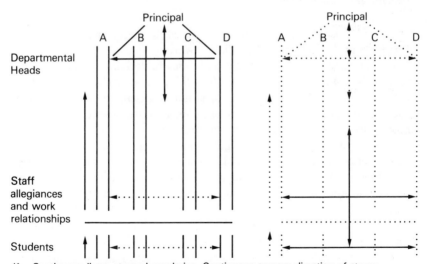

Key Continuous lines: strong boundaries. Continuous arrows: direction of strong relationships. Dotted lines: weak boundaries. Dotted line arrows: direction of weak relationships.

Fig. 4.2 Ideal typical organisational structures
(Bernstein, B. *Classification and Framing of Educational Knowledge*)

schools, in Nuffield science courses and in many inter-disciplinary CSE mode 3 syllabuses.

Knowledge is still largely organised through a series of well-insulated subject hierarchies. The school thus tends to be run as an oligarchy through meetings of the senior staff and the Academic Board made up mainly of Heads of Department. Senior staff have strong horizontal work relationships (i.e. peers in other subject hierarchies) and strong vertical work relationships within their own department. Junior staff are likely to have vertical rather than horizontal allegiances because they are subject to strong subject loyalties and compete with other departments for resources (see Fig. 4.2).

> Thus the collection code within the framework of oligarchic control creates for senior staff strong horizontal and vertical based relationships, whereas the work relationships of junior staff are likely to be vertical and the horizontal relationships limited to non-work based contacts. This is a type of organisational system which encourages gossip, intrigue and a conspiracy theory of the workings of the organisation for both the administration and the acts of teaching are invisible to the majority of staff.
>
> (Bernstein, B. *Classification and Framing of Educational Knowledge*)

• *The hidden curriculum*

Since the 1970s, sociologists have emphasised the importance of the *hidden curriculum* as distinct from the official, overt curriculum to which official curriculum documents refer. The basic idea underlying the hidden curriculum is that pupils learn many other things apart from what is taught to them about school subjects. So it is not sufficient, in the curriculum research, to concentrate upon specialisation versus non-specialisation, the importance of minority subjects, the proportion of time that should be spent on manual work as distinct from mental work, or whether a subject-based system is preferable to a course-based system of inter-disciplinary studies. Phenomenologists in particular have tended to separate public knowledge from hidden messages which are transmitted to pupils.

Jackson (*Life in School Classrooms*) first introduced the concept of the hidden curriculum. The hidden curriculum is less concerned with academic knowledge, and more concerned with teaching pupils to respect authority, maintain the status quo and acquiesce in an acceptance of existing social hierarchies. None of these things are ever admitted to be among the principal aims of schooling. The official objectives of the educational system are the selection, classification, distribution, transmission and evaluation of knowledge. It may be argued that unofficially society is most concerned with the distribution of power and with principles of social control.

> When considering the generation of pupils' identities, for example, the pupils' opportunity structure for acquiring any particular identity relates not merely to the teacher's working conceptual categories in her or his consciousness, but also to facets of the structure of classroom organisation which has to be understood in relationship to a range of extra-classroom as well as intra-classroom pressures which may be or may not be appreciated by the teacher or the pupils.
>
> (Sharp, R. and Green, A. *Education and Social Control*)

Pupils are influenced by the rules, regulations and rituals of the classroom. We saw in our study of the interactionist perspective in education (Section 4.1) that there is an unwritten body of shared understandings which makes for pseudo-concord in the classroom. Pupils have to learn what is expected of them if they are to succeed rather than merely survive. Nell Keddie ('Classroom Knowledge', in Young, M.F.D., ed., *Knowledge and Control*) found that 'A' stream pupils were more in tune with the teachers and less likely to have to attempt to bargain and negotiate. Middle-class conforming pupils frequently share the ideology of the teacher who is out of touch with the less able children. A lack of communication develops, relating to what he is trying to teach. Geoffrey Esland ('Teaching and Learning as the Organisation of Knowledge' in Young, M.F.D., ed., *Knowledge and Control*) believes that some teachers view children as deficit systems; the teachers become preoccupied in getting what they consider to be the right answer in what they consider to be the right way. There is not a one-dimensional or uniform quality of knowledge but rather a composite of different kinds of knowledge. Included in the broad knowledge required in the classroom is what is acceptable or unacceptable conduct from the teacher's point of view. Pupils are punished for asking what the teacher regards as stupid and irrelevant questions. Implicit demands are found in every classroom and it is up to the pupil to find out what they are and to comply with them. The ethical code is decided by authority and he must be subservient to it. So a pupil is compelled to learn to lie, evade and devise covert strategies which he takes with him to the world outside the classroom and retains for the rest of his life.

The hidden curriculum of the classroom is embedded in the organisation of the school. The formal structure is based upon pupils accepting the power of superiors and the hierarchy of authority. Even members of staff are subjected to social control because they are all dependent upon teachers with higher status, especially the headmaster. The teacher on a Grade 1 post hopes for promotion to a Grade 2: the deputy head has to comply if he is to be rewarded by a headship. The entire organisation of schooling depends upon an elaborate system of selection, sorting and sifting. Throughout his entire school life a pupil is involved in ranking, rewarding and competitive acts which symbolise the social order outside the school.

The hidden curriculum is not related to educational achievement or equal opportunity. It involves consequences of schooling which are not made explicit but nevertheless may be more important than what appears to be the purpose of the official curriculum. R. Sharp and A. Green (*Education and Social Control*) have emphasised the social-control function of education. They attempted to study and demonstrate some of the less subtle ways in which wider social structural forces impinge upon the social processes of the school. Even the child-centred radical teacher with well-intentioned motives may produce effects corresponding to the hierarchical differentiation of pupils as produced by formal methods. We have already seen in our consideration of the re-assessment of Neville Bennett's researches that there are dangers in trying to differentiate between formal and informal teaching methods. Sharp and Green suggest that the radicalism of progressive teachers may be a modern form of conservatism and therefore an effective form of social control. The hidden curriculum is successfully hidden even to the teacher himself; but nevertheless there is no doubt that it effectively inculcates the values, beliefs and attitudes which society wishes to be maintained.

Pierre Bourdieu ('Systems of Education and Systems of Thought', in Hopper, E. ed., *Readings in The Theory of Educational Systems*) has questioned whether patterns of thought and language transmitted by the school fulfil the function of the unconscious patterns which govern the thinking of people belonging to traditional societies, or do they operate only at the most superficial level of consciousness? He argues that the culture that comes from schooling provides individuals with a common body of thought. Those trained in a certain way have the same mentality and homogeneity which facilitates communication and communion between them. As the school is the principal transmitter of culture, it is the fundamental factor in the cultural consensus. Individuals owe to their schooling a whole collection of common things. It is these common things which link a thinker to his period of time and links a person to his social class within his own time. The sharing of a common culture which is transmitted by the school is one of the surest foundations of the deep underlying fellow-feeling that unites elite members of the governing class. All nations are conditioned by their educational systems and the organisations of their schools: there is no escape from it.

Dennis Smith ('Power, Ideology, and the Transmission of Knowledge', in Hopper, E., ed., *Readings in The Theory of Educational Systems*) considers the educational system in terms of the process of knowledge and transmission. Three characteristics may be located:

1 The power structure
2 The process of educational transmission
3 The structure of meaning embodied in the transmission process and attempts to impose specific patterns upon it.

The educational power structure involves the agencies which control the transmission process and the social groups which exercise control over the structure. The transmission of educational knowledge is concerned with norms and values embodied in the institutional arrangements which may be identified in streaming and other curricula organisation. The prestige accorded to institutions, teachers and pupils is also vitally important. When all educational institutions within a particular educational system are considered there are many overlaps and inconsistencies. Changes in the curriculum can often be best explained by studying competing power groups. There is an uncharted maze between those public statements of policy which relate especially to the curriculum and the implementation of policies. It has been contended that, as Secretary for Education and Science, Mrs Margaret Thatcher initiated nursery school policies which proved abortive in the long run, mainly to shelve the advance of comprehensive education in the short run. Within an educational system, different initiatives may be introduced at different times depending upon the dominant power factor. We have seen how the Mechanics Institutes were used in nineteenth-century England in an attempt to gear educational instruction towards objective sciences and consequently away from more controversial studies such as politics and economics. P.W. Musgrave (*A Model for the Analysis of the English Educational System from 1860*) has argued that struggles among groups competing for control over the educational system are punctuated by periods of bargaining ending in 'truce' situations. Consensus is reached on some goals: by the 1870 Act, England was provided with universal education at an elementary level; by the 1902 Act education was extended to the secondary level; by the 1944 Act the tripartite system of modern technical and grammar schooling was established. Dennis Smith argues that rather than 'truces', only when there is a great disparity of power is it possible to make a great leap forward.

The sequence of change assumed by Musgrave to be typical bears little relation to the actual pattern of educational development. The 'truce situations' of 1870, 1902 and 1944 within the English system were in fact stages in the progressive accretion of power to statutory authorities, increasing their importance both relative to other agencies and in terms of the sphere of education over which they exercised control. Such 'truces' were a consequence of overwhelming disparities in power, not of some happy meeting of minds.

(Smith, D. 'Power, Ideology, and the Transmission of Knowledge', in Hopper, E., ed., *Readings in The Theory of Educational Systems*)

4.3 Equality of educational opportunity

● *Definitions of the concept*

The concept of equality of educational opportunity may be defined in at least three different ways (see Table 4.5).

Table 4.5 Definitions and applications of educational opportunity

Definition	Practical application
1 Those of similar ability should have equal educational opportunities.	1944 Education Act established three types of secondary schools (tripartite system) for children of different abilities or capacities. 'To treat all children of the same measured ability in the same way, irrespective of social class or other environmental factors.'
2 Each individual should have an equal share of educational resources irrespective of potential ability.	Comprehensive schools have been established in Britain since the 1960s.
3 There should be positive discrimination in favour of the disadvantaged.	Compensatory education was organised for children in Educational Priority Areas following the recommendations of the Plowden Report in 1965.

In the USA, the concept of equal educational opportunity has been based on *four* principles:
(a) *free* education
(b) a *common* curriculum
(c) children from different backgrounds should attend the *same school*
(d) equality should be provided within a *given locality*.

> There is disagreement, however, as to the priorities even within the generally declared aim of equal opportunity and, thus, disagreement regarding the best way of achieving this aim.
> (Evetts, J. *The Sociology of Educational Ideas*)

It has even been suggested that equality of educational opportunity is not a meaningful term because complete equality is impossible to achieve. It would be more realistic for society to aim at a *reduction in inequality*. Nevertheless, the Hadow Report (1926) accepted the desirability of equality of opportunity, while the Spens Report (1938) and the Norwood Report (1941) contended that equality of opportunity could only be advanced through the reorganisation of education after the age of eleven.

The attempt to provide equal opportunities was the basic reason for the transition from the tripartite system of secondary education to a comprehensive system in Britain. The deficiencies of the 11-plus examination, combined with failure to establish parity of esteem between different types of secondary schools, have, to some extent, been mitigated by comprehensive schooling, but equality of opportunity still remains a very distant, if not mythical, goal. Factors which work against greater equality of educational opportunity are indicated in Table 4.6.

- *Limitations on equality of educational opportunity*

Table 4.6 Limitations on equality of educational opportunity

---

1 Variations exist in class sizes, facilities, teaching methods and criteria for selection.

2 Streaming and banding of pupils is still practised and this helps to maintain the traditional class bias of educational selection. (Holly, D.N. *Profiting from a Comprehensive School – Class, Age and Ability*, BJS, 1965)

3 There is no common curriculum, but rather a diversifying of the curriculum.

4 The New Sixth is mainly comprised of selective middle-class pupils who have greater opportunities of progressing to higher education than do working-class pupils.

   Students accepted by universities through UCCA in 1977 from the professional classes amounted to 36 per cent of the total compared with 35 per cent in 1976 and 34 per cent in 1974. By contrast children of blue-collar workers dropped from being 26 per cent of the total in 1974 to 24 per cent in 1977. . . .

   GCE A level results running from three As down to ABB were gained by 18 per cent of students from professional homes compared with only 11.6 per cent among children of blue-collar workers.

   (Statistical supplement to the Fifteenth Report, 1976–77, UCCA)

5 Fee-paying schools which still exist for a privileged minority reflect an elitist class system in accordance with R.H. Turner's model of sponsored mobility.

6 The access to a particular school by children in a limited catchment area means there is little social mix and leads to middle-class or working-class comprehensives. Julienne Ford's study of a London comprehensive (Ford, J. *Social Class and the Comprehensive School*) revealed that pupils' friendship patterns were determined by their social class.

Apart from the educational system, sociologists believe that there are two other basic aspects influencing equality of opportunity: these are genetic factors and social environmental factors such as family size, housing conditions and parental encouragement. Different educational starting points reduce inequalities of opportunity. There can never be anything approaching equality in an unequal society. Halsey has argued that liberal policies failed because:

> the major determinants of educational attainment were not schoolmasters but social situations, not curriculum but motivation, not formal access to the school but support in the family and the community.
> (Halsey, A.H. *Educational Priority*, HMSO)

Sociologists such as Brian Jackson and Dennis Marsden (*Education and the Working Class*), J.W.B. Douglas (*The Home and The School*) and Basil Bernstein have documented numerous instances of the ways in which social background restricts educational opportunities. The disadvantages include:

1 Great inequalities in the *distribution of wealth and income* as revealed by the reports of the Royal Commission on the Distribution of Income and Wealth, 1975 and 1976. (See Section 2.4.)

2 The cumulative restraint of poverty. (See W.G. Runciman's *Relative Deprivation and Social Justice*.)

3 Different standards of housing. J.W.B. Douglas (*The Home and The School*) conducted numerous tests in order to measure the influence of housing on educational ability and concluded that:

> When housing conditions are unsatisfactory, children make relatively low scores in the tests.

4 The pervasiveness of *sponsored mobility* ensures a controlled selection process by which the elite, or their agents, are deemed to be best qualified to judge merit.

5 Lack of encouragement given to girls compared with boys. The findings of J.W.B. Douglas remain largely true:

> The parents are rather less concerned about the progress of their daughters than of their sons.

6 The majority of teachers have middle-class backgrounds and are attempting to impose an alien culture on working-class pupils.

> A wedge is progressively driven between the child as a member of a family and community, and the child as a member of the school. Either way the child is expected, and his parents as well, to drop their social identity, their way of life and its symbolic representations, at the school gates.
> (Bernstein B. 'Education Cannot Compensate for Society', *New Society*, 26 February, 1970)

Schools may even have a negative effect upon the equality of educational opportunity. James Coleman's studies of educational attainment of whites and Negroes in the north and south of the United States indicated that contrary to offsetting cultural deficiencies, schools may be instrumental in causing children to move away from each other educationally. Compare the diverging curves representing the scores of urban whites with those of Negroes of the rural south in Fig. 4.3.

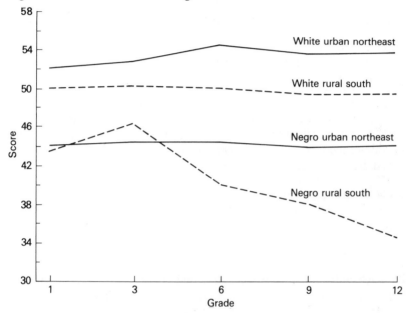

Fig. 4.3 Patterns of achievement in verbal skills at various grade levels by race and region
(Coleman, J.S. *et al.*, *Equality of Opportunity*)

● *Progress towards less inequality*

Although sociological research reveals continuing inequalities, the changes listed below indicate that progress has been made.
1 Active Parents'-Teachers' Associations have led to more parental co-operation and involvement in education. The US Headstart programme and the British EPAs proved that schools were unable to offer equal opportunities without bringing in parents as partners.

The Taylor Committee's Report, in 1978, recommended that parents should have equal participation on the governing bodies of schools. The move towards greater equality of educational opportunity is advanced as the school becomes more of a sharing and caring community.

These publics – parents, students, teachers and administrators – for our purposes make up 'the community', that is, the school community.

> (Fantini, M.D. in Raynor, J. and Harden, J., eds, *Cities, Communities and the Young*)

2 A greater diversity of opportunities are provided to enable a young person to reach the full poténtial of which he or she is individually capable. A more realistic spirit prevails with fewer people believing in the possibility of attaining complete equality of opportunity.

> One hundred years after the first great Elementary Education Act the Englishman still does not believe in equality. What he wants is equal opportunity to be unequal.
>
> (Pedley, R. *The Comprehensive School*)

3 Mixed-ability teaching (instead of streaming) allows children to be grouped by criteria other than mere ability: for instance by friendship, neighbourhood or common-interest patterns. Mixed ability groups present difficulties but,

> The general consensus appears to be that gains made, particularly in pupil-teacher relations and social development generally, as well as in the encouragement of independent learning, far outweigh the difficulties....
>
> (Benn, C. and Simon, B. *Half-Way There*, Report on British Comprehensive-school reform)

Evidence of the move away from streaming, in recent years, is provided by Benn and Simon and by the NFER research outlined in *A Critical Appraisal of Comprehensive Education*, 1972.

4 Compulsory schooling until the age of sixteen combined with the acceptance of the CSE examination, especially when combined with Mode 3 syllabuses, results in more children leaving school with some educational qualifications.

4.4 Community and compensatory education

● *Community education*

Although there are a variety of connotations to the term 'community education', the two most usual meanings are:

1 the involvement of the community or the neighbourhood in the activities of schooling;

2 the development of a community spirit within an educational institution. J. Raynor and J. Harden ('Communities: concepts and actions', in

Cities, Communities and the Young, Readings in Urban Education, Vol. 1) draw a further distinction with the term community used in different, though related, ways:

1 a 'residence community' in the sense of a defined geographical area;
2 a 'moral community' in the sense of belonging to a group with shared values or beliefs.

Neighbourhood schools can be classified in the first category, whereas public schools might well be classified in the second.

Gary Easthope (*Community, Hierarchy and Open Education*) believes that the origins of the educational concept of community lie in the public schools of the nineteenth century. The public schools developed a hierarchical community where social order took primacy over the individual. The individual's importance lay in his potential to serve the school while he was in it; when he was outside the school he existed solely as a representative of the school. The ultimate sanction was expulsion of the individual from the community. Public schools had to persuade the middle class to send their sons to join their community.

> They therefore had to offer something to attract the parents. What they offered was the promise that if you sent your son to them they would turn him out as a young gentleman fit to act as a leader in society. This promise attracted both those who were themselves gentlemen and wished their sons to be confirmed in that status and also those who, although rich, were not accepted as gentlemen and wished their sons to acquire the social behaviour appropriate to their wealth. It is not suggested that the schools or rather the headteachers and governors, sat down and thought out the problem in this way but rather that the successful schools were those who found the formula to attract clients. That formula was the liberal curriculum.
>
> (Easthope, G. *Community, Hierarchy and Open Education*)

In the context of a neighbourhood, community education has a long history. One of the tragedies of the 1980s has been the closure of village schools which were at the heart of the community. In the inter-war years, Henry Morris inspired the village colleges of Cambridgeshire. Community education of a neighbourhood type offers many advantages to the community which it serves. Schools can become focal points of the local community. The Hewett School in Norwich provides an example of a community-minded school which acts as a centre for playgroups (in which pupils studying child-care are involved), a youth club, evening institute classes, local gym and swimming clubs and numerous humanities projects which serve elderly and handicapped people in the vicinity of the school. However, it is more difficult to inculcate a community educational spirit in an urban setting; indeed, Michael Hill considers that:

> the search for communities in an urban environment is likely to be a fruitless

one, though this is not to say that one will not find patterns of neighbourliness and patterns of interdependence of a complex kind.

(Hill, M. 'Community concepts and applications', in Raynor, J. and Harden, J., eds, *Cities, Communities and the Young*)

Attempts to organise a community (neighbourhood) school are likely to flounder in the face of the hard facts of modern urban life with its deep-rooted social and economic problems. A successful community school would have to cut across class lines, but in most areas social classes are separated residentially. Educationalists have talked glibly about securing a good social mix but the affluent middle class and the less privileged working class have different orientations to the neighbourhood. The middle classes are more free to choose a particular locality in which to live: some will prefer to remain cosmopolitans orientated to a wider social network outside their neighbourhood community while others may become deeply involved in the community of their choice. The working classes have less freedom of action and this especially applies to immigrants who are more likely to feel socially attached to other immigrants than to the neighbourhood as a whole. Even when individuals feel commitments to a particular community their loyalties are to a specific locality which is itself often a relatively small part of an extensive urban area. If a number of individuals were asked to draw maps of the communities to which they thought they belonged, it would be found that different individuals, although living nearby, would perceive of themselves as living in very different communities. Additional complications arise when generalisations about geographical localities are compared with the social networks with which people associate. These ambivalences make community education very difficult in urban areas. Urban schools are likely to be handicapped by a lack of common values and an absence of a sense of belonging to a community.

Nevertheless some successful community schools have been established in urban areas. The development of pupil-counselling in recent years has meant that teachers maintain closer links with pupils and parents. The Seebohm Committee's original plan of a unified social service department in each local authority, embracing all neighbourhood welfare provision, included the involvement of school social workers based in schools. Such developments raise problems relating to the vexed question of school boundaries. Schools tend to defend their boundaries against outsiders. The answer to the simple question 'To whom do the schools belong?' is 'The ratepayers'. But anybody involved in contemporary English education will know that most schools jealously guard their boundaries against too much intrusion by administrators, governors, parents, careers advisors, welfare officers and social workers.

Some teachers are orientated more towards their subject than towards the children. They feel that it is no part of a school's function to be concerned more than is absolutely necessary with the wider aspects of the children's development. It would seem to them unnecessary and irrelevant to employ a social worker within the school. Other teachers and local education authorities may feel that for a school to have a social worker immediately brands it, in the eyes of the public, as a 'problem school'. They may seek to avoid such an appointment, or alternatively to take steps to disguise the real purpose of the job by changing the title and the role of the worker in some way.

(Avery, P. and Adamson, R. 'Attaching Social Workers to Schools' in Craft, M., ed., *Linking Home and School*)

Cyril Poster's account of the Lawrence Weston school at Bristol indicates how it is possible to practise community education even in an area with few middle-class parents and where the initiative has to be taken by the school. Poster was appointed headmaster of Lawrence Weston in 1959, before the school was built. As there was no public library on the large housing estate in which the school was to be sited, Poster recommended that the proposed school library should be resited and enlarged with a view to serving the needs of both the school and the community. When the library was opened in 1962 it was used exclusively by the school during the mornings, but open to both pupils and public in the afternoon and evenings. The library was far better stocked than the average secondary school library and had the additional advantage of being staffed by a qualified librarian with two assistants.

There were some early misgivings that the presence of adults on the school premises would be a distraction to the pupils, or that adults might be disinclined to use a library that required them to mix with large numbers of young people. In practice, from the outset, a strong sense of communal use rapidly developed, and in many cases there is a 'family' approach to the library ... But perhaps the greatest gain is in continuity: the library continues to serve the school's pupils at weekends and during the holidays. School leavers continue as members of the library whose routine and facilities they have grown used to over the years; and, most important, many primary pupils already have a sense of community with the school through the library which makes transition at eleven very much easier.

(Poster, C. 'The Head and the Community School', in Allen, B., ed., *Headship in the '70s*)

After the success of the communal library, Lawrence Weston extended its community education into the realms of arts and crafts (where for three evenings a week parents supervised the activities), recreational activities and social services. In order to meet the demand for leadership in community education, an Activities Organiser was appointed who acted as vice-principal of the evening institute centred on the school, supervised all the school activities which took place during the evening sessions and taught in the school in order to gain a real identification with staff and pupils. His teaching commitments released members of staff to run voluntary evening sessions.

> The advantage of the system at Lawrence Weston is not only that it coordinates the expertise of the staff more effectively but that it actually extends the voluntary principle to include help from outsiders – parents in particular.
> (McGeeney, P. *Parents are Welcome*)

The real involvement of parents in community education should go deeper than most Parent-Teacher organisations. PTAs in England, are usually confined to social involvements and fund-raising; headmasters exercise a form of guided democracy which carefully excludes discussion of vital educational issues such as curriculum reform or teaching methods.

> Parent-teacher associations have usually been heavily oriented (in terms of key personnel, etc.) to the teachers, and their views, perspectives and plans. PTAs in the past have all too easily been the mere mouthpiece of the local 'teaching establishment'; they have been perceived as such by minority group members, and have done little to elicit genuine feedback from a representative cross-section of the parents. It is also notable that most PTAs have excluded the one group who can provide true experiental links between parents and teachers – the students themselves.
> (Morton, D.C. and Watson, D.R. in Raynor, J. and Harden, J., eds, *Equality and City Schools*)

In the USA, parents play a far more active part and often participate in the appointment of staff and the general running of the school. Mario D. Fantini (*Educational Leadership*) suggests that real community education necessitates parents playing a conflict role. It is argued that parents and students form the major participants in the school community. Fantini regards the individual parent as the key figure, as the parent has intrinsic ties with the student and his welfare. The individual student is also looked upon as a key figure both as a community resident and as a central figure in the education institution we call the school. The student is seen as a legitimate party in the government of his educational future with basic rights which must be protected. Fantini acknowledges that the teacher is also a central party in the school community but in order to develop a new concept of community education the professional should form a revitalised partnership with parents and students. It is worthwhile to give considera-tion to this reversal of the usual order in which schools view the community: instead of teachers, students and parents, Fantini would place (in order of centrality) parents, students and teachers. If such priorities were accepted PTAs would be organised on the parents' terms rather than upon the teachers'. It has been argued (by D.C. Morton and D.R. Watson) that parents could teach the teachers many things about their children and their experiences. This is especially recommended in the light of compensatory education where a teacher must do all he can to relate to working-class children who are so readily labelled culturally or linguistically deprived.

● *Compensatory education*

Compensatory education is intended to compensate children who are considered socially disadvantaged because of cultural and linguistic deprivation. Community education and compensatory education can be practised together, but community education need not include compensatory education, i.e. there may exist community or neighbourhood schools which are not especially concerned with compensating pupils for any deprivations, social or otherwise.

Compensatory education began in the USA with educational programmes, in the 1950s and 1960s, such as Project Headstart. These were pre-school programmes intended to enrich the education of less fortunate children. They started by focusing particularly on the child in the family and in the classroom, but later switched to research studies of schools in general. Many programmes were aimed at helping black children compensate for a poor start in life. Operation Headstart has been subjected to criticism by those who were only too pleased to accept Professor Jensen's contention that the intelligence of black children could not be boosted by pre-school programmes. However more recent studies by the American Department of Health, Education and Welfare have indicated that these early attempts at compensatory education may have important lasting effects. The researchers pooled the data from independent experiments and then collected follow-up material in 1976–7. They thus assembled records of the performance of 3 000 deprived children who were involved in educational programmes intended to help them compensate for their poor environment.

It was found that there were five important benefits of compensatory nursery education.
1 The children are less likely to be assigned later to remedial classes.
2 There are fewer drop-outs from schooling and fewer cases of pupils being held back to repeat a year's schooling because of poor performance.
3 Achievement in mathematics at the age of ten is significantly improved.
4 The children scored higher than average on tests, for up to three years after their compensatory education.
5 The children retain more achievement-orientation and their mothers develop higher vocational aspirations for them than they have for them-

Table 4.7 How many under-achieving students did better after Headstart?

Headstart project *good experimental design*	failure rate of project children	failure rate of control children	reduction in failure by attending project	total
	%	%	%	
Gordon	39.1	61.5	36.0	82
Gray	55.6	73.7	24.6	55
Palmer	24.1	44.7	46.1	221
Weikart	17.2	38.5	55.3	123
median	31.6	53.1	41.1	481
quasi-experimental design				
Beller	48.6	53.1	8.5	69
Levenstein	22.1	43.5	49.2	127
Miller	20.6	11.1	–	125
Zigler	26.6	32.3	17.6	144
overall median	25.4	44.1	36.4	920

NB   'Failure' is defined as being placed in special education classes, and/or retained in grade, and/or deprived out of school. 'Reduction' is % control minus % project, divided by % control. Children's data were collected in different grades. The design of the Miller project permits no 'reduction' conclusion. The numbers in the total are of project children plus control children.

(Halsey, A.H. 'Education Can Compensate', *New Society*, 24 January, 1980)

selves. The expectations and values of working-class parents have been significantly changed.

So there is a resurgence of optimism concerning compensatory education in the USA. In spite of Christopher Jencks' conclusion that 'ingenious manipulations of marginal institutions like schools' (Jencks, C. *Inequality*) could not compensate for poverty and that inequality could only be tackled through radical housing, employment and social policies, further Headstart programmes have been given the go-ahead in the USA. These programmes, in the 1980s, are aimed at a quarter of children below the poverty line and even escaped President Reagan's public expenditure cuts in 1981 when the Headstart's budgets were increased from $800m to $950m.

In England, the Plowden Committee (*Children and Their Primary*

Schools, 1967) reported in favour of establishing educational priority areas in certain 'poor' locations. Plowden found that many teachers were unwilling to work in neighbourhoods where the schools were old, where the housing of the sort they desired was unobtainable and where educational standards were lower than they expected for their own children. The Plowden Committee found many schools caught in such vicious circles: grim approaches and incessant traffic noise; antiquated buildings with cramped conditions; difficulties in finding good headteachers and with a rapid turnover of staff. The deprived areas experienced a migratory school population and many children left school at the first opportunity.

> We ask for 'positive discrimination' in favour of such schools and the children in them, going well beyond an attempt to equalise resources. Schools in deprived areas should be given priority in many respects. The first step must be to raise the schools with low standards to the national average; the second, quite deliberately to make them better. The justification is that the homes and neighbourhoods from which many of their children come provide little support and stimulus for learning. The schools must supply a compensating environment.
>
> (*Children and Their Primary Schools*, The Plowden Report, Vol. 1)

The criteria to use as yardsticks by which to measure deprivations which might be overcome by compensatory education are shown in Table 4.8.

Plowden recommended a national policy of positive discrimination in favour of schools where children were severely handicapped by home

Table 4.8 Plowden's suggested criteria for assessment of deprivation

---

1 *Occupation* of parents, e.g. children of unskilled and semi-skilled workers are more likely to require educational compensation.

2 *Size of families*, e.g. the larger the family the more likelihood of deprivation.

3 *Supplementary benefits*, e.g. needy parents receive help from the state in other ways which could be reinforced by extra-educational help.

4 *Overcrowding*, e.g. children suffer greater pressures from shared accommodation.

5 *Poor attendance and truancy*, e.g. children are often absent from school for inadequate reasons.

6 *Proportions of retarded, disturbed or handicapped children*, e.g. proportions are highest in schools in deprived districts.

7 *Incomplete families*, e.g. single-parent families.

8 *Children unable to speak English*, e.g. multi-racial schools.

conditions. It was intended that a start should be made with 2 per cent of the most severely deprived pupils, building up to 10 per cent over five years. Five areas were eventually chosen to be granted extra resources in terms of finance, accommodation and special allowances to attract and retain teachers. The areas were in Liverpool, Birmingham, West Riding, London and Oxford; the national director of the project was A.H. Halsey.

Halsey was particularly impressed by two things in the Plowden Report. One was the principle of positive discrimination and the other was the call for action-research. Positive discrimination entailed raising schools with low standards to the national average and then deliberately attempting to make them better; it was anticipated that if deprived children were given the advantage of above-average schools then this would compensate, in some measure, for their inadequate social background. The action-research has four main aims:

1 to raise educational standards
2 to lift teacher morale
3 to solder home and school links
4 to assist in giving communities a sense of responsibility.

Unfortunately both positive discrimination and action-research raised serious operational problems.

Eric Midwinter, who was Director of the Liverpool EPA project, has highlighted some of these problems (Midwinter, E. *Priority Education*). It was found that the school, where children spend only five hours per day was comparatively powerless, on its own, to compensate adequately for home circumstances, social class and neighbourhood factors. Even allowing for positive discrimination there was never any real chance of equality of opportunity. Midwinter uses an analogy of a race which is unfair because some of the competitors are nobbled from the start. He also found that the action-research programme brought problems because of the conflict between the men of action who resented the inhibiting attentions of researchers, and the researchers who were driven neurotic by the wild ventures of the actionists. There were those, like one Senior Education Officer, who considered the only research necessary was 'to look out of the bloody window', while the academics believed that no one would take any notice of the work of the projects unless they were based upon sound experimental research. Even if practical attempts at compensatory education proved to be successful, children who gained from the extra help might be tempted to leave the area and seek advancements elsewhere. Thus deprived areas could become more deprived and priority areas need more priority. It was found necessary for compensatory education to be community education in the sense of aiming at the majority of children who would live out the remainder of their lives in that particular community.

In 1991 the population of Liverpool's inner ring will be 73 000 or so, the planners predict. Many of the children in our project schools will have children of their own at school by then. It is unlikely that the 73 000 will mainly be sales representatives, managers and even school teachers. It is more likely that many will fall into the nineteen-nineties equivalent of classes 4 and 5 on the Occupational Register. It is not quite *Alice in Wonderland*, where everyone won a prize. There are likely, even with greatly improved facilities in education as it stands, to be more losers than winners, for, in the last analysis, there is simply not room for everyone in the higher socio-economic grade. It struck us that, while obviously remembering the needs of local boys with the latent talent to make good, our preoccupation should be with the huge majority who will live forever in the deprived area.

(Midwinter, E. *Priority Education*)

A further problem of compensatory education is that it may well be counter-productive. Bernstein has argued that if children are labelled as deprived and inadequate, 'Teachers will have lower expectations of the children which the children will undoubtedly fulfil.' ('Education cannot compensate for society', *New Society*, 26 February 1970)

The labels do their own sad work. Bernstein argued that Plowden's concentration upon the child directs attention away from the internal organisation, and educational context of the school. 'Compensatory education' raises problems because it implies that something is lacking in the family and in the child. It ignores worthwhile elements in the working-class culture of the child.

One way to overcome the separation between the parents' culture and the school's culture is to draw the parents and the community into the life of the school. This is where 'compensatory education' and 'community education' complement each other. Bernstein's criticisms of 'compensatory education' are by no means completely borne out in practice. Based upon his EPA experiences in Liverpool, Midwinter describes the extension of social education including studies of the pupil's environment, the widening of the curriculum to make it approximate more closely to the pupil's own experiences, the attempts to improve home and school relations and the forging of useful links with industry. Some would want to argue that there is a danger, in such a scheme, of over-emphasising the educational significance of the neighbourhood area. The closer links forged between the pupils and their home community may reinforce desires to remain in a slum area, whereas the school might be better employed as an agency for the promotion of mobility as children moved away from an area of deprivation. A counter-argument is that if EPA youngsters become more community conscious and remain in EPA areas, the best brains will remain in the area rather than deserting it. On the other hand, if compensatory-cum-community education results in an increase in geographical mobility then the slum area might well become more disadvantaged than ever.

The 'compensatory education' initiated by Plowden, and based upon the principle of positive discrimination, wilted in England under a welter of financial cuts. But there is more than a grain of truth in Halsey's contention that the enthusiasm of the EPA venture has left 'a permanent mark on thought and opinion about the relation between education and upbringing and especially about the nature of the partnership between parents and teachers.' (Halsey, A.H. 'Whatever happened to positive discrimination?', *Times Educational Supplement*, 21 January 1977).

4.5 Educational achievement

- *What are the dimensions of educational achievement?*

Educational achievement refers to the standards of attainment reached by pupils in schools and students in colleges. Investigations conducted by sociologists and psychologists indicate that educational achievement is closely related to social factors such as social class, parental attitudes, neighbourhood environments, housing, family sizes and lifestyles (see Table 4.9).

We have seen from our study of community and compensatory education that, within limitations, progressive changes in social factors may improve levels of educational achievement. Social factors affect the educability of pupils and students because social differences result in significant differences in motivations, aspirations, language, attitudes and values. The achievement values of parents are likely to be internalised by

Table 4.9 Some social factors affecting educational achievement

1 *Social class and status* (occupations of parents)
2 *Family structure* (birth order and size of family)
3 *Social environment* (housing, poverty/affluence, and employment/unemployment)
4 *Parental attitudes* (child rearing – support for schooling, reading habits, and general aspirations)
5 *Language* (middle-class elaborate language code, or working-class restricted language code)
6 *Values* (esteem in which education is held, motivations toward short-term goals or long-term deferred gratification)

the child. Some sociologists have argued that even more important than social class, regarding high educational achievement, is the parental home which offers love, warmth, encouragement and praise. In this respect, fathers are less important than mothers: fathers may have a high mobility pessimism and pass on to the child disappointment at their own lack of success, while aggressive fathers may try to help with homework and consequently cause friction; mothers have more emotional contact with their children, tending to display affection and maternal care. Love-orientated families, who hold physical punishment in disfavour, have been found to produce more achieving children.

It is well-established that the middle class has a higher level of achievement than does the working class. The middle class work better, spend more time at educational institutions and are easier to control and guide towards high heights of educational achievements; they are likely to be more willing to shoulder responsibility, be keener participators in extra-curricular activities and they leave school with better qualifications which help them to go on to secure the best jobs and retain their middle-class orientation. The relationship between social class and educational achievement has been found to exist in the junior school (Douglas, J.W.B. *The Home and The School*), and in the secondary school (Douglas, J.W.B. *et al. All Our Future*).

The middle class have the advantages of higher grade occupations, preferential status, supportive homes and a greater esteem for education. In respect to educational achievement, it is more important where you come from than where you get to (Turner, R. *The Social Context of Ambition*) – the working-class achiever may move a few steps up the ladder, but as he starts lower down, he is still likely to trail behind his middle-class peers. The working class often do not expect their children to succeed and the working-class child may become more isolated from his fellows if he achieves more (Miller, G. *Educational Opportunity and The Home*). Children of skilled workers achieve more than children of manual workers; children of foremen are more inclined to mix with middle-class children while their parents have more hopes of upward social mobility for their offspring (Banks, O. and Finlayson, D. *Success and Failure in The Secondary School*).

For many years it was thought that middle-class children were more intelligent than working-class children. Sir Cyril Burt, the father of educational psychology, was convinced of the higher inherited intelligence of the middle class and his ideas were fundamental in influencing British education for half a century, from the late 1920s to his death in 1971. But in 1976 it was revealed by *The Sunday Times* that Burt had been accused of faking his research findings in order to support his preconceived notions. Some leading educational psychologists are now convinced that Burt published false data and invented crucial facts in order to support his theory that intelligence is largely inherited. The indictment of Burt has far-reaching implications, because Burt's findings helped to inspire the controversy over supposed race and intelligence correlations which have been propounded in Britain by Hans Eysenck and in America by Arthur Jensen, a former post-doctoral student of Eysenck. Burt has been charged on four main counts.

1 Burt frequently guessed at the IQs of parents whom he interviewed, but later used these guesses as if they were incontrovertible scientific data.

2 He miraculously produced identical answers accurate to three decimal places from different sets of data; this is a statistical impossibility and could only have been accomplished by working backwards to ensure that the observations fitted his answers.

3 He used this method of working backwards, by supplying data to fit predictions of his own genetic hypotheses.

4 Two of his collaborators, who are named as authors of research papers, probably never existed and Burt himself wrote the papers under fictitious names (*The Sunday Times*, October 24, 1976).

The accusation that Burt may have falsified his evidence was first revealed by Princeton's Leon J. Kamin who carefully scrutinised Burt's figures and contended that they varied significantly from one paper to the next. Kamin concluded that these frequent arithmetical consistencies and mutually contradictory descriptions cast serious doubts upon the entire body of Burt's later work. Dr Ann Clarke, and her husband Professor Alan Clarke of Hull University, also checked the inconsistencies of Burt's statistics and concluded that scientifically Burt's results were a fraud. Burt was so eminent during his lifetime that his work went unquestioned. We have dealt, at some length, with the charges that his work may have been scientifically fraudulent because his educational theories had such a profound and lasting effect upon education. Burt advised teachers that innate general intelligence, as measured by IQ tests, was the most important factor in determining educational achievement; he thus underrated the importance of social factors and caused teachers to do likewise. Burt's conclusions strongly influenced the 1944 Education Act by which three types of secondary schools (grammar, technical and modern) were provided for three different types of children. In theory it was possible for pupils to be switched between the different types of school, but such switches were rarely made in practice; in the light of Burt's ideas relating to genetic intelligence such changes in schooling seemed unnecessary. It was believed that an individual's IQ could be measured with a high degree of accuracy at the age of eleven and that subsequent changes would be insignificant. However, D.F. Swift ('Who Passes the 11+?', *New Society*, 5 March 1964) found that the lack of balance in IQ performance between middle- and working-class children was due to the fact that middle-class children were better able to score on intelligence and attainment tests. The fact that middle-class pupils performed better proved that they were better at doing the tests, but not that they were more intelligent overall. The tests tested the testers as much as they tested the children. The testers were of middle-class origin and designed tests at which middle-class children performed well. Elizabeth Fraser (*Home Environment and the School*) found that parental education and reading habits, income, occupation and living space all related significantly with IQ scores and subsequent educational achievement at school.

Burt's theories led him to regard the commonest cause of educational retardation as 'inborn inferiority of general intelligence' (incorporated in the Wood Report of 1929). These ideas played a leading part in confirming the policy of segregating the mentally sub-normal so that they could not reproduce. It is only in recent years that it has been accepted that sub-normal children are likely to achieve more if they are educated alongside normal children.

● *Educational achievement in the primary school*

We have already considered briefly (section 1.5) the longitudinal studies of children in primary schools, conducted by J.W.B. Douglas (*The Home and The School*). The key to differences in educational achievement was found to be home background. Although intelligence test scores were found to rise with social class level, children from good homes and schools improved their test performances between 8 and 11 years of age, while the scores of children from poorer homes were found to deteriorate. Parental interest in schooling and encouragement given to schoolwork were found to be crucial factors. For middle-class children, the primary school and family environment were found to reinforce each other positively, whereas for working-class children they worked in a negative direction. Douglas found that streaming affected educational achievement, but the abolition of the 11-plus, and the establishment of comprehensive schools, have made streaming somewhat less important. No longer are 'A' stream pupils coached to pass the 11-plus while the 'C' stream concentrates upon craftwork. In 1964, when Douglas published *The Home and The School*, children in the upper streams improved their scores as they passed through their primary schools, whereas the scores of those in the lower streams deteriorated. The fact that manual working-class children were found to deteriorate more when placed in the lower streams, illustrated the effect of the social organisation of the school upon educational achievement.

There are many reasons why children from good homes achieve better at school. Middle-class children are likely to have background books available, parents to take them on educational visits, a separate room in which to do their homework and the use of a telephone to chat with school friends about problems arising (see Table 4.10).

Douglas found that there was a clear correlation between standards of housing and awards of grammar school places at the conclusion of primary education (see Table 4.11). The mothers' aspirations for their children also played a part in 11-plus selection. In the light of grammar school places gained, middle-class children had a higher level of educational achievement.

The best primary schools are in prosperous residential areas. Children from all five social classes make higher achievement scores in these schools, but working-class children improve their scores less than middle-class children. This provides proof of neighbourhood and educational institutional influences upon educational achievement. Social class rather than intelligence determines one's fate from the earliest stages of education. Some reasons for a lack of educational achievement are given in Table 4.12.

In spite of the accusations of the Black Papers in Education, edited by C.B. Cox and Rhodes Boyson, there are a large number of statistics available indicating that on the whole educational standards are not falling. The Inner London Education Authority published figures in 1980 showing that the standard reached by London 11-year-olds has been rising steadily since 1974. Devon County Council has been testing eight-year olds' reading for five years and the results have shown a steady improvement year by year. The surveys of primary and secondary schools carried out since 1974 by Her Majesty's Inspectors of schools found no evidence of falling educational standards. On the contrary, there was no evidence that too little attention was paid to basic subjects (reading,

Table 4.10 Home circumstances of children by social class

| | Middle class | | Manual working class | |
	Upper %	Lower %	Upper %	Lower %
Satisfactory housing	85.7	61.9	38.1	27.7
Room for homework	59.4	36.6	30.5	19.2
Television	59.7	64.1	57.6	56.0
Telephone	71.4	38.1	7.6	3.2
Car	59.5	37.9	17.7	11.9

(Douglas, J.W.B. *The Home and The School*)

Table 4.11 Standard of housing by social class – award of grammar school places, comparison of observed and expected (percentages)

| Social class | Standard of housing | Grammar-school places | | | |
| | | Awarded | Measured ability at 11 | Expected from | |
				Teachers' assessment	Mothers' wishes
Middle:	Satisfactory	42.5	41.7	59.2	49.9
	Unsatisfactory	27.5	28.9	37.0	41.4
Manual working:	Satisfactory	19.0	18.0	29.0	33.0
	Unsatisfactory	11.4	11.9	17.3	21.5

(Douglas, J.W.B. *The Home and The School*)

Table 4.12 Educational reasons for lack of achievement

> 1 Teachers are mainly middle-class and tend to deprecate working-class traditions, values and culture.
>
> 2 Schools lack resources, especially in urban areas and twilight zones.
>
> 3 Children internalise the teachers' labels of 'disobedient' and 'disruptive' and react accordingly.
>
> 4 The content of the curriculum is limited in relation to so-called less able children.
>
> 5 School organisation is often selective with streaming, setting and banding.
>
> 6 The docility of children who find life easier if they act out the role of 'good' pupils in the light of the teacher's definition of the situation.

Table 4.13 Some recommendations of the Bullock Report

> 1 Close checks on reading standards
> 2 Improved methods of testing and recording
> 3 National centre for language in education
> 4 Detailed reading policy in every school
> 5 Screening to pick out backward readers
> 6 Extra help for slow readers
> 7 Local authority clinics to assist schools to teach reading
> 8 Parents' evenings to gain their cooperation in English teaching
> 9 Well-stocked libraries
> 10 Improved teacher-training to ensure that all teachers know how to teach the English language

writing and arithmetic) or that behaviour was a serious or worsening problem. School attendance figures have improved and pupil-teacher ratios have been favourably altered.

On the other side, the Bullock Report of 1975 stated that research evidence pointed to a decline in the standards of reading and writing among 7–11 year-olds in the previous ten years. The report contained 333 recommendations – and ten of the most important are given in Table 4.13.

● *Educational achievement in the secondary school*

Much of the sociological evidence relating to educational achievement in secondary schools was collected prior to the large-scale adoption of the comprehensive system. J.W.B. Douglas *et al.* (*All Our Future*) conducted a longitudinal study of secondary education and reported in 1968. They found that the effect on educational achievement of social class differences which we have so far considered at the primary stage have increased at the secondary stage and extended to pupils of high ability. Nearly half the lower manual working-class pupils of high ability left school before they were $16\frac{1}{2}$ years old. Early leaving and low job aspirations made it likely that as many as five per cent of the next generation of manual workers will be recruited from pupils, who in more favourable circumstances, might have qualified for the professions. Parental influences, family structure, school staffing and regional differences play a major part in differences in educational achievement at the secondary stage. Manual working-class pupils are least handicapped when they are in the best-staffed and best-equipped schools. The interest and encouragement that parents give to their children is closely linked with the parents' own educational history. Insecurity in a family, whether from father's absence, unemployment, illness or death is associated with poorer performance at school. It was found that children from large families make low scores in all attainment tests at all ages. The more young children there are in the family the lower the pupil's score in the eight-year old vocabulary test and it is significant that this early language deficiency is not made up at the secondary stage. Pupils from large families leave school earlier than expected at each level of measured ability. First-born boys in families of two or three score higher in attainment tests and are academically more successful than their younger brothers and sisters; this difference was not found for girls in the survey. 77 per cent of middle-class pupils obtained a good GCE certificate (at least three subjects covering three or more of the main academic fields, e.g. mathematics, science and English) compared with 37 per cent of lower manual working-class pupils. Among pupils of higher ability the proportion of the upper middle class achieving a good certificate was found to be twice that of the lower manual working class.

Very few manual working-class pupils who gain a GCE 'O' level certificate obtain a good one. In their aspirations for further education the manual working class fall considerably short of their teachers' hopes mainly because of the low ambitions of their parents. At fifteen years of age, the social class gap in attainment is at a maximum: the upper-class pupils clearly obtain the best achievement in mathematics and English, whereas the lower working-class score the worst results.

The Crowther Committee examined the education of boys and girls aged 15 to 18. The Report in 1959 revealed a similar story of high middle-class compared with working-class educational achievement (see Table 4.15). It was found that educability is determined by the subtle interaction of social influences of homes and schools. The social climate of the school, the social distance between pupil and teacher and the level of

Table 4.14 Proportions staying at school and gaining certificates related to ability and social class (percentage table)

Social class		60 and over	55–59	50–54	45–49	44 and less
		Ability at 15 years				
		% completing session 1961–62				
Middle	Upper	97	93	86	69	40
	Lower	94	79	59	36	17
Manual	Upper	90	67	35	22	6
	Lower	80	46	27	12	3
		% starting session 1962–63				
Middle	Upper	90	82	71	42	20
	Lower	78	52	37	20	8
Manual	Upper	67	43	20	10	3
	Lower	50	20	12	4	2
		% gaining good certificates				
Middle	Upper	77	33	11	4	–
	Lower	60	18	6	–	–
Manual	Upper	53	15	2	1	–
	Lower	37	9	3	–	–
		% gaining general certificates				
Middle	Upper	94	79	54	27	20
	Lower	87	59	38	13	1
Manual	Upper	86	45	17	5	–
	Lower	69	31	12	2	–

(Douglas, J.W.B. *et al. All Our Future*)

competitive tension, all help to explain why middle-class teenagers achieve better.

The Newsom Report, *Half Our Future*, 1963, provided evidence of the close correlation between the type of neighbourhood and educational

Table 4.15 Who achieves four 'O' level passes?

Father's occupation	Proportion of men in the top 10% of ability who had not achieved 4 'O' level passes in GCE %	Proportion of men in the middle range of ability who achieved 4 'O' levels %
Professional and managerial	5	20
Clerical	14	8
Skilled manual	23	6
Semi and un-skilled manual	34	3

Table 4.16 Mean scores in reading tests

School mean score	Sample		Special group schools in the slums
	All modern schools	Schools in problem areas	
25	2		
24	7		
23	22	3	1
22	38	7	1
21	28	3	3
20	27	6	1
19	14	4	5
18	3	2	4
17	5	4	2
16	1	1	
15			1
14			
13			1
Total Mean score per school	147 21.15	30 20.07	19 18.79
Standard deviation per school	1.72	2.05	2.37

(Newsom Report, *Half Our Future*)

achievement. The lowest scores in reading tests were from slum area children; those from problem areas had reading ages twelve months higher; those from mixed neighbourhoods, with a high proportion of owner-occupied dwellings, had the highest reading scores. (See Table 4.16.)

Even today, pupils in large urban areas tend to achieve less. A report from HMIs, in 1980, accused London comprehensives of expecting 'too little from their pupils at all levels'. The inspectors contended that during the vital examination years from 14 to 18, the teaching in two-thirds of London's classes was just not good enough. A quarter of London's children were leaving school without qualifications – more than any other authority expect Bradford. A similar picture would probably be revealed in the inner-city schools of other conurbations such as Manchester, Liverpool and Birmingham where examination passes are also well below the national average. London is an example of an urban area with great social problems: 14 per cent of its children are from one-parent families, nearly 30 per cent were born outside the UK and nearly three-quarters live in inferior rented accommodation. London's problems in the 1980s are a magnified form of those faced by every large urban authority.

The Robbins Report on Higher Education 1963 showed that the percentage of all ages with two or more 'A' level passes related to social background.

The percentages according to father's occupation were:

1 Professional and managerial   37%
2 Clerical   26%
3 Skilled manual   22%
4 Semi-skilled and unskilled   11%

Other significant factors affecting the educational achievement of school children and their entry to higher education included parents' educational level and attitudes, and the quality of primary and secondary education especially in relation to the size of classes and the qualifications of teachers. It was reiterated that many working-class children leave school without reaching their full potential.

It is impossible to make any accurate assessment of educational achievement in comprehensive schools as we stand too close to contemporary events and circumstances. Caroline Benn and Brian Simon recognised this fact when in 1970 they entitled their Report on British comprehensive school reform *Half Way There*. The same social class handicaps and inhibitions restrict the working class but there are some trends facilitating greater educational achievement of the less well-to-do. According to Benn and Simon these trends include:

1 a positive trend away from streaming;
2 the increased intake into the 'new sixth';

3 more working-class children going on to HE and FE, although 80 per cent still come from a middle-class background;

4 the acceptance of the CSE, and the use of Mode 3 type of examination whereby the teacher gears content and teaching methods to the children's abilities;

5 mixed-ability teaching, which theoretically contains an equal proportion of children of high, medium and low academic ability (the charge that the bright children are held back is largely discounted);

6 compulsory schooling until the age of sixteen (if the achievement of the working class is restricted, it could be argued that they need more education, rather than less);

7 more resources are spent on remedial education although they are still disproportionate;

8 the greater interest of parents in education, as evident by the increased number of PTAs, is likely to be more supportive to children and encourage them to achieve more.

In 1979, Lancaster University's educational research institute began processing data which will enable some comparisons to be made between comprehensive and grammar-school pupils. Preliminary analysis suggested that the most able ten per cent of the boys in comprehensives do better than the top ten per cent of boys in state grammar schools or direct grant and independent schools in terms of 'O' level passes. These results were based on a response of 73 per cent to a postal survey.

As grammar schools declined in numbers, the results of comprehensives inevitably improved. The curve for all maintained schools shows that the net effect of the changeover has not been dramatic (see Fig. 4.4). There has been an upward trend of young people leaving school with at least one 'A' level. Whether or not educational achievement would have been greater with or without comprehensives is an unanswerable question for a number of reasons:

1 We can never determine what would have happened if comprehensives had not been invented.

2 It is an inadequate statistical test to compare the results from remaining grammar schools and secondary modern schools with comprehensives.

3 There is the difficulty of deciding just what exam results to compare, e.g. the number of passes, or the number of students who have gained passes.

4 The particular time period which is used may be of considerable importance.

Julienne Ford (*Social Class and The Comprehensive School*) has cast doubts upon the ability of comprehensive education 'as it is practised at the present' to modify the relationship between social class and educational achievement. She suggests that by adopting comprehensive education

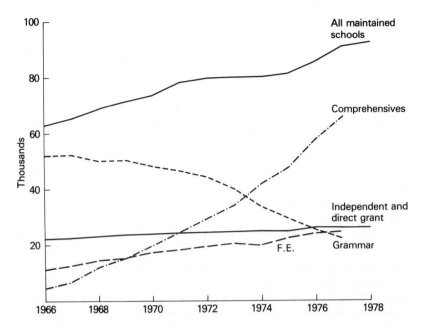

Fig. 4.4 School-leavers with one or more 'A'-levels in England and Wales, 1966–78
(*Times Educational Supplement*, 18 January 1980)

we are merely attempting to manipulate one variable (i.e. the educational system) in order to alter another variable (i.e. the class system). While schools continue to serve the function of selecting individuals for placement in the occupational structure, educational reform cannot influentially affect social change. Ford's critical book questions the advisability of experimenting with the life-chances of millions when the results will not be known for many years. We have seen that there is a direct relationship at all ages between social class and educational achievement, so if comprehensives do not cut across social barriers and lead to a fairer society, they will not contribute towards a significant advance in equality of opportunity or the higher educational achievement of the great mass of children in the lower social classes. However Ford's sampling methods have been severely criticised and her account, in 1970, was in the very early days of comprehensives. She has been accused of constructing an 'ideal type' of comprehensive school based on the meritocratic ideals of Anthony Crosland, then Secretary of State for Education and Science, and conducting her tests in the light of a rigidly streamed London comprehensive school which did not have a full ability range. Over a decade later, it is possible to take a more objective look. It is true that most comprehensives still use the selective process and that selection accentuates social class differences and enables middle-class children to achieve better. Comprehensives have not led to complete equality of opportunity, but a contribution has been made towards greater opportunity for those with equal talent and a widening of pupils' occupational horizons. Mixed-ability teaching, less-formal and less authoritative teaching methods and a widening of the curriculum have contributed to an atmosphere where broader-based educational achievement, cutting across social class barriers, is a distinct possibility. It is worth asking whether a truly comprehensive system of education is possible in a society where such wide social inequalities exist outside the school. There are so many other influences acting upon educational achievement apart from schooling, not least the social class background of the pupils and the quality of the teaching.

Michael Rutter *et al.* (*Fifteen Thousand Hours: Secondary Schools and Their Effects on Children*) made a meticulous study, carried out over six years, of twelve secondary schools with findings based on objective data. The study considered academic achievement, attendance, behaviour and delinquency. Rutter *et al.* concluded that high achievement depends mainly on the teachers – what sort of people teachers are and what they do. It does not depend on teaching methods so much, whether formal or informal, but rather upon teachers creating and maintaining certain norms, including the use of encouragement, a consistent set of values, and acting as models for their pupils in the sense that a punctual and achieving teacher makes for punctual and achieving children. The close correlation between attendance, behaviour and educational achievement led the researchers to stress the importance of the ethos of the school. Michael Rutter's message is that the teachers are a major important contributory cause of achievement; it is up to the teachers to insist upon agreed standards and establish a common understanding with their pupils about the necessity of securing consistent norms of attendance, behaviour and subsequent high educational achievement.

4.6 Educational reform

- *Education and alienation*

It is a truism that many children are alienated by schools and formal education. A large proportion of the world's children do not go to school and many of those who do so drop out at the first opportunity. When they are not at school they are happy, and when they are at school they are unhappy.

Sit still! Be quiet! These are the great watchwords of school. If an enemy spy from outer space were planning to take over earth, and if his strategy were to prepare mankind for this takeover by making men's children as stupid as possible, he could find no better way to do it than to require them, for many hours a day, to be still and quiet. It is absolutely guaranteed to work.

(Holt, J. *The Underachieving School*)

The ideology behind the alienating influence of teachers, schools and the educational system rests upon the Marxist notion of individuality. A human being only realises his true individuality when he finds satisfaction in his work; when work is outside his control it is meaningless and he feels powerless. It is argued by those who wish to abolish schools (i.e. the deschoolers) that children in society feel this way while they are attending school. Children feel that their education is separate from their real selves. The only solution to this problem would be to do away with schools altogether and give the children control over their own education. They would then seek knowledge of their own free will, and enjoy the realisation of their individuality by determining their own education.

In my view, the sooner we all get out of the stuffy classroom, the better it will be for everybody. Life is much more interesting if you can go out and see something instead of just sitting in a desk and being loaded with information about it.

Lynne, 15

What a bore school is nowadays, the same as it has been for hundreds of years. What we get is the same old thing – teacher, outdated textbooks, and a class fed up to the teeth with the teacher and the school. What we need is one vast change in the educational system of this country. Children do not want to be taught at, but want to find out things for themselves. If a child is interested in the way a dogfish's heart works, let him go and find out, by cutting one up.

Robin, 16

(Blishen, E., ed., *The School That I'd Like*)

The major exponent of the application of the Marxist concept of alienation to schooling is Ivan Illich (*Deschooling Society*). Whereas Marx applied the idea of alienation to man's manual labour in the productive process of a capitalist society, Illich applied alienation to mental labour in the educational process. The functions of school are regarded as having little to do with education, but everything to do with passing on middle-class values to working-class children. As these children reject alien values they end up by hating the school which propagates them. A distinction must be made between teaching and learning: deschoolers would regard conventional teaching as the compulsory dissemination of knowledge, whereas learning should be an enjoyable, personal gleaning of knowledge. Illich believed that a compulsory educational system, which enforces attendance at school, not only alienates the pupils, but also alienates the teachers from the products of their mental labour. The curriculum is formulated by people who are a long way from the classroom situation; most teachers are little involved in the compilation of the curriculum while the children are not consulted at all. Deschoolers regard school knowledge as irrelevant and find educational organisation as bad in itself, while the cost of education in modern industrial societies is believed to be far too high and disproportionate to its value to the children whom it is intended to serve. Illich claimed that compulsory school attendance is supposed to be an indication to the pupil, and to society at large, that school knowledge is superior to other forms of knowledge; otherwise it would not be so important to enforce school attendance and employ school welfare officers to 'hunt the kids'. In fact, attendance at school is not a legal requirement in Britain; education as approved by the state is compulsory, so in practice compulsory education means compulsory attendance at school. Illich is critical of the hidden curriculum (see section 4.2) whereby knowledge becomes a commodity and the task of teaching that of packaging the commodity so that it appeals to the consumers who are the pupils. The main function of education under the present system is seen to be the placing of pupils in a class structure based on attaining certificates which will enable them to secure employment in the occupational structure approved by the dominant middle class. Learning should be an end in itself: but learning at school is only a means to an end, i.e. a good job. Deschoolers are against compensatory education (see section 4.4) because they regard such measures as merely ways of making the underprivileged conform to conventional societal norms. Illich disagrees with the authority model of society, believing that nothing should be made obligatory – especially school. Deschoolers would argue that faced with alienation, an irrelevant curriculum, authoritarian teaching and overcrowded classes, children become over-dependent upon teachers and schools. Young people are not accepted into society unless they have been to school: the main criterion of acceptability is educational achievement judged by national qualifications, e.g CSE, GCE 'O' or 'A' level passes. Illich believes that society deliberately impresses upon pupils that they are only children, thus giving them an inferior status. In primitive society there is far less of a gap between childhood and adulthood. Illich would go so far as to regard childhood as a bourgeois invention; the school maintains the status quo and subsequently the capitalist system. A weakness of this argument is that an educational system and schools are still regarded as vital in countries such as the USSR and the People's Republic of China, although full-blooded deschoolers would argue that such countries are not organised on true communist lines. Societies which force people to go on 'progressing' from one education process to another are forcing people into institutionalised anomie.

To avoid the alienation of knowledge from the individual, Illich argues, it is necessary to give back to the individual control over knowledge production. This implies what he calls 'deschooling society' by which he means 'above all the denial of professional status for the second oldest profession, namely teaching'. The deschooling ideology seeks to give back to the individual control over the production of knowledge and in so doing attacks the hierarchy between professional teacher and pupil-client, by calling for the abolition of schools and the abolition of teachers as professionals.

(Easthope, G. *Community, Hierarchy and Open Education*)

• *Deschooling society*

Most of us would recognise that schools do not have a monopoly of learning. Everett Reimer (*School is Dead*) regards schools as mere 'institutional props for privilege'. Yet schools are major instruments of social mobility. How can we effectively deschool society and manage without schools?

Reimer argues that alternatives to schools must be more economical than schools and cheap enough to allow everybody to share in them. Schools must not be replaced by other institutions whereby students compete against each other and learn at the expense of others. Alternatives to school should not manipulate individuals but learners should play a positive role. Education should not be separated from the world of work and the rest of life, but be regarded as a resource upon which willing learners can draw. Schools suffer from the almost universal predilection that those in authority know best what is in the interest of those who are taught. Schools teach pupils what other people want them to know, so preferable alternatives to schools should teach pupils what they want to know. For example, ecologists would contend that we have sufficient technological knowledge at least for the present time and that we should concentrate upon learning how to utilise the resources which we have for the benefit of mankind.

What do people really want to know? As people understand the world by means of language, effective communication is one thing which everybody needs to learn. This knowledge is even more relevant to life if one joins Suzanne Langer (*Philosophy in a New Key*) in including with it music, dancing, poetry and all other affective modes of communication. Reimer believes that children suffer from a culture of silence as they are excluded from knowledge about grown-up things. This is less true than it was even a decade ago but it is still true that children often learn only what adults want them to learn. Rather than being forced to learn ancient history, plant-classifications and a host of highly specialised things, they should learn how society really works. If they wish to learn about why they feel as they do or why other people treat them in the way that they do, then they should be encouraged to do so. Paul Goodman (*Compulsory Miseducation*) condemns institutionalised learning and prescribes an increased involvement in the natural learning patterns of the family and the community.

Teachers, libraries, museums, etc. should be regarded as knowledge resources which children can seek out. Instead of schools, 'networks' of knowledge-sources (people and things) and 'skill exchanges' would encourage learners to seek help from those who possess the specialised knowledge which they wish to acquire. Innovatory ideas of ensuring equitable distribution of these resources have been suggested, e.g. the issue of educational credit cards which would give a specific number of contact hours with educational resources. The pupils could use these contact hours at any time they felt the urge to learn. Learning would no longer be compulsory. A child might withdraw and abstain for a time from the learning process, but with the present alienation to organised education removed, the time could come when of his own volition he would seek out knowledge resources. These resources would still be scarce and the child would look upon it as a privilege to be allowed to use an educational resource. When compared with the irrelevance of many subjects taught at present, plus the amount of time spent in keeping order at schools and forcing children to attend them, the deschooling society provides a useful critique to the present unsatisfactory state of education.

Teachers would be more, rather than less, necessary; teachers will again be honoured, once schools are abolished. They will be sought out by those who want to learn rather than wasting their time forcing unwanted knowledge upon those who do not wish to learn. Instead of having to concentrate upon 'crap detecting' (Postman, N. and Weingartner, C. *Teaching as a Subversive Activity*) children will be eager consumers, and see teachers as cooperators in the learning process. Postman and Weingartner go on to contend that the basic function of all education is to increase the survival prospects of the group. In this nuclear age it is essential that the young, with their lives before them, be allowed to choose that this function should be fulfilled. Herein lies the revolutionary role of education.

> Effective alternatives in schools cannot occur without other widespread changes in society. But there is no point in waiting for other changes to bring about a change in education. Unless educational alternatives are planned and pursued there is no assurance they will occur no matter what else happens. If they do not, the other changes are likely to be superficial and short-lived. Educational change, on the other hand, will bring other fundamental social changes in its wake.
>
> True education is a basic social force. Present social structures could not

survive an educated population even if only a substantial minority were educated. Something more than schooling is obviously in question here; indeed, almost the opposite of schooling is meant. People are schooled to accept a society. They are educated to create or re-create one.

(Reimer, E. *School is Dead*)

• *Radical school reform*

There are fundamental differences between deschoolers and free-schoolers. Whereas deschoolers envisage education and learning processes without schools, free-schoolers would modify the curriculum to make it more relevant to children and give their pupils more freedom within schools. Among important writers about free schools are A.S. Neill, (*Summerhill*) and D. Holly (*Society, Schools and Humanity*).

Free-schoolers are critical of schools as mere institutions for certificate-collecting and of pupils' instrumental attitudes to learning, i.e. children display a tendency not to wish to learn things for their own sake but only as a means to an official recognition of conventional educational achievement. Free-schoolers argue that schools should not be separated and isolated from society. Schools should not be abolished but rather resist the pressures of a society committed to alienated knowledge.

> They are bored because the things they are given and told to do in school are so trivial, so dull, and make such limited and narrow demands on the wide spectrum of their intelligence, capabilities and talents.
>
> They are confused because most of the torrent of words that pours over them in school makes little or no sense. It often flatly contradicts other things they have been told and hardly ever has any relation to what they really know – to the rough model of reality, that they carry around in their minds.
>
> (Holt, J. *How Children Fail*)

Illich, Reimer and other deschoolers are valuable critics of the present schooling system and lead us to consider a more individual approach to education. Opponents of the deschoolers would argue that a complete deschooling of society would create an intense amount of anomie; Durkheim would surely have regarded such a free-for-all as chaotic because people, on a large scale, would find it difficult to accept such a lack of what they regard as social reality. It is useful to criticise constructively what exists already in relation to education; free-schoolers would want to reform existing schools and make them more democratic institutions existing on behalf of the child. The most famous free-schooler, A.S. Neill, founded Summerhill school in 1921, in the town of Leiston in Suffolk. The children board at the school from the age of five to sixteen. It is a cosmopolitan group of about twenty-five boys and twenty-five girls.

The children are left free in their rooms and free in learning situations. Neill regarded schools that make active children sit at desks studying mostly useless subjects as bad schools; he believed that such schools produce uncreative citizens who want docile, uncreative children who fit into a civilisation whose standard of success is merely money. At Summerhill, the child is regarded as innately wise and realistic; if left to itself without adult suggestion, a child will develop as far as he is capable of developing.

> Education should produce children who are at once individuals and community persons, and self-government without doubt does this. In an ordinary school obedience is a virtue, so much so that few in later life can challenge anything. Thousands of students in teacher training are full of enthusiasm about their coming vocation. A year after leaving college they sit in staffrooms and think that education means subjects and discipline. True they dare not challenge or they will get the sack, but few challenge if only in their minds. A lifetime of moulding is hard to break. Another generation grows up and it imposes on the new generation the old taboos and morals and pedagogical insanities, the dear old vicious circle.
>
> (Neill, A.S. *Summerhill*)

Summerhill pupils are not pushed towards levels of educational achievement based upon adult standards. Theoretically it is a place where those who have innate ability to be scholars, and wish to be scholars, will develop as scholars; while those who wish to develop into street cleaners will do so. Perhaps it is because of the individualistic nature of the pupils, or the social environment of the school, they have not yet produced a street cleaner; Neill, in the last resort, would argue that he would rather produce a happy street cleaner than a neurotic scholar.

Lessons at Summerhill are optional. Children can go to them or stay away from them for years if they so desire. The timetable which exists is for the guidance of the teachers rather than the pupils. No new methods of teaching are used, because Neill and his staff do not consider that teaching is of paramount importance. It does not matter whether a school has a special method of teaching long division, because the child who really wants to learn long division will learn it no matter how it is taught. Pupils who come to Summerhill from other schools often vow that they will never attend any lessons. They are allowed to play and get in people's way while they fight shy of lessons sometimes for months. According to Neill, 'The recovery time is proportionate to the hatred their last school gave them.' The record case was a convent girl who loafed about for three years, but the average period of recovery from lesson-aversion is three months. There are no internal examinations of a formal type but it is claimed that Summerhill children display far more originality than children who have been to a normal school.

At General School Meetings, all school rules are voted by the entire school, pupils and staff. At one meeting, it was proposed that a certain culprit should be punished by being banished from lessons for a week. Although the philosophy of the school is anti-examination-orientated, Summerhill staff are qualified to teach to the set standard expected of external examination bodies and will teach pupils to prepare for these examinations if requested to do so by the children themselves.

> Summerhill is possibly the happiest school in the world. We have no truants and seldom a case of home-sickness. We very rarely have fights – quarrels, of course, but seldom have I seen a stand-up fight like the ones we used to have as boys. I seldom hear a child cry, because children when free have much less hate to express than children who are downtrodden. Hate breeds hate, and love breeds love. Love means approving of children, and that is essential in any school. You can't be on the side of children if you punish them and storm at them. Summerhill is a school in which the child knows that he is approved of.
>
> (Neill, A.S. *Summerhill*)

There are those who would wish to argue that the Summerhill experiment could not be practised on a large-scale and therefore has no significant message for society as a whole. It is a small boarding school which has proved that it is possible to rear children without unhappiness and alienation. It provides food for thought for those who stifle children's enthusiasm in traditional schools and believe that formal teaching of conventional subjects is the only way to think of the educational process. Alienation will be removed when open education is practised, either within schools or without, and when children choose what they want to learn and the way that they want to learn it.

4.7 Mass media

- *Influence of the mass media*

We saw in section 4.6 that language and communication are fundamental to education and the acquisition of knowledge. The media has enormous power in influencing opinions and attitudes, especially those of impressionable adolescents.

'Media' is an umbrella term which includes many means of mass communication such as TV, radio, newspapers, magazines, books, films, etc. All these forms of media are one-way systems of communication by which mass opinion is influenced. They contrast with the telephone which is a two-way medium by which individuals communicate with each other. Sometimes the different forms of media may be combined; the phone may become an instrument of the mass media, when used for a 'phone-in' to a radio programme. Even in such apparently two-way programmes, the audience has limited access, because their telephone calls are routed through a 'gatekeeper' who will select the questioners and their questions, consequently determining the substance of what is communicated.

Selectivity is the basis of the media's influence. Far more information pours into the newsroom than is printed in newspapers or broadcast over the air. Sociologists have conducted a great deal of research in recent years into the way the media selects items and thus creates or manufactures its particular product. News does not select itself: it may be argued that some aspects of the news are so important that they demand some coverage, but the actual presentation, including time and space given to items, is the product of judgements relating to the social and political relevance of the event. Somebody, or some group of people, must decide how newsworthy an event is. All news reports are constructed within a certain framework of interpretation. News is largely a cultural product with built-in social and political values. Newspapers especially tend to present a picture of the world intended to support their particular standpoint. The right-wing *Daily Telegraph* would be expected to select and present news in a very different way from the left-wing *Morning Star*. Television and radio are supposed by law and convention to attempt to exercise objectivity in their treatment of the news. However, detachment usually gives way to commitment, combined with the desire to support the system as it is. It is a myth that news priorities are largely dictated by the desire to show exciting film on TV news; the dominant visual element of TV news is a newsreader talking at millions of passive listeners.

An agenda, or list of topics, is set out for debate by the media, and anything which is not on the agenda is unlikely to receive coverage. Sociologists argue that the media 'sets the agenda' for public debate by including issues which the media wishes to discuss and by ignoring issues it has decided should not be discussed. Most professional journalists disagree with this point of view or are unaware of its operation; they contend that the content of news is beyond their control and that they start each day in expectation that something newsworthy will occur. Journalists try to keep on good terms with those who supply them with their stories (i.e. their sources of information). As their sources are usually superordinates rather than subordinates, journalists tend to portray the officials' view of reality. They do not wish to offend their papers' proprietors, editors or contacts so they are likely to write the story which the ruling elite wants them to write.

Newspaper circulation is closely related to social class (See Table 4.17 and Fig. 4.5) and education. In 1974–5, most people who left school at the age of 15 or under read the *Mirror* (35 per cent) or the *Sun* (32 per cent). Newspapers attempt to capture readers of a certain social class according

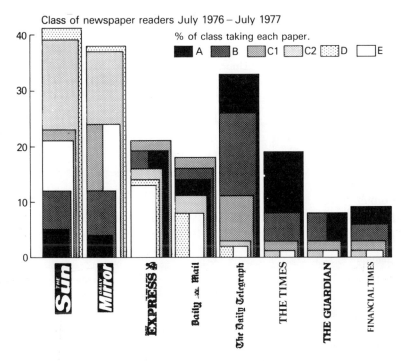

Class of newspaper readers July 1976 – July 1977

% of class taking each paper.

■ A   ▦ B   ▨ C1   ☐ C2   ▨ D   ☐ E

Fig. 4.5 Social class of readership, 1976–7
(*New Society*, 15 February 1979)

to the type of advertisement they print. Quality papers (*The Times, The Financial Times,* the *Daily Telegraph* and the *Guardian*) obtain about 60 per cent of their revenue from advertising, whereas popular papers may only receive about 30 per cent. Although advertisers carefully choose the newspaper whose readership is likely to be attracted to their product, there is little evidence that advertisers interfere directly with the content of news. However, as newspapers which circulate among people of low income find it difficult to attract advertising, several have had to close in recent years. Eight national dailies and Sunday papers have been forced to shut down since 1957, resulting in a decrease in the spectrum of news presentation. The popular papers are frequently of the tabloid type and are likely to concentrate upon sensationalism, human interest stories, sport, prominent headlines and many photographs, while the quality press is of the large broadsheet format and concerns itself with informative journalism and commentaries upon politics, economic problems, literature and the arts.

Age and regional distribution play a significant part in determining readership patterns. Readers of the *Sun* are overwhelmingly young, 47 per

Table 4.17 Readership profiles by social grades: estimated percentage of adult
population

	Upper middle class and middle class	Lower middle classes	Skilled working classes	Lower working classes
Morning Star	14	22	33	31
Daily Mirror	5	18	42	36
Daily Express	14	27	32	27
Sun	5	17	44	37
Daily Mail	16	30	29	24
Daily Telegraph	42	34	15	9
Daily Record	3	15	44	38
Guardian	42	34	15	8
The Times	51	27	13	9
Financial Times	53	29	12	5
News of the World	5	16	41	38
Sunday People	5	19	41	36
Sunday Mirror	6	20	43	31
Sunday Express	22	31	28	19
Sunday Post	8	19	36	37
Sunday Times	43	30	19	8
Observer	36	34	20	10
Sunday Mail	5	19	40	36
Sunday Telegraph	40	32	18	11

(Joint Industry Committee for National Readership Surveys)

cent being under thirty years of age. Readers of the *Express* and the
Telegraph are generally much older. National newspapers have a concentration of readership in the south-east and London. Provincial papers are
far less important than the nationals, probably because of London's
dominant position compared with other capitals in the political, economic,
cultural and communications spheres. In 1976 London evening papers
outsold provincial dailies by 15 million to 8.5 million. In recent years most
newspapers have been through difficult times with the advent of new
printing technologies and subsequent industrial unrest. The sales of
quality papers have held up better than sales of populars, while campaigns

for devolution may undermine the London press at the expense of provincial papers.

Some of the ways in which the press influences public opinion are worth considering.

1 *Selectivity*

> The *Telegraph* is obsessed by the colour issue. This is not to say it is racist ... colour gets big coverage: Southall's last English cinema goes Asian with photographs: 'Good Riddance to Obote' is followed by 'Good Luck to General Amin – a popular man with the troops'....
>
> (Duncan, B. 'The Daily Telegraph', *Society Today*, 20 January 1978)

2 *Omission*

The selection of some news items entails the omission of others. This truism is very important in practice. For example, it is now known that Geoffrey Dawson used his power as editor of *The Times* to omit references to Nazi atrocities before the war. If these omissions had not taken place the British people would have been aware far earlier of the Nazi danger to civilised society.

3 *Comment*

A great danger to unthinking readers is that it is so easy for a reporter to begin an article with a simple factual statement and then to introduce insidiously biased comment so that readers hardly know where the news ends and the comment begins. News and comment may be cunningly interwoven; merely one word can cause the reader to be unwittingly influenced. A correspondent who begins an article '*Even* the Conservative Party', or '*Even* the Labour Party', may be endeavouring to suggest that the Party has a low standard of morality, but that even the members of *this* party are capable of showing a small measure of virtue on some particular issue.

4 *Character assassination*

During the 1980s many people have been persuaded to adopt a low opinion of Tony Benn, largely because of adverse press coverage. Similar treatment was afforded to Harold Wilson in the 1970s.

5 *Special Campaigns*

The most important example of a successful newspaper campaign in recent years was the one conducted by the *Sunday Times* against the Distillers Company resulting in far more generous compensation for thalidomide victims.

6 *Errors*

Newspapers are prone to make light of errors in previous editions. Apologies and corrections are given little prominence.

7 *Headlines*

Figure 4.6 provides an example of what the *Observer* termed 'An

Fig. 4.6 An extraordinarily loaded front page
(*Daily Mail*, 26 April 1979)

extraordinarily loaded front page'. This may be regarded as emotive journalism intended to unduly influence those who merely read headlines and large type. The biased way in which different newspapers headline and report the same event is illustrated in Fig. 4.7.

Jim's sweet win in poll

By PETER PRENDERGAST
Political Correspondent

IT was the Pontefract cake-walk for Labour early today.

Premier James Callaghan's party romped home in the by-election in the Yorkshire constituency, but with a reduced majority.

The victory was a boost for the Premier's policy of keeping a curb on pay rises.

The result:

Geoff Lofthouse (Lab) 19,508

Hugo Page (Con.) 8,080

Les Marsh (Lib.) 2,154

Lab. majority 11,428

The by-election was caused by the death in June of Labour MP Joe Harper. At the last General Election he had a majority of 23,242.

The new MP, 52-year-old Mr. Lofthouse, is a former miner, now a Coal Board Manager.

POLL SHOCK FOR JIM

By WALTER TERRY

Labour won the Pontefract by-election this morning – though its vote dived and many voters failed to turn out in the Yorkshire town.

Two by-elections yesterday – the other at Berwick and East Lothian – were the first major test of public opinion since Premier James

Callaghan decided against an Autumn General Election.

Many Labour experts thought apathy was inevitable. Pontefract is one of the safest seats in Britain. Labour's majority

in October, 1974, was 23,242.

The result showed Labour needs a far more energetic campaign to get itself on the move.

RESULT:
G. Lofthouse (Lab)
               19,508;
H. Page (C)   8,080;
L. Marsh (L)   2,154.
Lab majority 11,428

The swing to Tories was 7.9 per cent.

Fig. 4.7 Two contrasting headlines for the same news story
(*Daily Mirror* and *Sun*, 27 October 1978)

Television is arguably more influential than the press. Marshall McLuhan believed that television was the main agent in the modern reorganisation of our sensorium, analogous to that provided by the invention of printing over five hundred years ago. According to McLuhan, TV was making the world into a 'global village'; this evening's TV news will bring the triumphs, disasters, crimes, politics and violences of the wider world into our living rooms. The audio-tactile is changing our whole sense of social reality (McLuhan, M. *Understanding Media*). He considered radio as 'hot' (i.e. high in information content), while TV is 'cool' (low in information). McLuhan was probably wrong when he suggested that the viewer participated in some measure. TV viewing is a passive occupation, but that does not mean that the watcher remains uninfluenced by the programmes he watches. However, the extent of the influence of television is impossible to assess accurately. Consider, for example, the possible relationship between violence portrayed on television and the incidence of violence in real life.

In 1977, Dr William Belson told the British Association for the Advancement of Science that his research suggested that boys exposed to high levels of violence on television were 50 per cent more likely to commit acts of violence than boys who had not been so exposed. Belson's survey studied more than 1500 London boys aged between 13 and 16. He called for immediate action on his recommendations to reduce the content of television violence; naturally his recommendations were endorsed by Mrs Mary Whitehouse. However, there have been six previous important studies on this subject and none of them have shown any very significant relationship between TV violence and real-life violence. Belson's questions went back twelve years, so the boys were being asked about their memory of how they responded to programmes when they were two to four years old.

It is difficult to conduct serious scientific media studies when research moves away from the academic field and is influenced by commercial groups. C. Wright Mills (*The Sociological Imagination*) warned against research sponsored by commercial organisations:

> The formation of these costly techniques makes them especially serviceable in providing the very kind of information needed by those capable and willing to pay for it.

In spite of charges that are made about the adverse effect of television and cinema programmes, sociological studies 'lead us to doubt very strongly whether screen violence has any direct effect on the real behaviour of young people' (*Violence on the Screen*, by Andre Glucksmann, British Film Institute, 1971). The world in which we live may be no more violent than the world of yesteryear; it is merely that, through the medium of television in particular, violent deeds in Ulster are seen on our TV screen within a few hours of their happening.

As sociologists we must be objective and therefore be wary of those who continually point to the supposedly bad effects of TV upon young people. Sociological research has suggested that 'any connection between the mass media and overt behaviour will be indirect' (L. Bailyn, *Mass Media and Children*). Perhaps the soundest contribution to the controversy about the influential effects of television has been made by James Halloran in *Television and Delinquency*; Halloran's approach to the research into the importance of television in shaping social values has been to place TV's influence in relation to all the other factors in modern society.

It does seem likely that the more a person is exposed to TV, the less likely that person is to be much moved by what he sees. Certain of Dr Hilde Himmelweit's investigations (*Television and the Child*) suggest the more used a child is to films, the less he seems alarmed by them. The Annan Committee felt that television has more of an impact where attitudes and opinions are uninformed, particularly on children. They criticised the showing of violence between 9 and 10 p.m., as too many children were still watching at this time, but they rejected the argument that TV violence had a cathartic or 'cleansing' effect. Television violence clearly has its dangers, but these must not be exaggerated.

- *Sociological perspectives of media studies*

1 *The consensus perspective*
Even if communicators wished to do so, it would not be possible to be completely impartial in the selection and portrayal of news. It would be a simple matter if news could be separated from comment in the way that C.P. Scott, the famous editor of the *Manchester Guardian* once suggested in his newspaper, over fifty years ago:

> The newspaper is of necessity something of a monopoly and its first duty is to shun the temptations of monopoly. Its primary office is the gathering of news. At the peril of its soul it must see that the supply is not tainted. Neither in what it gives nor in what it does not give, nor in the mode of presentation, must the unclouded face of truth suffer wrong. Comment is free but facts are sacred.

The Annan Committee, in its *Report on the Future of Broadcasting*, appreciated that such neutrality is more apparent than real. The Annan Committee argued that what is demanded from broadcasters is not simply 'impartiality' but 'due impartiality' which is by no means the same as neutrality. In keeping with a liberal-democratic perspective, the Annan Committee Report said,

The broadcasters are operating within a system of parliamentary democracy and must share its assumptions. They should not be expected to give equal weight or to show an impartiality which is not due to those who seek to destroy it by violent, unparliamentary or illegal means.

This is the 'hyperdermic model of the media' whereby communicators inject their programmed message into their audiences, in accordance with a consensus which is presumed to be acceptable. It is assumed that society agrees that certain things (such as crime, strikes, terrorism and racialism) are anti-social, while other things (such as the monarchy, the party system and the mixed economy) are worthwhile and therefore should be preserved. According to this argument, controllers of the media should exercise due impartiality which is in effect partiality within a defined area. It is thought to be the duty of newspapers and broadcasters to reflect this consensus. The controllers of the media support the existing order of things.

Those with minority views naturally feel aggrieved at this approach. How can a minority view ever become a majority view if it is not given a fair airing by the media? However, the Annan Committee did not expect the controllers of the media to give equal weight to all opinions: according to the committee's report the majority viewpoint is entitled to receive the greatest coverage.

> Broadcasters must take account, not just of the whole range of views on an issue but also of the weight of opinion which holds these views. Their duty to let the public hear various voices does not oblige them to give too much weight or coverage to opinions which are not widely held. While it is right that the orthodoxies should be challenged, equally it is essential that the established view should be fully and clearly put and that the status and implications of the challenge should be made clear.
>
> (Annan Committee Report, *The Future of Broadcasting*)

Although the BBC and IBA are supposed to be independent, it is clear that, in reality, they support the political status quo and the underlying social and economic order. This does not mean that they do not appreciate that the status quo itself is subject to change over time.

> ... the range of views and the weight of opinion are constantly changing. What may be an acceptable approach to an issue at any one time will not necessarily remain so for all time.
>
> (Annan Committee Report, *The Future of Broadcasting*)

The BBC and IBA perform their permitted roles like actors in a morality play and consequently reap the reward of a large measure of independence. They can be relied upon to 'play the establishment game' and support existing institutions. They are free from political interference in their day-to-day activities, although they are aware of outside pressures always at hand, ready to act if they step out of line. When they attempt to make minor modifications to the status quo they have to bear in mind just how far they can go in shaping public opinion or how far they should be led by their audience. The extent to which either the media or the masses lead in changing the status quo is a difficult area of compromise. Whether or not one thinks the media obtain the right balance depends upon the coverage given to one's own particular point of view.

Consensus involves agreement about what is normal and acceptable. The media regards the majority of people in any society as sharing a consensus about reality and, consequently, news coverage is geared to reinforce the consensual image of society. People who do not conform to the present boundaries of normality are considered to have deviated. They are exceptionally newsworthy because they can be held up as abnormal and dysfunctional, so that they do in fact indirectly strengthen the consensus. It is easy for the media to rouse the ire of the public against murderers, rapists, homosexuals and those labelled as social security scroungers. Tax-evaders are less newsworthy, as they are less deviant, according to middle-class values. Stan Cohen and Jock Young (*The Manufacture of News*) argue that the deviant's own knowledge of how 'normal' people see him derives from the way the media portrays him. However, the media may help towards modifications in public opinion. For example, nudity was marginally a deviant act a quarter of a century ago. There has undoubtedly been an increase in displays of nudity on TV; it is hard to say whether this is largely because TV has created a climate conducive to the greater acceptance of nudity or whether this is in accordance with viewers' changing attitudes. In other words, is nudity more acceptable and less of a deviance? Mrs Mary Whitehouse's National Viewers' and Listeners' Association express their desire for less nudity on TV. The broadcasters are open to criticism for being impartial either to nudists or to Mary Whitehouse. Presumably they consider that the consensus is in favour of the acceptability of more nudity and that Mrs Whitehouse reflects a minority voice. The consensus perspective thus extends from political questions of national importance to deviant acts by individuals. However, the most important sociological implication of the consensus approach is in the realms of political action and the underlying economic ideology. This can be seen clearly by examining the opposing conflict perspective of the media.

2 *The conflict perspective*

The conflict perspective of the media concentrates upon its ownership and control. It is contended that in a capitalist society, the final control over what is broadcast or printed is in the hands of a relatively small section of society. The political views of this powerful group is reflected in the selection of news and the content of programmes which influence the masses, such as current affairs items. There is a great deal of well-documented evidence which reveals the close relationship between the ownership and control of newspapers and the power structure of society.

Although the inter-relationships between financial concerns are continually subject to change, there is no doubt that the press is a capitalist organisation linked with other instruments in the capitalist system. In recent years, the *Daily Mail* and General Trust Group owned Associated Newspapers which was involved in commercial TV and fifty subsidiary industrial and commercial companies. The International Publishing Company (the *Daily Mirror* Group) merged with the Reed Group of companies which was responsible for about 400 associated companies including subsidiaries concerned with TV, films and theatres. The *News of the World* organisation had diverse interests in retail newsagents, betting shops and transport. Until 1981, the Thomson Organisation (*The Times* and the *Sunday Times*) owned nearly 200 subsidiaries and associated companies and enjoyed substantial interests in Scottish TV. Even the *Observer*, which prides itself on editorial independence, had a chairman with numerous directorates in other financial enterprises. All newspapers have on their Boards of Directors, men who hold interlocking directorates with other businesses motivated by profit. Claims that most national newspapers are independent over large important issues are highly debatable.

The press is an agent of capitalist propaganda in our advanced industrial society, just as it is an agent of communist propaganda in Russia and China where powerful elites control the destiny of the masses. However, in recent years, sociological studies have revealed that TV is also an important instrument working in favour of the governing class. It is claimed that in the conflict between employers and employees, TV journalists deliberately take sides. We have seen that the Annan Committee accepted that broadcasters should share the assumptions of our society. However, it has been claimed by the Glasgow University Media Group that broadcasters exercise more than 'due responsibility' and come down deliberately but insidiously on the side of the interests of the dominant social class. This is going further than asserting that TV journalists should come down against 'sin' and expose illegalities.

> Contrary to the claims, conventions and culture of television journalism, the news is not a neutral product.
> (Glasgow University Media Group, *Bad News*)

The Glasgow University Media Group carefully analysed the *Nine O'Clock News* on BBC and *News at Ten* on ITV. Over twenty million viewers watch one or other of these programmes each day. In spite of

Britain's mass-selling newspapers, TV news is probably the most influential mass medium concerned with shaping political attitudes.

In *Bad News*, the Glasgow University Media Group analysed TV news bulletins in 1975. The group found that the bulletins displayed a 'systematic presentation of a particular and narrow view . . . alternatives to the dominant view have little chance of surfacing in a meaningful way.' During a long strike by Glasgow dustcart drivers, not one of the strikers was invited to participate in any of the twenty-one interviews which took place. In industrial conflicts, management was always presented in a better light than the workers. In broadcasts earlier in the day, a brief mention might be made about inefficient management and low investment, but in many succeeding broadcasts of the same news item adverse comments about employers would be omitted while ultra-critical postures were adopted against workers.

In the second volume, *More Bad News*, describing further work by the Glasgow University Media Group, a myth propagated by the medium of TV was clearly exposed. The myth concerned TV broadcasters' contention that inflation was caused solely by high wages, whereas most agree that there are many contributory causes. Professor Friedman and the monetarists would go so far as to claim that only the government can cause inflation by increasing the money supply and that therefore wages have no direct effect upon inflation. This belief was unrepresented by both BBC and ITV because it was not the consensus view at the time. Many apparently factual news broadcasts analysed statistics incorrectly and ignored views which disagreed with the TV consensus approach. There were 96 references to excessive wages increases as the cause of our economic crisis, compared with 33 blaming poor investment and 29 blaming the oil crisis. Although the Price Commission indicated that, in its opinion, a number of factors, including the price of oil, were responsible, ITN still broadcast distorted accounts.

Today's message from the Price Commission is grim and is no less grim because it's not a new one. Inflation is now rampant and according to the Commission, wage inflation is almost entirely to blame: Ominously they say the pace of prices explosions has so far been understated. In the three months covered the Retail Prices Index went up five point eight per cent, and wholesale prices six point five per cent, but the Commission's own index, which should be more up to date, rose seven point five per cent. For this the Commission firmly blames wage cost increases.

(ITN News, April 1975)

In the conflict between politicians about proposed solutions to Britain's economic crisis, those who advocated views unacceptable to the TV authorities were unlikely to have their voices heard. Study Table 4.18, and

Table 4.18 Proposed solutions to the economic crisis as portrayed on TV news

Proposed solution	Number of references
Wage restraint/lower wages	287 (+17 negative)
Defence of living standards	79 (+15 negative)
Expansion of the public sector, the need for a government investment programme, proposals to reverse decline in industrial investment	47 (+50 negative)
Cuts in government expenditure	21 (+ 1 negative)
Better communications in industry	14 (+ 6 negative)
More progressive taxation 'cuts at the top' 'tax the rich', etc.	12 (+ 4 negative)
Abolition of price control	11 (+ 6 negative)
Increased profits for industry	10
Statutory wage control	8 (+20 negative)
Increased investment in private industry (including government aid)	9
Import controls	7
Reduction of 'complex' VAT rates	6
A ban on the export of capital	2
Lower interest rates	1

note the comparatively small number of references to tax increases for high income earners, government aid to industry, import controls or banning capital exports. (The table is based on data recorded throughout the first four months of 1975.)

The media faces the charge of reporting in terms of 'us' (the employers and general public) and 'them' (the workers and trade unions). The generally accepted news image is one of strikes and other industrial conflicts being against the national interest. The public are considered to be always being held to ransom by selfish workers: the workers are portrayed as being exploited by the dominant group in an advanced industrial society. The media continues to assume that there is a consensus in the face of continual conflict.

Just as attention must be directed at the evidence we present rather than at assumptions as to our ideological stance, so too we would not argue that the broadcasters are engaged in simple-minded conspiracy to distort or bias their work. The prevailing professional ideology encompassed by the myths of impartiality, balance and objectivity allows the broadcasters to tacitly trade upon the unspoken and dominant ideology of our society – the liberal notion that there is a fundamental consensus.

(Glasgow University Media Group, *More Bad News*)

Further Reading

Benn, C. & Simon, B. *Half-way There, Report on the British Comprehensive-School Reform* (Penguin)

Berg, L. *Risinghill: Death of a Comprehensive School* (Penguin)

Brown, J. (ed.) *Knowledge, Education and Cultural Change* (Tavistock)

Bruner, J.S. *The Process of Education* (Harvard University Press)

Burgess, T. *Education after School* (Penguin)

Cashdan, A. (ed.) *Language in Education* (Routledge & Kegan Paul)

Cosin, B.R. (ed.) *Education: Structure and Society* (Penguin)

Cosin, B.R. (ed.) *School and Society* (Routledge & Kegan Paul)

Craft, M. (ed.) *Linking Home and School* (Longman)

Dale, R. (ed.) *Schooling and Capitalism* (Routledge & Kegan Paul)

Davis, R. *The Grammar School* (Penguin)

Delamont, S. *Interaction in the Classroom* (Methuen)

Easthope, G. *Community, Hierarchy and Open Education* (Routledge & Kegan Paul)

Eggleston, J. (ed.) *Contemporary Research in the Sociology of Education* (Methuen)

Evetts, J. *The Sociology of Educational Ideas* (Routledge & Kegan Paul)

Ford, J. *Social Class and the Comprehensive School* (Routledge & Kegan Paul)

Golding, P. *The Mass Media* (Longman)

Goodman, P. *Compulsory Miseducation* (Penguin)

Halloran, J. *The Effects of Television* (Panther)

Halloran, J. *Television and Delinquency* (Leicester University Press)

Halsey, A.H. (ed.) *Educational Priority* (HMSO)

Hargreaves, D. *Social Relations in a Secondary School* (Routledge & Kegan Paul)

Himmelweit, H. *Television and the Child* (OUP)

Holt, J. *The Underachieving School* (Penguin)

Holt, J. *How Children Fail* (Penguin)

Hopper, E. (ed.) *Readings in the Theory of Educational Systems* (Hutchinson)

Hoyle, E. *The Role of the Teacher* (Routledge & Kegan Paul)

Illich, I. *Deschooling Society* (Penguin)

Jackson, B. *Life in School Classrooms* (Penguin)

Jackson, B. & Marsden, D. *Education and the Working Class* (Penguin)

Lawton, D. *Social Class, Language and Education* (Routledge & Kegan Paul)

McQuail, D. *Sociology of Mass Communications* (Collier-Macmillan)

Neill, A.S. *Summerhill* (Penguin)

Pedley, R. *The Comprehensive School* (Penguin)

Raynor, J. & Harden, J. (eds) *Cities, Communities and the Young* (Routledge & Kegan Paul)

Raynor, J. & Harden, J. (eds) *Equality and City Schools* (Routledge & Kegan Paul)

Reimer, E. *School is Dead* (Penguin)

Robbins, Lord *The University in the Modern World* (Macmillan)

Shipman, M.D. *Sociology of the School* (Longman)

Smith, W.O. Lester *Education* (Penguin)

Swift, D.F. (ed.) *Basic Readings in the Sociology of Education* (Routledge & Kegan Paul)

Young, M.F.D. (ed.) *Knowledge and Control* (Collier-Macmillan)

FIVE
Work

5.1 Comparison of work in pre-industrial and industrial societies

- *Work in pre-industrial societies – the structural-functionalist perspective*

There are FOUR principal distinctive features of pre-industrial societies which are of great sociological significance.

First, in pre-industrial societies, working life and social life were unified. A person's work was prescribed by social relationships.

> The outstanding discovery of recent historical and anthropological research is that man's economy, as a rule, is submerged in his social relationship.
> (Polanyi, K. *The Great Transformation*)

Before the development of the market economy, the community looked after its members. The maintenance of social ties were of paramount importance and the social system was based on the principles of *reciprocity* and *redistribution*. Individuals reciprocated in respect of work done and services rendered, while the tribal chief redistributed surpluses accompanied by social activities such as ceremonies, festivities, dances and communal feasts. Work was not determined by the market forces of wages and prices but was performed in a communal or cooperative way by members of the tribe, the clan or the family. R.W. Firth has described how he witnessed the repair of a canoe in Tikopia when a chief requested the help of close kinsmen and neighbours and how others turned up when they heard that the work was taking place. Another social anthropologist, Bronislaw Malinowski, has recorded a similar organisation of economic life in Melanesian New Guinea.

> Communal labour is an important factor in the tribal economy of the Trobriand natives. They resort to it in the building of living-huts and storehouses, in certain forms of industrial work, and in the transport of things, especially at

harvest time, when great quantities of produce have to be shifted from one village to another, often over a great distance.
(Malinowski, B. *Argonauts of the Western Pacific*)

Cooperative labour did not exclude the division of labour in the sense that different groups of people did different tasks. The 'primary division of labour' (to use the term of Thurmwald, R. *Economics in Primitive Communities*) was between men and women. In his account of the Maori, Firth lists large numbers of tasks which were either men's tasks or women's tasks. Even where men and women combined in the work of planting and fishing, men and women did not do the same work in the same way. Division of labour also extended to varying age groups.

> The children assisted their relatives in many technical occupations and so helped to get their training.... Old people who were past their prime did not remain in idleness, but occupied themselves in work requiring no great expenditure of energy.
> (Firth, R. *Primitive Economics of the New Zealand Maori*)

The natural expectation of work by the very young and the very old is foreign to most industrial societies.

Under the feudal system, tasks were required as obligations which themselves presupposed a number of social relationships. Serfdom consisted of a complex set of obligations to the lord of the manor. The tenant serf was given the right to work upon a number of strips on the open field and was thus able to provide for his family, but in return he was obliged to do specific tasks on the lord's land. The serf's economic obligation was to work for his lord. The network of complex social relationships was bound up with three important social institutions:

(a) *vassalage* – a feudal lord protected his vassal in return for services rendered:

> The lord, at every level of the hierarchy, would be answerable for his 'man' and would be responsible for holding him to his duty.
> (Bloch, M. *Feudal Society*)

(b) *fief* – a grant of land to a vassal (subordinate) in return for military services;

(c) *the church* – the church was the greatest landowner in feudal Europe and collected a tithe or tenth of all the annual produce from those who worked its lands.

The Indian caste system, which for centuries has regulated social life for 300 million Hindus, is deeply rooted in the economic structure and in work situations.

> Each caste is traditionally associated with a separate occupation. Some of the earlier students of caste were so impressed with this feature of caste that they

ascribed the origin of caste to the systematization of occupational differentiation. In rural India the bulk of the castes continue to practise their respective traditional occupations, though agriculture is common to all castes from the Brahmin to the Untouchable.

Some occupations are considered defiling because of the contact with some defiling object or other necessary to their practice. Swine-herding is defiling because swine defile. Leather defiles, and consequently the making and repairing of shoes is an occupation of the Untouchables.

(Srinivas, M.N. *Religion and Society among the Coorgs of South India*. A short extract from this book is reprinted in Beteille, A., ed., *Inequality*)

A second important characteristic of pre-industrial society was that work roles were **ascribed** *rather than* **acquired**. After rudimentary specialisation (division of labour) had evolved, then particular occupations were passed on from one generation to another. One of the main functions of the pre-industrial family was that the father should teach his sons the skills of the trade. This aspect of the economic function of the family is of diminishing importance in modern society, but it was once the natural societal trait that sons should adopt the same occupation as their fathers. Ascribed work roles are still found to varying degrees in industrial societies, but the majority of the work-force today acquire their jobs by dint of training and qualifications. Whereas industrial societies largely use an achievement system to match people to work roles, pre-industrial societies used an ascriptive system.

Under an 'ascriptive' system of bringing people and jobs together it is assumed that some categories of persons have, from birth, qualities that automatically fit them better than others for entry into certain occupations. Under an 'achievement' system, occupations are not reserved in this way but are left open to be reached through competition and individual effort.

(Sofer, C. in Williams, W.M., ed., *Occupational Choice*)

Thirdly, work in pre-industrial societies was not dominated by the clock. This does not mean that there was no notation of time in pre-industrial societies, but rather that there was *task-orientation* instead of *clock-orientation*. The Nuer of the southern Sudan work by 'cattle time': they awake with their cattle, feed and milk them when required, and generally regulate their social life in accordance with tasks associated with cattle. Fishermen's work had been governed by the tides even before the invention of clocks led to artificial time-barriers dominating our lives. Time, in the context of task-orientation, is far more meaningful and less alienating than clock-timed work, for the work is seen to be necessary and has to be done. Task-orientation leads to less demarcation between work and social life. The working day was extended or contracted according to the time required to finish the work. When the tasks were completed there was no need to work; there was more time available for leisure. According to H. Wilensky, in *The Uneven Distribution of Leisure*, the thirteenth-century skilled artisan worked only 194 days a year. In places where the people, such as the Spanish Americans of New Mexico (Mead, M. *Cultural Patterns and Technical Change*) are as yet not absorbed in industrial work,

> It is possible to observe a round of seasonal activities set within an established framework and linked to the calendar of sacred festivals and holy days.... Work and rest are not seen in opposition to each other, but as part of the same process – work a little, rest a little.
> (Eldridge, J.E.T. *Sociology and Industrial Life*)

In such conditions it is not considered immoral to be idle. Irregular patterns of work enable people to enjoy numerous 'holy days' (holidays) or saints' days.

A fourth distinctive feature of pre-industrial societies was that no sharp dividing-line existed between work and leisure (or work and non-work, see section 5.8). Kinship groups, in pre-industrial society, joined together in both working and leisure activities. Under the domestic system, the cottage industries were operated by women and children doing the spinning, while the men did the weaving. When the work was done they were free to join in communal leisure activities.

- ● *Work in industrial societies – the conflict perspective*

In industrial societies, work and social life are physically separated. One 'goes to work'. The home and the family are distinct from factory, workshop, office or shop; two different sets of social relationships exist. Work is no longer 'embedded' in social life. Apart from the separation in location, as work is now done in workplaces, the work is performed at specific times and these times are distinct from the times of social activities.

Industrial societies are so arranged that there is a 'working day', with set hours of work. Clock-orientation has led to a changing notion of time. The worker 'clocks in' and 'clocks out'.

> I work in a factory. For eight hours a day, five days a week.... Work to me is a void and I begrudge every precious minute of my time that it takes....
> My working day starts with the time-honoured ritual known as 'clocking in'. For the uninitiated: a lever is pressed and, in blue ink, a time is recorded on one's card. It's so mechanical that one expects the time to be always the same. But it isn't. Just have the effrontery to be late: then you will find that your time has been stamped in RED ink. The management may condone bad time-keeping, but that blasted clock seems to shed blood in anguish.
> (Johnson, D. in Fraser, R., ed., *Work*)

The worker expects to be paid extra for any 'overtime'. He is paid an hourly or daily rate, or a weekly wage, or an annual salary.

Under the capitalistic mode of production, the measurement of time became a means of exploitation.

> **Question 5118.** At the time they worked those long hours, would it have been in their power to work a shorter number of hours, taking the three shillings?
> **Answer.** They must either go on at the long hours, or else be turned off.
> **Question 5129.** What time did you begin work at a factory?
> **Answer.** When I was six years old.
> **Question 5133.** What were your hours of labour in that mill?
> **Answer.** From 5 in the morning till 9 at night, when they were thronged.
> **Question 5134.** For how long a time together have you worked that excessive length of time?
> **Answer.** For about half a year.
> (*Report of Select Committee on Factory Children's Labour 1831–32*)

There is no longer a natural time sequence in relation to work, but time is looked upon as something that should be 'saved', 'used efficiently' and not 'wasted'. The phrase 'time is money' invariably means the employers' time. Workers eventually realised that if time is money, then time is a weapon with which they can fight back.

Many trade unions are now campaigning for the working week to be reduced to 35 hours. The modern worker, in industrial societies, is insistent upon being paid time-and-a-half or double time for work which extends beyond his normal commitment. He expects to receive sick-pay, holiday pay and to be paid during tea-breaks. Since 1974 legislation has been passed in order to allow workers to be paid for 'time off' to attend union meetings.

The worker has turned the tables on the entrepreneur, but not without a great deal of industrial friction lasting for over two centuries. Marx, in *Capital*, illustrates the conflict approach. He drew attention to the conflict which arose between the capitalist and the worker through the fixing of piece-work rates. According to E.P. Thompson the workers' fight to use time-orientation of labour to their own advantage evolved over three stages.

> The first generation ... were taught by their masters the importance of time; the second generation formed their short-time committees in the ten-hour movement; the third generation struck for overtime or time-and-a-half. They had accepted the categories of their employers and learned ... their lesson, that time is money, only too well.
> (Thompson, E.P. 'Time, Work-Discipline and Industrial Capitalism', *Past and Present*, No. 38, Dec. 1967)

So in industrial societies the principal obligation to work is through the cash-nexus and there are rarely any social obligations which bind a worker to an employer. The inducement of overtime and piece-work rates symbolises the employer's own philosophy in relation to work and his acceptance of a close connection between the amount of work done and the rewards offered to the worker. Much industrial work is, in the nature of things, extrinsic.

> The worker feels himself at home only outside his work and feels absent from himself in his work. He feels at home when he is not working and not at home when he is working. His work is not freely consented to, but is a constrained, forced labour. Work is thus not a satisfaction of a need, but *only a means to satisfy a need outside work*.
> (Marx, K. *Capital*; my italics)

Work tasks are but fragmentations in a man's experience and it has been argued that work has lost its former position as 'the central life interest' (Dubin, R. *Industrial Workers' Worlds: A Study of the Central Life Interests of Industrial Workers*). We have moved a long way (though not necessarily in the right direction so far as job-satisfaction is concerned: see section 5.3), since the workers in pre-industrial societies toiled in the field to produce crops which they themselves would consume.

● *The logic of industrialism – the convergence perspective*

Industrial societies have certain common characteristics. The fact that one industrial society is very much like every other industrial society is known to sociologists as *the logic of industrialisation*. This development is in accordance with the convergence (organicist) theory and its main features are summarised in the following charts from *Industrialism and Industrial Man* (Clark Kerr *et al.*).

Other similarities of industrial societies include industrial locations (largely dependent upon the proximity of raw materials, good transport facilities, power, markets, etc.), the existence of an occupational hierarchy and job similarities. The work of dockers, miners, car workers and factory workers is similar in all industrial countries. Containerisation first affected US dockworkers in the 1960s, but has since spread to the UK and all industrial countries (see Wilson, D.F. *Dockers*).

The so-called logic (or universality) of industrialism is based on universal knowledge and progress in science and technology. It can be argued that it is not the capitalist organisation of production which is responsible for the universality of work-tasks; the alienation (see section 5.5) of the factory worker may occur in the Soviet Union and in the USA.

Table 5.1 The logic of industrialism

Work force	Increased skills and widening range of skills.
	Increasing occupational and geographic mobility.
	Higher levels of education more closely related to industrial function.
	Structured work force.
Scale of society	Urbanisation and decline of agriculture as a way of life.
	Larger role for government.
Consensus in society	Increasing ideological consensus in a pluralistic society.
World-wide industrialism	Industrial society spreads out from the centres of advanced technology.

(Clark Kerr, *Industrialism and Industrial Man*)

Clark Kerr *et al.* contend that industrialism is value-neutral. Marxists would be likely to contest this view on the grounds that the social relations of production are different in capitalist and communist countries. The Marxist would disagree with Kerr's convergence perspective arguing that the capitalist exploits the industrial workers by appropriating surplus value, and that contentious managerial techniques bring fundamental conflicts of interest which make capitalist industrial countries different from collectivist industrial countries.

● *Conflict in industrial societies*

From the conflict-structuralist perspective the changing nature of work has brought increasing antagonisms. In accordance with the *organic (functionalist) perspective*, it is useful to view society as a whole; however, the whole has interdependent parts and there may well be conflicting interests between the parts. So the *conflict perspective* helps us to understand that industrial work may be manipulated for the benefit of a particular group. Marxists contend that the important question is not how can the economic system best function for the good of the whole, but rather which class gains from the arrangement? The conflicts which have emerged since the arrival of industrialism are summarised in the table below.

Table 5.2 Reasons for conflict in industrial society

1 The decline in traditional skills has brought about a loss of job satisfaction.

2 Mechanisation and factory production have resulted in jobs which are boring and alienating.

3 Individual workers feel self-estranged in large bureaucratic organisations; Schumacher has advocated the reverse of this trend by encouraging small-scale technology whereby

   people have a chance to enjoy themselves while they are working, instead of working solely for the pay-packet.
   (Schumacher, E.F. *Small is Beautiful*)

4 There is an unbridgeable gulf between workers and managers (e.g. in multinational companies).

5 Industrial relations have become anomic (i.e. without norms) and a 'them' and 'us' attitude prevails (see section 5.6).

6 Even office work has become increasingly repetitive (C. Wright Mills, *White Collar*).

7 The worker has lost control over the work and the whole productive process has become meaningless to him. (Blauner, R. *Alienation and Freedom*. (See section 5.5.)

● *Durkheim's mechanical and organic solidarity – the reconciliation of the consensus and conflict perspectives*

The consensus and conflict models of working life do not necessarily exclude each other. The consensus or organic perspective can be reconciled with conflicts of interest at work; the economic system has many imperfections.

Emile Durkheim contrasted *organic solidarity* with *mechanical solidarity* which he regarded as the basis of the pre-industrial social structure. Mechanical solidarity was a simpler structure based on the belief that individuals closely resembled each other because they cherished the same values. In pre-industrial societies, workers were largely interchangeable because there was very little specialisation. But in an industrial society there is complex differentiation based upon division of labour. Where mechanical solidarity exists:

> ... not only are all members of the group individually attracted to one another because they resemble one another, but also because they are joined to what is the condition of existence of this collective type; that is to say, to the society they form by their union.
> (Durkheim, E. *The Division of Labour in Society*)

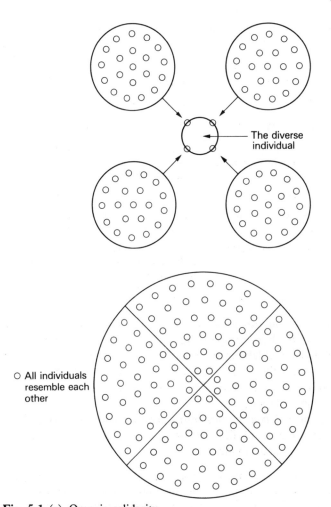

The diverse
individual

O All individuals
resemble each
other

Fig. 5.1 (a) Organic solidarity
(b) Mechanical solidarity

● *Simple and complex societies*

The move from mechanical solidarity to organic solidarity is the most
important feature of any comparison between pre-industrial and industrial
societies. *A priori*, it might seem that the division of labour would bring
people together because it necessitates cooperative tasks. However, organic solidarity creates conflicts because it involves a movement away from a
social structure based on *personal relationships* to a structure based on
impersonal relationships. In pre-industrial society morality depended upon
doing what everybody else did, but in an industrial society, based on

Table 5.3 Summary of simple and complex societies

SIMPLE SOCIETIES	COMPLEX SOCIETIES
Population sparsely distributed	Population densely distributed
Little division of labour	Highly specialised work
MECHANICAL SOLIDARITY	ORGANIC SOLIDARITY
Solidarity derived from resemblances, linking the individual to society.	Enormous social and economic differentiation caused by industrialisation.
Uniformity of beliefs and values.	Plurality of beliefs and values.
Religion pervades everything; all that is social is religious.	An ever-decreasing number of collective beliefs and sentiments.
Supreme value attaches to society as a whole.	Supreme value attaches to individual freedom and equality of opportunity.

organic solidarity, an individual has to comply with social roles relating to many different groups. For example, family life is separated from working life. The social division of labour in modern society creates a large number of role conflicts. According to Durkheim there are abnormal forms of the division of labour: two of the most important are (a) the anomic and (b) the forced division of labour.

(1) *Anomic division of labour* comes into operation when society fails to adjust to modern industrial life and serious conflicts arise especially between management and labour.

> As the market extends, great industry appears. But it results in changing the relations of employers and employees. The great strain upon the nervous system and the contagious influence of great agglomerations increase the needs of the latter. Machines replace men; manufacturing replaces handwork. The worker is regimented, separated from his family throughout the day.
> (Durkheim, E. *The Division of Labour in Society*)

2 *Forced division of labour* takes place when individual workers are not adequately fitted to perform their work tasks.

> . . . the division of labour produces solidarity only if it is spontaneous . . . labour is divided spontaneously only if society is constituted in such a way that social inequalities express natural inequalities.
> (Durkheim, E. *The Division of Labour in Society*)

Spontaneous division of labour can only operate:
(a) if social inequalities are drastically reduced;

(b) if society is reclothed in moral character by the economic order being once more integrated into social life (Fig. 5.2(a) and (b)).

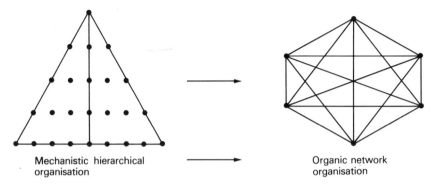

Mechanistic hierarchical
organisation

Organic network
organisation

Fig. 5.2 (a) Mechanistic hierarchical organisation
(b) Organic network organisation

5.2 Occupations

- *Occupations and the division of labour*

Viewed from the structural-functionalist perspective, a study of the sociology of occupations and occupational differentiation facilitates understanding of the implications of the division of labour. Different occupations may be categorised in 'banded groups' of varying degrees of 'occupational crystallisation'. Occupations with a high degree of crystallisation are those which can be clearly defined. They are occupations which tend to be associated with intense specialisation. The work of a brain surgeon, for example, is highly specialised and could not be undertaken without long training, expert knowledge and a high degree of competence for which considerable reward would be expected and obtained. Occupations with a low degree of crystallisation are not easily classified because they could be performed by a very large number of people and without prior training. Such occupations may be referred to as 'jobs' because they involve routine, manual, lowly-paid work.

- *Occupations and social class*

An individual's occupation is of vital sociological importance because it is the chief criterion of social stratification. The importance of a person's occupation as a yardstick of social classification is not just a fetish of sociologists; it is the main criterion used by the Registrar General when compiling the standard five-point scale of social classes. There is a general consensus about the relative social standing of occupations. An order of social esteem from high regard to low regard might run as follows: doctor, school teacher, policeman, bricklayer, railway porter and roadsweeper. Such orders of occupational esteem might vary between countries.

Social class groups, based on a person's occupation, can thus be objectively assessed and are widely used.

> A sociologist worth his salt, if given two basic indices of class such as income and occupation, can make a long list of predictions about the individual in question even if no further information has been given.
> (Berger, P. *Invitation to Sociology*)

Berger goes on to argue that a sociologist who has knowledge of the income and occupation of an individual should be able to make intelligent guesses about his housing, living conditions, and social activities.

> The backbone of the class structure, and indeed of the entire reward system of modern Western society, is the occupation order. Other sources of economic and symbolic advantage do exist alongside the occupational order, but for the vast majority of the population these tend, at best, to be secondary to those deriving from the division of labour.
> (Parkin, F. *Class Inequality and Political Order*)

● *The occupational continuum*

A study of occupations presents definitional problems. It is convenient to use a continuum (or spectrum) depending on the degree of crystallisation involved in particular occupations (see Fig. 5.3). The polar ends of the continuum would be
(a) *jobs* (with a low degree of visibility and identity);
(b) the *professions* (with a high degree of determinates).

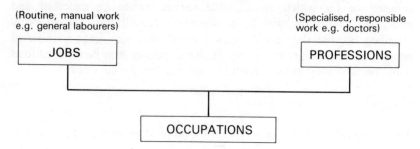

Fig. 5.3 The occupational continuum

The study of 'jobs' is of great interest to those examining society from the conflict perspective, while the study of the 'professions' is more in keeping with the structural-functionalist perspective.

As one moves towards the 'jobs' end of the continuum, the work is likely to be extrinsic and have an instrumental orientation. This type of work is regarded as mere labour and is performed as a means to an end. The job is not regarded as the central life-interest and a sharp distinction is made between work and non-work. The worker is likely to endeavour to maximise returns while at the same time minimising effort.

> When I asked them to select three out of 17 attributes of the ideal job (on the hypothetical assumption that they were looking for a new job) dockers most frequently chose high level of pay and long-term security – both of them extrinsic attributes. The intrinsic attribute of the opportunity to develop skills and potential came a long way behind.
>
> (Stephen Hill, 'Dockers and Their World', article in *Society Today*, No. 8, 28 January 1977)

Towards the 'professions' end of the continuum, the work is intrinsic by nature and is more likely to represent the central life-interest. There is no definite dichotomy between work and non-work. Admission into a profession is by a 'one-portal entry' controlled by existing members of the profession. Thus the Law Society is the sole arbiter of who should be allowed to join the legal profession.

● *Dimensions of occupational crystallisation*

There are various dimensions of occupationateness and these are best examined according to the concept of crystallisation. The following table illustrates the extremes of occupational crystallisation.

Table 5.4 Occupational crystallisation

LOW OCCUPATIONAL STRATA		HIGH OCCUPATIONAL STRATA
Working (manual)	Social class	*Middle* (non-manual)
Inadequate (hourly or weekly wage)	Pay	*High* (annual salary)
Insecure (possibly temporary)	Job security	*Very secure* (permanent staff)
Instrumental (extrinsic)	Motivation	*Expressive* (intrinsic)

Table 5.4 Occupational crystallisation (Cont.)

LOW OCCUPATIONAL STRATA		HIGH OCCUPATIONAL STRATA
Organisational ('I work at Ford's')	Orientation	*Occupational* ('I am a farmer)
Indeterminate (work can be done by almost anybody)	Determinateness	*Very determinate* (specialised, e.g. a dentist)
Little (responsible TO others)	Responsibility	*Great* (responsible FOR others)
Close (no chance of using initiative – answerable to foreman)	Supervision	*Little* (freedom and autonomy)
Low (unskilled and untrained)	Level of marketable transferable skill	*High* (qualified and certificated)
Poor (few 'perks' and no pension scheme)	Fringe benefits	*Good* (many 'perks' and excellent pension scheme)
Few (one or two weeks annually)	Holidays	*Many* (four to six weeks annually)
Poor (hot, cold, noisy, dirty, dangerous)	Working conditions	*Good* (air-controlled, sedentary, quiet, safe)
Many (unsocial hours)	Working hours	*Few* (normal hours or flexi-time)
Fragmented (repetitive)	Work task	*Complete* (satisfying)
Localised (little or no travelling)	Situation	*Cosmopolitan* (much travelling, with expense account)
Trade unions (attempting to obtain higher pay)	Representation	*Professional body* (attempting to maintain standards)
Great (hates the work)	Alienation	*Little* (loves the work)

Table 5.4 indicates polarised positions between work performed according to low or high occupational strata. In real life these extreme positions are rarely met. However, Table 5.5 provides examples of the extreme divergences which occur in the earnings and hours of certain occupations.

Table 5.5 Occupational divergences in earnings

Occupation	Average gross weekly earning (£)	Average weekly hours
Accountants	107.4	37.0
Firemen	79.9	49.6
General labourers	68.6	45.7
Office managers	116.1	37.0
University academic staff	136.3	36.1

(*Department of Employment Gazette*, October 1978)

'Jobs' have a low degree of crystallisation and would normally be categorised in the 'low occupational strata' column, but even 'jobs' are amorphous, varying in content depending upon organisation of the workplace. Factory and office jobs are generally regarded as unskilled, but they may be relatively skilled in a particular firm or industry.

> Although the personnel men classify a hundred-odd positions in the cotton mill, it is unrealistic to suppose that each one of them is a separate occupation.
> (Caplow, T. *The Sociology of Work*)

● *Changes in occupational structure*

We saw in section 5.1 that according to the logic of industrialism all industrial societies tend to develop similar work patterns. This particularly applies to the occupational structure of industrial societies. There has been a decline in the proportion of UK workers employed in primary industries such as agriculture and fishing and an increase in the proportion of the working population occupied in providing services (see Fig. 5.4).

Daniel Bell has argued that most advanced industrial societies are becoming service economies. Services rather than goods predominate. The occupational structure has changed as white-collar workers constitute an increasing proportion of the workforce at the expense of manufacturing workers. An increase in professionalisation has been accompanied by the new role of theoretical knowledge and industrial technology. (See Bell, D.

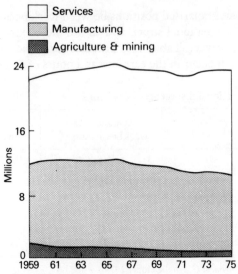

Fig. 5.4 Employees in employment: by industry, UK, 1959–75
(*Social Trends*, HMSO, 1977)

Table 5.6 Division of the workforce in the UK, according to occupational
sectors

Sector	1881 (per cent)	1971 (per cent)
Primary	13	3
Secondary	50	44
Tertiary	37	53

The Coming of Post-Industrial Society and *Cultural Contradictions of Capitalism*.)

The post-industrial society, it is clear, is a knowledge society in a double sense: first, the sources of innovation are increasingly derivative from research and development (and more directly, there is a new relation between science and technology because of the centrality of theoretical knowledge); second, the weight of the society – measured by a larger proportion of the Gross National Product and a larger share of employment – is increasingly in the knowledge field.

(Bell, D. *The Coming of Post-Industrial Society*)

Similar ideas have been propounded by other sociologists such as A. Touraine in *The Post-Industrial Society* and J. Habermas in *Towards a Rational Society*. The increasing influence of both central and local government is reflected in the increased proportion of people working for government bureaucracy. Recognition of the increase in the power and prestige of white-collar workers caused C. Wright Mills, in *White Collar* (1951) to refer to them as the 'new middle class'.

> 'Class situation' in its simplest sense has to do with the amount and source of income. Today occupation rather than property is the source of income for most of those who receive any direct income.
> (C. Wright Mills, *White Collar*)

Mills, as a conflict theorist, argued that white-collar workers were entitled to be termed the 'new middle class' mainly because they were far better paid than manual workers. It is possible that in the future this trend may be reversed. There is an increasing tendency for people to shun manual occupations such as dock work and mining. According to the economic laws of supply and demand, the income from such occupations is likely to increase as people reject manual work and opt for comfortable white-collar jobs. The greatest occupational increase in the past in the white-collar sector has been in those engaged in clerical work, but the most important white-collar occupations in a technological age are those of scientists and engineers. The emergence of new occupational requirements in the field of computers and automation are of sociological significance when considering the allocation of time between work and non-work (see section 5.8).

Table 5.7 is based upon some of the implications and speculations about the service economy suggested by V.R. Fuchs, in *The Service Economy*.

Table 5.7 Possible consequences of the service economy

1 Non-profit operations account for one-third of the service sector's employment.

2 'The large corporation is likely to be overshadowed by the hospitals, universities, research institutes, government agencies and professional organisations that are the hallmark of a service economy.'

3 New instruments of regulation and control will be necessary to replace the profit motive as a spur to efficiency.

4 Many occupations in the service sector do not require the physical strength necessary in traditional occupations so women can compete on equal terms with men.

5 More older and part-time workers can be utilised in the service industries.

6 It is likely that automation will result in less alienating work.

7 Because many service occupations are extremely rewarding the line between work and leisure will be more difficult to draw (see section 5.8).

5.3 Job satisfaction

• *The meaning of work*

A proper understanding of work, according to interactionists, requires an analysis of the *meaning* which people attach to their work. The degree of satisfaction a worker gains (or does *not* gain) from work depends upon how he regards the work. The dichotomy between *intrinsic work* (where the worker finds the job satisfying for its own sake) and *extrinsic work* (where the worker is only there because of the pay and what he can purchase with it), is over-simplistic when considering the *social meaning* of work.

> ... a man may work because he must, or because he should or because he wants to. In the first instance his satisfaction lies in escaping the results of not working. In the second he has the satisfaction of duty fulfilled. In the third he has the satisfaction in the pleasure of work for its own sake.
>
> (Balchin, N. *Occupational Psychology*)

According to the conflict perspective, in an industrial society only a minority of workers find job satisfaction in the pleasure of work itself. When a post-industrial society is fully established things may be otherwise; but in industrial societies job satisfaction mainly revolves around whether or not the job enables a worker to buy the latest car or a favourable package holiday.

Satisfaction at work can be more easily measured in *negatives* than positives. How short are the hours? Is the work not too boring, noisy or dirty? Where work is regarded 'as a necessary evil' then it is not possible to make the work really satisfying, but only less dissatisfying. The various managerial techniques discussed in the latter part of this topic rarely engender positive job satisfaction but rather they remove some of the antagonism against work and therefore give a semblance of meaning to it. The more contented the worker the more effective is his work and the greater will be his production.

It is impossible to measure accurately degrees of job satisfaction. In 1935, Hoppock made one of the first studies of job satisfaction by asking workers very generalised questions, such as:

'Do you *love* your job?'

or

'Do you *hate* your job?'

Likert used a similar but more sophisticated type of questioning which enabled work attitudes to be measured according to the Likert Scale based upon five responses. A worker might be asked a series of five questions relating to conflict at work; e.g.

In your department is there:

1 a very great deal of friction?
2 a lot of friction?
3 average friction?
4 not much friction?
5 no friction?

General Motors organised an essay contest where workers wrote about their job, but the results were unsatisfactory as many of the workers dwelt upon trivia (such as 'I like the cafeteria'), without commenting upon their attitude to the job itself.

- *The social psychology of work*

Interactionists suggest that job satisfaction depends upon the *personality* of the worker. Some workers like to be autonomous and feel free to make decisions, while others prefer to work in a structured environment. Some would rather be part of a large-scale operation, while others wish to work with a small group. Social psychologists believe that intelligence is the best predictor of which jobs people will choose and whether they will be able to do a job well and consequently be happy in it. People with high IQs find more satisfaction in doing interesting and creative work, while those with low IQs find repetitive work less distressing. Some jobs call for a particular kind of personality: an extrovert may make a happy actor, politician, spy or lion-tamer, while an introvert could well gain a high degree of job satisfaction as a lighthouse-keeper or nightwatchman.

> More than any other job I have ever done, nightwatching showed up the truth of this dream-life. Its heart was really nothing but the relief-sensation of escape, like a holding of the breath as the curtain rose.
>   (Nairn, T. 'The Nightwatchman', in Fraser, R., ed., *Work*)

Whether or not satisfaction is obtained from working indoors or outdoors, with things or with people, depends on an individual's interests and sense of values. Personality traits may change as workers become socialised by a particular job: for many people work personality is essentially part of a *work subculture*.

There are workers who are able to resist the over-socialisation effects of work: for some the retention of inherent personality traits contributes to unhappiness at work. For others, their special traits (e.g. introvertism) may make them especially suitable for the particular work and contribute towards job satisfaction.

> For example, neuroticism leads to low job satisfaction, and introversion to being able to withdraw from conflicting sources of social pressures in role conflict.
>   (Argyle, M. 'Personality and Work' in *Society Today*, No. 8, 28 January 1977)

• *Comparisons of job satisfaction*

From a consensus perspective, the logic of industrialism implies considerable uniformity in national comparisons of job satisfaction. Inkeles
(*Industrial Man*) has attempted to document this uniformity in a survey of
six industrial countries. Table 5.8 suggests that similarities apply to a
worker's social class, status and position in the hierarchy.

Table 5.8 National comparisons of job satisfaction, by occupation: percentage
satisfied

USSR		USA		Germany	
		Large business	100		
		Small business	91		
		Professional	82	Professional	75
Administrative, professional	77				
Semi-professional	70			Upper white-collar	65
White-collar	60	White-collar	82	Civil servants	51
				Lower white-collar	33
Skilled worker	62	Skilled manual	84	Skilled worker	47
Semi-skilled	45	Semi-skilled	76	Semi-skilled	21
Unskilled	23	Unskilled	72	Unskilled	11
Peasant	12			Farm labour	23
Italy		Sweden		Norway	
		Upper-class	84	Upper-class	93
		Middle-class	72	Middle-class	88
Skilled worker	68				
Artisan	62	Working-class	69	Working-class	83
Unskilled	57				
Farm Labour	43				

(Landsberger, H.A., ed., *Comparative Perspectives on Formal Organisations*, 1970)

• *Orientation to work and* The Affluent Worker *studies*

One of the most important pieces of research dealing with job satisfaction
is *The Affluent Worker* studies of Goldthorpe, Lockwood *et al.* The
researchers found that car workers, at the Vauxhall plant in Luton, gave
up jobs which offered intrinsic satisfactions for jobs which offered higher

wages and extrinsic satisfactions. In *The Affluent Worker: Industrial Attitudes and Behaviour* they found that:

1 many workers found no satisfaction from their work, but were content with their jobs in the sense that they did not wish to leave Vauxhall for a job with another firm;

2 the workers studied had an instrumental attitude to their jobs and two-thirds had moved from jobs which gave more intrinsic satisfaction;

3 workers' orientation to work is more important than what actually goes on at work.

> ... the question of satisfaction from work cannot in the end be usefully considered except in relation to the more basic question of what we would term orientation to work. Until one knows something of the way in which workers order their wants and expectations relative to their employment – until one knows what the meaning of work has for them – one is not in a position to understand what overall assessment of their job satisfaction may most appropriately be made in their case.
>
> (Goldthorpe, J.H. *et al.*, *The Affluent Worker: Industrial Attitudes and Behaviour*)

Goldthorpe, Lockwood *et al.* set out three 'ideal typical' orientations to work.

(a) *Instrumental orientation* – the work is entirely extrinsic and satisfaction is gained only from the monetary rewards received.

(b) *Bureaucratic orientation* – the purpose of work is found in service to the organisation in return for improved rewards and security.

(c) *Solidaristic orientation* – the work is given meaning because it is a group activity, e.g. Hull fishermen (see Tunstall, J. *The Fisherman*) or coalminers (see Dennis, Henriques and Slaughter *Coal is Our Life*).

The main importance of *The Affluent Worker* studies is that they made clear that explanations of job satisfaction should not be sought merely from studying people *at work*. An individual's orientation to work is the most significant sociological factor. The degree of job satisfaction obtained from work depends, to a great extent, upon workers' attitudes. Herzberg, F. (*Work and the Nature of Man*) found that advancement was the factor which many workers regarded as most important. Those Luton workers who had aspirations for their children were those whose *reference group* workers were doing jobs with a higher status but which they themselves hoped to reach through upward social mobility.

- *Male and female attitudes to job satisfaction*

Women, despite lower pay and status, are less dissatisfied than men with their jobs. According to the General Household Survey carried out in the

UK in 1971, less than half of the men questioned were 'very satisfied' with their jobs compared with over 60 per cent of women. The answers to the survey revealed distinct differences between the sexes. Men were more dissatisfied with pay, possibly reflecting their continued position in society as 'breadwinners', while many women apparently regarded pay as a peripheral extra. A higher percentage of women disliked the type of work they were required to perform, although men were more dissatisfied with a lack of opportunity for advancement and physical conditions. Both men and women rated dissatisfaction with the administration or organisation as one of the three main reasons for discontent at work (see Table 5.9).

Table 5.9 Job satisfaction and dissatisfaction, 1971

	Percentages	
	Men	Women
Degree of satisfaction:		
Very satisfied	47	61
Fairly satisfied	40	31
Neither satisfied nor dissatisfied	6	4
Rather dissatisfied	4	3
Very dissatisfied	3	1
Main reasons for dissatisfaction:		
Pay	38	23
Dissatisfied with administration/organisation	20	22
Did not like the kind of work	18	27

('General Household Survey' in *Social Trends* No. 5, 1974, HMSO)

- **The complexity of job satisfaction**

Interactionists believe that there are no simple answers to questions of job satisfaction. Complex problems of conceptualisation arise. In the first important book on job satisfaction, in 1935, Hoppock wrote:

> The problem is complicated by the ephemeral and variable nature of satisfaction. Indeed, there may be no such thing as *job* satisfaction independent of the other satisfactions of one's life. Family relationships, health, relative social status in the community, and a multitude of other factors may be just as important as the job itself in determining what we tentatively choose to call job satisfaction. A person may be satisfied with one aspect of his job and dissatisfied with another. Satisfactions may be rationalized, and the degree of satisfaction may vary from day to day. A person may never be wholly satisfied.
>
> (Hoppock, R. *Job Satisfaction*)

Some of the difficulties of assessing the significance of factors relating to job satisfaction will become obvious to students who attempt to place the items in Table 5.10 in order of importance, with reference to their views of what constitutes job satisfaction.

Table 5.10 Factors affecting job satisfaction

Advancement (promotion)
Autonomy (freedom to make decisions)
Company policy
Control (e.g. of speed of the job)
Creativity (originality)
Democracy (consultation)
Esteem
Fringe benefits
Group (large or small organisation)
Holidays
Hours (including shift work, flexitime, overtime, etc.)
Incentives (pay, status, etc.)
Intelligence (IQ rating)
Interaction (with other workers)
Job rotation (swapping jobs)
Management (administration)
Recognition (of work done)
Security (of employment)
Supervision (of others)
Working conditions

It is impossible to decide the most vital aspects of job satisfaction for an individual unless one knows the worker's:
1 orientation to work;
2 actual job;
3 personality;
4 desire to satisfy intrinsic and/or extrinsic needs.

● *Managerial techniques*

In accordance with a structural-functionalist stance, managers appreciate the desirability of comprehending what constitutes job satisfaction. Various managerial techniques have been employed to reduce dissatisfaction on the understanding that the more satisfied the workers the greater will be their productive efforts.
1 *Taylor's scientific management*
In the early part of this century F.W. Taylor conducted research based on two main premises.

(a) Workers regard work as extrinsic and wish to receive the highest possible pay packet.
(b) In order to gain high wages, workers must obey instructions implicitly and leave all planning decisions to management.

He felt that the *planning* of a job should be separated from the *doing* of it. The doing of the work could be entrusted to the workers themselves, but the planning was a highly complex activity that required the application of special techniques.
(Vroom, V.H. *Work and Motivation*)

Taylor's ideas were tested at the Bethlehem Steel Company's works, in the USA, where labourers were loading $12\frac{1}{2}$ tons of pig-iron a day. After careful observation Taylor calculated that a really efficient worker should be able to load between 47 and 48 tons a day. He decided to select the best man for the job, instruct him in the most efficient methods and offer him high rewards.

There was to be no argument, no 'back-talk', no initiative, nothing but the bare carrying-out to the minutest detail what he had been ordered to do. When he was told to lift, he was to lift; when he was told to walk, he was to walk; when he was told to put the iron down, he was to put it down; when he was told to rest, he was to rest. By the end of the day, this labourer had loaded $47\frac{1}{2}$ tons of pig-iron, and for the three years he was under observation he continued to load this amount and was paid 60 per cent higher than his former wage.
(Brown, J.A.C. *The Social Psychology of Industry*)

Taylor had a mechanistic perspective of people at work and regarded them as machine-like units. From his research developed modern ideas of time and motion study, but 'Speedy' Taylor became a hated figure and 'Taylorism' was much resented by workers. Although he appreciated that production could be increased by extrinsic job satisfaction and improved working conditions, Taylor adopted a one-sided approach by looking at work merely from the employers' viewpoint.

2 *Elton Mayo's Hawthorne Studies*
Elton Mayo was responsible for a series of work studies carried out at the Hawthorne Works, in Chicago, in the 1930s. His research methods were superior to those of Taylor. Mayo's meticulous control of his experiments and his analysis of the apparently incongruous results were in the best tradition of social science investigation. Mayo began by altering the lighting provided for workers assembling and checking electrical components. The output went up, both for workers enjoying improved illumination but also for the control group which had no such advantages.

In the second series of tests, girls assembling telephone relays were carefully observed over a period of five years. Various changes were introduced for test periods of four to twelve weeks. The changes included the use of piece-work rates, varying rest periods and shortened hours. Most of the strategies resulted in improved production.

> Finally, all the improvements were taken away, and the girls went back to the physical conditions of the beginning of the experiment: work on Saturday, forty-eight-hour week, no rest pauses, no piece-work, and no free meal. This state of affairs lasted for a period of twelve weeks, and output was the highest ever recorded, averaging 3000 relays a week.
> (Brown, J.A.C. *The Social Psychology of Industry*)

At first sight the results appeared inexplicable, but subsequent interviews of workers caused Mayo to come to two conclusions.

(a) The girls worked harder as a result of being observed. At last somebody was really interested in what they were doing at work. By requesting the workers' help, the investigators made them feel the job was worthwhile. (This 'Hawthorne effect' provides a problem which will always exist for social science researchers: whenever people are studied, they begin to behave differently as social actors. They indeed 'put on an act'.)

(b) Improvements in group relationships resulted in increased output. This conclusion was in direct opposition to the notion of the worker as a machine; Taylor's ideal worker, Schmidt, had loaded pig iron in isolation. Mayo's work emphasised the importance of social relations at work and of purposeful group activity.

> People do not just get together, they get together for a purpose.
> (Homans, G.C. *The Human Group*)

Mayo found that particular groups insisted upon conformity to certain standards and that workers whose output exceeded the accepted norm were pressurised by other members of the clique. Evidence of this practice emerged in Mayo's study of nine workers wiring telephone equipment.

> They worked in rows of three, each row behind the other and were attended by two soldermen and supervised by two supervisors. The ones in front worked on 'connector' equipment, which was paid at a slightly higher rate and conferred prestige; the ones at the back worked on 'selector' equipment, which carried rather less prestige. They were paid by group piece-rates, divided into differential shares, so it was to their interest to raise output as high as possible. In point of fact the output remained extraordinarily constant, and below their actual capacities. This uniform and restricted rate was a controlling agency in the group, giving rise to protests when any individual exceeded it or fell below it.
> (Sprott, W.J.H. *Human Groups*)

The significance of Mayo's work to the sociologist is in the importance he placed upon work as a *group activity*. Mayo's ideas gave rise to the

Human Relations school of work studies. The term is now applied to a heterogeneous number of management techniques aimed at increasing production by encouraging self-actualisation by the worker. The Human Relations school stresses vital psychological factors. Man is a creature of sentiment and wishes to be approved of by his fellows. Mayo found that group activity could be used to overcome the worker's conception of himself as an isolated, atomised man. Mayo's emphasis upon group satisfactions has a parallel with Durkheim's solution to anomie. (See anomic division of labour, section 5.5.)

The task of management is to take cognizance of human-social facts and to organise sustained cooperation among workers. The establishment of good group relations promotes good human relations.

3 *Maslow's hierarchy of needs*

In recent years, a school of neo-human relations has developed based upon Maslow's *needs hierarchy (A Theory of Human Motivation)*.

Maslow contended that man has an ascending order of needs leading to self-actualisation (see Fig. 5.5). The worker's first concern is to satisfy physiological needs such as having enough to eat and drink. As one need is satisfied, so the worker moves up the hierarchical scale to higher needs such as a safe job, a sense of belonging, improved status, and finally (at the apex of the pyramid) to self-actualisation by which he realises his full potential.

The ideas of Maslow have been expanded by F. Herzberg (*Work and The Nature of Man*) and D. McGregor (*The Human Side of Enterprise*). Herzberg's

basic assumption was that motivation is generated by the opportunity to satisfy needs in work and that if you want to know what the worker's needs in work are then look at the types of satisfaction he gets out of work. He therefore asked

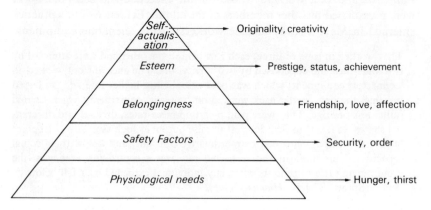

Fig. 5.5 Maslow's hierarchy of human needs

workers to recount to him incidents, events, and occasions in their jobs when they experienced a feeling of satisfaction.

(Daniel, W.W. 'Understanding Employee Behaviour in Context' in Child, J., ed., *Man and Organisation*)

An analysis of workers' replies caused Herzberg to suggest that job satisfaction can be brought about in five main ways:

1 Achievement – satisfaction in fulfilling a task;
2 Recognition – receiving acknowledgement and praise;
3 Responsibility – enjoying a degree of trust;
4 Promotion – advancing to new opportunities;
5 Intrinsic interest – satisfaction in the job itself.

The management philosophy of neo-human relations is based upon power-sharing, job-restructuring and schemes of job-enrichment which give more meaning to work thus leading to self-actualisation and a higher degree of job satisfaction.

Job enrichment and its antecedents, job enlargement (in which an employee may be allowed to perform a sequence of tasks rather than a single repetitive one) and job rotation (in which employees circulate among different functions), attempt to reverse the specialization trend by giving employees more varied tasks which, it is claimed, will interest them more in their work and also make them more productive .... job enrichment differs from its predecessors in that employees

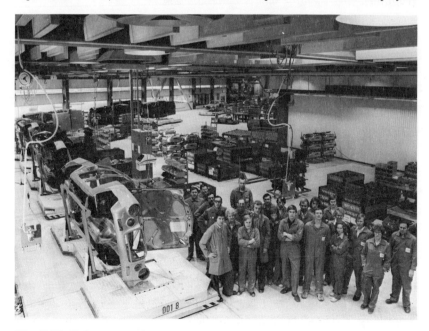

Fig. 5.5A Volvo car workers

are asked to take over some of the responsibilities previously held by superiors or by colleagues at a slightly higher level in the organization.

(Hesper, G. and Little, A. in Warr, P.B.W., ed., *Psychology at Work*)

Large companies (such as Volvo, ICI and Philips) have organised successful job-enrichment schemes. The Volvo experiment has been particularly successful. A group of workers acting as a team build the whole car. (See Fig. 5.5A.) Within the team everyone earns the same with the exception of the elected chargehand. Absenteeism, wildcat strikes and high staff-turnover have been radically reduced. In contrast assembly-line workers, these groups of Volvo workers take a pride in their work. The workers have the satisfaction of knowing that they have produced the car as a group effort in a congenial work environment. Professor Lupton has argued that scientific management and human relations do not provide all the answers: management theory must consider the *total environment* of the worker. (Lupton, T. 'Social Science and the Manager', in *Work, A New Social Science Study Reader*, published by *New Society*.)

5.4 Ownership and control in modern industry

• *Capitalist and socialist modes of production*

In a capitalist society the material means of production (factories, machines and raw materials) are owned by private capitalists who employ the labour necessary to operate the means of production. In accordance with the conflict perspective, the social relations of capitalism involve the owners of capital controlling the wage-earners. Marx argued, in the nineteenth century, that the social relations of a capitalist society were responsible for a constant class struggle between the *bourgeoisie* who owned the means of production and the *proletariat* who constituted the labour force.

In the early days of the industrial revolution the capitalist was both owner and controller of the means of production. Early capitalists in Britain, such as Richard Arkwright and Josiah Wedgwood, owned the means of production as private property and personally controlled the labour process in an attempt to maximise their profits. Labour power was regarded as a commodity to be bought on the labour market.

In both capitalist and socialist societies, surplus labour exists in the sense that more labour is demanded by the organisers of production than is necessary to supply the basic human needs which make possible the conditions of reproduction of labour power. The great difference which exists between the conceptual models of capitalism and socialism is that under capitalism surplus labour is appropriated privately, whereas under socialism it is appropriated collectively. In a capitalist society surplus labour is appropriated in the form of *surplus value*.

> But by paying the daily or weekly *value* of the spinner's labouring power, the capitalist has acquired the right of using that labouring power during the *whole* day or week. He will, therefore, make him work say, daily, twelve hours. Over and above the six hours required to replace his wages, or the value of his labouring power, he will, therefore, have to work six other hours, which I shall call hours of surplus labour, which surplus labour will realize itself in a surplus value and a surplus produce.
>
> (Marx, K. *Wages, Price and Profit*)

The owners of the means of production put to use the labour of the worker and sell the finished product at a price which enables the capitalist to exploit the worker by appropriating the surplus value created (see Fig. 5.6).

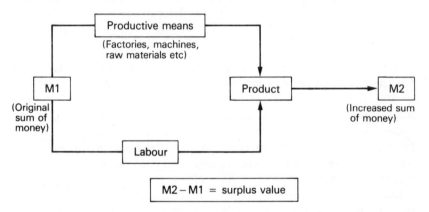

Fig. 5.6 The capitalist appropriates surplus value

Table 5.11 Capitalist and socialist modes of production

Capitalist mode	Socialist mode
1 Private ownership of the means of production	1 Public ownership of the means of production
2 Surplus value appropriated privately	2 Surplus labour appropriated collectively
3 Production determined by market forces	3 Production planned according to community needs

The socialist mode of production is typified by public ownership of the means of production. Socialist planning of production still necessitates the existence of managers, but the surplus value is appropriated by the community rather than by the individual. The main contrasting points of the two modes of production are summarised in Table 5.11.

- ● *The separation of ownership and control in capitalist enterprises*

The tendency for there to be a divorce between ownership and control in capitalist businesses was suggested by Berle and Means.

> Economic power, in terms of control over physical assets, is apparently responding to a centripetal force, tending more and more to concentrate in the hands of a few corporate managements. At the same time, beneficial ownership is centrifugal, tending to divide and sub-divide, to split into even smaller units and to pass freely from hand to hand. In other words, ownership continually becomes more dispersed; the power formerly joined to it becomes increasingly concentrated; and the corporate system is thereby more securely established.
>   (Berle, A.A. and Means, G.C. *The Modern Corporation and Private Property*)

Their analysis, in 1929, of the 200 largest US corporations, revealed that 65 per cent of these corporations, with 80 per cent of their combined wealth, were management-controlled. Although the statistics of Berle and Means were refined by P. Sargant Florence (*Ownership, Control and Success of Large Companies*), there is little doubt that a far larger proportion of companies are now controlled by managers or by a very small proportion of owners who supervise the running of the business on behalf of a majority of passive shareholders.

During the last fifty years, the control of large companies has been passing from the owners (i.e. shareholders who invest their capital) to paid managers who undertake the vital entrepreneurial functions of decision-making and planning. As the control of shareholders over large capitalist enterprises has declined, so managers have ceased to act merely as agents of the owners and have assumed control of businesses. The trend from owner-orientated to management-orientated businesses has evolved in Britain since the Limited Liability Acts of 1855–6 enabled individuals to invest in companies without being liable for more than the value of their own holdings; the liability of a shareholder who invests £1000 in a joint stock company is limited to £1000. Before the limited liability acts were passed, owners of shares were at risk of being sued for company debts far beyond the amount of their holdings.

The corporate paradigm of managerial supremacy is accepted in large measure by sociologists such as Dahrendorf and Aron. Baran and Sweezy

(*Monopoly Capital*) have singled out three characteristic features of large modern capitalistic enterprises.

1 Control rests in the hands of the management.
2 Management is a self-perpetuating group.
3 Company funds remain at the disposal of the management.

It is the modern tendency for managers of large companies to own no appreciable share of the business. They are chosen by a self-selected Board of Directors. A large firm may even be controlled by one all-powerful manager who has a monopoly of knowledge of the business.

> With growing size and complexity of operation, smaller or more passive owners tend to lose their power of decision. The number of stockholders usually increases; the share in the voting power of each owner thus declines. More important is the failure of knowledge. Those who are not active in the management of the enterprise have less and less knowledge of what is happening. . . . The individual or individuals who are immediately in authority, by contrast, retain the knowledge that goes automatically with such association. This knowledge often accords an individual full authority over the enterprise in the absence of voting control. Others have no alternative but to accept his lead.
> (Galbraith, J.K. *The New Industrial State*)

Below top managers in the hierarchy, are numerous junior executives who have used the process of upward social mobility to become part of the management team of the organisation. These middle managers do not merely work for the firm; they devote their lives to furthering its aims. Their loyalty to the large organisation is motivated by a feeling of 'belongingness'.

> it is they who are the mind and soul of our great self-perpetuating institutions.
> (Whyte, W.H. *The Organisation Man*)

James Burnham (*The Managerial Revolution*) also believed in the primary importance of the role of managers, but he did not confine his ideas of a new managerial elite to a capitalist society. Burnham argued that the managerial revolution was of wider significance than that of capitalistic owners being superseded by professional managers. He contended that the new management elite was also an important aspect of *state* enterprises. Burnham's thesis has been severely criticised. Dahrendorf has written of Burnham's inability to distinguish property from authority as evidenced by his reiteration of the misconception that 'ownership means control' so that 'those who control are owners' (Dahrendorf, R. *Class and Class Conflict in Industrial Society*). Nevertheless, in spite of ambiguities and contradictions, Burnham was the most successful publicist of managerialism.

What Berle and Means had done for the academic world, Burnham did for the masses, or more accurately their leaders. It is largely as a result of his influence that the phrase 'managerial revolution' is now used by journalists, economists and politicians with a greater degree of ambiguity and assurance than perhaps any other.

(Nichols, T. *Ownership, Control and Ideology*)

• *Is the separation of ownership and control sociologically significant?*

It is clear that owners of stocks and shares are decreasingly influential in the running of capitalist enterprises. The separation of ownership and control has been made possible by industrial expansion and the accompanying issue of an increasing number of shares. A minority of owners (shareholders) control the fate of businesses while the majority passively acquiesce. The dispersal of share-ownership has resulted in shareholder-absenteeism.

> The consequent power vacuum is filled by an increasingly entrenched management.
>
> (Child, J. *The Business Enterprise in Modern Society*)

So ownership and control are effectively divorced from each other, but there are those who argue that this separation is of very little sociological significance.

Although the ownership of shares has been diffused, they are owned by a very small proportion of people in the UK, and there has been no significant statistical change in the last thirty years.

> Some 93 per cent of all adults in 1970 held not even a single share, or, for that matter, any government bond. Most of the 7 per cent or so who did had only small or modest holdings. A minority of 1 per cent owned about four-fifths of all capital of this kind in personal hands. There is massive concentration even within the ranks of the small group of shareholders. And there has been very little change on that score. It was much the same in 1950.
>
> (Westergaard, J. and Resler, H. *Class in a Capitalist Society*)

According to C. Wright Mills, a remarkably similar pattern of stock-holding existed in the USA in the 1950s; there is little to suggest that the pattern shows much sign of change.

> The six and a half million people who owned stock in publicly held corporations in 1952 made up less than 7 per cent of all adults in the population.
>
> (C. Wright Mills, *The Power Elite*)

Those holding the structural-functionalist perspective believe that the divorce of ownership and control in modern business is of little importance and argue that a general consensus exists between shareholders and managers. In spite of the incumbents having two sets of conflicting roles, they share an overall homogeneity of values and beliefs.

> ... the fact remains that in any sense that seriously matters it is not true that the managerial function alienates those who perform it from those on whose behalf it is performed; the differences of purpose and motivation which may exist between them are overshadowed by a basic community of interests.
> (Miliband, R. *The State in Capitalist Society*)

The Royal Commission on Employers' Associations and Trade Unions (1965–8) recognised that owners and managers may sometimes have opposing aims and policies, but considered that, in the long run, a compromise is reached. This compromise is in the interest of both owners and managers for both have the success of the organisation at heart.

> With a continuing growth in the size of industrial units and the amalgamation of companies there has developed a managerial society in which ownership has been divorced from control. The running of large businesses is in the hands of professional managers. They are responsible to boards of directors who can be regarded broadly as trustees for the general body of shareholders. While in the long term shareholders, employees and customers all stand to benefit if a concern flourishes, the immediate interests of these groups often conflict. Directors and managers have to balance these conflicting interests, and in practice they generally seek to strike whatever balance will best promote the welfare of the enterprise as such.
> (*Royal Commission on Employers' Associations and Trade Unions, 1968*)

Both owners and managers have middle-class beliefs; they want the capitalist system to continue; they are vitally interested in the success of the business enterprises in which they are involved and in whose fruits they indulge; and they share an ideology which arises from the capitalist mode of production and the acquisition of private property. They enjoy the same middle-class life-style and have the same attitude towards the working class who provide the labour which makes production possible.

> The manager shares with the capitalist two important social reference groups: his peers and his subordinates.
> (Dahrendorf, R. *Class and Class Conflict in Industrial Society*)

There are, however, those theorists who wish to argue that the separation of ownership and control is of great sociological significance. According to this view, the maximisation of profit is no longer the main goal of the business enterprise and managers are able to choose their own goals free from the interference of capitalistic owners. Managers, there-fore, have a wide-ranging span of responsibilities including social and benevolent obligations to employees, customers and the community at large.

The implications of this doctrine of the 'soulful corporation' are far-reaching. The truth is that if it is accepted, the whole corpus of traditional economic theory must be abandoned and the time-honoured justification of the existing social order in terms of economic efficiency, justice, etc. simply falls to the ground.

(Baran, P.A. and Sweezy, P.M. *Monopoly Capital*)

The belief that the modern managerial elite may use their power for the benefit of society has been put forward by other modern sociologists. While Daniel Bell (*The Coming of Post-Industrial Society*) points to the social control of the new managerial class, Alain Touraine (*The Post-Industrial Society*) sees technocrats as the top social class equipped with knowledge to benefit mankind. Jurgen Habermas (*Towards a Rational Society*) also stresses the social aspects of the technical knowledge of professional managers.

If managers do really act benevolently and conduct long-term business-planning with the benefit of the community in mind, then we have indeed moved a long way from the exploiting, profit-maximising owners who typified the entrepreneurs of the early industrial revolution. There are many sociologists, however, who are frankly sceptical of this type of 'organisation theory' associated with Herbert A. Simon in the USA. The 'satisficing' behaviour of managers as described by Simon, is perhaps less apparent as an indication of the behaviour of corporate managements than their constant endeavours to increase profits with apparent disregard for the social consequences.

5.5 Alienation

• *Alienation and capitalism*

According to Karl Marx and the conflict perspective, alienation is a pathological condition of man in capitalist society; workers find themselves powerless in industrial organisations dominated by machines which are *privately owned*. Marx used the concept of alienation in this context as a 'unit idea in his model of capitalism'. He contended that the property relations of capitalist societies were the root cause of the alienation of employees. Industrial workers in a capitalist society hated their work, the product of their work and those for whom they worked. Alienation is a most important concept for conflict theorists.

From the Middle Ages down to our own times the power of alienation has been regarded as a necessary and natural element of property .... In primitive social orders alienation is quite unnatural [but] With the increase of trade and the improvement and expansion of political organisation, community property in chattels and later in land slowly broke down and disintegrated into individual ownership, with broadening powers of alienation . . . .

(Vance, W.R. *Alienation of Property. Encyclopaedia of the Social Sciences*)

Marx argued that the property institutions of capitalism are at the root of the worker's sense of isolation from the productive system and its goals.

In his *Economic and Philosophical Manuscripts*, Marx considered four main facets of alienated labour.

1 *Alienation of man from the object of his labour*
The worker comes to loathe the product which he helps to produce. He is regarded by his employers merely as a commodity which becomes relatively less valuable in relation to that which he produces. The object of the labour is thus regarded by the worker as an alien being. Thus a Ford worker who owned a Morris Oxford car, expressed himself on the subject of Ford cars.

I wouldn't touch the bloody things; not what I see going on in this plant.
(Beynon, H. *Working for Ford*)

According to Huw Beynon this denial of any identity with the Ford product is a general phenomenon amongst Ford workers. Partial escape from plant tensions is provided by denying identity with the Ford car that has been the source of great agony on the assembly line.

Marx argued that the worker externalised himself in his work and the more powerful the alien world he helps to create the poorer becomes his own life because the less of it he can truly claim as his own.

2 *Alienation of man from the act of production*
Alienation shows itself not only in the final product of a man's labour but also in the act of production. Indeed it follows from the fact that the worker regards the object of his labour as alien that he will regard as loathsome the processes by which the objects are made.

'You don't achieve anything here. A robot could do it. The line here is made for morons. It doesn't need any thought. They tell you that. "We don't pay you for thinking" they say. Everyone comes to realize that they're not doing a worthwhile job. They're just on the line. For the money. Nobody likes to think that they're a failure. It's bad when you know that you're just a little cog. You just look at your pay packet – you look at what it does for your wife and kids. That's the only answer.'

He begins to watch his arm, as if it were being moved by what it is holding instead of by his shoulder. He thinks of water pumping his arm. . . . He knows that what he is doing is separate from any skill he has. He can stuff a saddle with straw. He has been told that the factory makes washing machines.

(Berger, J. and Mohr, J. *A Seventh Man*)

The product is merely the summary of the activity of production. Hence when the worker is *not* at work he is happy but while he is at work he is unhappy and alienated. In a factory based on the division of labour and the conveyor-belt system, the nature of the work is alienating because apart from a sense of powerlessness and loneliness, the worker is also faced with boring, repetitive, dangerous and soul-destroying work.

> Occasionally men did die. One, a man of about forty, lay by the side of the line as his mates worked.... His face was an awful grey colour. We all rushed around him like and the buzzer went. The line started. The foreman came across shouting 'get to work ... get on the line.' And there we were sticking things on the cars and he was lying there. He must have been lying there ten minutes ... dead. In front of us.
> (Beynon, H. *Working for Ford*)

Labour in which man *externalises* himself is a labour of mortification. Marx argued that most work performed in an industrial environment is *external* to the worker: it does not belong to his essence, it is not part of his nature. Therefore the worker does not confirm himself in his work, but rather denies himself so that he has a feeling of misery. He deploys no free physical and intellectual energy, but mortifies his body and ruins his mind. He feels physically exhausted and mentally debased. His work is not spontaneous, but *forced labour*. The act of production is not the satisfaction of a need but only a means to satisfy needs outside work itself. Proof of the alienation of the work process is exemplified by the willingness with which labour is shunned when there is no compulsion to do it. This is largely because the work is external in character; neither the means of production nor what is produced belongs to the worker.

> Alienated labour is work done for reasons other than its intrinsic interest and delight; it is work done for someone else – the person who controls and owns the work situation.
> (Salaman, J.G. *Community and Occupation*)

3 Alienation of man from his species-being
Alienated labour not only alienates nature from man, and man from himself, but it also alienates the species from man. Productive life is species-life, i.e. life producing life. For the essential generic character of the species to be sustained man must be involved in vital activity; free conscious activity is the species-characteristic of man. Marx argued that work which denies man this conscious vital activity is alienating work. Man is alienated when he has to adapt to nature instead of being the master of nature. It is mastery over nature which makes man different from animals. If he is alienated from those characteristics which are the essence of his humanity, then he is alienated from his species-being.

4 *Alienation of man from man*
It follows from the characteristics of alienated labour so far discussed that
man will be alienated from his fellow men. As man is alienated from his
species being, so one man is alienated from another, each man being
alienated from the human essence. According to Marxist analysis,

> ... in a society based upon capitalist exploitation ... men's relationships will be
> characterised by calculation, selfishness and self-interest.
> (Salaman, J.G. *Community and Occupation*)

This brings us back full circle to Marx's belief that alienation is basically
a feature of a capitalist society with its emphasis upon private gain, private
property and private profit. Marxists define alienation in terms of the
structure of capitalist society. The worker's sense of alienation arises from
the property relations of capitalism.

Aron has argued that the worker and the capitalist both experience
alienation.

> The entrepreneurs themselves are in a sense alienated, because the commodities
> they produce do not answer needs which are truly experienced by others but are
> put on the market in order to procure a profit for the entrepreneur. Thus the
> entrepreneur becomes a slave to an unpredictable market which is at the mercy
> of the hazards of competition. Exploiting the wage earner, he is not thereby
> humanised in his work, since he himself is alienated in the interests of the
> anonymous mechanism of the market.
> (Aron, R. *Main Currents in Sociological Thought*, Vol. 1)

● *Alienation and the organisation of work*

If it is accepted that alienation is a direct consequence of the private
ownership of the means of production, then it would follow that there
should be no alienated workers in the Soviet Union or in the People's
Republic of China or in any other communist country. Marxists define
alienation in terms of the structure of *capitalist society*. However, non-
Marxists employ the concept of alienation in a wider context to include the
revulsion from work found in industrial society.

It can be argued that workers in any *industrial society* (whether capitalist
or communist) are likely to feel self-estranged and look upon work merely
as a way of earning a living. The purpose of industrial production is
obscure; work becomes an instrumental activity subordinated to basic
needs (see Maslow's hierarchy of needs, section 5.3). Non-Marxist
sociologists argue that alienation results from the fact that industrial work
is organised in accordance with intensive division of labour and elaborate
specialisation which obscure the goals of the productive organisation.

Miklos Haraszti found that workers in a Hungarian factory felt themselves just as exploited as workers in the West (*Workers in a Worker's State*).

Robert Blauner, an American sociologist, has made one of the most important contributions to the study of workers' alienation in an industrial environment. Blauner excludes private property as the basic cause of alienation but agrees that there are powerful alienating tendencies, the effects of which differ according to four variables: technology, division of labour, social organisation and economic structure.

Although Blauner accepts that no simple definition of alienation is satisfactory, considering all the complexities of industrial work, he considers in detail four facets of alienation.

1 *Powerlessness* results from the control and manipulation of management. This sense of powerlessness is felt most acutely in a capitalist society because of the enormous gulf existing between the workers and the owners of the means of production. However, in all industrial societies where large organisations exist and work is performed by means of machinery, the worker is powerless to influence managerial policies, immediate work processes and his conditions of employment.

2 *Meaninglessness* derives from the worker's lack of understanding of the nature and purpose of the work he is directed to perform. The effects of standardisation and specialisation have made insignificant the worker's contribution to the final product.

3 *Isolation* occurs when the worker does not experience any sense of belonging to a work-based community or purposeful group. This is a type of social alienation accentuated by the worker not identifying with the business organisation and its goals. Such a feeling of isolation is in keeping with Durkheim's account of the evolution from a simple social structure involving mechanical solidarity to a very complex social structure involving organic solidarity (see section 5.1). The intense social and economic differentiation found in an industrial society results in uncertainty and a lack of norms (anomie).

4 *Self-estrangement* arises when the worker is prevented from realising his true self at the work place. Work is regarded as primarily instrumental and depersonalised; there is no opportunity for creativeness or satisfaction in the work itself.

Blauner analyses alienation in relation to four types of work: printing, assembly-line work, textile work and continuous process work in the chemical industry. His descriptions of the feelings of alienation are similar to those of Karl Marx, but whereas Marx regarded alienation as a direct effect of the capitalistic structure of society, Blauner and some other modern sociologists see alienation as arising from complex bureaucratic-industrial work-situations.

● *Degrees of alienation*

Blauner's most basic assumption is that

> the alienation perspective can be used scientifically . . . to elucidate the complex
> realities of present-day industrial society.
> (Blauner, R. *Alienation and Freedom*)

Whereas Marx theorised, Blauner attempted to apply the concept of
alienation to actual work situations.

It is impossible to measure with any precision the degree of alienation
experienced by a particular worker, but it is possible to illustrate by an
inverted U-curve, an evolutionary perspective of alienation (Fig. 5.7).

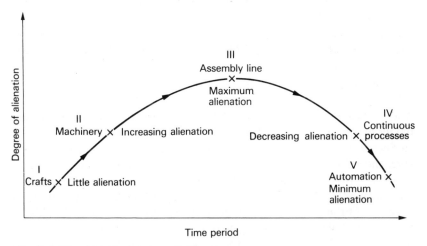

Fig. 5.7 Five historical stages of alienation

I *Craft industry* In the early stages of industrial society, workers laboured
in craft industries rather than in factory industry. The work provided
some scope for originality and workers enjoyed far more autonomy than is
experienced in the modern work-place. Consequently there was little
alienation.

II *Machine industry* The introduction of machines increased the worker's
feeling of alienation. It was convenient for owners of the means of
production to employ large numbers of workers in factories where
water-powered or steam-powered machines were located. These machine-
minding workers were subjected to severe discipline and became increasingly alienated.

III *Assembly-line industries* The repetitive, moronic work associated with
conveyor-belt organisation of production results in the maximum degree

of alienation. The curve of alienation reaches its apex with the assembly-line worker, especially in the car industry.

IV *Continuous-process industries* The integrating of various processes in modern factories has tended to decrease the worker's alienation.

> Since work in continuous-process industries involves control, meaning and social integration, it tends to be self-actualising instead of self-estranging.
> (Blauner, R. *Alienation and Freedom*)

V *Automated industries* The worker gains a sense of responsibility combined with control over the work process. The inverted U-curve is completed as alienation is minimised.

There are those who would argue that complete automation will make workers into mere robots. However, automation may be seen as the opposite of that division of labour which leads to the disintegration of the worker's skill. Automation allows the worker to control and superintend (see Touraine, A. *An Historical Theory in the Evolution of Industrial Skills*).

• Alienation and anomie

Alienation and anomie are two sociological concepts which help to explain the ills of industrial society from two different perspectives (see section 1.4 on Sociological Perspectives). They are fundamental concepts which have been the subject of detailed analysis by two of the founding fathers of sociology. From the conflict perspective, Karl Marx explained the conflicts of modern industrial society by distinguishing different aspects of alienation. From the structural-functionalist perspective, Emile Durkheim believed that the pathological state of the economy was brought about by the prevalence of anomie caused by a lag in the growth of new norms and rules as simple pre-industrial societies were replaced by complex industrial societies.

The concepts of alienation and anomie differ in the hypotheses they embody. They both throw light upon industrial unrest but it is wrong to consider them as synonymous sociological concepts. The terms have been used ambiguously in the literature; the alienated worker has been considered as anomic, i.e. without norms. (*Nomos* = order; *a/nomos* = lack of order; anomie = without order or norms.) Nisbet provides an example of an attempt to define one concept in terms of the other.

> Alienation is a historical perspective within which man is estranged, anomic and rootless when cut off from the ties of community and moral purpose.
> (Nisbet, R.A. *The Sociological Tradition*)

Although alienation and anomie are diseases of industrial man, they presuppose a fundamental divergence of view relating to the effects of the division of labour. Marx argued that the division of labour, under capitalism, was a major contributory cause of alienation; it impoverished the worker and enslaved him. Durkheim believed that when the division of labour was properly regulated it linked men together and produced solidarity (see section 5.1). But when new forms of division of labour or specialisation are introduced, anomie is created because workers take time to become adjusted to new methods of production with their attendant rules and regulations. In extreme cases a worker's feeling of disillusionment, discontent and disturbance may cause him to commit *anomic-suicide* (as distinct from altruistic suicide or egoistic suicide – see section 7.6).

Both alienation and anomie are socio-psychological concepts which help to explain the ills of modern society: man becomes alienated from himself, his work and the product of his work. Anomie arises when man does not comply with the norms of society. Alienation is experienced when man suffers from too much regulation: anomie occurs when there is too little regulation. The unrest experienced in Britain in recent years, especially in the field of industrial relations (see section 5.6), has been accentuated by a large increase in norm-fixing groups. Workers are subjected to an ever-increasing number of authorities and normative systems.

> An excessive proliferation of normative systems can therefore produce social consequences that are similar to those resulting from the absence of any norms to regulate conflict. Both situations can be seen as a breakdown of social regulation. Both can be described in the terms of Durkheim's characterization of anomie.
>
> (Fox, A. *A Sociology of Work in Industry*)

5.6   Trade unions and industrial relations

● *The purposes of trade unions*

It is generally considered that the main purpose of trade unions is to improve the pay and working conditions of their members. There are those who assume that the aims of trade unions should be different from what they are. On the extreme left, Marxists argue that unions should attempt to overthrow capitalism and completely transform society. On the political right, there are those who assume that trade unions should regard themselves as responsible bodies acting as agents of the existing social order. From the structural-functionalist perspective:

> The trade-union leader's main responsibility, to judge from the sort of comment one reads in the press and hears from middle-class lips, is 'to keep his chaps on line' or 'knock some sense into them'. . . . In practical terms, the main function

of a union leader according to this view is to deter his members from putting in ambitious wage claims, stop them from going on strike, and behaving in other anti-social ways, and encourage them to work harder and increase their productivity.... Having done all that, he can gracefully retire with a peerage.
(Shanks, M. *The Stagnant Society*)

Should trade unions aim to be instruments of social change? Functionalists argue that trade unions are nothing more than the creatures of social change.

... the original organiser of the trade union movement is the shop, the factory, the mine and the industry. The agitator or the labour leader merely announces the already existing fact.
(Tannebaum, F. *The True Society: A Philosophy of Labour*)

According to the functionalist argument, trade unions emerged when workers associated in spontaneous groups to strive for necessary improvements in wages and working conditions; therefore trade unions should be regarded as essential within an industrial, capitalist framework. If trade unions did not exist someone would have to invent them.

A trade union comes into existence to fill a void caused by innovations which represent a break with the past, but it has no power to innovate of its own volition.
(Banks, J.A. *Trade Unionism*)

Conflict-structuralists hold an opposing view and argue that trade unions have been directly instrumental in improving the lives of working men and women; it is only by organised industrial action, whether in the form of collective bargaining or strikes, that change has been brought about. Union militancy, is seen as a causal factor in changing things for the betterment of workers.

... the period in which the unions have grown has witnessed a great improvement in the whole economic condition of the classes which formed them.
(Hobhouse, L.T. *The Labour Movement*)

As is so often the case in sociological studies, the truth probably lies somewhere between the views of the functionalist and conflict schools. The changes brought by industrial society have necessitated the establishment of trade unions which are now accepted as necessary institutions. They are recognised by employers and government, and enjoy clearly-defined legal rights.

The integration of trade unions into the structure of society has been given meaning in occupational and social terms.
(Allen, V.L. *The Sociology of Industrial Relations*)

However, trade unions have extended their purposes beyond those envisaged by the original founders. They are primarily concerned with improving wages and conditions of employment, but they are involved in far more than this.

> ... one thing is at once certain, and it applies to all trade unions and has applied throughout the greater part of their history. The activity to which they devote most of their resources and appear to rate most highly is collective bargaining. So the question we have to ask is what purposes do unions pursue in collective bargaining? The conventional answer is that they defend and, if possible, improve their members' terms and conditions of employment. They are out to raise wages, to shorten hours and to make working conditions safer, healthier and better in many other respects.
> This answer is right as far as it goes, but it does not go far enough.
> (Flanders, A. *Management and Unions*)

Allan Flanders goes on to argue that trade unions are concerned not merely with raising wages, but also with regulating them. Union strategies, such as wage negotiations, strikes, working to rule, go slows, and control of apprentices are all directed towards this end. A study of trade-union history reveals that they have also been involved in the regulation of many other aspects of social and economic life. The early unions protected the worker within the confines of the work situation. As unions evolved they adopted political aims outside the work situation. They advocated the regulation of industry through nationalisation and the regulation of welfare by the creation of a welfare state. It is ironic that since the 1950s they have attracted the greatest public attention because of their secular, instrumental goals.

Table 5.12 distinguishes between three categories of trade union aims.

Table 5.12 Three categories of trade union aims

Immediate aims	General aims	Ideological aims
higher pay	negotiating machinery	socialism
shorter hours	legal status	nationalisation
improved conditions	recognition	welfare
superannuation	political representation	education

• *Types of trade unions*

It is convenient to consider four main types of unions or collectivities of workers, although any typology is bound to be structurally ambiguous.

Any student of trade-unionism will be familiar with the inadequacy of the classifications commonly used to describe the diverse external forms it may assume. Such categories as 'craft' or 'occupational', 'industrial' and 'general', may sometimes indicate a union's original shape or the recruiting doctrine by which it has at some time been influenced, but as a guide to its present character they are rarely very illuminating.

(Turner, H.A. *Trade Union Growth, Structure and Policy*)

1 *General unions*

The membership of general unions is dependent upon the principle of *inclusion* of all types of workers (whereas the craft union emphasises *exclusion* of workers not possessing recognised skills). A belief in comprehensiveness has enabled general unions to grow very large as an increasing number of low-status workers have joined their ranks. In 1978 the Transport and General Workers' Union had over two million members. The three largest trade unions are general unions. (see Table 5.13).

Table 5.13 The largest British trade unions (1978)

Union	Total membership ('000s)
Transport and General Workers (TGWU)	2073
Amalgamated Union of Engineering Workers (AUEW)	1494
National Union of General and Municipal Workers (NUGMW)	965

A very large proportion of members of general unions are unskilled manual workers with an instrumental commitment. There is a tendency for members to pledge their loyalty to the shop stewards rather than to paid trade union officials. The shop steward wields considerable power at shop-floor level within the individual plants. The ambivalent role of the shop steward affords him flexibility as a link between management and men. Many employers prefer to negotiate local agreements with shop stewards who are in close contact with those working at a particular plant than with union officials committed to national agreements which may not be upheld by the rank and file.

2 *Industrial unions*

Industrial unions also adopt the practice of inclusion, but differ from general unions by attempting to include different types of workers in a particular industry. Examples of UK industrial unions are the National Union of Mineworkers and the National Union of Railwaymen. Industrial unions in the UK are not as strong as in the USA where the US Auto

Workers' Union represents all the workers in the automobile industry; employers in the British car industry may have to negotiate with many different unions, separately representing engineers, electricians, transport and general workers. An example of the divisive nature of unionism in Britain is provided by the position in the rail industry where the NUR attempts to safeguard the interests of the majority of railway workers while the so-called craft union of ASLEF fights for differentials for locomotive drivers. Industrial unions have been particularly adversely affected by high unemployment in early 1980s. The Amalgamated Textile Workers' Union lost 5000 members in 1980–81 and total membership fell to 30 000.

3 Craft unions

Craft unions represent occupational groups of highly trained workers who have acquired skill, expertise and technical know-how. There are 250 craft unions with membership of less than 1000 each. The smallest union affiliated to the TUC in 1981 was the Cloth Pressers' Union with a relatively stable membership of 30.

Skilled craftsmen were described by Lenin as 'the aristocracy of labour'. For many years the craft union has limited the labour supply in a particular trade by means of a sponsored system of long apprenticeships. Unskilled workers have been downgraded by restriction of job-entry which has resulted in relatively high wages for members of craft unions. The exclusiveness of craft unions has left the way open for the general unions to expand both membership and industrial muscle.

4 White-collar unions

Membership of white-collar unions has increased far more than membership of any other type of union.

Table 5.14 Increase in white-collar unionism

	1948	1974
Union membership ('000s)		
White-collar	1964	4263
Manual	7398	7491
Union density (%)		
White-collar	30.2	39.4
Manual	50.7	57.9

(Bain, G. and Price, R. Union Growth Revisited, British Journal of Industrial Relations, Vol. XIV, No. 3, 1976)

From 1948 to 1968 membership of white-collar unions affiliated to the TUC increased by 36 per cent. These unions are no longer restricted to office clerks whose situation was analysed in David Lockwood's famous

304 SOCIOLOGY IN CONTEXT

study *The Blackcoated Worker*. They represent workers in such diverse fields as finance, science, government, technology and the professions.

- **The sociological significance of the growth of white-collar unions**

In *The Blackcoated Worker* David Lockwood examined white-collar workers in relation to three situations.

1 *The market situation*

In the old 'counting house' and in many modern offices, workers are more interested in job security, pensions, opportunities for promotion and fringe benefits, than in wages. However, there has been a marked tendency in recent years for white-collar workers to be concerned primarily about pay. They are no longer satisfied with enjoying better working-conditions and higher status than manual workers. White-collar workers have proved themselves willing and able to adopt militant union strategies to gain improved material rewards. They have moved closer to the aims of general, industrial and craft unions in a struggle to command more goods and services.

2 *The work situation*

White-collar work has lost much of its personalisation as large, bureau-cratic-administrative units have developed. The work situation of the white-collar worker in an office-factory based upon intensive division of labour proximates more closely to that of the manual worker. The counting-house clerk was not subject to rigid discipline, but today the social relations of white-collar workers are more formal and impersonal.

3 *The status situation*

In the past the white-collar worker regarded himself as a member of the administrative staff on the side of management. He was most likely to adopt a unitary rather than a conflict perspective. He saw the firm as a family concern; the interests of management and men were one and the same. The ideology of white-collar workers has changed as they look for something more tangible than situations of prestige and esteem.

Lockwood's approach to the social class position of white-collar workers is neo-Weberian; he centres upon the market situation rather than upon the social relations of production which form the basis of Marxist analysis. Both Weberian and Marxist views are relevant. White-collar workers are placed in positions which are structurally ambiguous because they belong to an occupational group associated with both capitalists and collective workers. They may be asked to act as 'middle-men' between the two elements:

(a) the capitalist who controls the labour force;
(b) the collective worker who is actively involved in the work.

When the white-collar worker is conveying the orders of management to other workers his conception of class may be defined in terms of 'management', although he is still part of the labour process. The ambiguity of the class position may be illustrated by the work of a technician who both:

(a) controls production;
(b) participates in production.

Apart from the major structural ambiguities there are sectional ambiguities, such as distinctions between:

(a) government and non-government work;
(b) productive and non-productive workers.

Employers in the private sector have resisted the growth of white-collar unions. This applies particularly to banks and insurance companies.

> The best illustration of the importance of employer policies and practices as a factor in union growth is provided in Great Britain by contrasting the public and private sectors of the economy. The density of white-collar unionism in the civil service, local government and the nationalised industries is extremely high, even among managerial and executive grades.
>   (Bain, G.S. *The Growth of White-collar Unionism*)

As post-industrial society has evolved a smaller proportion of workers are engaged in primary industries and manufacturing; in a service economy (see section 5.2) the largest proportion of workers participate in 'non-productive work'. A proliferation of white-collar jobs has strengthened white-collar unionisation. As the capitalist mode of production develops further, even within a mixed economy, there will be further increases in white-collar jobs intended to increase surplus value (see section 5.4). As the white-collar worker realises that his surplus value is appropriated by global capital, he is prepared to take militant action, in concert with other workers, to improve his market situation. From the interactionist perspective the increasing strength of white-collar unionism is inspired by a move from *group consciousness* (whereby the interest of the group is accepted) to a measure of *class-consciousness* (whereby common interests shared by all groups of workers are recognised). Class consciousness is less developed by white-collar workers but it is emerging and can be seen in the militant strategies employed by modern white-collar unions. Association with manual workers in large organisations has affected the growth of white-collar unionism, but there is little evidence that such association is of primary importance.

> Degree of contact with manual workers and their unions, then, is one of those factors which affect the distribution of membership within clerical unions, but is not generally decisive in determining the differences in the degree of concerted action between one union and another. Civil servants, for example, are not a

group of black-coats who frequently come into contact with manual workers in their day-to-day routine, yet they are highly organised.

(Lockwood, D. *The Blackcoated Worker*)

The following tables summarise the main reasons for the growth in white-collar unions and evidence of new attitudes adopted by the white-collar workers.

Table 5.15 Reasons for growth in white-collar unionism

1 Rejection of their previous false consciousness, and the emergence of class-consciousness as white-collar workers recognise their common interests with other workers.

2 Division of labour and mechanisation have led to impersonal labour relationships and increased alienation at work.

3 White-collar workers are in a stronger bargaining position in a service economy which relies so much upon their contribution.

Table 5.16 New attitudes adopted by white-collar unions

1 Staff associations aiming at workers' welfare replaced by active unions, e.g. insurance workers have left the Guild of Insurance Officials to join the Association of Scientific, Technical and Managerial Staffs (ASTMS).

2 White-collar unions affiliated to the TUC,
  e.g. NUBE (National Union of Bank Employees)
       NUT (National Union of Teachers)
       NALGO (National Associationof Local and Government Officers).

3 Greater militancy in occupational strategies designed to protect the interests of their members, i.e. a higher degree of *unionateness*.

● *Occupational strategies*

The structural-functionalist would contend that a normative consensus exists regarding disputes between management and workers.

In most Western societies, values and norms have of course favoured, within varying limits and on a somewhat fluctuating basis, the right of collectives to form, mobilize power, and exercise it against management in the pursuit of their normative aspirations.

(Fox, A. *A Sociology of Work in Industry*)

A diversity of occupational strategies are employed by associations of workers in an attempt to maintain or improve their wages and working conditions. These strategies range from negotiations to strikes.

1 *Negotiation* acts as an initial stage in collective bargaining between the two collectives of employers and employees. The Royal Commission on Trade Unions and Employers' Associations, 1968 (The Donovan Commission) drew attention to two systems of negotiating machinery which are often in conflict.

(a) *Formal negotiations* are national and industry-wide. They can only operate efficiently if employers' and employees' collectives have the power to impose their decisions upon their members. In Sweden, the Employers' Federation and the Central Labour Federation are so powerful that nationally-negotiated agreements are almost universally accepted.

> ... no Swedish employer tries to weaken the union or deal at arm's length with the union representatives.
> (Myers, C.A. *Industrial Relations in Sweden*)

This helps to explain Sweden's excellent record in the minimisation of industrial disputes (see Fig. 5.8).

It is a commonly-held supposition that 'the greater the number of trade unionists, the greater the industrial unrest'. The Swedish experience is contrary to this view: three-quarters of the work force are members of powerful trade unions but the general acceptance of these unions by management and workers makes for industrial harmony and successful wage and work negotiations.

(b) *Informal negotiations* are increasingly the reality as workers want shop-stewards to represent them in local negotiations with management.

> Without shop-stewards, trade unions would lack for members, for money, and for means of keeping in touch with their members. Even so none of them is the most important of the British shop-steward's tasks. That is the service which he performs by helping to regulate workers' pay and working conditions and by representing them in dealings with management.... Consequently it is often wide of the mark to describe shop stewards as 'trouble makers'. Trouble is thrust upon them. In circumstances of this kind they may be striving to bring some order into a chaotic situation, and management may rely heavily on their efforts to do so.
> (*Royal Commission on Trade Unions and Employers' Associations 1968*)

Failure to appreciate the present close relationship between workers and shop-stewards was evidenced by Prime Minister James Callaghan's indictment of them during the industrial unrest of early 1979 when he accused shop-stewards of not fully understanding 'basic tenets' of trade unionism (interview on Thames TV's *TV Eye*, 8 February 1979). If Donovan's advocacy of both systems (formal and informal) had been accepted,

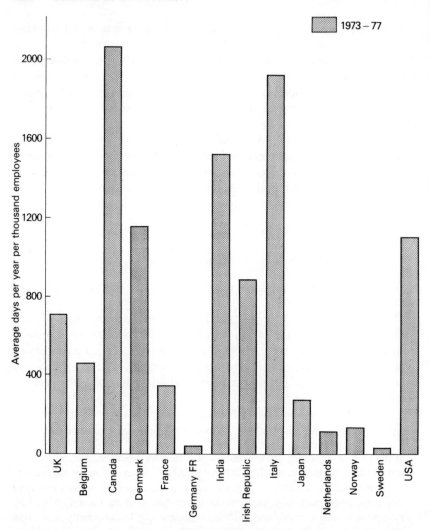

Fig. 5.8 Average number of working days lost per thousand employees (mining, manufacturing, construction and transport industries), 1968–72 and 1973–7
(*Department of Employment*)

negotiations in recent years might well have been more realistic, and the collective agreements reached as a result of such negotiations more lasting. 2 *Conciliation and arbitration* takes place when normal negotiations break down. The Secretary of State for Employment has power to appoint conciliators in industrial disputes under authority derived from the Conciliation Act of 1896 and the Industrial Courts Act of 1919. The advice of conciliation officers has been sought infrequently by disputing parties, but in recent years ACAS (The Advisory Conciliation and Arbitration Service) has been given power to conduct inquiries, on its own initiative, into 'any question relating to industrial relations generally or to industrial relations in any particular industry ... or undertaking.' The CAC (Central Arbitration Committee) has power to impose legally binding arbitration awards in certain circumstances.

The appointment of a third party to settle industrial disputes raises the question of whether arbitration can ever be 'value-neutral'. Arbitration is sometimes thought to result in a 'golden mean' award approximating to that which would have resulted if the disputants had fought out the matter, in the industrial field, until one party was exhausted. In this case it could be argued that arbitration shortens the disputes. However, there is evidence to suggest that arbitration is less of a compromise and more of a settlement dependent upon the industrial muscle or power of the rival parties.

> A comparison of two recent national disputes referred to third-party settlement after lengthy strike action is also relevant: the local authority manual workers, who caused considerable disruption with their stoppage at the end of 1970, received a far larger award than the postal workers, whose strike in early 1971 was comparatively ineffectual. This is strong evidence that the power relationship of the parties – shaped ultimately by an assessment of the damage that each can inflict in open conflict – provides the background to any resort to arbitration.
>
> (Hyman, R. *Strikes*)

3 *Restrictive practices* are used by workers to exert pressure upon employers. They take many forms but usually their main purpose is restricting output and causing inconvenience in an attempt to compel management to recognise the workers' claims. Absenteeism, sickness and even industrial accidents may be used to further workers' demands. More important as occupational strategies are collective actions such as work-to-rule, go slows, demarcation disputes (connected with rate-fixing and the effort-bargain) and even sabotage.

> All you do is put the bags on lop-sided. They fall off the conveyor and you get a huge pile of spillage in no time. And there's the foreman jumping up and down and cursing.
>
> (Nichols, T. and Armstrong, P. *Workers Divided*)

4 *Strikes* represent a last resort measure constituting the complete withdrawal of a worker's labour. They are such an emotive issue that they warrant a more detailed analysis than all other forms of occupational strategies.

● *Strikes*

It may be argued that strikes are unduly focused-upon, especially by the media; pickets and mass-union meetings are sufficiently photogenic to provide sensational news material which particularly serves the purpose of a capitalist press. Those who rely on the media might be forgiven for believing that the British worker is always on strike. It is a popular assumption that strikes are the 'English sickness'.

Yet a survey conducted by the Department of Employment showed that in the period 1971–3, there were no strikes in 95% of British manufacturing plants; four out of five workers were employed in plants where no strikes occurred. In those places where strikes did occur only a third had more than one strike per year. Furthermore, the majority of the time lost through these strikes was accounted for by prolonged action in 150 firms. The whole thing is brought into perspective when one considers that out of the 60 000 manufacturing plants in Britain, only 100 were affected by a strike on an average day. Figure 5.8 indicates that important countries such as the United States, Canada, and Italy had far worse records for industrial disputes over a ten-year period. Even a semi-industrial country, such as India, was more strike-torn. The following table depicts some sociologically significant reasons why strikes attract attention.

Table 5.17 Sociological significance of strikes to the public

1 reminder of *conflict* existing in society;
2 signify *non-cooperation* between management and workers;
3 provide the media with anti-working-class *propaganda*;
4 represent an *overt action*;
5 indicate a *loss of production*;
6 allow a *measurement* of working-days lost through a breakdown of normal industrial relations.

Strike statistics can never be completely accurate: there may be under-reporting of smaller strikes, by employers who wish to maintain public confidence in the image of the firm, while there may be over-reporting by employers who wish to give an impression of a total breakdown of relations. A strike has to meet two criteria to be included in the official statistics:
1 at least ten workers must be involved;
2 the strike must last a day.
Three main indices of strike measurement are employed:
1 the number of stoppages;
2 the number of strikers;

3 the number of working days lost. (This is the index generally considered the most reliable.)

Industrial relations in the UK became so soured in the early 1970s that 24 million working days were lost in 1972 following the Industrial Relations Act of 1971. In 1979, 29 million working days were lost through strikes; this was the largest total since the General Strike of 1926. In 1980, the number of days lost through strikes dropped to 11.9 million; increasing unemployment weakened the power of the trade unions. In the early 1980s there has been very little dialogue between the TUC, the CBI and the government. Tripartite talks attempting to reach a consensus and to cut down on strike action have largely been abandoned. According to surveys by the ILO and the EEC, in 1980 the UK maintained a mid-ranking position in terms of the number of recorded strikes in a world survey of strikes.

There are many difficulties appertaining to strike statistics. Political strikes are generally excluded from official figures although there is a close correlation between political and economic factors. The uneven spread of days lost through strikes makes any statistical 'average' of doubtful validity. A small number of major strikes may distort the picture and the disproportionate effect of miners' strikes is significant.

Table 5.18 Types of strike

Type of strike	Working definition
1 Official	with union approval
2 Unofficial	no union backing
3 Wildcat	no consultation with management
4 Unconstitutional	failure to participate in all procedural stages

Ninety-five per cent of strikes in the UK are unconstitutional. One of the main reasons for the increase in unofficial, wildcat and unconstitutional strikes is the greater importance of the local level of informal negotiations. The shop-steward is an unpaid official whose wage is paid by the firm. We have seen that the firm increasingly relies, for industrial peace, upon the shop-steward, rather than upon the paid union official. The shop-steward may be allowed the use of office and telephone. Under the Employment Protection Act of 1975 he is allowed time off for union business. It can be argued that shop-stewards are becoming *institutionalised*.

... a social form becomes an institution when it takes on a fixed and distinctive character ... or when it serves as a receptacle for vested interests.

(Broom, L. and Selznick, P. *Sociology*)

Evidence that some shop-stewards liaise closely with management in return for personal advantages has been documented by Theo Nichols (writing of 'ChemCo' in *Workers Divided*) and Huw Beynon (writing of Ford workers at Halewood in *Working for Ford*). As a general rule, however, the shop-steward is regarded as 'one of the lads' who is doing a similar job to that of his mates. The rationalisation of trade unions has made for larger unions, and for a lack of communication between management and workers; but a shop-steward is more likely to know what is really going on concerning new technology and related wage rates. Combinations of shop-steward convenors in Shop Stewards Committees constitute a powerful and militant body. These lay trade-union officials are the instigators and leaders of most UK strikes.

The change in the real power base of unionism can be seen in an analysis of two distinct periods of strike incidence.

1 *1950–69*

The period from 1950 to the end of the Donovan Commission was a period of short strikes involving relatively few workers, compared with some of

Table 5.19 British strike statistics 1919–69

	Number of strikes	Workers involved ('000)	Striker-days ('000)
1919–21	1241	2108	49 053
1922–5	629	503	11 968
1926	323	2734	162 233
1927–32	379	344	4740
1933–9	735	295	1694
1940–44	1491	499	1816
1945–54	1791	545	2073
1955–64	2521	1116	3889
1965	2354	868	2932
1966	1937	530	2395
1967	2116	731	2783
1968	2378	2255	4719
1969	3116	1654	6925

the critical periods in the inter-war years (e.g. in 1926, 162 million striker-days were lost). From 1965 to 1967 only about $2\frac{1}{2}$ million striker-days were lost annually.

Although the British strike record was comparatively good, the most disturbing feature was that the unconstitutional strike became the norm in the 1960s. The proliferation of such strikes was one of the main considerations of the Donovan Commission.

2 1970–80

During this period there was an increase in
(a) the number of strikes;
(b) the number of workers involved;
(c) the big set-piece strike;
(d) the length of strikes.

Worsening industrial relations led to the passing of the 1971 Industrial Relations Act, by a Conservative government which was eventually forced to resign in the face of a prolonged miners' strike combined with general industrial unrest. Militant action against the 1971 Act caused 24 million days to be lost by strike action in 1972. The subsequent Labour government repealed the 1971 Act, and passed the Trade Union and Labour Relations Act (1974) and Amendment Act (1976) which restored the position and extended the privileges of trade unions. The Employment Protection Act (1975) placed the Advisory Conciliation and Arbitration Service (ACAS) on a statutory basis, provided for the appointment of a certification officer to whom trade unions have to submit records, and established an Employment Appeal Tribunal to hear appeals concerning the decisions of the certification officer.

The early 1980s saw unemployment exceed three and a quarter millions, and a Conservative government's Employment Act (1980) which was intended to:
(a) restrict so-called 'secondary picketing';
(b) encourage the use of secret ballots for unions contemplating strike action;
(c) provide greater protection for individual employees faced with a closed shop situation;
(d) allow employers to dismiss workers more easily, the onus of proof relating to unfair dismissal resting upon employees.

• Consensus and conflict views of industrial relations

According to the consensus perspective of industrial relations, management and workers share the same interests because they both gain from the achievements of the organisation. The success of the firm requires the cooperation and commitment of both sides of industry. The firm may be considered as 'a family'. The workers should be thankful to the boss who gives them work and organises that work. Such a unitary view of industrial relations is in keeping with management ideology and the neo-human relations school (see section 5.3 for the ideas of Maslow and Herzberg). The consensus depends upon the 'rules of the game' being accepted by both sides; reasonable claims by workers may be met so long as the existing framework of society is preserved.

The conflict perspective of industrial relations is based upon the assumption that management and workers have opposing interests arising from the relations of production in a capitalist society. If it is believed that capitalists aim to maximise profit while workers aim to maximise wages, their interests are diametrically opposed. There is continuous interaction between management and workers as both profits and wages come out of the same kitty. This interaction starts with collective bargaining between the two sides, but if agreement is not reached, more militant strategies may be employed: the ultimate weapon of organised labour is the strike while the employer may go to the extreme of enforcing a lock-out of workers. Agreement between the opposing sides will be temporary. There may be a lull until the next 'battle' or round of bargaining begins. The underlying conflict always remains.

The consensus and conflict perspectives of industrial relations can be analysed empirically in relation to the 1971 Industrial Relations Act. The consensus school would argue that the Act provided a legal framework intended to encourage management and workers to cooperate. Following the recommendations of the Donovan Commission, the Act was passed with the intention of reducing the chaos caused by the disproportionate number of unofficial strikes. Although workers retained the right to strike, the Act set out measures intended to make the incidence of strikes less frequent. These measures included:

(a) the registration of trade unions with a Registrar;
(b) the power to impose:
    (i) a sixty-day cooling-off period,
    (ii) ballots by trade unionists to ascertain their opinion about the advisability of strike action;
(c) the establishment of a Commission on Industrial Relations to further the operation of the law;
(d) a Code of industrial relations practice for general guidance.

The conflict school would argue that the Act was passed by representatives of the dominant middle class using the legislative machinery to impose their will upon the workers. Industrial relations were controlled and institutionalised. The Act attempted to confine conflict and mitigate militancy by legislative clauses intended to keep the worker in his place. A National Industrial Relations Court was empowered to fine a trade union up to a maximum of £100 000 if convicted of unfair practices. The Act failed to diminish conflict and the workers strenuously resisted it. The TUC organised a one-day general strike as a protest against the Bill and ordered its affiliated unions not to register. Unions refused to appear before the NIRC and the TGWU declared its intention not to pay fines imposed upon it. The 1971 legislation was so divisive that the Conservative government hesitated to enforce its own Act. When five dockers were imprisoned by order of the NIRC, a relatively obscure civil servant, the Official Solicitor, secured their release in order to avert a national dock strike. The Prime Minister accused the dockers of causing the Midland Cold Store to lose £2000 a week thus forcing the firm into bankruptcy.

> A few days later news leaked out that the brave little Midland Cold Store was an offshoot of one of the country's biggest conglomerates, the Vestey group. They had been closing down riverside facilities where dockers worked, at the same time as it opened the Midland Store with its identity concealed as a nominee. The news was excavated by *The Sunday Times....* But the picketing dockers had suspected it all the time.
>
> (Ferris, P. *The New Militants*)

• *The anomic state of UK industrial relations*

From the conflict-perspective, a case can be made out for regarding industrial relations in the UK as anomic. The concept of anomie (see section 5.5) can be applied to macro-situations such as industrial disputes or to the pathological state of the economy. We have seen (in section 5.1) that Durkheim used the term anomie to refer to an absence of social norms or situations where norms are unclear or conflicting. Anomie is likely to increase when people in an industrial society are not aware of moral obligations. Contractual agreements must rest upon conventions and codes accepted by everybody in society. Industrialisation has brought so many changes to society that people find it difficult to adjust to modern economic life.

> Very violent changes can produce what since Durkheim we speak of as 'anomie' – the vacuum of standards which results from the dislocation of a stable social context.
>
> (Runciman, W.G. *Relative Deprivation and the Concept of the Reference Group*)

Modern technological changes, combined with great inequalities in society have led to feelings of injustice based upon the lack of relationship between natural aptitudes of individuals and rewards received for services. It is this moral injustice which Durkheim relates to the problem of anomie.

The economic cartography of British society has been brought into focus by the reports of the Royal Commission on the Distribution of

Income and Wealth. These reports uphold past evidence of deeply entrenched inequalities. In 1972, 5 per cent of the population, aged 18 and over, owned 56.3 per cent of the country's wealth, leaving the other 95 per cent owning less than half (RC Report No. 1, Table 56). Existing inequalities create future inequalities. There has been little change in marked inequalities of income (see section 2.4). J.H. Goldthorpe has argued that the anomic condition of British society is brought about not merely by inequalities in remuneration, but also by

> the inequalities in the content of work tasks and roles. There is, however, by now ample evidence to show that *wide* differences exist between occupations and jobs in the extent to which they offer possibilities of *intrinsic* satisfaction to the individuals engaged in them or, on the other hand, are a source of psychological or social deprivation.
>
> (Goldthorpe, J.H. 'Social Inequality and Social Integration in Modern Britain', *Advancement of Science*, December 1969)

A. Fox and A. Flanders (in 'The Reform of Collective Bargaining: from Donovan to Durkheim', *British Journal of Industrial Relations* 7, No. 2, 1969) contend that the anomie in industrial relations could be tackled in three ways:

1 the company or plant should be seen as the only unit of regulation able to integrate the conflicting normative aspirations of work groups;
2 a prices and incomes policy should secure productivity agreements in keeping with work roles and rewards;
3 there should be an authoritative articulation of norms.

This is less than convincing. The remedies Fox and Flanders recommend have either been tried and found wanting or they will not eradicate the gross inequality which is the underlying cause of anomie. The measures suggested would be unlikely to achieve a stable, normative system of industrial relations.

Even if the Bullock Committee's recommendations of workers' directors were accepted, the anomie associated with economic and social inequality is unlikely to be much affected. If the anomie is to be anything but a normal condition of present-day society, there must be a new morality based upon a closer correlation between natural aptitudes and social justice.

5.7   The professions

● *The professions in pre-industrial societies*

The knowledge necessary for the existence of 'professions' in a modern context did not exist in pre-industrial societies. In such societies most adult members shared the same skills and the division of labour was used only in a simple way. Nevertheless an examination of some of the few specialised activities in pre-industrial societies leads to an understanding of what a sociologist, using the structural-functionalist perspective, would look for in determining the criteria of a profession.

Firstly, professions are associated with very specialised knowledge not possessed by laymen. For example, the 'priest' or religious expert, in primitive society, studies religious rites, magic, sacred things, myths and taboos. Religious practices are established over a long period and the 'priest' is expected to absorb a large body of specialised knowledge and to understand its implications and practical applications. Modern social anthropologists no longer doubt the significance of specialised knowledge to those who are closely involved in religious practices.

> Whereas the nineteenth-century anthropologist sought to answer such questions as 'What is the sociological significance of religion?' no anthropologist or, at any rate, no sensible anthropologist, would ask such a question today. Rather, he seeks to determine, for instance, the part played by the ancestor cult in a social system ... among certain African peoples.
> (Evans-Pritchard, E.E. *Social Anthropology*)

Specialised knowledge of what one's ancestors understood and practised in the realms of religion and magic gives prestige to the tribal priest and allows him to be respected as a 'professional'. The development of esoteric knowledge increases the *social distance* between the initiated and the uninitiated and gives the expert power over other members of the community.

> Magic is similarly inseparable from mythology. The belief in magic power rests on the inherited myths, which are full of descriptions of magical feats. Equally, magic also creates and constantly replenishes its own 'running mythology of magic miracles' which relates all the presumed magic successes that can be remembered (or presented as would be memories), and hence validates in advance any future magic effort.
> (Nadel, S.F. 'Malinowski on Magic and Religion', in Firth, R., ed., *Man and Culture*)

So the priesthood came to be regarded as a profession, and religious organisations became powerful in society. Their representatives had a monopoly of religious knowledge, which allowed them to extend their power into the field of government and politics.

Secondly, the specialised knowledge is jealously guarded and confined to a select few (an elite). Entry into the profession is carefully controlled. Potential physicians in Ancient Greece served under a master who was himself regarded as an expert. In medieval England, medical knowledge was controlled by the church and only over a long period of time did medicine become a secular profession. However, a hallmark of a profession is that it should have a controlling body comprising its own members; in medicine this came about with the establishment of the Royal College of Physicians.

Thirdly, when a group monopolises an area of knowledge, new specialised tasks develop. Before the Reformation, law was administered by the church, but the growth of trade encouraged the work of lawyers specialising in commercial cases. New sub-sections of the profession emerged as fresh needs arose. While certain lawyers were recognised as being expert in commercial affairs, others specialised in cases involving crime or property. Canon lawyers were replaced by common lawyers.

This brief account of professions before industrialisation demonstrates the emergence of four vital aspects of a profession.

1 The possession of very specialised knowledge.

2 The profession becomes a monopoly and entry is confined to a select few.

3 A controlling body rigidly supervises professional conduct.

4 The profession sub-divides and certain members undertake very specific tasks.

● *The attributes of professions in modern society*

The four basic criteria of what constitutes a profession still prevail but as the professions have developed, other aspects of professionalisation have emerged. Table 5.20 sets out the main attributes of a profession in a modern society.

Although the term 'professional' is ambivalent, it is generally true that membership of a profession is earned only after many years of arduous training during which specialised knowledge and skills are acquired. This is true even of soccer players or highly-trained soldiers; the work of the latter has been portrayed in TV advertisements appealing for recruits to 'Come and join the professionals'. Yet footballers and private soldiers are not members of a profession in the generally recognised sense of the term. It is not sufficient for an occupation to satisfy merely one or two of the criteria enumerated in Table 5.20.

Although a profession is associated with norms of practice enforced by a central regulating body, nevertheless the conduct of the true professional is motivated by individuality, originality, judgement, responsibility and autonomy.

> Creativity is basically an individual act and the individual professional has the ultimate responsibility for his professional decision; for example, the surgeon

Table 5.20 Some attributes of a profession (ideal type)

1 Possession of a high level of systematic knowledge.

2 A central body determines entry to the profession.

3 Knowledge is sub-divided as members concentrate upon specific fields.

4 Professional behaviour is regulated by an accepted code of ethics.

5 Members' primary orientation is to the community which they serve.

6 Prolonged academic training is determined by the profession itself.

7 Special relationship with the client.

8 The reward system (originally fees) is to some extent symbolic and not necessarily the primary motivation.

9 Members of the profession are held in high esteem by the community.

10 Members strongly identify with the profession and protect other members.

11 Certificates are awarded to denote an agreed standard of professional competence.

12 Members are highly rewarded in terms of income, power and prestige.

has to decide whether or not to operate. Students of the sociology of the professions have pointed out that the autonomy granted to professionals who are basically responsible to their consciences (though they may be censured by their peers and in extreme cases by the courts) is necessary for effective professional work. Only when immune from ordinary social pressures and free to innovate, experiment, and take risks, without the usual repercussions of failure, can a professional carry out his work effectively.

(Etzioni, A. *A Sociological Reader on Complex Organisations*)

The professional is likely to operate most effectively if given freedom from lay evaluation and control. In any case, it is almost impossible for a layman to judge the full effectiveness of the skills of a surgeon or an architect. Society is prepared to grant autonomy to professions which successfully control their members. The norms of practice established by such professional bodies as the General Medical Council, the Royal College of Physicians, the Royal College of Surgeons or the British Medical Association are often stricter than the legal controls imposed upon members of the medical profession.

Admission Boards to the professions are comprised of respected members determined to safeguard an honourable public image of the profession as a whole. The licence to practise a particular profession is often awarded in the first place by the regulating board and subsequently legally recognised. After initial acceptance, novices are subjected to a long period of adult socialisation by senior members of the profession. Initiates have to learn the jargon of the profession. The use of highly specialised technical terms increases the social distance from laymen, associates members of the same profession and acts as a shorthand of professional expediency. In this way the profession is able to exercise a monopoly which some laymen regard as being against the public interest.

Mr Whatsisname's campaign to end solicitors' monopoly

Do-it-yourself legal expert Mr Francis Whatsisname told a court yesterday that he was conducting a political campaign to try to break the solicitors' monopoly of house conveyancing work.

Mr Whatsisname, formerly Mr Reynolds, changed his name by deed poll last November in protest at the Law Society's advertising campaign which said: 'Don't listen to Whatsisname – see a solicitor.'

He told Worcester magistrates that the solicitors' monopoly 'is not in the best interests of the public no matter how much they may plead otherwise.'

Mr Whatsisname (43), a law lecturer at Birmingham Polytechnic, made his remarks while applying for permission to call a large number of witnesses including Lord George-Brown and Lord Hailsham. But the chairman of the Bench refused.

Mr Whatsisname, of Hylton Road, Worcester, denies a total of six charges of either preparing or drawing documents for house-purchase conveyancing without proper qualifications. The charges were brought privately by the Law Society.

Mr Alistair Hill, who appeared for the Law Society, said the alleged offences related to three transactions at Feltham, Middlesex; Sutton, Surrey; and Bromley, Kent. Acting for the purchaser of the property in each case was an 'unincorporated' body known as the Property Transfer Association. It was an unqualified conveyancing association, composed of unqualified persons operating from a number of addresses, he said.

Mr Hill showed the court a brochure produced by the PTA which set out a scale of charges. He asked: 'What were these charges for if not for the purpose of the whole exercise, namely the transfer of the titles to land and property?'

Mr Hill submitted that an offence had been committed by Mr Whatsisname, contrary to the Solicitors Act of 1974, if the preparation of certain instruments had been carried out for, or in the expectation of, a fee or reward for himself or anyone else.

Mr Whatsisname admitted that within the meaning of the Solicitors Act 1974 he was not a qualified person.

Mr Hill said there was no evidence in the Law Society's possession that Mr Whatsisname had received a personal fee or reward for the transactions before the court.

The hearing was adjourned until today.

(*The Guardian*, 10 January 1978)

A profession may be analysed as a community. The work is likely to provide a lifetime career associated with long-standing social relationships.

It is accepted that only fellow professionals can pass judgement upon the work and the professional expects to be protected if anything goes wrong.

Table 5.21 Stages of entry into a profession

> 1 Academic training in approved educational institutions.
>
> 2 Success in qualifying examinations.
>
> 3 Entry by certification with letters designate, e.g. ARIBA, and the entrant's name added to a register.

State registration enables the general public to distinguish between the qualified and the unqualified. The more highly qualified an individual, the greater the loyalty to the profession. A hierarchy is imposed as those with the highest status have power over those below them in the professional ranks. The highest-ranking professionals would be expected to have a great degree of specialised skill, experience and service, together with a sense of collective responsibility for the profession as a whole.

● *The aspiring professions*

From the interactionist perspective, Howard Becker has argued that if a radical sociological view is taken of the professions, there is no such thing as a true profession; rather there are only groups of workers who are esteemed by others to belong to a profession. Perhaps such acknowledgement is the best recognition of what constitutes a true profession.

In modern times, professional recognition has been accorded to such occupations as dentistry, accountancy, architecture, science, engineering, and pharmacy. Yet there are those who would regard pharmacy, for instance, as only a marginal profession. The pharmacist is in an ambivalent position in two respects. Unlike the industrial chemist, the pharmacist acts professionally in everyday life while he is dispensing medicines, but at other times is engaged 'in trade' as an entrepreneur organising a chemist's shop. He is also subordinate to members of the medical profession, and carries out their directions after the same manner as physiotherapists, radiographers and other medical auxiliaries. Other marginal professions are those of nursing and midwifery where the work is performed under the direct supervision of members of the medical profession. Occupations which supplement the work of the medical profession are less than full professions because their members are not part of any vital decision-making process. Neither do they control their own entry, nor have they the power to strike a member off the professional register. Their rewards are less than those of more powerful professions because they have a lower status in the hierarchical administration of an institution.

Other similar marginal professions include those of social worker, probation officer, and community worker. It is in the nature of things, in advanced technological societies, that new occupations should evolve and that many of these occupations should aspire to professional status. Before the Second World War it was unthinkable that some workers would serve as 'professional' economists, conservationists, computer programmers, environmentalists or nuclear physicists.

The apparent domination of industrial societies by professionals and quasi-professionals has given rise to the claim that a professional society is emerging.

> The increase in the number of professionals and the growth of professionalism has been generally accepted by social scientists as a major if not a determining characteristic of industrial societies.
> (Johnson, T.J. *Professions and Power*)

However, although it is true that certain facets of professionalism are apparent in many occupations, a true profession must qualify according to *all* the accepted criteria (see Table 5.20). For example, the service ethic may prevail in many occupations ranging from health workers to trade union officials. It is increasingly commonplace that work techniques and procedures are controlled by a central body. However, that body does not fulfil the functions of control found in the case of the ideal-type professions such as medicine and law. Millerson, in *The Qualifying Associations*, contends that the primary functions of a professional body include the organisation of the profession into a community, organisation of qualifying examinations, encouragement to further study, registration of competent professionals and the promotion of high standards of conduct.

Secondary functions of a professional body include acting as a pressure group and endeavouring to gain professional status for the occupation. Although people speak loosely of the teaching profession, teachers are not held in such high esteem as doctors or lawyers. The National Union of Teachers is an influential body which protects its members and acts as an educational ginger group. But the NUT does not control the qualifying examinations for teachers nor entry to the occupation. There are many occupations which have developed *some* of the characteristics of a profession. The importance of knowledge, as Giddens has stressed (see section 2.3), means that many workers possess expertise which laymen are inadequate to evaluate. Engineers have specialised knowledge of electronics or motor cars or television sets. A service economy, based on expert knowledge and science, tends to be part of the natural evolution of a society which moves from being less developed to more developed. While not denigrating the expertise of a large number of modern workers, it seems too far-reaching to acclaim the arrival of a professional society.

● *Professions and bureaucracy*

An ever-increasing number of professional workers are engaged in working for large institutions and especially for state concerns. The old client/fee relationship is fast disappearing as the professional becomes a salaried, dependent worker responsible to a government agency or to a large public joint stock company. The dwindling number of autonomous professionals makes independence a less important facet of professionalisation in modern society.

As it is increasingly difficult to assess the complex skill of the specialist, a great degree of trust is essential when the modern professional deals with the public. Even in a very large hospital a gynaecologist must have clinical freedom to practise in a controlled situation; the organisation of a large institution may be conducive to controlled relationships by reason of the numerous other workers engaged, including many pseudo-professionals. A large number of other patients sharing similar situations means that encounters can take place without embarrassment. Some of the dangers to the professional working within a bureaucratic organisation are shown in Table 5.22.

Professionals profess; i.e. they profess to know more than their clients. This is a fact of life which is important for both independent professionals and members of a profession who work in bureaucratic organisations.

Table 5.22 Dangers to a professional in a bureaucracy

1 Decreased power, e.g. resources withheld by politicians and administrators.

2 Less altruism – the professional serves the institution and deals with a suspicious public.

3 Less control – who makes the policy decisions?

4 Temptation to be less than professional, e.g. it may be convenient for babies to be induced in order to promote the smoother running of the institution.

5 The 'nationalisation' of the professions means that the state, rather than the profession itself, decrees what services will be provided.

6 The 'commercialisation' of the professions has led to corruption and manipulation.

Role-conflicts may occur within the organisation if the professional has to choose between allegiance to the profession to which he has been socialised or to the organisation which pays his salary. C. Wright Mills, in *The Sociological Imagination*, has warned of the dangers of subservience to the bureaucratic ethos by those who work for large institutions such as the state, public corporations, the army and advertising concerns.

The possibility of professionals being disturbed by role-conflicts may well be less in under-developed countries where the professions have emerged under the auspices of government control. The danger here is that the professional ethic may be lacking, for even workers with highly specific knowledge may regard themselves as servants of the state rather than the servants of their clients.

5.8   Work and non-work

• *Relationships between work and non-work*

Work may be defined as activity carried out under conditions where there are normally THREE principal specific demands relating to: (a) time; (b) place; (c) effort.

Where work is instrumental and extrinsic (providing merely a means to an end) there is less ambivalence between the terms work and non-work. The alienated industrial worker has a clear idea of what he regards as work, because he hates every moment of it. For a certain period of *time* (say 8 a.m. to 5 p.m.), he has to be in a certain *place* (say the factory where he is employed), to do a certain piece of work which requires *effort*. He is not free to chose the time or the place or the particular piece of work that he has to do. His alienation from work may become alienation from life itself.

The distinction between work and non-work is very ambivalent in the case of professional and higher-grade workers. Their work is intrinsic; it is an end in itself. A surgeon gains satisfaction from performing a heart transplant and will be prepared to expend the maximum effort even if the operation lasts for many hours beyond his normal working-day. And what is the normal working-day for a dedicated schoolteacher who spends many out-of-school hours in lesson preparation and marking?

Apart from time spent on activities related directly to earning a living, there are also *work-related tasks* and *work obligations*. A carpenter will wish to ensure that he has the right tools to do the work in hand. A landscape gardener may service his rotary cultivator, sort out plants, and ensure he has other necessary raw materials. A bank manager is expected to groom himself carefully. The majority of workers must spend time travelling to and from work. Time spent strap-hanging in a tube train, or at the steering wheel of a stationary car caught up in traffic congestion with others making their way to work, is all work-related time. Time spent on a subsidiary job, closely associated with an individual's main work, can be categorised as work-related time. A sociology lecturer may use work-related time to write books or act as an examiner. Unpaid work such as attending conferences or professional meetings may also be placed in the same category. A peculiar example of work-related time includes the modern practice of 'moonlighting' whereby extra work done as part of the so-called hidden economy has been calculated by the Inland Revenue to cost over £3500 million a year in lost taxes.

Work obligations include work-related activities which have to be performed because of an individual's main work or employment. A husband may help with the household chores, so that his wife has time to prepare his meals or pursue her own career outside the home. Elizabeth Bott, writing in the 1950s, described how some husbands and wives had moved from segregated conjugal roles to joint conjugal roles.

> At the other extreme was a family in which husband and wife shared as many activities and spent as much time together as possible. They stressed that husband and wife should be equals: all major decisions should be made together, and even in minor household matters they should help one another as much as possible. This norm was carried out in practice. In their division of labour, many tasks were shared or inter-changeable. The husband often did the cooking and sometimes the washing and ironing.
> (Bott, E. *Family and Social Network*)

Today the tendency towards 'the symmetrical family', to borrow Young and Willmott's term, whereby both husband and wife each have two jobs, working both inside and outside the home, makes distinctions between work and non-work even less clear.

> Husbands also do a lot of work in the home, including many jobs which are not all traditional men's ones – which is one reason why the distinction between work and leisure is now a great deal less clear for men than it used to be.
> (Young, M. and Willmott, P. *The Symmetrical Family*)

Productive effort is considered as work whether paid or unpaid. The role of a housewife and mother involves hard work which may be either enjoyable or tedious. Although a housewife is not paid a wage, she may consider that she gains great satisfaction from looking after the house and bringing up the children. Supporters of the women's liberation movement would contest the viewpoint of such a housewife.

> ... the modern concept of work, as the expenditure of energy for financial gain, defines housework as the most inferior and marginal work of all.
> (Oakley, A. *Housewife*)

Dr S.R. Parker (*The Future of Work and Leisure*) considers that there are three main non-work areas:

1 *Existence time* is used for meeting physiological needs such as sleeping, eating, washing and eliminating.

2 *Semi-leisure time* is a term used by Joffre Dumazadier (*Towards a Society of Leisure*) to describe activities associated with leisure pursuits. A yachtsman may spend hours working upon his boat so that he can enjoy the leisure activity of sailing. Children must feed and clean out their pets, while the dog has to be taken for a walk. These may be regarded as onerous obligations: distinctions between work and leisure (non-work) are again ambivalent.

3 *Leisure-time* is free time, during which an individual is free to choose his own pursuits. Demands made upon him are self-imposed. He may well work during his leisure-time but he does so at his own discretion.

Parker's summaries of work time and non-work time provide a useful broad guide to problems of definition.

	Work time	*Non-work time*		
work	work obligations	physiological needs	non-work obligations	leisure

	Constraint	*Activity* ⟵——————————⟶		Freedom
Work Time	Work (employment)	Work obligations (connected with employment)		'Leisure in work'
Non-Work	Physiological needs	Non-work obligations		Leisure

(Parker, S.R. *The Future of Work and Leisure*)

Any measurement of leisure time depends upon how people define leisure. Parker's survey of middle-class residents in Islington ('Professional Life and Leisure', *New Society*, 10 October 1974) revealed that:

(a) just over half of the working sample thought of leisure as the only time they had free to do what they liked;

(b) nearly a quarter considered that leisure was all the time they were not employed at work (residual time);

(c) a fifth regarded it as all the time, except when doing things essential for the maintenance of life such as eating and sleeping.

● *Leisure*

The following table of boxes indicates ten significant positive and negative aspects of leisure.

1 Opportunity to leave behind stereotyped behaviour and conformities	+	
2 Extension of work skills to non-work areas	+	
3 Opening up of new horizons	+	
4 Development of individual personality	+	
5 Removal of work fatigues (diversion from work)	+	
6 Free time without duties		−
7 Unnecessary to expend energy (rest period)		−
8 Absence of work-related time and obligations		−
9 An escape from alienation		−
10 Time remaining after primary obligations have been fulfilled		−

In industrial societies people work longer and consequently have less time for leisure than in the past. The thirteenth-century skilled artisan worked only 194 days a year (Wilensky, H.L. *The Unseen Distribution of Leisure*). In the UK the average *basic* working week amounts to 40 hours but this is increased to an *actual* average of 44 hours when overtime is included. This may appear a relatively short working week compared with the 70-hour week worked by nineteenth-century workers, but nonetheless it represents far more time than that spent at work in pre-industrial societies.

In pre-industrial societies there was no sharp division between work and leisure; families and kinship groups spent their work and non-work time together. The emphasis upon work, as separated from and opposed to leisure, developed as part of the Protestant ethic whereby the exploited workers were expected to labour tirelessly and not waste time upon frivolous leisure activities. Max Weber (*The Protestant Ethic and Spirit of Capitalism*) argued that the social ethic of protestantism was an important contributory factor in the growth of capitalism and was responsible for some of its worst features. Weber's maxim, 'The Puritan wanted work to be his vocation; we are forced to want it,' expressed his disillusionment with the culture of capitalism. The conscientious protestant was a work addict or workaholic who strove for his own profit and exploited others for the same end. People are still socialised to the idea that leisure must be earned.

Leisure pursuits have changed rapidly as society has changed. *The Concise Oxford Dictionary* definition of leisure as free time spent 'without hurry' applied to most leisure pursuits of past generations in Britain, and is still relevant in societies little affected by industrial changes. An important influence upon leisure pursuits is the state of technology; today 'leisure has certain traits that are characteristic only of the civilisation born from the industrial revolution' (Dumazadier, J. *International Encyclopedia of the Social Sciences*). Modern leisure presupposes an infinite variety of contemporary activities such as hang-gliding, motor racing, losing money to one-armed bandits and playing chess against your own computer.

> This is not to deny the existence of work and play in non-industrial societies but rather to stress their articulation through religion and communal ceremonial and, by contrast, their sharp separation in the organisation of modern industrial society.
> (Halsey, A.H., ed., *Trends in British Society since 1900*)

Looked at from the conflict-structuralist perspective, differences in leisure pursuits have always depended upon social class differentiation. The middle classes are more likely to indulge in world cruises or spend their free time in yachting, mountaineering, skiing, or hunting, shooting and fishing. Such activities require a great deal of space once enjoyed only by owners of large estates. The rewards of hunting, shooting and fishing came to the working class by means of illegal poaching until the twentieth century. The great inequalities of incomes associated with different occupations clearly influence leisure activities. Those with low earnings are unable to afford expensive types of leisure, although they are now able to indulge in mass entertainment such as cheap package holidays. However, sociologists who support the idea of *embourgeoisement* would argue that a dichotomy of leisure activities according to social stratification is too simplistic. Modern leisure pursuits increasingly cut across social class barriers. Leisure has been democratised by the mass media, cheap transport, greater affluence and leisure organisations catering for the masses.

> It is for instance, far less easy to assign people to their appropriate social category on the basis of the clothes they wear when not at work, or how lavishly their houses are equipped. The milkman is almost as likely to have a car and go on a continental holiday as the bank clerk.
> (Newson, J. and E. *Patterns of Infant Care in an Urban Community*)

The most significant development in leisure pursuits in recent years have been television and increasing car ownership. See Table 5.23 and 5.24.

Sociologists recognise that an individual's occupation is often the most important influence upon the way he spends his leisure. The use of

Table 5.23 Television viewing in the UK

	1971	1973	1975	1976	1977
Average weekly hours viewed by age group					
5-14	20.7	24.5	24.0	22.0	22.0
15-19	16.6	16.8	17.3	18.4	17.6
20-29	17.0	18.1	18.2	19.1	18.2
30-49	18.4	18.4	18.4	19.0	17.9
50 and over	18.9	19.0	19.6	20.4	20.0
Social class of adults (15 and over)					
A	14.0	15.0	14.0	16.7	14.4
B	16.8	16.8	16.6	17.7	16.8
C	19.1	19.3	20.0	20.3	20.1
Overall average weekly hours viewed by all persons aged 5 and over	18.6	19.3	19.7	19.9	19.3
Television broadcast licences current at 31 March (millions)					
Monochrome	15.3	13.8	10.1	9.1	8.1
Colour	0.6	3.3	7.6	8.6	10.0

(*Social Trends* No. 8, 1977)

Table 5.24 Private transport in Great Britain

	1966	1971	1973	1974	1975	1976
Number of private cars and private vans (millions)	9.5	12.1	13.5	13.6	13.7	14.0
Percentage of households with regular use of						
one car	39	44	45	45	46	46
two cars	6	8	9	10	10	10

(*Social Trends* No. 8, 1977)

non-work time in general, and leisure in particular, depends largely upon a person's type of work and the income he receives from it.

> Studies of leisure which have hitherto focussed on social class differences are now developing the theme that there are occupational differences within class and status groupings which play a large part in determining the style of leisure, family behaviour, political orientations, as well as more general values.
>
> (Parker, S.R. 'Work and Non-work in Three Occupations' in Butterworth, E. and Weir, D. *The Sociology of Modern Britain*)

When workers form a close-knit unit, their associations at work are likely to extend into their leisure time. Work and non-work friendships apply particularly to manual workers who are likely to live near each other. The coalminer, who shares occupational hazards with his fellow workers, is inclined to spend his free time with his mates. He is intensely class-conscious. Similarly a trawlerman is drawn to his fellow workers by sharing in the dangerous work of deep-sea fishing, and

> has indelibly printed on him certain habits, reflexes, patterns of spending, attitudes to life ....

Professional workers, such as dentists, who are separated from colleagues performing similar tasks, are less likely to spend their leisure together; they work separately and play separately.

The way an individual spends his leisure is related to his occupational status. Golf or bridge may be played as a means of achieving social status: they are leisure activities providing contacts for advancement. When occupational status is achieved, leisure pursuits may be carefully chosen to reflect status: it may be considered appropriate to join a club held in high esteem by others in the community. Willmott, P. and Young, M. (*Family and Class in a London Suburb*) found that 35 per cent of the middle class in Woodford attended at least one club a month, compared with 18 per cent of the working class. Bottomore's survey of 'Squirebridge' revealed clubs which demanded

> a standard of behaviour unattainable (or seemingly so) for individuals of low occupational status.
>
> (Bottomore, T. *Social Stratification in Voluntary Organisations*)

Office-holding in clubs and charitable organisations is largely confined to those of high occupational or social status.

Thorstein Veblen argued that the working classes copied the behaviour of what he termed 'the leisure class'. Veblen was particularly critical of *conspicuous consumption* by those of independent means who spent their wealth and leisure in attempts to impress others. Veblen saw their prime motivation as a desire for status.

In order to gain and to hold the esteem of men it is not sufficient merely to possess wealth or power. The wealth or power must be put in evidence, for esteem is awarded only on evidence.

(Veblen, T. *The Theory of the Leisure Class*)

Dr Mark Abrams has classified *five ages of leisure*. The young are naturally involved with physical activities enjoyed with their peer group. Both young and old have fewer obligations and thus more leisure than other members of society. Table 5.25 gives a generalised overview of the five principal ages of leisure.

Viewed from a structural-functionalist perspective, both work and leisure are vital to the economic system. Firstly, workers must have free time and opportunities to enjoy their leisure, in order that they may be revitalised for work, thus improving their contribution to the economy; their hours of work must be so arranged as to allow evenings and weekends to be available for leisure activities. Secondly, leisure industries employ large numbers of workers in both the private and public sectors of the economy. Many leisure activities are profitable commercial concerns: these include ITV, cinemas, public houses, bingo halls, race meetings, holiday camps, hotels, restaurants and many clubs. Central and local authorities provide public leisure amenities such as parks and gardens, recreation grounds, museums, libraries and art galleries. The BBC is financed from licence fees and government grants.

As it is increasingly difficult, in these days of mass TV viewing, to make a profit from performances by live ballet, opera, orchestral and theatrical groups, these leisure activities are frequently sponsored by government grants. Some leisure industries are successful at the expense of others; radio and cinema audiences have declined as television viewing has increased. Even by 1964, 90 per cent of the homes in the UK were equipped with a TV set. The average TV viewing by people aged over five in the UK is over 19 hours a week. Weekly cinema audiences have declined from 25 million in 1953 to fewer than 3 million in 1980. Young people are big spenders upon leisure, and cinemas today largely cater for those between 15 and 24 who are free and able to spend their leisure outside the home: they are free because of few domestic obligations and they are able to indulge in comparatively expensive activities because of the affluent position in which modern society places them. In the latter respect working-class youngsters can often afford to spend more upon leisure than those of the middle class who are involved in further or higher education (and have to rely upon parental contributions to augment their government grants), or who receive relatively low remuneration in the early days of long professional training. Apart from spending upon cigarettes, drink, hi-fi equipment, tape recorders and cassettes, over 70

Table 5.25 The five ages of leisure

1st Age Teenager/Youth Culture	2nd Age Young marrieds	3rd Age 35 to 45 years	4th Age 45 to 64 years	5th Age Over 65 years
Much time spent outside the home in company with peer group; working classes have more spending money than middle classes in many cases.	Set up home and have children; 70% women and 55% men married before they reach 25; essentially home-centred.	Home ties decrease as children are less demanding; more time spent outside the home.	Most affluent age; very few have responsibilities of children; less physical energy; status-seeking.	Retirement of women at 60 and men at 65; physical and mental decline; little spare cash.
Mass sports; sexual freedom; luxury spending on non-essentials; search for danger to ease boredom.	Purchase of home and car; child-caring; TV, reading; DIY and hobbies; home and car maintenance.	Public houses; visiting friends; dinners and dances; church and small group activities; camping and caravanning.	Eating and drinking more expensively; golf and bridge; colour TV; continental holidays.	Inexpensive pursuits, e.g. reading, gardening, knitting, whist, bingo, walking (often cannot afford pubs and cinemas).

million LPs were bought annually in the 1970s.

It may be argued that leisure time is increasingly a time of passivity rather than activity. The boredom of work may produce mental stagnation and apathy. On the one hand there are leisure pursuits (such as TV, radio, cinema and professional sport) which encourage people to be mere spectators, while package holidays free people from the effort of planning their own holidays. On the other hand, there are far more people today actively engaged in golf, fishing, sailing, athletics, show-jumping, squash, tennis, chess, etc. Television has been indicted as the principal instrument of passivity but it does encourage people to participate by introducing them to new activities or by instructions aimed at improving skills and techniques in existing leisure activities.

An important sociological consideration is whether or not the mass media is instrumental in producing a *cultural democracy* or a *cultural class system*. A cultural democracy entails meeting the demands of the masses, perhaps for soap operas or continuous pop-music. A cultural class system involves class distinction between high-brow and low-brow tastes such as classical and pop music. An interesting overview of radio entertainment is that channels 3 and 4 cater for the middle classes, whereas channels 1 and 2 are geared towards working-class tastes. Similarly the quality newspapers (*The Times, Daily Telegraph* and *Guardian*) attract middle-class readership whereas the tabloid papers (*Daily Mirror, Daily Express, Daily Star, Sun* and *Daily Mail*) are far more popular with working-class readers. The larger the number of instruments of communication the greater the opportunity for a compromise whereby the tastes of the majority are satisfied without neglecting the interests of the minority groups. It is a controversial question whether the media should adopt the conscious social purpose advocated by Lord Reith (the first Director General of the BBC) and aim at attempting to raise standards of taste. Obvious vexed questions centre around what is the nature of good taste and what are worthwhile cultural values?

Further Reading

Baran, P.A. & Sweezy, P.M. *Monopoly Capital* (Penguin)

Blauner, R. *Alienation and Freedom* (University of Chicago Press)

Brown, J.A.C. *The Social Psychology of Industry* (Penguin)

Burns, T. (ed.) *Industrial Man* (Penguin)

Child, J. *The Business Enterprise in Modern Society* (Collier-Macmillan)

Child, J. (ed.) *Man and Organisation* (George Allen & Unwin)

Dennis, N., Henriques, S. & Slaughter, C. *Coal is Our Life* (Tavistock)

Dore, R. *British Factory – Japanese Factory* (George Allen & Unwin)

Durkheim, E. *The Divison of Labour in Society* (Free Press, Macmillan)

Eldridge, J.E.T. *Sociology and Industrial Life* (Nelson)

Fox, A. *A Sociology of Work in Industry* (Collier-Macmillan)

Fraser, R. (ed.) *Work* (Penguin)

Galbraith, J.K. *The New Industrial State* (Penguin)

Goldthorpe, J.H. *The Affluent Worker: Industrial Attitudes and Behaviour* (Cambridge University Press)

Hyman, R. *Strikes* (Penguin)

Johnson, T.J. *Professions and Power* (Macmillan)

Kerr, C. *et al. Industrialism and Industrial Man* (Penguin)

Lockwood, D. *The Blackcoated Worker* (George Allen & Unwin)

McCarthy, E.J. (ed.) *Trade Unions* (Penguin)

Miliband, R. *The State in Capitalist Society* (Penguin)

Nichols, T. *Ownership, Control and Ideology* (George Allen & Unwin)

Nichols, T. & Armstrong, P. *Workers Divided* (Fontana)

Parker, S.R. *et al. The Sociology of Industry* (George Allen & Unwin)

Sprott, W.J.H. *Human Groups* (Penguin)

Tunstall, J. *The Fisherman* (Macgibbon & Kee)

Warner, M. (ed.) *The Sociology of the Workplace* (George Allen & Unwin)

Weir, D. (ed.) *Men and Work in Modern Britain* (Fontana)

Whyte, W.H. *The Organisation Man* (Penguin)

Williams, W.M. (ed.) *Occupational Choice* (George Allen & Unwin)

Wilson, D.F. *Dockers* (Penguin)

Zweig, F. *The Worker in an Affluent Society* (Heinemann)

SIX

Politics and social order

6.1 Power and authority

• *What is power?*

Power cannot be held in isolation, but must be exercised over others. It is the way in which one man or a group of men exert their will over other people. Some would go so far as to argue that power can never be the sole property of one individual; a person who is 'in power' needs the support of a group. Power extends to every aspect of political, social and economic life. It is derived from force of arms or status or property or money or influence. It includes the general who orders an army to move, a prime minister who appoints her cabinet, an entrepreneur who runs a business, a local councillor who is party to a decision about footpaths, and a mother who allocates household duties to other members of the family.

Simplistically, when power is held to be legitimate, and accepted by those who are subject to it, it is termed 'authority'. Consequently parents and teachers are obeyed: the laws of a country are respected. In the last resort, however, it may be argued that all power rests on force or coercion. Parents and teachers may take punitive action against children: the police force sees that people comply with the law.

> Authority means the probability that a specific command will be obeyed. Such obedience may feed on diverse motives. It may be determined by sheer interest situation, hence by the compliant actor's calculation of expediency; by mere custom, that is, the actor's inarticulate habituation to routine behaviour; or by mere effect, that is, purely personal devotion of the governed. A structure of power, however, if it were to rest on such foundations alone, would be relatively unstable. As a rule both rulers and rules uphold the internalised power structure as 'legitimate' by right, and usually the shattering of this belief in legitimacy has far-reaching ramifications.
>
> (Weber, M. 'The Three Types of Legitimate Rule', in Etzioni, A., ed., *A Sociological Reader on Complex Organisations*)

Max Weber went on to describe the three principal types of authority within social relations. Assuming pure types, each is connected with different sociological structures of executive and administrative organisation.

1 *Legal-rational authority*

Laws are enacted and changed by an elected, or appointed, governing body. The administrative staff are appointed by the ruler to form a bureaucratic system in which officials are bound by rules. The rulers' right to govern is legitimised by enactment. The pure type of legal-rational authority is a bureaucracy where the operation of the system rests on organisational discipline. This type of 'legal rule' comprises the power structure of modern states, cities, capitalist enterprises, public corporations and voluntary associations. Obedience is not owed to any particular person but to enacted rules which even the top person has to obey. The whole power structure is based upon the belief in the legality of patterns of normative rules and the right of those elevated to authority under such rules to obey commands.

2 *Traditional authority*

Immemorial traditions allow certain people to exercise authority over others. Patriarchal authority is the purest type: the father ruled the household, while the lord ruled over his obedient servants. If the lord violated tradition then the legitimacy of his personal rule would be violated; thus Charles I's divine right to rule was challenged and ultimately defeated. Generally, tradition deems that the lord rules at his pleasure, following personal considerations, using relatives or favourites as henchmen. He is not bound by rules and the bureaucratic concept of competency is absent. The individual servant depends upon his personal loyalty to the ruler on whom he is personally dependent. Traditional authority is likely to result in despotic government such as the rule of estates represented by the aristocracy in feudal society (see section 2.1). In such cases power usually corrupts, while absolute power may corrupt absolutely. It is very difficult to challenge those who have traditional power and the weakness of the system is its static nature.

3 *Charismatic authority*

The leader commands devotion and obedience from his followers or disciples, but that obedience is only forthcoming so long as he retains his charisma. The administrative staff are selected according to their personal devotion to the leader and do not possess any special qualifications to govern. The administration lacks all orientation to rules and regulations, whether enacted or traditional. For the sociologist, the charisma is value-neutral: the maniacal ravings of Adolph Hitler and the subsequent murder of millions of Jews are as much part of charisma as the sufferings of Jesus and his teachings of love. When the personal representative of the charisma is eliminated, the authority structure tends to routinise and change into traditional or legal-rational authority.

Weber argued that authority in a modern industrial society was likely to be of a 'legal-rational' nature. He detailed an 'ideal type' of bureaucracy. The ideal type is a useful concept, because by overemphasis and crystallisation it helps us to study a situation or organisation with greater clarity. The ideal type does not accurately reflect social reality and is unlikely to be obtained in practice. The use of ideal types provides a means by which comparisons can be made between social phenomena; it helps us to compare the organisation, functions, merits and demerits of bureaucracy with other forms of power structure.

- *Sociological perspectives of power*

The two broad paradigms of consensus and conflict attempt to explain the existence and operation of power in society. The perspectives are mutually exclusive so that sociologists who accept one perspective are unlikely to agree with the fundamental maxims of the other.

Adopting the consensus or functionalist perspective, Talcott Parsons sees power as the ability to mobilise the resources of society for the attainment of common goals. The amount of power in society is judged by the degree to which collective goals are attained. The goals are defined by the members of society so the general public makes a commitment towards them. The competence of a social system can be judged by goal-attainment: the more efficient a social system, the nearer it will come to its goal-achievement and the more power will exist in society. In a democracy, politicians attempt to obtain the recognised goals of society in exchange for votes and continuing support. Although differences exist, political parties share a common framework of values. Differences are aired, within accepted institutions, such as parliament or the courts, and the status quo is maintained. In an advanced industrial society, the mass of the people are committed to technological advance and a higher standard of living. Those who advocate such goals will receive approval; the greater the levels of economic growth 'the more power to their elbow'. Supporters of the Green or Ecology Party do not gain power, because, given the present consensus, the majority of people do not concur with their goals. Political power according to the consensus perspective or liberal tradition goes to those who, society believes, desire the good of the whole. The public's belief may be miguided but *vox populi* rules for the time being. It is up to minority groups to try to change the consensus. The variable-sum concept of power holds that power is not constant or fixed.

Conflict theorists see society as divided into the oppressors and the oppressed. Power rests with the dominant group, who use that power to further their own interest. This constant-sum concept of power means that the rulers always rule at the expense of the ruled, who constitute the

majority of members of society. Whereas consensus theorists see cooperation between members of society as essentially good and worthwhile,
conflict theorists see no virtue in cooperation while one group is exploiting
another. In an advanced industrial society, based on specialisation, the
division of labour enables people to cooperate in order to increase
production; but if increased production generates a disproportionate
amount of wealth for the few while mass labour is exploited, then only
conflict will bring a greater measure of justice in society. Karl Marx
believed that the basis of all power lies in the economic infrastructure of
society. The dominant group controls the means of production, property
and wealth for its own ends. Their power is derived from their privileged
economic position. Some sociologists regard the whole power structure
(whereby the dominant group exerts its power through socialising agencies, e.g. the family, school and media) as a conspiracy whereby the
middle class propagates the myth that society is united and all members
should work for the national interest. Whether it is a conspiracy or not,
the dominant group in the economic infrastructure exerts power throughout the superstructure. We have seen that schools are organised according
to middle-class ideologies and that the media is controlled in a similar way
for sectarian interests. The middle class are also all-powerful in the
judiciary, the executive and the legislative fields of government. The legal
system reinforces the power of the dominant group. Property owners are
legally endowed with more power than the propertyless. The trade unions
and other opposing pressure groups are drawn into the establishment and
rewarded with social honours. Although consensus may exist at specific
periods, such as wartime, conflict must re-emerge. From the conflict
perspective, society is seen as a number of groups, often opposing each
other. Whether or not the conflict is contained or results in revolution,
depends upon the degree of change which is permitted by the social
system.

6.2 Types of power

- *Elitism*

Elitism exists when a minority group is socially acknowledged to be
superior and consequently exercises power over other groups in society.
Most elitist writers (Pareto, Mosca and Michels) see the ruling elite as a
minority who hold power over the majority who are subject to that power.
Pareto (*Mind and Society*) distinguished between the governing elite, the
non-governing elite and non-elite. Mosca (*The Ruling Class*) used a simple
dichotomy dividing the class that rules and the class that is ruled: in all

societies the rulers are always less numerous, perform all political functions, monopolise power and enjoy the advantages which power brings; the ruled are always more numerous, provide the rulers with material means of subsistence and are subject to direction and control by methods which may have a semblance of legality or may be arbitrary and violent. Michels (*Political Parties*) pointed to the elite's ability to preserve its dominant position: according to his iron law of oligarchy, leadership is essential for the success and survival of society; the group of leaders who possess power and expertise are in such a favoured position that it is a matter of utmost difficulty to dislodge them.

C. Wright Mills (*The Power Elite*) sees elitism in the USA as constituting three spheres of power – the business, political and military elites. Other institutions are peripheral and subordinate to the three elite domains. Religious, educational and family institutions are decentralised and shaped by the big three.

> No family is as directly powerful in national affairs as any major corporation; no church is as directly powerful in the external biographies of young men in America today as the military establishment; no college is as powerful to the shaping of momentous events as the National Security Council .... Families and churches and schools adapt to modern life; governments and armies and corporations shape it ....
> (C. Wright Mills, *The Power Elite*)

According to Mills, the power elite are not solitary rulers. The elite is made up of advisers, consultants, spokesmen and opinion-makers; they are supported by professional politicians, pressure groups and celebrities. Within the big three, the typical institutional unit has become enlarged, administrative and centralised. The power of the elite rests on institutional position because institutions determine the means of power.

1 *The economy* was once a scatter of small productive units, but is now dominated by two or three hundred powerful business corporations.

2 *The political order* was once made up of many states, but has now become a centralised, executive establishment.

3 *The military order* was once a collection of state militia, but is now the largest and most expensive feature of government.

However, the domains of elitism really stem from a single power elite, because of a similarity of social origins and family relationships. As the activities of each elite sphere become greater its interconnections with other elites increase.

> The decisions of a handful of corporations bear upon military and political as well as upon economic developments around the world. The decisions of the military establishment rest upon and grievously affect political life as well as the

very level of economic activity. The decisions made within the political domain determine economic activities and military programs.

(C. Wright Mills, *The Power Elite*)

There is a frequency of interchange of personnel between the business, political and military domains. Mills was particularly interested in what he called the 'mass society'. He considered that as organisations become more powerful the masses lose contact with the power elite and are therefore unable to exert any real influence. It is a myth that the Great American Public is the seat of all legitimate power. The public is being transformed into a powerless mass society.

1 Far fewer people express opinions than receive them.

2 It is extremely difficult for the individual to answer back and give his own point of view.

3 Opinion is controlled by the authorities.

4 Agents of authorised institutions penetrate this mass and minimise the formation of opinion by discussion. C. Wright Mills, at many points of his sociological analysis, comes close to Karl Marx's notion of a ruling class holding power over a subjugated mass.

Marx's analysis of power was based on distinguishing between a ruling class and a subject class. Whereas most elitist theorists argue that the elite, although maintaining an element of exclusiveness, must remain accessible to the non-elite, and recruit members from it, if it is to maintain its elite position, Marx saw a polarisation of the ruling class and the masses. The ruling class did not owe its dominance to recruitment from the masses, but from ownership of the means of production consolidated by control of political institutions and military forces. Marx's concept of a ruling class was economically determined, whereas elitist theory would hold that the elite rules, but is not completely cut off from the mass; the elite is socially favoured and uses its traditional expertise to control other groups within society. Marx believed that economic dominance alone provided the means for the ruling class to exercise oppressive political dominance. The ruling class uses its economic power to manipulate the political sphere in order to maintain the status quo and its own dominant position in society. The minority elitist group always closes its ranks to provide a cohesive opposition to the proletariat who are in the majority.

Some of the basic ideas of classical elitist theories are in opposition to Marx: Pareto's non-governing elite included high-ranking influential individuals such as professors and doctors, while Mosca's organised minority was composed of individuals who might be joined, from the ranks, by others who displayed superiority. Classical elitist theories believed the circulation of elites prevented a closed ruling class, whereas Marx assumed the ruling class constituted a closed group; he argued that there would be

Table 6.1 Some comparisons between elitist and Marxist concepts

Elitist	Marxist
1 Some individuals are endowed with superior ability and they will form an elitist minority who will govern.	1 A small ruling class governs because it owns and controls the means of production and the wealth of society.
2 Elites are continually circulating and new recruits come up from below.	2 The ruling class maintains the status quo and there is no significant social mobility.
3 A classless society is impossible; there will always be inequalities and the minority will always govern the majority.	3 A classless society will come about as a result of economic development, class conflict and in the last resort, revolution.

no social mobility as there was no opportunity for members of the proletariat to join the ruling class.

Opponents of Marxist philosophy argue that although a ruling class did exist, particularly during the early days of the industrial revolution, there is now a separation between those who control and those who own the means of production. The diffusion of company share-ownership has meant that the ownership of economic resources is now shared by hundreds of thousands of people many of whom participate because of their contributions to pension funds and their subscriptions to trade unions which invest in companies. The control of business has passed to paid managers. (For a fuller account of this argument, see section 5.4) It is further contended that the ruling class is no longer such a closed group; upward social mobility is still difficult but it is not impossible. T.B. Bottomore (*Elites and Society*) uses a historical continuum to illustrate his contention that industrial societies are moving from a class system to a system of governing elites and from a social hierarchy based upon property and the ownership of the means of production towards one based upon merit and achievement.

> The concepts of 'ruling class' and 'governing elite' are used in descriptions and explanations of political happenings, and their value must be judged by the extent to which they make possible reasonable answers to important questions about political systems. Do the rulers of society constitute a social group? Is it a cohesive or divided, an open or closed group? How are its members selected? What is the basis of their power?
>
> (Bottomore, T.B. *Elites and Society*)

We still have a long way to go before we reach a meritocracy. A study of

British elites (Stanworth, P. and Giddens, A. *Elites and Power in British Society*), gathered material on the background of directors of some of the most powerful business organisations in Britain. 73 per cent of the directors of industrial corporations were found to have had a public school background. Three important conclusions emerged from the study.

1 Elite positions in our major institutions continue to be heavily dominated by people with a privileged social background (see Table 6.2).

2 The public schools and Oxbridge still play a pre-eminent part in recruitment to the elite.

3 In most elites, the proportion of recruits drawn from a public-school background remains relatively stable.

There are few opportunities for sociologists to study the extent to which kinship ties influence economic and political power, but one occasion was provided by the Bank Rate Tribunal 1959, set up to investigate claims that

Table 6.2 Elite recruitment

year	category	origin	%
1970	Labour MPs	working class★	27
1970	Tory MPs	working class★	1
1955–70	Labour cabinets	working class★	35
		middle class★	62
1955–70	Tory cabinets	aristocracy★	3
		middle class★	79
		working class★	0
1900–72	company chairmen	working class	1
		middle class	13
		upper class	86
1960–69	millionaires (dead)	manual/lower clerical	19
		established upper class	66
	half-millionaires	manual/lower clerical	7
		established upper class	79
1966–67	civil service entrants	white collar/skilled manual	19
		semi-unskilled/manual	5
1967	upper grade civil service	white collar/skilled manual	25
		semi/unskilled	6
1960–74	bishops	not professional/landed	28
★defined by own first job, rest defined by father's job			

(Stanworth, P. and Giddens, A., ed., *Elites and Power in British Society*)

a change in the Bank Rate had been leaked for purposes of monetary gain, before the official announcement. The tribunal made possible the chartering of kinship connections existing between leading figures appearing in the report of the tribunal.

Cameron Fromanteel Cobbold was governor of the Bank of England.

> C.F. Cobbold (since 1960 Baron Knebworth) is a man from a family of landed gentry. He is related through the paternal line to Lieutenant-Colonel John Cobbold, who married a daughter of the ninth Duke of Devonshire. John Cobbold's sister married Sir Charles Hambro, a member of the leading banking family and a director of the Bank of England. Lieutenant-Colonel H.E. Hambro married the widow of the sixth Earl of Cadogan; her grandson married a daughter of John Cobbold.
>
> (Giddens, A. 'An Anatomy of the British Ruling Class', *New Society*, 4 October 1979)

In a capitalist society, the ruling class rules insofar as it forms an elite whose members control the state for the furtherance of its own elitist interests. They do not bother to govern, but they do possess the power. In Karl Kautsky's famous phrase the elite 'contents itself with ruling the government'.

Table 6.3 Elites in British society

Institutional category	elite	administrative substratum	recruitment substratum
polity			
monarchy	monarch	royal household	royal family
House of Commons	members of parliament	(administrative class, civil servants plus senior diplomats)	adopted candidates
House of Lords	'active' peers		'passive' peers
economy			
100 largest industrial firms, large banks, insurance and finance houses, nationalised industry	directors, large shareholders, board members	senior management	senior management plus members of other elite groups
judiciary	judges	court officials	barristers

Table 6.3 Elites in British society (Cont.)

Institutional category	elite	administrative substratum	recruitment substratum
civil service			
home	under-secretary and above	administrative class civil servants	administrative class civil servants
foreign	officials grades 1 & 2	officials, grade 5 and above	officials, grade 5 and above
military	general officers and equivalent ranks in other forces	colonels and above, and equivalent ranks plus senior civil servants	colonels and above and equivalent ranks
trades unions	TUC council members	senior union officials	TUC delegates
Church of England	archbishops and bishops	assistant bishops, bishops suffragan and senior clerics	assistant bishops and bishops suffragan
mass media newspapers BBC and ITA	directors and larger shareholders, board members	editorial staff and senior management	members of other elite groups
universities and colleges	vice-chancellors, masters of Oxbridge colleges, heads of 'top nine' schools	professors and heads of department	professors and heads of department

(Giddens, A. 'Elites', *New Society*, 16 November 1972)

● *Pluralism*

Pluralism exists when power is in the hands of a number of groups in society. In modern industrial societies, power becomes dispersed as the increased specialisation of labour involves different occupational groups who organise themselves in order to fight for their rights. Such protective interest groups include professional associations and trade unions. Other promotional interest groups are concerned with promoting a cause or securing legislation; the Campaign for Nuclear Disarmament attempts to persuade people that Britain and the world would be safer if we did not possess nuclear weapons. The extension of the powers of one particular group may limit the powers of another. For example, the livelihood of fishermen could be adversely affected by those who wish to set up marine nature reserves (see Fig. 6.1). Pluralist theories consider politics to be involved with different groups competing for power, each seeking its own interest. As no single group is dominant, power depends upon negotiations and compromise. A democratic framework allows different interests to compete. Pluralists believe that power in society is fragmented into interest groups and political parties.

Danger in new powers proposal

Mr Bob Rushmer, secretary of the North Norfolk Fishermen's Society, outlined yesterday how proposals to set up marine nature reserves seriously threatened the livelihood of local crab and lobster fishermen. In a statement issued to the press he said, 'This has to be treated with great respect and needs to be looked at very carefully because it could be a very dangerous move as far as the professional fisherman is concerned'.

One of the most contentious aspects of the proposals is that very wide powers of control are being sought. If the Bill is approved, these powers would enable the authorities to introduce a marine reserve up to ten miles long and three miles wide. This area would be large enough to cover all the crab and lobster fishing grounds from Weybourne to Trimington. As Mr Rushmer emphasised, the implications of such a decision could be drastic.

Fig. 6.1 Powers 'could mean dangers'

Robert A. Dahl (*Who Governs?*) examined the decision-making of American local politics in New Haven, Connecticut to see how power was distributed. Dahl selected widely-varying issues such as urban renewal, mayoralty elections and educational issues concerned with school-siting and teachers' salaries. He found that no single group monopolised power and that there was no ruling elite in the town.

Arnold M. Rose (*The Power Structure*) accepts pluralist theories and rejects the idea that the USA is governed by a power elite. Rose examined the policies of business interest groups, such as the National Association of Manufacturers and the US Chamber of Commerce, and concluded that decisions made by the President and Congress indicated that they were not unduly influenced by the business lobby. Limited democracy existed and decisions were generally a compromise between the claims of opposing interest groups.

Christopher J. Hewitt examined twenty-four British parliamentary issues which arose in two decades between 1944 and 1964. Judged from the basis of decisions ultimately reached, Hewitt found that no single interest group was consistently dominant. Decisions reflected the public opinion polls in all cases except for the abolition of capital punishment. Hewitt's work supported the pluralist conception of consultation between a number of conflicting interests without one dominant interest prevailing.

However, there have been a number of criticisms of those who adopt the pluralist viewpoint of western democracies.

1 There are hidden elites who work behind the scenes, whose power is not fully discernible, e.g. the British Establishment comprises a powerful elite which exercises power although it is not democratically accountable.

2 Studies purporting to support pluralism in practice are based upon open decision-making by the government, whereas the crucial decisions in society are made behind closed doors and are not subject to debate. Even a government minister will be dismissed if he expresses an opinion counter to the established view (see Fig. 6.2). Irrespective of parties, British governments follow one another without any important change in the distribution of power or any fundamental reduction in the inequality which exists in society.

3 Democratically elected representatives often use their power to further business or trade union interests rather than the interests of the constituents who elected them. It is not uncommon for MPs to say something like, 'I represent the motor trade', or 'I represent the mineworkers.' (See Tables 6.4 and 6.5.)

Anger over attack on defence cuts
THATCHER SACKS NAVY MINISTER

Mrs Thatcher has sacked Navy Minister Mr Keith Speed, who challenged the Government's policy on defence spending, it was disclosed early today.

Mr Speed warned in a speech last Friday that cutting the Navy's fleet of destroyers and frigates would scupper Nato and endanger every man, woman and child in Britain.

A brief statement from 10, Downing Street said: 'The Prime Minister has this evening seen Mr Keith Speed and asked him to place his office at her disposal.'

Fig. 6.2 A minister may lose his job if he attacks in public decisions made in private

4 Not all interest groups are adequately represented: the poor, the black, the young, the old and the unemployed, have not the resources to organise themselves effectively in order to affect important decision-making.

Table 6.4 Occupations of MPs elected October 1974

	Lab.	Con.	Lib.	Others
Barristers	33	48	2	–
Solicitors	10	11	–	3
Journalists	27	22	1	1
Publishers	–	3	–	1
Public relations	1	2	–	–
Teachers, lecturers	76	8	1	5
Doctors, surgeons	6	3	–	–
Farmers, landowners	–	21	2	1
Company directors	3	72	2	1
Accountants	4	7	1	1
Underwriters and bankers	1	16	–	–
Managers, executives and administrative staff	29	20	1	2
Other business	25	22	–	3
Clerical and technical	17	1	–	–
Engineers	29	3	1	–
Trade union officials	19	–	–	–
Party officials	3	4	–	–
Mine-workers	17	–	–	–
Rail-workers	4	–	–	–
Other manual workers	7	–	–	–

(*The Times*)

5 Steven Lukes (*Power*) criticises the pluralistic or one-dimensional view of power because 'it inevitably takes over the bias of the political system under observation ...'

Pluralism and elitism are not necessarily mutually exclusive. The pluralist position allows for a multiplicity of elites; it may be best to think of 'democratic elitism' and elite theories of democracy. J.A. Schumpeter (*Capitalism, Socialism and Democracy*) argues that, within a democracy, rival elites compete for power. Institutional arrangements, such as political parties representing different interests in society, vie with each other for the people's vote. The advantage of Schumpeter's redefinition of the concept of democracy is that it closely coincides with the political systems

Table 6.5 Trade unions sponsoring MPs

National Union of Blastfurnacemen	1
Union of Construction Allied Trades & Technicians	3
Electrical, Electronics & Telecommunications & Plumbing Trades Union	3
Amalgamated Union of Engineering Workers (AUEW)	16
Amalgamated Union of Engineering Workers (constructional section)	1
Amalgamated Union of Engineering Workers (technical and supervisory section)	4
National Union of Furniture, Timber and Allied Trades	1
British Iron, Steel and Kindred Trades Association	1
General and Municipal Workers' Union	14
National Union of Mineworkers	18
Musicians' Union	1
Post Office Engineering Union	2
Union of Post Office Workers	2
Association of Professional, Executive, Clerical & Computer Staff	6
National Union of Public Employees	6
National Union of Railwaymen	6
Association of Scientific, Technical & Managerial Staffs (ASTMS)	10
National Graphical Association	1
National Union of Seamen	1
Transport Salaried Staffs Association	3
Union of Shop Distribution and Allied Workers	5
Transport and General Workers' Union (TGWU)	22
National Union of Agricultural & Allied Workers	1

('Political Britain', *The Economist*)

characterised by political parties opposing each other at elections in a democratic state. The idealistic idea that democracy is 'government of the people, for the people, by the people' is replaced by the reality of a leadership group such as the cabinet oligarchy which rules in Britain. According to Schumpeter, the principal part played by the citizens in a democracy is the election or rejection of political leaders. Once leaders are elected they will make the decisions upon all important issues. They are only restricted by the necessity to submit themselves to the electorate every five years. Although different groups have the ear of the leadership, it is the cabinet oligarchy which rules between elections.

W. Korphauser (*The Politics of Mass Society*) argues that the activities of intermediary groups in a pluralist liberal democracy safeguard it from totalitarianism. Different groups have access to the channels of power and individuals are able to work through these groups. If individuals are left without limited representation by interest groups, then they would become atomised and consequently apathetic. Pluralism prevents the evolution of a mass society where people have no active involvement or participation in the power structure.

● *Bureaucracy*

We have seen that Max Weber saw bureaucracy as the most efficient form of organisational power structure. Yet bureaucrats are frequently depicted by the media as petty officials, tied up with red tape, operating in large inefficient organisations which grind to a halt. As sociologists we are value-neutral towards bureaucracy and must study it objectively as a form

Table 6.6 Weber's ideal-type bureaucracy

1 *Appointment of officials* according to technical qualifications and merit; officials are not elected.

2 *Rules and regulations* govern the official's specialised work; officials work impersonally showing neither fear nor favour to anyone.

3 *Promotion* allows efficient officials to climb higher in the hierarchical power structure; officials enter a career and do not expect preferential treatment, or property rights related to the office.

4 *Full-time officials* devote themselves to the work of the organisation; officials are expected to carry out their duties impersonally and competently.

5 *Continuous business* is carried on faithfully by the officials; the office does not come to an end with the death of the holder.

6 *Written documents* are used to conduct official business; everyone is subject to formal equality of treatment.

7 *Public and private life are divided* by the segregation of organisational activity from the official's private life; public monies and property are separated from the official's private property.

8 *Limited compulsion* by officials is allowed but without hatred or passion, and hence without affection or enthusiasm.

of complex organisation. The term bureaucracy is derived from the French *bureau* meaning 'office'; literally bureaucracy means that power is in the hands of officials. Table 6.6 outlines the criteria of Max Weber's ideal type of bureaucracy.

Weber thought that bureaucracies would be technically superior to other organisations in the same way that machine production is superior to non-mechanical production. Bureaucratic administration may be compared to the way an assembly line is used in the manufacture of motor cars; each worker specialises in a specific expertise and works more efficiently than if he were asked to perform multitudinous tasks. Weber saw power, in a bureaucracy, to be in the hands of experts who would work faithfully for a regular salary with prospects of advancement. The official would exercise his authority impersonally, in accordance with his contract. Supporters of bureaucracy would contend that large organisations can only function if power is diffused. In a large public joint stock company, paid officials supervise personnel, finance, sales and advertising, etc. (see Fig. 6.3). In a one-man business, the sole proprietor carries out all the entrepreneurial functions: he is responsible for designing the product, selecting the factory site, ordering raw materials, supervising personnel and marketing the finished product. As the business increases in size he requires the assistance of partners or fellow directors to share the burden of power and responsibility. A large organisation inevitably becomes bound up with power-sharing and requires a central administration run by full-time professional officials or bureaucrats. This applies to organisations in the private sector of the economy, such as large companies, and also to public corporations such as the Gas Corporation or the British National

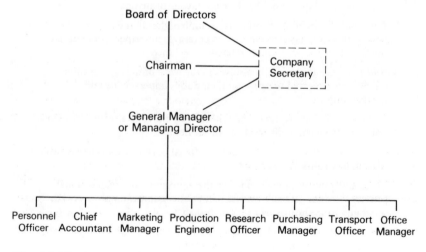

Fig. 6.3 The bureaucratic organisation of a large company

Oil Corporation. Bureaucracy is also prevalent in other large organisations such as the civil service, the armed forces and the national health service. In theory, bureaucracy is the most efficient way of running large organisations for it allows highly complex administrative tasks to be broken down into manageable areas. Weber believed the specialisation of bureaucratic roles enabled an efficient chain of command to be constructed. The power structure is essentially hierarchical and there always exists a higher authority to whom any doubtful decision can be referred. Bureaucracy should therefore be superior because it is precise, unequivocal, continuous and uniform in its operation.

Weber's analogy of bureaucracy as similar to a machine leads us to see why it is subjected to severe criticism. Bureaucrats are considered to be too impersonal, too officious and too much bound by regulations from which they cannot escape. It is contended that faceless bureaucrats do not care enough about people but are obsessed with rigid rules, the advance of their own careers and the expansion of their organisation. C. Northcote Parkinson (*Parkinson's Law*) has described how the bureaucrat's 'work expands so as to fill the time available for its completion', while the number of unnecessary officials escalates. He gives an example of the way in which the number of Admiralty officials almost doubled while the number of ships decreased by over a third (see Table 6.7).

Table 6.7 The growth of bureaucracy in the Admiralty

Classification	1914	1928	Increase or decrease %
Capital ships in commission	62	20	−67.74
Officers and men in RN	146 000	100 000	−31.5
Dockyard workers	57 000	62 439	+9.54
Dockyard officials and clerks	3249	4558	+40.28
Admiralty officials	2000	3569	+78.45

(C. Northcote Parkinson, *Parkinson's Law*)

R. Michels (*Political Parties*) considered that bureaucracy arose in response to demands made by the educated elite for more powerful positions in society. He believed that bureaucracy was not the most efficient form of organisation and its aims would often conflict with the goals and aspirations of the working class. The aims of bureaucracy were not necessarily the aims of society as a whole.

R.K. Merton (*Bureaucratic Structure and Personality*) contended that the merits of the Weberian official could become exaggerated as in practice he acted over-zealously and over-methodically. He believed that bureaucracy could work against the common people when

> primary concern with conformity to the rules interferes with the achievement of the purpose of the organisation, in which case we have the familiar phenomenon of the red tape of the official. An extreme product of this process is the bureaucratic virtuoso, who never forgets a single rule binding his actions and hence is unable to assist many of his clients.
>
> (Merton, R.K. *Bureaucratic Structure and Personality*)

Merton noted two possible dysfunctional aspects of bureaucracy; it tends to produce in officials a state of 'trained incapacity'; and the means to bureaucratic ends may become ends in their own right.

A.W. Gouldner (*Patterns of Industrial Democracy*) documented how employees in a bureaucracy had to bend the rules in order to get things done. He examined the plan of a new manager to introduce a bureaucratic structure at a gypsum mine. The plan worked out in the plant above the ground was resisted successfully by those below ground, because the miners knew that the scheme was too rigid to work in practice. Gouldner also attacked writers who accept the inevitability of bureaucracy. Bureaucratic institutions do not necessarily result in a loss of individual freedom. The degree of impersonal relationships varies according to status levels within organisations. Although Weber called for impersonal dealings between bureaucrats and clients, in reality officials may operate various degrees of impersonality and exercise some sympathy and compassion.

Peter Blau (*The Dynamics of Bureaucracy*) also found that in spite of orders that all clients must be treated equally, in practice some were treated better than others. Middle-class clients are treated better than working-class clients, whites receive preferential treatment over blacks while the middle-aged come off better than the young or the old. If a rigid bureaucracy were applied then there should be no favouritism.

Organisational structures need to be adapted to circumstances. Qualified officials must be given power, but not too much power. They should use their power in a disciplined, but not over-disciplined way. T. Burns and G. Stalker (*The Management of Innovation*) in their study of the electronics industry suggested a more fluid, organic organisational structure. An organisation may operate efficiently if officials do not cling too much to their own areas of power. Burns and Stalker recommended that there should be cooperation across official boundaries. This would cut across Weber's ideal type of bureaucracy which involves each office having a clearly defined area of competence.

Dr Ernst Schumacher's doctrine that small is beautiful has produced a catchphrase which warns us that large bureaucratic institutions pose a danger to democracy.

> Bureaucracies seem to be necessary for, and simultaneously incompatible with, modern democracy . . . . Yet by concentrating power in the hands of a few men in business and government, bureaucracies threaten to destroy democratic institutions. Our democratic institutions originated at a time when bureaucracies were in a rudimentary stage and hence are not designed to cope with their control. To extend these institutions by developing democratic methods for governing bureaucracies is, perhaps, the crucial problem of our age.
> (Blau, P. *The Dynamics of Bureaucracy*)

6.3 Political participation and organisations

● *Political socialisation*

Political socialisation is the process by which the individual learns about the political system. It determines the individual's perception of political organisations and his subsequent participation or non-participation in political activity. A person's reaction to political phenomena is largely determined by his social class and his economic environment. The experiences, beliefs and values of a middle-class farmer are likely to lead him to vote for the Conservative Party, while the working-class manual labourer is likely to vote Labour. We must therefore examine the main channels through which an individual's experiences, attitudes, beliefs and values are determined.

Political socialisation does not in itself determine adult political participation, but it does create dispositions that influence political involvement in later life. In most cases what is learned in the earlier formative years is simply reinforced by later life; we read the papers we have been accustomed to read, listen to opinions we have learnt to respect and are receptive to arguments that accord with our social background. Socialisation continues throughout life, so it is possible that adult socialisation will bring about a change in political attitudes, but it is more than likely that views once learned are merely strengthened in the course of our experiences. The family, the school and the media (see section 4.7), all play their part in our political socialisation.

1 *The family*

The family is first in the process of political socialisation, both from aspects of time sequence and social significance. Political attitudes related to childhood are well-entrenched because they are deeply rooted in the primary attitude to the family. Individuals learn their patterns of political participation at a very early age. David Easton and Robert Hess (*The*

Child's Political World) found that in the United States, political socialisation begins at the age of three and is well established at the age of seven; by the age of eight the majority of American youngsters could identify with either the Democratic or Republican parties. The young child saw the President as the state authority figure corresponding to the father-figure of the family; the child is taught to orientate himself to the hierarchical structure of authority.

Basic attitudes reflected in the political culture change very slowly. Children learn to accept the normative consensus which includes support for the monarchy, the capitalist system and the liberty of the individual. Conservative families accept the status quo and place little store upon improving conditions of social equality. Although the children of Labour parents may be taught to struggle against social injustice, they come to accept the institutionalised position of the Labour Party and the fact that it is 'unwise' to attempt to overthrow the established system. Any changes to be made must come about through the framework of parliamentary government and the party system.

Political socialisation is important in two major respects: it influences voting behaviour in later life and it causes a small number of people to seek positions of power in both local and national politics.

In a BBC interview in 1964 Harold Wilson said:

My mother, who died four years ago, had a very big influence on me .... Her brother who was very politically conscious when he was in England, left at the age of twenty to become Speaker of the West Australian parliament. My mother went out to visit him when I was a very small boy, and I think I got the political bug from seeing them perform in the West Australian parliament there. My father also was very politically-minded. He voted Labour in Manchester in the 1906 election. But I think my biggest influence as far as they were concerned – and this was true of my grandparents as well as my parents – was the church or chapel background, the Non-conformist background.'

('The Family Background of Harold Wilson', in Rose, R., ed., *Studies in British Politics*)

Sir Winston Churchill's father had been an MP. Harold Wilson's 1966 Government included five ministers of cabinet rank whose fathers had been MPs – they were Benn, Caradon, Foot, Greenwood and Jenkins. That this should have been true of a Labour Government is most significant; generally speaking, political recruitment to high-ranking positions have come from a relatively small number of high-status families. Ron Hall's analysis (*The Family Background of Etonians*) found that about a quarter of all Tory MPs were educated at Eton and that they dominated positions in the Cabinet and other important high offices; the influence of Eton parents upon their children and subsequently upon

British politics is reflected in the types of residences in which they live, the lifestyles which they pursue, the social statuses which they inherit and the political attitudes which they pass on to their offspring.

2 *The school*

After the family, the school is probably the most important agency of political socialisation. Ron Hall's account of Etonians indicates that Eton furnishes a disproportionate number of Britain's political leaders; for example, he found that in the Cabinet Etonians outnumbered their nearest rivals, the Wykehamists, by seven to two. Family background facilitates entrance into Eton and other status-conferring and status-confirming public schools where political aspirations are inculcated and encouraged. The top public schools in general, and Eton in particular, furnish a disproportionate number of those who reach the top in politics. In Mrs Thatcher's government of 1979 only two members of the Cabinet had not been to a public school – Mrs Thatcher and Mr Biffen. The Cabinet included six old Etonians, three Wykehamists and one old Harrovian.

While a tiny minority are socialised for roles of political leadership in the public schools, the majority attend state schools where they generally accept politically passive roles. The English educational system implicitly emphasises cultural norms which are based on inequality. Lord Eccles, when Minister of Education, contended that English schools are 'one of the chief instruments which create a gulf in our society.' This social gulf which begins with the social class of the family is reinforced by a middle-class school system which adopts the structural-functionalist standpoint and presents social inequality as necessary and inevitable.

We saw that according to Ralph Turner's sponsored and contest mobility systems (see section 4.1) that the English educational system is based on sponsored mobility, favouring a controlled selection process; the middle class are considered best able to judge merit and for advancement they choose individuals who have supposedly superior qualities. The mass are considered suitable for only a basic education and are taught to defer to the elite who provide a governing class suitable to take over the positions of political power in society.

The universities continue as instruments of the social divide. Oxbridge especially provides far more than its fair share of political leaders. Seventeen members of Mrs Thatcher's Cabinet of 1979 were graduates of Oxford or Cambridge.

● *Political parties*

In Britain, there are four main political parties. The Conservative Party is identified with the interests of property owners, private business, individual initiative and affluent middle-class members of society. The Labour

Party believes in the extension of public ownership of industry, the welfare state, and a steeply progressive tax system whereby the burden of taxation falls more upon the rich than the poor; it is closely linked to the trade union movement. The Alliance of the Liberal Party and the Social Democratic Party stand between the Conservative Party on the right and the Labour Party on the left (see Fig. 6.4); they derive their strength from both the working and middle classes without obtaining the overwhelming support of either.

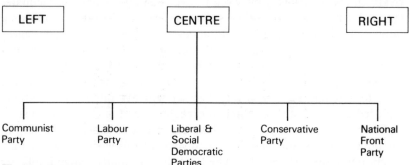

| LEFT | CENTRE | RIGHT |

Communist	Labour	Liberal &	Conservative	National
Party	Party	Social	Party	Front
		Democratic		Party
		Parties		

Fig. 6.4 British political parties

Membership of the political parties may be divided into activists, who are energetically involved in politics, and those who give very limited support, such as helping the party at election time. The Conservative Party claims to have a membership of 1.5 million, while the Labour Party numbers about 300 000 individual members, but this number is increased to about six millions if affiliated trade-union members are included. The Conservative Party receives extra financial support from private companies, while the Labour Party augments its finances from trade unionists unless they contract out of paying the political levy. About a third of the members of Conservative associations are politically active, whereas about two-fifths of the Labour membership are actively involved in party activities.

The constituency party is the lifeblood of political participation at grass-roots level. It is at constituency level that candidates are selected and elections are organised for local councils and parliament. At election times the party agents arrange for distribution of literature, canvassing the electorate and 'knocking up' supporters to try to persuade them to vote. Between elections, members are eligible to attend branch meetings where party policies are discussed, and delegates elected to represent the branch at regional or national level. The parties hold annual national conferences, in the autumn, in order to debate issues of national policy.

In spite of the Labour Party's claim to represent the working class,

Table 6.8 Who holds power in British political parties (1981)

Party	Leader	Shadow Cabinet	Party HQ	Election manifesto
Labour	Elected by: trade unions 40% constituency parties 30% MPs 30%	Elected by MPs	Controlled by National Executive Committee elected by annual conference	Approved jointly by Cabinet/Shadow Cabinet and NEC
Conservative	Elected by MPs	Appointed by leader	Controlled by leader	Issued by leader who consults Shadow Cabinet
Liberal	Elected by party members	Appointed by leader	Controlled by National Executive elected by annual assembly	Issued by leader who consults informally

people of middle-class origins and occupations comprise the officials and
the candidates in all four major parties. Jean Blondel (*Voters, Parties and
Leaders*) found that even in traditional working-class areas more than half
the Labour Party officers were middle-class, while in the Conservative
Party more than three-quarters were middle-class. MPs are predominantly
middle-class: more than half have had university background and only a
tiny proportion have not received education beyond the age of eighteen.
Table 6.8 shows who elects or appoints the people of power in the major
parties.

The method by which the leader is elected is of utmost importance
because it is the party leader who is the dominant figure of modern British
politics. Party leaders are usually more extreme in their political views
than party voters, but more moderate than party activists (see Fig. 6.5). If
a party is returned to power at a General Election, it is the leader who will
select the cabinet. There is a great deal of evidence that, in recent years,
cabinet oligarchy has begun to be replaced by government by the party
leader. According to Hugo Young,

> the myth of collective decision has been substituted by the reality of collective
> endorsement.
>
> (Young, H. 'The Death of Cabinet Government', *The Sunday Times*, 24
> May 1981)

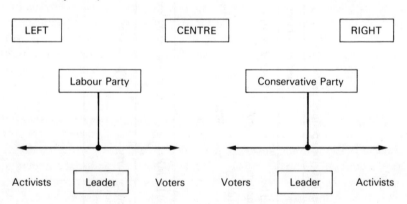

Fig. 6.5 The position of party leaders in relation to party activists and voters

The cabinet still exists as a body of about twenty leading politicians
selected from one party by its leader. The cabinet continues to meet every
Thursday but it only discusses those things which the party leader/prime
minister places on the agenda. When exchange controls were abolished in
1979, the majority of cabinet ministers did not know of the decision until
they read about it in their newspapers. The £7000m-plus expenditure on

Trident missiles is one of the most important issues of current politics but it has never been subject to a collective decision in cabinet. In the 1970s prime ministers Wilson and Callaghan succeeded in keeping secret from the cabinet a £1000m programme to modernise Polaris missiles.

Considering the great power held by the leader of the party, it is no wonder that in the 1980s the Labour Party is re-examining the way in which its leader is elected. Previous Labour leaders blatantly ignored decisions of party conferences and an attempt has been made to establish a wider democratic franchise (see Table 6.8). The Conservatives have comparatively recently adopted democratic elections for the leadership; the first leader not to be selected by an elite clique was Edward Heath who became Prime Minister in 1970.

The vast majority of MPs have been described as lobby fodder as it is very unusual for them to disobey the party whips and vote against the party. They can, however, exercise influence through pressure groups: Conservative Party policy is influenced to a limited extent by the 1922 Committee, the Monday Club and the Bow Group; similarly Labour leaders must take some notice of the Tribune Group or the Manifesto Group or the Solidarity Group.

For the last fifty years in British politics, the Conservative and Labour parties have dominated the national political scene. Their powerful positions have been maintained by election of MPs according to 'the first past the post' system which has militated against parties of the centre such as Liberal and SDP. Party politics have been mainly concerned with mobilising support for two alternative government teams. However, in recent years the two major parties have come under pressure which has manifested itself in four principal ways. Both the main parties have suffered from:

1 *Decrease in number of MPs* In 1974 devolutionist parties gained fourteen parliamentary seats (Scottish Nationalist 11 and Plaid Cymru 3). Probably more important, in the long run, has been the loss since 1981 of moderate MPs from both the major parties in order to form a new social democratic party which agreed to cooperate with the Liberal Party in future elections.

2 *Decrease in membership* Since their peak membership year of 1953, both parties have lost paid-up members: Conservative membership has decreased from 2.8 to fewer than 1.5 million while Labour's individual membership has fallen from 1 million to about 300 000. Members lost from the Conservative and Labour parties have not provided a compensatory rise for the smaller parties (apart from those attracted to the SDP): members lost to the two major parties have generally lapsed into political inactivity.

3 *Decrease in funds* The loss of membership has brought about an acute financial crisis for all political parties. It is necessary for both the major

parties to rely less upon the support of individual members and seek
extraneous financial aid. The wealthier Conservative Party receives most
of its funds from donations by big business whilst the Labour Party relies
greatly upon the trade unions.

4 *Decrease in voting support* The percentage of votes cast jointly for the
Conservative and Labour Parties dropped from a record 96.8 per cent at
the 1951 general election to 75 per cent in October 1974. It appeared as if
this decline in Conservative and Labour votes might lead to a number of
indecisive 'hung' parliaments, but in the 1979 general election the major
parties combined polled 80.9 per cent. However, this result probably
provided a freak kink in an otherwise downward curve (see Fig. 6.6). It is
likely that the middle ground in British politics will find increasing
support in the 1980s. Much depends upon whether the centre parties
(Liberal and SDP) can force the major parties to accept the proportional
representation system of voting at elections. PR would provide more
representation for minority parties, with fewer wasted votes, and the
composition of the legislature would reflect voting figures more accurately.

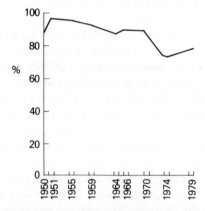

Fig. 6.6 Conservative and Labour shares of the votes cast at general elections,
1950–79

● *Voting behaviour*

The study of voting behaviour is known as psephology. The techniques of
psephological analysis of voting behaviour have become far more reliable, with various types of sample analyses by means of opinion polls.
Although these polls are frequently denigrated, in recent years they have
been relatively accurate. The polls that have interviewed right up to the
last moment before an election have been remarkably precise. For
example, in 1979, the Market of Opinion Research International (MORI)

poll, published in the *Evening Standard* on the polling day itself was extremely accurate: Marplan in the *Sun* was a close second, while nearly all the polls were accurate to 2 per cent. The National Opinion Poll (NOP), the *Observer*'s poll and the Gallup Poll were probably less accurate than MORI only because they conducted their interviews at an earlier stage in the election run-up. The general accuracy of the polls is significant because it indicates that actual voting behaviour can be scientifically analysed. For the 1979 general election, a weighted average of all five polls can be compared with both the final MORI survey and the actual result (see Table 6.9).

Table 6.9 Comparison between opinion poll forecasts and voting in 1979 general election

Party	Five polls %	MORI %	Actual result %
Conservative	44.5	45.0	43.9
Labour	39.0	37.0	37.0
Liberal	13.5	15.0	13.8

The British electorate consists of approximately 40 million people over the age of eighteen. On average about three-quarters of the electorate cast their votes at general elections (see Table 6.10); this proportion is relatively high compared with other western democracies such as the United States. As the British people are not compelled to vote, as are the citizens of Australia, it is important to distinguish between positive abstainers and negative abstainers: positive abstainers deliberately stay away from the polling booth whereas negative abstainers make no deliberate decision to abstain but merely do not bother to vote. The rate of abstention can have a profound effect upon the result of an election: for example, the difference between the Labour and Conservative parties in

Table 6.10 Percentage voting at general elections 1950–79

Date	%	Date	%
1950	84.0	1966	75.8
1951	82.5	1970	72.0
1955	76.7	1974 (Feb.)	78.7
1959	78.7	1974 (Oct.)	72.8
1964	77.0	1979	76.0

the 1964 general election was only 204 000 votes (see Table 6.11); Harold
Wilson's government had a majority of four seats, and in one seat the MP
was elected by a majority of only seven votes. The effect of abstention is
even more marked in local council elections when the turn-out averages
about 40 per cent for the country as a whole.

Table 6.11 Votes cast at general elections 1964–79 (thousands)

Date	Conservative	Labour	Liberal	Others
1964	12 002	12 206	3093	349
1966	11 418	13 066	2327	453
1970	13 144	12 179	2117	900
1974 (Feb)	11 928	11 661	6056	1695
1974 (Oct)	10 458	11 458	5348	1909
1979	13 698	11 532	4314	1678

The identification of social class both objectively in surveys of voting
behaviour and subjectively in the minds of voters is a source of great
interest to sociologists. Analyses made during the 1960s (e.g. Butler, D.
and Stokes, D. *Political Change in Britain*) suggested that class-alignments
to the political parties were weakening; the cohorts of voters coming on to
the registers were less politically influenced by social class than their
parents' generation. However, analyses of the 1974 general elections
indicated that, at that time, the two major parties were still very
dependent on their social class bases (see Table 6.12 and Fig. 6.7).

Generally, the Labour Party wishes to be clearly identified with the
working class, while the Tories aim their image and propaganda primarily
at the middle class, although the Conservative Party persistently picks up

Table 6.12 Voting allegiance by social class, October 1974

Party	All	Middle-class (A, B, C1)	Working-class (C2, D, E)
	% (100)	% (35)	% (65)
Conservative	36	55.5	24
Labour	39	19.5	53
Other	25	25	23

(Butler, D. and Kavanagh, D. *The British General Election of October 1974*)

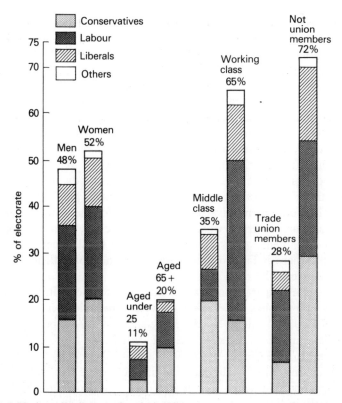

Fig. 6.7 Voting allegiances, October 1974
(adapted from Butler, D. and Kavanagh, D. *The British General Election of October 1974*)

a larger share of the working-class vote than the Labour Party does from the middle class. As 65 per cent of the electorate are working-class it would seem to be obviously advantageous for a party to be identified with that class. Mrs Thatcher's success in the 1979 general election suggests that class divisions are somewhat arbitrary, and that the Conservatives attracted middle-of-the-road voters whose self-identification with a particular class was not clearly drawn.

Working-class and lower-middle-class electors who vote Conservative may be divided into deferentials and pragmatists (Nordlinger, E.A. *The Working Class Tories*): deferentials vote Conservative because they believe that political leaders should be drawn from the upper middle class; pragmatists vote Conservative because they think the Tories are likely to run the country more efficiently. At one time there were probably more deferentials than pragmatists, but in later years working-class Tories have been more pragmatic.

We had in our sample a number of respondents who could be described as pure specimens of the socially deferential. But we were much more impressed by the fact that the Conservatives attracted working-class support for many of the same reasons they attracted support throughout the country.

(Butler, D. and Stokes, D. *Political Change in Britain*)

The tie between class and party is probably decreasing but it is stronger in Britain than in other Western democracies. R.R. Alford (*Party and Society*) made a comparative study of Britain, Canada, Australia and the United States, and found that social class had more effect on voting in Britain than in the other countries surveyed. Class remains the major factor underlying the political cleavage. The term 'adversary politics' is used by those who consider that there is too much political cleavage in Britain with consequent adverse consequences for the country as important policies are reversed when a Conservative government replaces a Labour government, and vice-versa. From the conflict perspective it is argued that there is far too much consensus and not sufficient political cleavage between the main parties.

Other factors, apart from class, contribute to the political cleavage. Religious opinion has little effect on voting behaviour in most of the United Kingdom, but in Northern Ireland the way a person votes is largely determined by whether he is a catholic or a protestant. Older people tend to vote Conservative. Several possible reasons have been put forward for this. Firstly, although the mass of voters remain loyal to the party they choose initially, there is a tendency for people to adopt radical stances early in life in a desire to change society, but as they grow older they wish to preserve the society they have come to accept. Secondly, upward social mobility causes some people to accept the political ideologies which match their new lifestyle, while those who experience downward social mobility are less likely to change their political allegiances. Thirdly, the middle-class live longer than the working-class and this favours the Conservative Party. Women live longer than men and they are more inclined to vote Tory: it has been suggested that women are more conservative by nature, and their voting behaviour is influenced by their occupation – about 60 per cent of female jobs are non-manual. It is difficult to assess the effect of immigration upon voting behaviour: although surveys indicate that the majority of immigrants vote Labour, this may be counter-productive because the political opinions of whites may harden, causing people who are racially prejudiced to switch their votes to the Conservatives.

Any study of voting behaviour indicates that it is a far more complex matter than it seems at first sight. As children tend to vote the same way as their parents, and working-class parents outnumber middle-class parents, it would appear that the Labour Party would have an increasing advantage as the years go on. However, we have seen that the Conservative Party gains political power by consistently managing to gain a large measure of working-class support. David Butler and Donald Stokes, in the second edition of *Political Change in Britain*, have suggested several important reasons for this political phenomenon. Firstly, upward social mobility (see Table 6.13) has meant that nearly 10 per cent more people have moved upward in the last generation than have moved down: a change in their state of affluence has meant a change in voting behaviour.

Table 6.13 Social mobility, 1970

		Father's social grade		
		I–IV	V–VI	
Head of household's social grade	I–IV	20.7	19.1	39.8
	V–VI	9.5	50.7	60.2
		30.2	69.8	100%

(Butler, D. and Stokes, D. *Political Change in Britain*, second edition)

Secondly, Butler and Stokes point to the unpopularity of trade unions and the tendency for Labour MPs to be drawn from middle-class people with a university education. These factors make younger voters less willing to regard politics as a conflict of class interest. Butler and Stokes's findings help to explain the arrival of the volatile voter and the increase in electoral swings. Figure 6.11 indicates the recent increase in the percentages of voters opting for parties other than the two major ones.

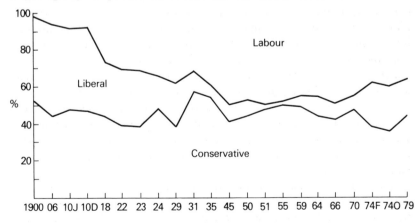

Fig. 6.8 Votes cast in general elections, 1900–79

The tendency towards uniform electoral swings would be severely undermined if the centre parties became strong enough to force the major parties to adopt proportional representation. Our simple plural electoral system (whereby victory goes to the candidate with most votes on the first count) allows the majority of constituencies to return candidates for one of the two major parties in every general election. This means that whether or not the Conservative or Labour Party is returned to power depends upon the whims of floating voters in a minority of constituencies.

6.4 Social order

- *Conformity and deviance*

Social order exists in society because the majority of people conform to certain rules both written and unwritten. Although people have widely different interests, they behave in a way which enables society to change but still endure. We internalise social rules during our early years of primary socialisation and the application of these rules ensure that we conform and behave in a way which allows the game of social life to be played out successfully.

There is an underlying unity and order in all social life. We assume other people will conform to social rules. For example, we know the milkman will deliver the milk for our early morning cup of coffee. We can be sure that the bus will be more-or-less on time, that the driver will pick us up at the bus-stop and obey the traffic signals which ensure the safety of his passengers. The caretaker will see that our school or college or office or factory is reasonably heated. We rarely bother to think about the innumerable cases of conformity which we meet, because we take other people's conformity to the rules for granted. We can be sure that the milkman, the bus-driver, and the caretaker will perform their social roles. We saw in section 1.6 that social interaction is largely predictable. People conform to the rules of social life in the same way that they conform to the rules of chess; the chess player decides which moves to make but all his moves must be in accordance with the rules of the game.

There is no single theory which satisfactorily explains why men conform to produce social order. But we do know that all societies establish rules intended to ensure that individuals and institutions behave in an orderly way; the rules may involve coercion, cooperation, consensus and continuity.

Percy S. Cohen (*Modern Social Theory*) discusses four theories of social order.

1 *Coercion theory* emphasises that order exists in society largely as a result of the power which some people hold over others. According to this theory

social order results from physical or moral coercion. If people do not obey the rules they may be physically punished by imprisonment or deprivation of property or rights. Moral coercion can only be exercised if people accept moral values: teenagers will obey their parents only if they accept that there is a certain degree of reasonableness about the orders given. The coercion theory is often associated with the idea of a conspiracy perpetrated by some people upon others: for example medieval rulers were expected to maintain social order because of the supposed divine right of kings. However, the coercion theory is not necessarily linked with such an assumption; it may be argued that those in power are there by popular consent.

2 *Cooperation or mutual interest theory* stresses that social order results from men realising that their own interests are best served by helping others who will in turn help them. One facet of this theory is that people enter into contracts setting out rights and obligations. More important is the subtle and complex idea that social order results from unintended consequences of people pursuing their own interest: people do not discover that social order is in their best interest and plan accordingly, but rather social order is established unwittingly and found to be in the best collective interest.

3 *Consensus theory* states that social order is based on a minimal consensus on certain values. When people accept the same values they recognise a common identity and aim for common goals. This value-consensus encourages individuals to devise means for reconciling or adjusting any conflicting interests which they may have. For example, people have different ideas about the way a town should develop: some wish to conserve old buildings while others wish to pull them down and build modern ones. Some degree of consensus or commitment to common values is a necessary condition for reconciliation and the maintenance of social order: as both groups share an interest in the best possible social life of the town, modification and adaptation is possible. In Norwich it has been agreed that sections of old city wall should exist beside the modern inner ring road. There is an obvious link between the consensus and cooperation theories as indeed there is between all four theories of social order.

4 *Continuity theory* states that there is a continuity or inertia appertaining to social life. It may seem like arguing in a circle to assert that if social order exists it provides the means for its own perpetuation. Despite the seeming absurdity and tautology of the theory, it does make it clear that some of the causal processes of social phenomena are indeed often circular in nature. Social order is maintained by a number of mutually reinforcing processes and tends to resist pressures for change from within society itself.

Fig. 6.9 Deviant behaviour?

Although conformity is the usual state of affairs, there are those who indulge in deviancy and break the rules of society. Deviant behaviour is not a simple concept; Albert K. Cohen has considered four states to which the term deviancy is applied.

1 *Behaviour that violates norms* is the most common understanding of deviancy. Crime is the prototype of deviancy in this sense: if people break the law of the land, they are considered deviants. However, there are also folk norms or moral standards which it is also regarded as deviant to violate.

> It is important to note that although deviance, in this sense, and conformity are 'opposites', they represent the poles within the same dimensions of variation; therefore a general theory of the one must comprehend the other.
>
> (Cohen, A. 'Deviant Behaviour', in 'The Sociology of the Deviant Act', *American Sociological Review*, No. 30, 1965)

The law may even be more permissive than folk norms. For example, the act permitting homosexuality between consenting adults was passed when the majority most probably accepted the folk norm which held homosexuality in disfavour and incidentally disagreed with the law.

2 *Statistical abnormality* is not necessarily deviant. People who behave unusually, but do not break significant social rules may be regarded as eccentric rather than deviants. This particularly applies to way-out dress fashions. Deviancy relates to something that is less good or less desirable and not merely less frequent.

3 *Psychopathology* is not necessarily synonymous with deviancy in a sociological sense. Illness or personality disorganisation may be included within the scope of deviancy, but behaviour is truly *deviant* if it departs from the normative rules of some social system, whereas behaviour is *pathological* when it proceeds from a sick or defective personality. However, although illness may not usually be considered as deviancy, a person's deviance may be caused by illness as in the case of alcoholism or drug addiction. There are those who consider that psychologically we help to create our own illnesses. Illness may be looked upon as a deviancy because society desires a person to work. So illness may be considered a deviance from a set of norms representing the situation of a healthy person.

4 *Socially-disvalued behaviour and states* such as mental deficiency, blindness, ugliness, vagrancy and other situations may be regarded as deviant by society. Erving Goffman (*Stigma*) subdivides such deviations into:

(a) people who have a licence to deviate, e.g. those who use an illness for their own ends and use their sick status as a permit to deviate from normal work-performance standards or to gain a social advantage such as jumping a queue.

(b) people who provide a symbol or mascot for a particular social group, e.g. the village idiot or the school fat boy become the focus of attention which welds others into a participating group around him.

(c) people who voluntarily deviate, openly accepting a degraded social position by acting rebelliously in connection with basic institutions, e.g. the family drop-out or the punk rocker who decides that society has written him off and who consequently writes off society.

(d) people who join together to form a sub-community of social deviants, e.g. groups of drug addicts and gangs of juvenile delinquents (see section 7.6).

A distinction may be made between a deviant person and a deviant act. A deviant person may be considered to be an individual who:

1 is formally described as a deviant, e.g. by the police or the courts;

2 is continually performing an act regarded as deviant, (if you only violated a norm once you are unlikely to be looked upon as a deviant);

3 admits to himself that he or she is a deviant, e.g. a prostitute is likely to have a deviant self-image and a self-description of herself as a common prostitute.

A deviant act violates norms existing in a certain social situation. There is nothing about an act which in itself makes it deviant. For example, it is socially acceptable for a youth to cheer at a football match where he is expected to get behind his team, but it is thought to be deviant if he cheers in church where he is expected to conform to an atmosphere of worship. An act which is looked upon as deviant in one society may be socially acceptable in another: in an Islamic society drinking alcohol is a forbidden and deviant act, but in most western societies partaking of alcoholic drinks is generally considered a pleasant pastime. Acts considered deviant in a certain period of time may become acceptable as societal norms change: at one time it would have been considered deviant for a woman to smoke in public – nowadays it is commonplace and not a deviant act so long as the woman does not smoke a pipe! Whether or not an act is looked upon as deviant depends upon who makes the rules in society: the smoking of marihuana may be the norm amongst some groups of young people but considered a very deviant act by the middle-class and the middle-aged. Similarly the well-to-do are likely to regard tax evasion as a far less deviant act than that which they label social-security scrounging. The mass media use the labelling process to build up stereotype impressions of deviant acts. Excess drinking is regarded as a deviant act, but the alcoholic has his own personal explanation for his behaviour. A deviant act violates norms and theories relating to deviancy.

Any theory of deviancy should attempt to answer four principal questions.

1 *What acts are defined as deviant and why?* Rightly or wrongly, for health reasons, the partaking of drugs is considered as a deviant act for students, but not for patients in hospital. It would normally be considered as morally wrong for a pilot to crash his aircraft purposely, but in wartime Japanese kamikaze pilots were hailed as heroes. Similarly, the killing of another human being is a deviant act in peacetime but acceptable in wartime: this helps to explain the different attitudes of the British Government and the Irish Republican Army concerning killings in Ulster; the IRA contend that they are in a state of war.

2 *Why do people commit deviant acts?* The deviance must be related to the social context. It is often difficult to examine the cause of a deviant act; the actors may give their reasons, but they are not always reliable because people tend to rationalise after the event. The functionalist would argue that in well-ordered societies deviancy should not occur, because deviancy is a dysfunction which works against consensus. Conflict theorists would argue that deviancy is of vital importance because change is necessary in

any society. It is the deviants who change the world. Religious leaders such as Jesus and Joan of Arc were regarded as deviants by their contemporaries.

3 *How do people react to deviants?* Jesus and Joan of Arc were punished by death, but later generations have acclaimed them. In our society, criminal acts may be viewed ambivalently in relation to deviancy. Far more people violate the law than are caught and sentenced; only a small minority are stigmatised as criminals. Sometimes the police will turn a blind eye as in the case of under-18 year-olds drinking alcohol in public houses. On occasions deviants may be forced to make restitution and pay for damage caused. On other occasions retribution may be demanded, e.g. a trade unionist blackleg may be sent to Coventry, a recalcitrant schoolboy may be subject to corporal punishment, while a first-degree murderer may be sentenced to capital punishment.

4 *What is the effect upon the actor upon being labelled a deviant?* Some actors may resist being stigmatised as a deviant while others will accept the label which society places upon them.

Structural-functionalists would argue that social forces determine our behaviour: the normative structure of accepted values and beliefs will determine our actions; non-normative structures are not internalised and their effects are less obvious, e.g. the development of modern technology – technical incompetence may be a deviancy. (Would you consider it a deviancy for a motorist not to be able to change a wheel?)

Conflict theorists believe that it is inevitable that rules will be broken and that deviancy will occur. Robert K. Merton put forward the view that rules are broken when people are unable to achieve the goals valued by society, such as academic success at school or promotion at work. Merton divided rule-breakers into four groups.

1 *Innovators* who try to achieve their goals by illegitimate means, e.g. criminals, hijackers, terrorists, etc.

2 *Rebels* who aim to change the rules of society completely so that they can succeed in the new order, e.g. political extremists of the right or left.

3 *Retreatists* who drop out of conventional society and adopt unconventional modes of behaviour, e.g. gypsies, winos, religious freaks, etc.

4 *Ritualists* who become passive social actors continuing to work within the system but no longer anticipate success, e.g. the silent majority.

Interactionists see individuals, and not social forces, as exercising their own influence. Individuals accept certain standards which are taken for granted, although these standards may change as individuals and society change. Whereas the structuralist sees deviancy as due to inadequate socialisation, the interactionist sees deviancy in the light of interpreting the actions and interactions of individuals and the way in which both the observer and the deviant sees the deviant act.

● *Formal and informal social control*

In order to achieve conformity, a society sets up and maintains a series of social control mechanisms with the intention of correcting deviancy. These social-control mechanisms may be either formal or informal.

The most obvious formal social controls are rules which constitute the law. In Britain we have three main types of law.

1 *Common law* has been passed down through the ages. For centuries there have been rules commonly recognised to be law. These were rules or laws common to the whole country.

2 *Statute law* consists of laws passed by Parliament and *written* in statute or law books. Every Act of Parliament adds to statute law.

3 *Case law* is so called because a court case has taken place and a judge has given a ruling on a point of law. The judge bases his decision on the law of the land and the interpretation previously given to it by other judges. The judge's decision forms the basis of future law.

Our laws are also divided into criminal law and civil law. Criminal law concerns offences committed by individuals against the community. These range from serious crimes such as murder to petty theft. Actions which break the law are known as offences and are of two types: indictable and non-indictable. *Indictable offences* were once tried before a jury but may now be tried by magistrates if the accused agrees. *Non-indictable* offences are heard in a magistrates' court with no jury. Of the 2 million or so cases each year where people are found guilty, the majority are non-indictable. Table 6.14 shows offenders by age, sex and the type of offence they committed, in 1979.

There are five main types of offence:

1 *Offences against persons*, e.g. assault, wounding (where the skin is broken), grievous bodily harm (GBH) where severe injuries are inflicted, manslaughter and murder.

2 *Offences against property*, e.g. theft, fraud, forgery, malicious damage and robbery.

3 *Traffic offences*, e.g. failing to obey traffic signs, riding a bicycle dangerously, having faulty brakes and riding on the footpath.

4 *Sexual offences*, e.g. bigamy, rape and incest.

5 *Offences against the state*, e.g. perjury (telling a lie on oath), treason or unlawful assembly.

Some crimes cut across these divisions, e.g. robbery with violence. The robbery is a criminal offence against *property* while the violence is a criminal offence against the *person*. The civil law deals with the rights, duties and responsibilities of individual members of the community to one another. A civil wrong or injury inflicted by one person on another is known as a *tort*. A civil offence is allowing your dog to bite the postman; whereas a criminal offence would be stealing the postman's mail.

Table 6.14 Offenders found guilty of, or cautioned for, indictable/triable either-way offences, England and Wales, 1979

	Males: age ranges					Females: age ranges				
	10 to 13	14 to 16	17 to 20	21 and over	All ages (000s)	10 to 13	14 to 16	17 to 20	21 and over	All ages (000s)
Indictable/triable either-way offences:										
Murder, manslaughter, or infanticide	0·3	3·4	21·1	75·2	0·4	–	1·5	14·9	83·6	0·1
Other violence against the person	3·1	14·0	28·8	54·1	47·9	6·0	25·7	19·4	48·9	4·8
Sexual offences	3·7	15·9	19·9	60·6	10·1	8·9	9·6	18·5	63·0	0·1
Burglary	16·1	30·2	24·9	28·7	66·1	23·4	32·2	22·8	21·6	3·0
Robbery	5·9	17·9	34·7	41·5	3·1	8·4	33·7	33·2	24·7	0·2
Theft and handling stolen goods	14·5	22·9	22·0	40·6	222·5	17·5	19·7	13·7	49·1	73·0
Fraud and forgery	2·0	5·7	18·3	74·0	17·1	2·2	7·8	24·3	65·7	5·0
Criminal damage	17·9	22·1	27·3	32·7	10·5	15·3	21·6	16·6	46·5	0·8
Other indictable/triable either-way (excluding motoring) offences	0·3	2·4	19·9	77·4	19·7	0·3	3·8	22·7	73·2	2·6
Triable either-way motoring offences	0·4	8·7	21·9	69·0	21·0	0·3	6·3	12·2	81·3	0·7
Total indictable/triable either-way offences	11·3	20·4	23·1	45·1	418·3	15·5	19·3	15·2	50·0	90·4
Number of offenders per 1000 population in age group	29	68	62	12	20	9	15	9	3	4

(*Social Trends* No. 11, 1981)

In order to ensure that people abide by these formal rules of social control, there are specific penalties, such as fines or imprisonment, which are imposed upon those found guilty of breaking the law. The authority of the law in society is underpinned by a number of complex agencies such as the police, the legal profession, the courts and penal institutions. All these agencies attempt to ensure that the law is enforced and that those who break the law are punished. The law is thus an important means of formal social control because if people think that they will be punished they will be more likely to conform and not deviate from the way in which society wants them to behave.

However, the law controls people's actions in a more subtle way. It is generally accepted that the law is morally right and consequently should be obeyed. Respect for justice underlies the following social functions of the law.

1 Maintenance of public order.
2 Protection of property.
3 Encouragement of co-operative action by all citizens.
4 Communication of moral standards.
5 Regulation of social life.
6 Moderation of the struggle for power by conferring legitimacy upon the recognised authority.

It is important to appreciate that law and morality do not necessarily coincide. Opinions can alter about what is thought to be morally right or wrong. The law can be changed but this takes time. Ideas about the morality of divorce changed more quickly than the law did. When A.P. Herbert introduced a parliamentary bill to change the divorce laws, he gave accounts of how couples contrived ridiculous situations because adultery was virtually the only grounds upon which a divorce would be granted. By 1969, the law had caught up with the social climate and it was accepted that the one ground for divorce was that the marriage had irretrievably broken down.

The law may even try to lead public opinion. This has been the case with the abolition of capital punishment. In 1969 the death penalty for murder was abolished in the Murder (Abolition of Death Penalty) Act, in spite of a public poll which showed that 84% of the population were in favour of hanging. Another poll conducted by ITN in 1977 showed that 85 per cent favoured the restitution of capital punishment, although two years earlier, parliament rejected such a move.

Informal social controls are based upon the acceptance of social norms, mores, folkways and customs learned through such agencies of socialisation as the family, school, peer group and mass media. Social norms have already been touched upon in section 1.2. These are standards of behaviour to which members of a social group are expected to conform.

They provide shared standards by which an individual's actions are judged by the rest of the group. Social norms are mechanisms of social control which generally take the form of unwritten rules. In Britain it is the norm that young children should grow up at home with their parents. It is still the norm for the young to remain living with their parents until they get married and start a home of their own, although in recent years there has been a tendency for teenagers to want 'a pad' of their own. An individual who breaks a well-established social norm is not subject to specific sanctions but any deviant action may be received with disgust, ridicule or ostracism. A person who conforms to social norms is accepted and possibly praised or rewarded. The majority of people accept social norms for granted and seldom consider alternative forms of action.

Each person's social role involves norms. We already know something about a particular social role before assuming it. We expect a teacher to be informative on his subject, to keep his class in order, to set and mark work, etc. If he falls down on any of these things, constraints backed by sanctions will be taken against him. His pupils may be inattentive or fail to turn up for his lessons. Parents may make protests. We are socialised into a role, and to the norms attached to that role, by the reactions of others.

Mores are very important norms relating to morality. Such norms are concerned with whether or not we deal with each other justly and honestly. Western societies have fundamental common mores; for example as we live in monogamous societies, a man or woman should not have more than one marriage partner at one time. In polygamous societies it would be normal for a man to have more than one wife at one time. Mores play a vital part in maintaining social order and are likely to be incorporated into the law of the land, e.g. it is regarded as morally wrong to steal or kill or injure another person.

Folkways are less important norms. Society could function without them and disregarding them does not result in strict penalties. Examples of folkways include eating with a knife and fork, forming a queue or celebrating birthdays. The term folkways was coined by Sumner in order to describe common modes of behaviour accepted as natural in a particular society. There is nothing specially right or wrong about observing folkways. We shake hands when we meet friends, the French kiss each other on the cheek, whereas the Chinese often shake hands with themselves. Folkways are embedded in the culture of a society and must be seen in a specific social context.

Customs are merely folkways which have existed in a society for a very long time. Holly and mistletoe have been used as decorations since pagan times. Customs are socially accredited ways of behaving, relating to every aspect of our lives. They involve the ways in which people in our society traditionally bring up their children, eat their food, practise their courtship and care for their old people.

• Religion in a secular society

Religion is another form of social control. Religious beliefs have a great deal of influence upon the actions of the people who hold them. If people believe in life after death and in the threat of damnation if they flout religious doctrines, this will affect their social actions. As sociologists we are not concerned with whether or not particular religious beliefs are true, but we are vitally interested in how people holding such beliefs are affected by them in their day-to-day lives. Similarly we are interested in the effect of rejecting religious beliefs. Durkheim and Weber were very concerned with the ways in which social experience relates to religious beliefs. Religion can play an important part in maintaining social order. Table 6.15 summarises some of the main functions of religion.

Table 6.15 Some important sociological functions of religion

---

1 Religion gives people an understanding of life and death and the purpose of human existence.

2 Religious rites, such as sacraments, reinforce people's beliefs and give people a feeling of comfort and cooperation which unites them in a moral community.

3 Religion gives sacredness to the values of society, thus contributing to conformity, group objectives and stability.

4 Religious ceremonies are traditional and link the past, present and future actions of members of society.

5 Religious beliefs help people to cope with problems of not conforming, e.g. they can be absolved from sins and reintegrated into the social group.

6 Religious beliefs help the individual to make sense of personal maturation experiences as he evolves through the various stages of life from infancy to old age.

7 Religion may perform a prophetic function and inspire believers to challenge established authorities if it is considered that they are out of alignment with the doctrines of religion.

When everyone in a particular society holds the same religious beliefs, religion unifies society. In Victorian England, religion was used by the middle classes as an important social control mechanism.

On Sunday evening he [the head of the household] is their spiritual guide, their chaplain: they may be seen entering in a row, the women in front, the men behind, with seriousness, gravity, and taking their places in the drawing room.... The master reads aloud a short sermon – next a prayer; ... lastly, he repeats the Lord's Prayer and, clause by clause, the worshippers respond.

(Taine, H. *Notes on England*, 1861)

It has been argued that religion plays a less important part today because we live in a secular society where the majority of people reject religious values. It is further argued that religion itself has become more secular; people may attend church but they live materialistic lives and their religious beliefs do not much influence their social conduct.

There is a great deal of evidence pointing to the secularisation of society and the decline of religion.

1 *Decline in church membership and in attendance*

Statistics relating to church membership are ambivalent, but by most criteria of measurement there appears to have been a decline. Anglicans include in their membership-figures all those who attend communion on Easter Day, even though for some it may be a once-a-year attendance. The membership criterion for Roman Catholics is infant baptism, although many backslide as they go through life. Methodists prune their membership annually and only include those who are active participants. Catholics claim an absolute increase of those attending Mass in Britain but

Table 6.16 Baptisms in selected churches (thousands)

	1951	1961	1966	1971	1975	1976	1977	Percentage change 1951–77
Church of England:								
infant	441	412	413	347	298	237	230	−48
other	9	11	10	8	7	8	10	+11
Church of Scotland:								
infant	39	45	39	32	23	23	22	−44
other	5	5	4	2	2	1	2	−64
Baptist churches	7	6	6	5	5	5	6	−24
Methodist churches	...	46	47	39	30	28	26	−44
Roman Catholic Churches:								
baptisms under age 7	92	131	132	108	76	71	68	−25
other baptisms	11	14	9	6	5	5	5	−55

(*Social Trends* No. 10, 1980)

Table 6.17 Marriages: religious and civil ceremonies, Great Britain

	1966	1971		1977		1978
	All Marriages	First* Marriages	All Marriages	First* Marriages	All Marriages	All Marriages
Manner of solemnisation (000's)						
Church of England/Church in Wales	175	155	160	112	117	120
Church of Scotland	22	18	20	13	15	15
Roman Catholic Church	51	46	48	32	34	} 70
Other Christian	38	29	37	19	32	
Jews and other non-Christian	2	1	2	1	1	
Register Office	138	107	180	89	195	200
Total marriages	426	357	447	266	394	405
Percentage of marriages solemnised in Register Offices						
England and Wales	32	30	41	34	51	51
Scotland	25	25	31	28	38	40
Great Britain	32	30	40	33	49	49

* i.e. first marriage for both parties
(*Social Trends* No. 10, 1980)

attendance has declined in proportion to the total population. Protestants have lost even more ground especially in Britain. Table 6.16 indicates the number of baptisms in the major British churches from 1951 to 1977. Note the last column which indicates the percentage change from 1951 to 1977. Many children who are baptised do not attend church as they grow older; but figures of the number of confirmations show that in 1977 there were 67 000 in the Roman Catholic Church and over 95 000 in the Church of England where confirmation is carried out at a later age.

2 *Increase in family breakdowns*

Harmonious family life is associated with religious observance and belief. The increases in the divorce rate, the illegitimacy rates, the number of one-parent families and people living together outside the framework of marriage, have all been suggested as evidence of a decline in religious influence. The number of church marriages has declined, while the percentage of marriages solemnised in register offices has increased markedly (see Table 6.17).

3 *Decline in the influence of religious institutions*

Bryan R. Wilson (*Religion in a Secular Society*) emphasised the historical dominance of Christianity in Western culture. The Roman Catholic Church ruled over medieval Europe: in England, Cardinal Wolsey occupied the highest political and religious positions. In nineteenth-century Britain the church controlled education, politics and welfare services. Schools are no longer under religious control, while religious instruction and assemblies in state schools have been watered down and largely transformed into ways of propagating liberal education. The links between the Anglican Church and the Conservative Party have decreased, while the Labour Party's claim to have originated from Methodism rather than from Marxism is not really relevant to politics today. The churches have lost their pastoral functions to the Welfare State and have modified their teachings to comply with changing views, e.g. on contraception and divorce.

In 1908 the Lambeth Conference had regarded 'with alarm the growing practice of the artificial restriction of the family.' In 1966 the Anglican Church, in advance of changes in the law, recommended that irretrievable breakdown of marriage should be substituted for previous grounds for divorce (Church of England Report, *Putting Asunder*).

4 *Fewer people believe in God*

Public opinion polls have suggested that fewer people have faith in a personal God although there are many who claim to believe in a creator or supernatural forces. There is evidence all around us that people are turning from Christianity and putting their trust in astrology, good luck charms and even black magic. The Bible is read less frequently (see Fig. 6.10).

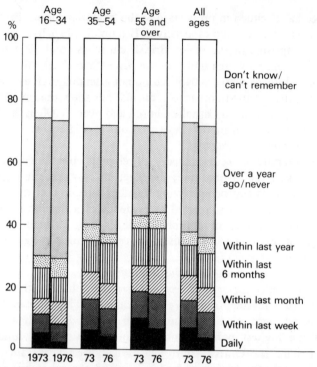

Fig. 6.10 Bible readership, by age (in households owning a Bible), Great Britain (*Social Trends*, 1980)

5 *Religion is regarded as irrelevant to modern life*
Many people still use symbolic services (*rites de passage*) provided by the church, but do not find services of worship meaningful. The four-wheeled Christians have evolved: they go to church in a perambulator to be christened, in a taxi to be married and in a hearse to be buried. At other times they are apathetic to religion and the church is ignored.

6 *Churches do not attract the working class*
E.R. Wickham (*Church and People in an Industrial City*) pointed to the fact that the working class are not absorbed into the activities of the church. They see the churches as middle-class institutions preoccupied with small-time fund-raising for various charities, but apparently unconcerned with wider issues of social justice. A cultural gap prevents the churches from communicating with the mass of the people. The working man indulges in more leisure pursuits on Sundays and is not attracted to the traditional idea of the Sabbath as a day of rest. David Martin (*A Sociology of English Religion*) found that areas with least religious activity are large housing estates and old-established working-class areas in large cities

where Church of England practice is 0.5 to 2.5 per cent. In Dagenham 83 per cent never went to church. Small towns are likely to have only a 7.5 per cent weekly attendance.

7 The middle class are drifting away from church

In Britain it is no longer necessary to go to church in order to climb the social ladder, gain promotion at work or establish respectability in society. The church finds it difficult to compete with increased leisure facilities such as golf and television.

8 The clergy have less influence

The Church of England has been especially hit by the secularisation process and the position of the priest in the community has declined. The clergy have suffered from low morale because of low stipends. They exert decreasing influence now that the Anglican Church is less of a national institution to which the majority of people identify. Consequently there have been fewer ordinations and the average age of the clergy has risen. The normal career structure is from 25 to 65 years, so it would be expected that the majority would be below 45 years, whereas over 60 per cent are over 45 years old.

9 People have turned to way-out sects

In Britain, sects such as Jehovah's Witnesses, Plymouth Brethren, Seventh Day Adventists and even 'the Moonies' have made an increasing impact as people have turned from traditional religious institutions. So far as individual belief is concerned, the increased activities of the sects may be a sign of religious rejuvenation rather than secularisation, but it does indicate a decline in the influence of the orthodox religious bodies to which the majority of people belong. The Moonies are members of the Unification Church run by the millionaire South Korean, Sun Myung; they use a technique called 'love-bombing' to brainwash their converts. But it would be a mistake to suggest that all sects resort to suspect methods or that they do not offer to many people a feeling of peace and comfort, combined with a real religious experience denied them in traditional churches. Nevertheless, the conduct of many sects is very suspect. In December 1979 more than 900 members of the People's Temple died in a ceremony of murder and suicide ordered by their leader at the sect's headquarters in Guyana. The activities of the People's Temple are illustrative of the power of a charismatic leader who is able to fill a gap left by the secularisation of organised religion.

10 Secularisation of the church itself

The best example of the secularisation of religion is provided by the United States where about 45 per cent of the population are regular attenders and 60 per cent are members of a church, but the society to which they belong is extremely secular and materialistic. From its inception, the state and the church have been kept separate. Will Herberg

(*Protestant, Catholic and Jew*) has explained that being a protestant, a catholic or a Jew are three ways of indicating that immigrants are members of a new nation. Over the last two centuries, different ethnic groups have settled in America and tried to establish a personal identity in a mass society. Membership of a religious group makes them part of the American Way of Life. Church membership is necessary for respectability and to enhance promotional prospects in business corporations. The churches act as social and community centres offering access to recreational clubs and a set of friends. Herberg's account helps to explain why American Churches have survived in an urban industrial society. They have responded to the society which they serve: they are led by its standards rather than setting standards for others to follow.

In considering the evidence for secularisation, we have already touched upon some of the reasons for secularisation. These include the weakening of family relationships, the failure of the churches to attract artisans or stop professional people from drifting away, and the advent of urbanisation and industrialisation. Other important reasons for the evolution of the secular society have been suggested.

1 *The growth of scientific thought and method*

People are no longer willing to believe things blindly. They have been taught to be more rational and are concerned with cause and effect. The advantages of applied science are all around to see and experience: everyday devices, gadgets and machinery work efficiently while space travel has broken through old barriers. Living in a world of high-geared technical progress makes people aware of the rational at the expense of the religious.

2 *Many Biblical assertions have been challenged*

Modern thought has questioned ideas long held to be sacred. In biology, Darwinian theories of evolution are generally accepted and fundamentalist or literalist approaches to creation are rejected even by most Christians. Similarly many Christians no longer accept the Virgin Birth and they attempt to explain (if not to explain away) the miracles attributed to Christ.

3 *Contemporary theologians have indulged in Christian apologetics*

There has developed a large following, especially among modern churchmen, committed to the teachings of Dietrich Bonhoeffer, Paul Tillich and others. Bonhoeffer has outlined a startling paradox of belief in ultimate reality and a non-religious understanding of God; his disciples in Britain, such as John Robinson (*Honest to God*) have popularised his beliefs. A leading Methodist, Leslie Weatherhead, has written *The Christian Agnostic*.

4 *Comparative sociology has illustrated the multifarious nature of religious belief in different cultures*

POLITICS AND SOCIAL ORDER   383

It is largely accepted that no one religion, and certainly no one Christian denomination, has a monopoly of the truth. Whereas Christian education was once a compulsory subject at school, today the study of comparative religions is regarded as useful and illuminating. There are those who search for a reconciliation between Christians, Jews, Moslems, Buddhists, Hindus, etc. In the modern world an individual's religious beliefs have become broader and possibly less valid.

5 *Political ideologies sometimes compete with religious beliefs*
Political ideologies may even become religious beliefs rather than mere substitutes for orthodox religion. It can be argued that nazism and communism are forms of religion. Communism in particular offers an alternative explanation of the world and social reality. This is of great sociological significance considering that two-thirds of the world population now live in countries with communist governments.

Although Bryan Wilson (*Religion in a Secular Society*) takes a pessimistic view of what is happening to religious belief in a secular society, David Martin (*The Religious and the Secular*) is inclined towards greater optimism. In spite of all that has been written about the causes of secularisation and the evidence for it, there are positive indications that religious belief is still of importance even in our urban, industrial society. These indications include the following:

1 *There remains a great deal of individual religious commitment*
We have seen that church membership and attendance figures are an unsatisfactory standard of measurement. Martin believes that the number of people who identify with the Church of England amounts to about 60 per cent of the population, while 25 per cent identify with the Roman Catholics and 10 per cent with noncomformists. Religious statistics are no guide to personal devotion and private prayer. People no longer attend church for ulterior motives, but those who do attend have a strong spiritual commitment. The majority of people, when pressed, express a belief in the supernatural. All this indicates a retention of religious belief; even belief in providence, fate or the protestant work ethic is of interest to sociologists. All belief affects social action and social order.

2 *The ecumenical movement has brought greater unity among the churches*
E.R. Wickham (*Church and People in an Industrial City*) found, in his investigations in Sheffield, that one important reason for people's disenchantment with Christianity was the disunity of the churches. In recent years there have been talks between Roman Catholics and Anglicans, Roman Catholics and Methodists, and Anglicans and Methodists, all intent upon finding a measure of common ground. Congregationalists and Presbyterians have joined to form the United Reform Church. Writing in 1981, conversations are proceeding between members of the Anglican, Methodist, United Reform, Churches of Christ and Moravian churches

with a view to covenanting for union. This would allow local churches to cooperate, and for unity to develop from grass-root levels rather than being imposed from the top. Such a move would have been unheard of even twenty years ago when the churches often opposed each other with intense bigotry. Any display of a united front is likely to add to the strength of the churches fighting to oppose the secularisation process.

3 *The charismatic movement and the growth of sects fulfil religious needs*

New religious movements which have been developed by leaders with charisma may be looked upon with distrust by traditional religious institutions and by society at large, but they may exemplify devout religious experiences. Norman Cohn (*The Pursuit of the Millenium*) shows how sects are no new phenomenon: millenarian sects arose during the middle ages and were based upon the Second Coming of Christ. It is difficult to differentiate clearly between sects and churches. Sects usually reject the values of society, whereas churches accept them. The noncomformists began as sects, but are now accepted as churches which conform. In this light the growth of sects may be seen as offering a spiritual challenge to churches which have grown conformist and even moribund.

4 *Worker-priests are closer to the people*

Although institutionalised religion has declined, many priests are now more involved in the community. People who do not attend church often feel a lack of comfort and peace which is reflected in the increasing numbers of psychiatric cases. In addition to industrial chaplains the concept of 'the priesthood of all believers' has led to the encouragement of all Christians to become actively involved in extra-mural Christian activities. Many people regard themselves as Christians without attending the churches. They are prepared to call upon the clergy when need arises and the clergy are more inclined to offer their pastoral care to non-adherents.

5 *The extent of recent secularisation has been exaggerated*

There is no real evidence to support contentions that the church has declined sharply in recent times. It is more likely that the church never gained the allegiance of the working class and that secularisation began about three centuries ago with the advent of industrialisation. It could be argued that the churches are nearer to the people today with their welfare work particularly among trade unionists and in industrial missions. Society relies upon religious bodies, such as the Salvation Army, to care for the homeless.

6 *The church is far less bigoted*

Apart from in Northern Ireland where religious fervour is shown at its worst, the churches in Britain live together far more harmoniously than in the past. Considering the fanatical actions undertaken in the name of religion in Ulster and Iran, it may be argued that the churches are better out of the political arena. The churches have a record of hindering social change as well as of helping it. There are many who believe that the churches should not become too involved in educational and political fields. The churches serve society best if they act as one important pressure group among many and concentrate upon the spiritual rather than the temporal.

Further Reading

Blau, P. *The Dynamics of Bureaucracy* (University of Chicago Press)

Blondel, J. *Voters, Parties and Leaders* (Penguin)

Bottomore, T.B. *Elites and Society* (Penguin)

Budd, S. *Sociologists and Religion* (Collier-Macmillan)

Butler, D. & Stokes, D. *Political Change in Britain* (Macmillan)

Cohen, A.K. *Deviance and Control* (Prentice-Hall)

Dahl, R.A. *Who Governs?* (Yale University Press)

Etzioni, A. (ed.) *A Sociological Reader on Complex Organisations* (Holt, Rinehart & Winston)

Giddens, A. *Politics and Sociology in the Thought of Max Weber* (Macmillan)

Goldthorpe, J.H. *et al. The Affluent Worker: Political Attitudes and Behaviour* (Cambridge University Press)

Gouldner, A.W. *Patterns of Industrial Democracy* (Collier-Macmillan)

Guttsman, W.L. *The British Political Elite* (MacGibbon & Kee)

Hindess, B. *The Decline of Working Class Politics* (MacGibbon & Kee)

Honerich, T. *Punishment* (Penguin)

Lukes, S. *Power* (Macmillan)

Martin, D. *A Sociology of English Religion* (Heinemann)

Martin, D. *The Religious and the Secular* (Routledge & Kegan Paul)

Michels, R. *Political Parties* (Free Press)

Mills, C. Wright *The Power Elite* (OUP)

Musgrove, F. *Youth and Social Order* (Routledge & Kegan Paul)

Nordlinger, E.A. *The Working Class Tories* (MacGibbon & Kee)

Parry, G. *Political Elites* (George Allen & Unwin)

Pizzorno, G. *Political Sociology* (Penguin)

Robertson, R. (ed.) *Sociology of Religion* (Penguin)

Rock, P. & McIntosh, M. *Deviance and Social Control* (Tavistock)

Rose, A.M. *The Power Structure* (OUP)

Rose, R. (ed.) *Studies in British Politics* (Macmillan)

Schumpeter, J.A. *Capitalism, Socialism and Democracy* (George Allen & Unwin)

Stanworth, P. & Giddens, A. (ed.) *Elites and Power in British Society* (Cambridge University Press)

Taylor, I. *et al. The New Criminology* (Routledge & Kegan Paul)
Urry, J. & Wakeford, J. *Power in Britain* (Heinemann)
Wilson, B.R. *Religion in a Secular Society* (Penguin)
Worsley, P. *The Trumpet Shall Sound* (MacGibbon & Kee)

SEVEN
Social problems

7.1 What is a social problem?

- *Difficulties of definition*

Sociological definitions are sometimes highly contentious. Hillery (*A Critique of Selected Community Concepts*) discovered ninety-four different definitions of 'community'. The term 'social problem' is similarly difficult to define. Some suggested definitions centre mainly upon aspects of urban society and the problems arising from urban living (e.g. alcoholism, drug-addiction, homosexuality and prostitution). There are 'voluntary' social problems such as crime, which may be differentiated from 'involuntary' social problems such as old age.

It can be argued that *specific* social problems are of doubtful value as subjects of sociological study. There are three main reasons for taking up this position.

1 If a sociologist considers a certain area of research as constituting a social problem, he is intimating an attitude of disapproval and is in danger of abandoning any semblance of a value-neutral position which a scientist (social or physical) might be expected to assume.

2 A sociologist who studies a specific social problem is likely to want to change things for what he considers to be 'the better'. A true scientific approach necessitates the researcher studying things as he finds them and not being influenced by subjective desires to institute changes. Researchers into the problem of poverty have put forward measures intended to change social conditions in order to mitigate poverty.

3 It is dangerous to generalise about the nature of a social problem and possible remedies because that which is considered a social problem in a particular society may not be considered to be so in a different society. For example, although most human societies invoke an incest taboo/avoidance,

> there are many examples of societies in which incest is either allowed or even enjoined for some sections of the population. (This perhaps gives the lie to the

idea that people 'see' the deleterious effects and therefore ban incest.) ... in some cases where advantages were not all that obvious, and where there might have been positive advantages to inbreeding, then inbreeding was allowed or even encouraged. (For example, royal families or religious cults wishing to preserve exclusiveness of blood might practise brother-sister marriage.)
(Fox, R. *Kinship and Marriage*)

Although it is not possible to put forward a definition of the term 'social problem' with which every sociologist will agree, two generally basic components may be suggested. Both structural-functionalists and social-interactionists are likely to find these criteria acceptable.

A social problem is:
1 considered to be a course of complexing anxiety by many people in a particular society;
2 a situation upon which society spends large sums of public money.

Structural-functionalists regard social problems as serious behavioural deviations hindering the functioning of society; social problems are regarded as inhibiting the needs and goals of society – bachelorhood could be so regarded. Social actionists are more concerned with attempting to find solutions to the problems of society; in such cases, it is difficult to remain detached and not to relate to people involved.

Sociologists do not regard people as social problems. As Durkheim pointed out, even deviant behaviour is socially-generated. The condition of being poor or old or black or a town-dweller does not constitute deviant behaviour. Poverty is a social problem brought about by a lack of this world's goods. The problem of old age is accentuated by the ageing population structure. A man is black by reason of genetics; it is racial disharmony which is the social problem and not the individual, irrespective of his colour. Urbanisation is associated with social problems largely because of inadequate, overcrowded living conditions and not because of any inherent shortcomings of town-dwellers.

● *Private troubles and public issues*

C. Wright Mills, in *The Sociological Imagination*, distinguished between the private troubles and public issues. Private troubles cause personal unhappiness to the individual, whereas public issues are social problems because they transcend individuals and affect adversely a large proportion of the members of society. Mills considered the problems of unemployment, war, divorce and urbanisation.

In these terms, consider unemployment. When, in a city of 100 000, only one man is unemployed, that is his personal trouble, and for its relief we properly look to the character of the man, his skills, and his immediate opportunities. But when in a nation of 50 million employees, 15 million men are unemployed, that is an issue, and we may not hope to find its solution within the range of opportunities open to any one individual. The very structure of opportunities has collapsed. Both the correct statement of the problem and the range of possible solutions require us to consider the economic and political institutions of the society, and not merely the personal situation and character of a scatter of individuals.

Consider war. The personal problem of war, when it occurs, may be how to survive it or how to die in it with honour; how to make money out of it; how to climb into the higher safety of the military apparatus; or how to contribute to the war's termination. In short, according to one's values, to find a set of milieux and within it to survive the war or make one's death in it meaningful. But the structural issues of war have to do with its causes; with what types of men it throws up into command; with its effects upon economic and political, family and religious institutions, with the unorganised irresponsibility of a world of nation-states.

Consider marriage. Inside a marriage a man and a woman may experience personal troubles, but when the divorce rate during the first four years of marriage is 250 out of every 1000 attempts, this is an indication of a structural issue having to do with the institutions of marriage and the family and other institutions that bear upon them.

Or consider the metropolis – the horrible, beautiful, ugly, magnificent sprawl of the great city. For many upper-class people, the personal solution to 'the problem of the city' is to have an apartment with private garage under it in the heart of the city, and forty miles out, a house by Henry Hill, garden by Garrett Eckbo, on a hundred acres of private land. In these two controlled environments – with a small staff at each end and a private helicopter connection – most people could solve many of the problems of personal milieux caused by the facts of the city. But all this, however splendid, does not solve the public issues that the structural fact of the city poses. What should be done with this wonderful monstrosity? Break it all up into scattered units, combining residence and work? Refurbish it as it stands? Or, after excavation, dynamite it and build new cities according to new plans in new places? What should those plans be? And who is to decide and to accomplish whatever choice is made? These are structural issues; to confront them and to solve them requires us to consider political and economic issues that affect innumerable milieux.

(C. Wright Mills, *The Sociological Imagination*)

According to Mills, public issues can only be solved by structural changes. The unemployment of millions of workers cannot be solved by individual action but it can possibly be mitigated by government policies such as spending upon public works or monetary measures. The ordinary individual is powerless to stop a war, or bring down the divorce rate, or improve the quality of life in the inner city areas. These are macro-social problems involving social cost and requiring collective action.

• *Should the sociologist take sides?*

In spite of attempts to be value-neutral, there are sociologists who argue that it is impossible not to sympathise with the underdog. Sociologists who study the social problems of poverty, old age, racial prejudice and urbanisation, are expected to recommend measures to alleviate these problems. Howard Becker (*Approaches to the Study of Social Problems*) argues that sociologists find themselves compelled to take sides. The important issue is, whose side do they tend to support?

Accusations of bias have occurred in studies of prisons, schools, hospitals, asylums and other institutions. The social researcher has to be careful not to be influenced unduly by superordinates who are in control of subordinates. The researcher is allowed into a prison only if the prison authorities approve, and he works under the guidance of the prison governor and other officers; he is likely to see and hear only that which they want him to see and hear. Similarly, headmasters and senior medical staff are superordinates who have the greatest influence upon those who attempt to ascertain what is really going on in schools and hospitals. Subordinates (such as pupils or patients) are not organised well enough to present their case adequately.

> Many total institutions, most of the time, seem to function merely as storage dumps for inmates, but, as previously suggested, they usually present themselves to the public as rational organizations designed consciously, through and through, as effective machines for producing a few officially avowed and officially approved ends. It was also suggested that one frequent official objective is the reformation of inmates in the direction of some ideal standard. This contradiction, between what the institution does and what its officials must say it does, forms the basic context of the staff's daily activity.
>
> (Goffman, E. *Asylums*)

If the researcher does not accept the views of superordinates, he is forced to analyse his own *definition of the situation*, although he may know less about the situation than those intimately involved. He has to tread warily. A hierarchy of credibility exists. The people at the top possess most knowledge in their particular field; if the sociologist refuses to defer to bureaucrats and administrators he is likely to be accused of ignoring those generally regarded as most informed. The sociology of knowledge cautions us to consider the circumstances in which judgements are made. On the one hand, the researcher attempts to avoid an unthinking acceptance of the status quo. On the other hand, if he accepts the subordinate's viewpoints, he is likely to be criticised for siding with the underdog. A researcher into any form of deviant behaviour is likely to sympathise with the deviants. The researcher into the problem of football hooliganism has a greater comprehension than the layman of the under-lying reasons for such anti-social behaviour.

> To travel on any British Rail football special is to come into contact with groups of supporters, led by slightly older men, solidified in a total support for individual teams and antagonistic in their behaviour to 'outsiders' ('innocent bystanders' or supporters of other teams)....
>
> This rump is not only experiencing the loss of its game to managers and millionaires; it is clearly isolated and segregated in its experience of life in general. There may indeed be grounds for seeing the violence around soccer as a reflexion, in some ambiguous sense, of a more total and material estrangement of the isolated group from the wider society.
>
> (Taylor, I. 'Soccer Consciousness and Soccer Hooliganism', in Cohen, S., ed., *Images of Deviance*)

Although Becker argues, as an interactionist, that it is impossible for the sociologist not to take sides, there are clearly dangers in taking a liberal overview of any social problem. Alvin Gouldner has attacked Becker for being preoccupied with an underdog identification. Gouldner argues that the sociologist's allegiance must be to the welfare of society as a whole rather than to competing factions. He sees no special virtue in the underdog who lacks power and authority, any more than there is any special virtue in those who have power and authority.

If the sociologist sides with authority he may gain the respect of those who exert the greatest influence. If he sides with the underdog he may gain the support of large numbers of people because there are more underdogs than 'overdogs'. Although it may be argued that the sociologist is probably on the safest ground if he gives his allegiance to values rather than to factions, the difficulty is to decide which are the 'best' values?

> ... the sociologist, qua sociologist, is in no better position than the layman to say whether or not a particular social end is to be desired.
>
> (Rex, J. *Key Problems of Sociological Theory*)

7.2 Poverty

● *Absolute poverty*

Looked at from structural-functionalist perspective, the simplest conception of poverty is expressed in terms of absolute poverty, e.g. a minimum weekly sum of money

> necessary to enable families ... to secure the necessaries of a healthy life.
>
> (Rowntree, S. *A Study of Town Life*)

The term 'absolute poverty' is associated especially with studies of the poor in London by Charles Booth from 1889 (*Life and Labour of the People of London*), and of studies of poverty in York by Seebohm Rowntree in 1899, 1936 and 1950 (the last investigation being undertaken in cooperation with G.R. Lavers).

Rowntree adopted a minimum subsistence level which erred on the side of meanness rather than extravagance. In accordance with the criterion of 'the lowest standards which responsible experts can justify', Rowntree compiled (with the help of the BMA) a dietary which was supposed to provide a family with adequate nutrition at minimum cost. The inflexibility of such a dietary is obvious; it included only one weekly egg for a man, wife and their three children. Rowntree added minimum sums for clothing, household sundries, fuel and light, and personal sundries. When all these items were taken into consideration, a family of five could avoid poverty in an absolute sense if their weekly income, in 1950, was not less than £5. Families whose incomes were too low to provide the minimum necessities of life were considered, by Rowntree, to be in *primary poverty*. Families whose incomes were marginally above the poverty-line, would place themselves in a state of *secondary poverty* if they spent part of their income on non-essentials or if they budgeted inefficiently.

Although Rowntree's subsistence-conceptualisation of poverty has been severely criticised, particularly in recent years, it was generally accepted and had certain distinct advantages.

1 Absolute poverty corresponded to a commonsense view of what it really meant to be poor, e.g. not having enough to feed your children.

2 Absolute poverty, according to Rowntree's criteria, was easy to measure.

3 Measurement of poverty was objective in terms of:
  (a) levels of family income;
  (b) calorific requirements of diets.

4 Research could be cheaply carried out, using Rowntree's definition of poverty, i.e. it was operational.

5 The concept of absolute poverty could be used over a period of time and minimum standards of living could be raised as diets improved.

Rowntree's changing assessments and upgradings in his later investigations suggest a link between absolute poverty and the concept of relative poverty which is more acceptable to modern sociologists.

- *Relative poverty*

Viewed from conflict and interactionist perspectives, the relative concept of poverty arises from the idea that people are poor if they suffer *relative deprivation* in the sense that they are unable to enjoy things which the majority of people in their particular society enjoy. The concept is particularly associated with the work of Peter Townsend. In the 1950s Townsend began to cast doubts upon the validity of the concept of absolute poverty. He argued that Rowntree's minimum level of subsistence was too narrow and that any realistic assessment of what constituted poverty must take into account the spending habits of the majority of people in a society. It was not necessary that the things people bought should be necessities or that people's choices should be regarded as wholly rational. If newspapers are to be included in a list of necessities but contraceptives are omitted, does this mean that the poor are to be denied a safe and happy sex-life?

> ... what is to be considered 'necessary' and what is not? If clothing, money for travel to work and newspapers are considered to be 'necessaries' in the conventional sense, why not tea, handkerchiefs, laundry, contraceptives, cosmetics, hairdressing and shaving, and life insurance payments?
> (Townsend, P. 'Measuring Poverty', *British Journal of Sociology*, 1954)

In accordance with the concept of relative poverty, families living in an affluent country today may consider the possession of a television set as essential. If all the other families in the street have the use of a TV set then it is a relative deprivation not to have one. Dennis Marsden found this to be so when he conducted a survey of over a hundred mothers (unmarried, separated, divorced and widowed) in a northern industrial borough during the mid-1960s.

> The fact that 84 per cent of the mothers had TV indicates that it was considered virtually essential in their lives.
> (Marsden, D. *Mothers Alone*)

An understanding of the relative nature of poverty is not new, but like the existence of poverty itself, it has recently been rediscovered. Marx appreciated that poverty was related to the prevailing social conditions of a society.

> Our needs and enjoyments spring from society; we measure them, therefore, by society and not by the objects of their satisfaction. Because they are of a social nature, they are of a relative nature.
> (Marx, K. *Selected Works*)

The relative nature of poverty explains why the poor are always with us. Although industrial societies have been growing progressively more affluent, there are always some citizens who are far less fortunate than others. In the relative sense of the term, poverty can never be eradicated. Even in the so-called affluent society, there are those whose incomes are below what J.K. Galbraith has termed 'the minimum necessary for decency'

> ... and they cannot wholly escape, therefore, the judgement of the larger community that they are indecent. They are degraded, for, in the literal sense, they live outside the grades or categories which the community regards as acceptable.
> (Galbraith, J.K. *The Affluent Society*)

Apart from 'pockets of poverty' which exist in any affluent society, the relative nature of poverty is a world-wide social fact. *A priori*, it seems obscene to consider that a family without a TV set is living in poverty while two-thirds of the world's population suffer from chronic malnutrition. How can anybody living in a modern western society be considered to be in a state of poverty compared with the lot of the mass of people who inhabit south-east Asia, Latin America, the Caribbean, the less-developed countries of Africa and other parts of the Third World? The answer lies in the relative nature of poverty; it is a dangerous assumption that there is a universally absolute minimum standard of life.

> To have one bowl of rice in a society where all other people have half a bowl may well be a sign of achievement and intelligence ... to have five bowls of rice in a society where the majority have a decent, balanced diet is a tragedy.
> (Harrington, M. *The Other America*)

- ● *The rediscovery of poverty in Britain*

There have been times when poverty in Britain has appeared to recede only to be rediscovered, e.g. in Britain at the end of the nineteenth century and during the Great Depression of the 1930s. The post-war Beveridge myth that poverty had been abolished by the Welfare State was challenged in a Fabian tract by Audrey Harvey (*Casualties of the Welfare State*). At a time when Prime Minister Harold Macmillan was declaring that the British 'had never had it so good', Mrs Harvey argued that:
1 many thousands were suffering real economic hardship;
2 the network of welfare agencies was so complex and bureaucratic that many who were in dire straits were not receiving the help they needed.
Complacent opinion about the success of the Welfare State was subjected to healthy scepticism. The challenge was more effective because it came, in the first place, from a social worker in London's East End, and not from an academic sociologist. Audrey Harvey's criticisms were followed by many pieces of research which supported her contentions.

Table 7.1 The rediscovery of poverty in Britain

Date	Author	Publication	Summary of findings
1960	Audrey Harvey	*Casualties of the Welfare State*	Welfare services were not preventing great poverty.
1962	Richard Titmuss	*Income Distribution and Social Change*	There had *not* been a substantial redistribution of income in favour of the poor.
1962	Dorothy Wedderburn	*Poverty in Britain Today*	A large proportion of the population (12%) was living at near subsistence level.
1963	Tony Lynes	*National Assistance and National Prosperity*	The subsistence scale adopted by the NAB (National Assistance Board) was far too low.
1964	Royston Lambert	*Nutrition in Britain 1950–60*	The diet of families had deteriorated below the standard recommended by nutritional experts.
1965	Brian Abel-Smith & Peter Townsend	*The Poor and the Poorest*	The proportion living in poverty had increased: (a) 1953, 7.3%; (b) 1960, 14.2% ($7\frac{1}{2}$ million).
1969	A.B. Atkinson	*Poverty in Britain and the Reform of Social Security*	NI and Supplementary benefits were inadequate and reforms were essential (e.g. increased allowances, a negative income tax, etc).

● Cycles of poverty

Seebohm Rowntree analysed the lifecycle of a member of the working class according to five stages relating to family income. Rowntree's analysis indicated that people may drift in and out of poverty during their lifetime.

> During early childhood, unless his father is a skilled worker, he probably will be in poverty; this will last until he, or some of his brothers and sisters, begin to earn money and thus augment their father's wage sufficiently to raise the family above the poverty line. Then follows the period during which he is earning money and living under the parents' roof; for some portion of this period he will be earning more money than is required for lodging, food, and clothes. This is his chance to save money ... this period of prosperity may continue after marriage until he has two or three children, when poverty will again overtake him. This period of poverty will last perhaps for ten years, i.e. until the first child is fourteen and begins to earn wages; but if there are more than three children it may last longer. While the children are earning, and before they leave home to marry, the man enjoys another period of prosperity – possibly however only to sink back into poverty when his children have married and left him, and he himself is too old to work.
> Rowntree, S. (*A Study of Town Life*, 1901)

Table 7.2 The cycle of poverty

Period	Time	Features of the period
1 in poverty	childhood	Low family income and children to rear.
2 out of poverty	working youngster	Earning more than is paid to parents for board and lodgings.
3 in poverty	young married	Sinks back into poverty as children are brought up.
4 out of poverty	middle-age	Children earning or have left home.
5 in poverty	old-age	Income falls; living on a pension.

Figure 7.1 is an attempt to update Rowntree's analysis taking into account two important trends in contemporary society:
(a) Young people do not start work until they are aged sixteen and an increasing proportion continue their studies beyond that age with the help of financial support from their parents.
(b) In the symmetrical family both husband and wife have jobs; the wife does not stop working until the first child arrives.

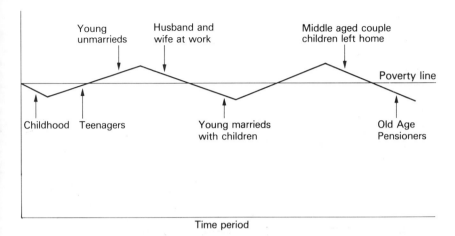

Fig. 7.1 A modern version of the cycle of poverty

Rowntree's account of the cycle of poverty indicates some of the main causes of poverty such as low wages and old age, although different causes are more influential at different times, e.g.

(a) 1899 inadequate income
(b) 1936 inadequate income and unemployment
(c) 1950 old age

The main causes of poverty remain comparatively constant in a modern industrial society such as Britain. Rowntree's 1901 list of the main causes

Table 7.3 A comparison of Rowntree's York studies

Cause of poverty	Percentage of those in poverty		
	1899	1936	1950
Unemployment of chief wage-earner	2.31	28.6	Nil
Inadequate wages of earners in regular employment	51.96	42.3	1.0
Old age	5.11	14.7	68.1
Sickness		4.1	21.3
Death of chief wage-earner	15.63	7.8	6.4
Miscellaneous (including large family)	24.99	2.5	3.2

(Coates, K. and Silburn, R. *Poverty: the Forgotten Englishmen*)

of poverty is almost identical to that outlined by Abel-Smith and Townsend in *The Poor and the Poorest*.

Table 7.4 Main causes of poverty

1 Death of chief wage-earner
2 Incapacity of chief wage-earner through accident, illness or old age
3 Chief wage-earner unemployed
4 Chronic irregularity of work
5 Large family
6 Low wage

Another poverty cycle has been termed the *cycle of deprivation* or *cycle of disadvantage*. This cycle is not based upon Rowntree's argument that although the number of people in poverty may not differ greatly at any time, the particular people who make up the number change according to their stage in the life cycle. Those who argue that there is a cycle of deprivation believe that the hard core remaining in poverty are largely the same from one generation to another, i.e. deprived children in their turn become parents of deprived children. The existence of a cycle of deprivation was recognised in 1972 by the then Minister of Health, Sir Keith Joseph, and on the basis of his comments the Social Science Research Council funded twelve study projects. A pilot study conducted by the University of Edinburgh traced back the social history of twenty-four families over six generations. It was found that poverty was most intensive when there had been intermarriages between poor families. There exists a close correlation between poverty and social class immobility. This is in line with Becker's *labelling theory*: families caught in the poverty trap are labelled as 'the poor' and their social behaviour is interpreted in the light of their poor circumstances.

There are areas of disadvantage which are generally accepted.

1 Low intellectual attainment correlates with low income and associated adverse environmental factors.

2 Regional unemployment rates remain similar over time, e.g. relatively high unemployment has existed for a long period in Scotland, north-east England, South Wales and Ulster.

3 Unhealthy habits of parents may cause health hazards for their children. The National Child Development Study showed that children whose mothers smoked during pregnancy gave birth to children who were one centimetre shorter than average in height and approximately four months behind in reading ability at the age of seven.

4 Teenage (often, shotgun) marriages are likely to provide unstable homes of shorter than average duration.

Michael Rutter and Nicola Madge (*Cycle of Disadvantage*, 1976) investigated multiple problem families. Where three of the following factors occurred they found that there was a real problem of deprivation:

(a) mental subnormality;
(b) temporary instability;
(c) ineducable children;
(d) squalid home;
(e) large numbers of children.

Problem families tend to remain on the housing lists of local authorities. It is a Catch-22 situation in which they cannot escape from being regarded as problems. It has been argued that sons remain in this situation longer than daughters, possibly because they are prone to copy the wayward habits of their fathers.

There are grounds, however, for regarding the cycle of deprivation with some scepticism.

1 The single notion of a 'cycle' is of doubtful validity as there are many cycles. (Apart from Rowntree's cycle of poverty already considered, there are Orlinsky's productive cycle, reproductive cycle and integrative cycle – see Coser, L.A. and Rosenberg, B., *Sociological Theory*, p. 113).

2 It would take a very long research period to verify the existence of a cycle of deprivation. If you asked child-batterers if they were battered, you would have to rely on the accuracy of their memories. The most suitable study would be a longitudinal one but this has yet to be carried out by trained sociological researchers.

3 Previous findings are suspect because they have been one-sided (e.g. if a phrenologist studies the bumps on the heads of convicts, he ought also to study the bumps of non-convicts before he can reach any logical conclusions).

4 There is little evidence of correlation between poverty and generations of deviants or maladjusted people (Jordan, W. *Poor Parents*). Records of higher-than-average rates of suicide, divorce and alcoholism relate to middle-class family histories as much as to those of poor families.

However, there is little doubt that some members of society are disadvantaged in relation to the lives of the majority. Disadvantages vary according to causes (e.g. genetic or environmental). The disadvantages tend to correlate although there is usually one basic disadvantage. Ralph Miliband ('Politics and Poverty', in D. Wedderburn's *Poverty, Inequality and Class Structure*) argues that poverty can only be seen realistically in terms of social class; the poor are always poor in the labour market and this continues from one generation to another. Poverty will only cease to be a cyclical phenomenon when a militant working class takes action to defeat the causes of poverty which they inherit (see Marcuse, H. *One Dimensional Man*).

● *The culture of poverty*

The culture of poverty is associated with Oscar Lewis and his studies of peasant cultures in South America. From a structural-functionalist viewpoint, Lewis argues that the poor have distinctive culture of their own. The poor constitute a society within a society.

The concept of a culture of poverty correlates with a belief in the cyclical nature of poverty. According to Oscar Lewis, the beliefs, values, attitudes and experiences of the poor are originally generated within their own communities and are passed on in a continuous cycle. The poor value their own culture and do not regard it as of less value than mainstream culture. They do not feel stigmatised while they remain with other members of their peasant class. Rather than seeing the poor as a disadvantaged class, Lewis found a great deal of joy and vitality existing in people whom the dominant middle class regarded as deprived. Similar claims concerning the peculiar worth of the culture of the poor have been made by Basil Bernstein, Brian Jackson and other sociologists writing in the field of education.

Oscar Lewis found that in Latin America the life of the poor went on at a different rhythm from that of society at large. Although the rest of society desired to eliminate poverty and absorb the poor into their midst, the poor themselves wished to perpetuate their particular culture. Mainstream society regarded the values of the poor as impoverished, but the poor had a different conception of the same values.

According to Lewis, the poor adopted this attitude as a reaction to the low status in which they were regarded by the rest of society; 'It's the poor what gets the blame'. Their way of countering attacks from the dominant culture was to protect their own distinctive cultural pattern.

Table 7.5 Conditions encouraging a culture of poverty (in accordance with the conflict perspective)

---

1 A capitalist society based on profit, private appropriation of surplus value and the cash nexus.

2 Low wages combined with exploitation of labour.

3 Unskilled work and a large army of unemployed.

4 Little political, economic, social and welfare organisation to help the poor.

5 The values of the dominant middle class are geared to the ownership of property and the accumulation of wealth.

6 Little possibility of upward social mobility to allow the poor to escape from their poverty.

Slum children are socialised so that they are loyal to their own class. They use their own networks of self-help: 'it's the poor what helps the poor'. Thus the culture of the poor is perpetuated. The poor are suspicious of capitalist society and all its trappings, such as banks, insurance companies, trade unions and welfare agencies. They distrust those in authority, particularly politicians and police.

Table 7.6 Characteristics of the culture of poverty (largely from the interactionist perspective)

Level	Characteristics
Individual	Inferiority complex; present-day orientation rather than having aspirations for the future; acceptance of male-superiority; feeling of resignation and hopelessness.
Family	Curtailment of childhood; early sexual relations; common-law wives; abandonment of wife and children; matriarchical family structure.
Community	Bad housing, even homelessness; overcrowding; minimum organisation; informal, temporary groups such as gangs.
Society	No commitment to national sentiment; little participation in major institutions; lack of resources; low level of education, literacy and political acumen.

Although Oscar Lewis's analysis of the so-called culture of poverty helps us to appreciate some of the attributes of the poor in an unconventional way, it nevertheless provides no answer to the plight of the poor. The knowledge that the poor have pride in their peculiar culture does nothing to provide shelter for the homeless or to feed the hungry.

> Culture . . . is that complex whole which include knowledge, belief, art, morals, law, customs, and any other capabilities and habits acquired by man as a member of society.
> (Tylor, E.B. 'Primitive Culture', in Coser, L. and Rosenberg, B. *Sociological Theory*)

To deny any group the benefits of society because they believe that their sub-stream culture is adequate, is questionable in the extreme. The social scientist finds it difficult to remain value-free in the face of the misery associated with dire poverty (see section 7.1).

> Theories which place responsibility for poverty with the individual or with 'the culture of poverty' are rejected. The concept of the culture of poverty concentrates attention upon the familiar and local setting of behaviour and largely ignores the external and unseen social forces which condition the

distribution of different types of resources to the community, family and individual.... Poverty is not just a lack of resources required to live a normal life. It is lack of resources in fact used, and felt to be rightly used, by the rich.
(Townsend, P. *The Concept of Poverty*)

7.3 Old age

- *Britain's ageing population*

The ageing population of Britain is best analysed by comparing the population structure of pre-industrial and industrial Britain. Figure 7.2 shows the pyramidical structure of two centuries ago and the significant 'house-shaped' structure of modern times.

The increase in the proportion of old people is often attributed simply to increased life-expectancy. It is true that the expectation of life at birth, for both sexes combined, has increased from approximately 41 years in 1941 to about 73 years in 1980. However, it is not so much that old people are living longer but rather that more people are reaching old age: one of the main reasons for this is that infant mortality has decreased (from at least 150 per 1000 births in 1800 to 14 per 1000 in 1980). If a far larger proportion of the population survives the first five years of life (and the first year in particular) then far more people will reach old age. Other reasons attributing to the ageing population include improvements in housing, the standards of nutrition, the medical care and the general quality of life. The modern 'house-shaped' population structure depicted

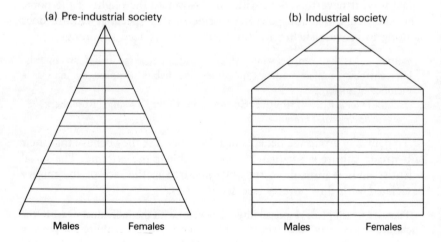

| (a) Pre-industrial society | (b) Industrial society |

| Males   Females | Males   Females |

Fig. 7.2 Simplified population structures of pre-industrial and industrial Britain

in Fig. 7.2 indicates that mortality is increasingly effective from about the age of fifty.

Old people in the population have steadily increased, both in proportion and in absolute numbers. There are now approximately 10 million old people in the population (i.e. males over 65 and females over 60 years). About one person in six is an old person. Between 16 and 17 per cent of the population is classified as 'old', i.e. of pensionable age. This percentage is likely to remain relatively constant for the next thirty years (see Table 7.7).

Table 7.7 The structure of the projected population of the UK

Age group	1973 (base)		1981		1991		2001		2011	
	'000	%	'000	%	'000	%	'000	%	'000	%
65 and over (M) 60 and over (F)	9291	16.6	9787	17.4	9871	17.0	9468	16.0	10 032	16.5

(*Population Projections, No. 4: 1973–2011*, HMSO, 1974)

The larger proportion of old people in Britain, compared with previous centuries and with most other contemporary societies, constitutes a far-reaching social problem. It is a problem in human relationships which demands collective social action. It affects a significant number of people and involves a large social cost.

● *Sociological implications of an ageing population*

Table 7.8 summarises the principal problems resulting from a large proportion of elderly people in the community.

The dependency ratio is the combined number of people of retirement age and children below the age of sixteen per 1000 people of working age. The proportion of dependent people in these two categories is likely to remain at about 40 per cent in the foreseeable future. The excess of emigration over immigration in recent years may be partly attributable to the high dependency ratio; young workers are not attracted to the idea of having to provide facilities for an increasing number of old people. Old people constitute a greater social cost than any other section of the community, in institutional care, welfare services, etc.

Pressure groups endeavouring to secure improvements in benefits provided by society for old people should be aware that the costs might be so excessive that Britain's economic progress is retarded. Movements such as Age Concern and the trade unions are increasingly active on behalf of old people. Sociologists must be concerned with society in its entirety. Is it

Table 7.8 Problems of an ageing population

---

1 An increased burden of dependency (i.e. a greater burden upon those gainfully employed).

2 High level of expenditure upon old people's homes, sheltered housing, hospitals and general geriatric care.

3 Special dilemmas for the families of the elderly.

4 A less adventurous and enterprising population as old people disengage themselves from the affairs of the world.

5 More people in poverty; old people often fall below the poverty line (see section 7.2).

6 Very large government expenditure upon social security benefits; retirement pensions already make up the largest single national insurance benefit.

7 Special problems of the elderly such as loneliness, hypothermia, terminal illnesses, etc.

8 An increasing proportion of elderly females (a society of 'old women').

---

justifiable to pursue the interests of a particular group to the extent of damaging the interests of society as a whole?

> Some economists have suggested that it is not so much that providing for this dependent population will *directly* put an undue strain on our economic resources, but rather that the necessary taxing of the economically productive section of the community to transfer resources on this scale to the non-producers may seriously reduce the incentives on which our economic well-being and progress depend. Such budgetary or transfer problem could, of course, be accentuated if the potential voting power of those over working age were ever used to raise pensions to a level likely to cripple the economy either directly or indirectly. This possibility was very much in the mind of the late Lord Beveridge when preparing his report *Social Insurance and Allied Services* (1942), and had much to do with his insistence that pensions under the state scheme should be tied to a level at, but not above, subsistence.
>
> (Kelsall, R.K. *Population*)

Some of the extra costs of caring for a large number of old people include:

---

1 expenditure on pensions;

2 expensive unit dwellings such as sheltered housing;

3 old people are more likely to require medicines and the services of a doctor;

4 old people are more likely to need institutional care including hospital treatment.

Klein and Ashley ('Old Age Health', *New Society*, 6 January 1972) made some significant projections of hospital beds needed by the elderly. By the year 1992 old people, i.e. those above pensionable age, will occupy:
  (a) 73.5 per cent of hospital beds provided for males.
  (b) 94 per cent of hospital beds provided for females.
It is not likely that those in younger or middle-aged groups would tolerate a situation where such a large proportion of hospital beds were occupied by about 17 per cent of the population. Unless there is a great increase in the availability of hospital accommodation many old people will die: those below the age of 65 are unlikely to acquiesce in their exclusion from essential hospital treatment. More government expenditure is clearly necessary upon hospital and other welfare services but we have already considered the possible adverse implications upon Britain's economic growth. The economic struggle of bushmen and Eskimos forced them to leave their old folks to die. It has been argued that to keep people alive beyond their allotted lifespan often involves unnecessary misery and pain.

The special dilemmas which face the old and their families include intensive care, communication, social life, housing, loneliness, illness and poor nutrition. Elderly people may require places in old people's homes or accommodation in sheltered housing. If they live on their own they may suffer loneliness: where they are cared for by relations the generation gap may cause conflicts and family unhappiness. Lifestyles change so rapidly in modern societies that communication is difficult, especially if three generations dwell in a single household and when the elderly have lost the crucial faculties of hearing and sight. Old people may find communication easier with the very young who are but partially socialised in the culture of modern society.

It is necessary to find a new role for old people in society. The old deliberately disengage themselves from contemporary society because they feel a loss of purpose in life. Retirement forces them to stop work at sixty or sixty-five. By marrying men older than themselves, women set themselves up for a long period of widowhood. This is inevitable as female expectation of life is higher. (The situation would be reversed if women married men younger than themselves but given traditional social norms such a change in custom would be considered an unnatural phenomenon.)

Grandmothers are less likely to be allowed to look after their grandchildren. Perhaps young mothers should be less arrogant, especially as they are inexperienced in bringing up children. The research work of Peter Townsend and others has shown that in working-class extended families, married daughters are prone to rely upon the experience and advice of their mothers. Some middle-class houses have granny annexes which give the elderly independence without cutting them off from their families. In pre-industrial societies old people were revered and their judgement esteemed. They were given the status and authority long associated with old age. Where the family retains its traditional influence old people are still respected. It will be interesting to see what happens in China as family cohesion is whittled away by industrialisation. In pre-industrial societies, old people were afforded prestige when traditional wisdom was important to a community; acquired knowledge and moral norms changed little. Today the young regard the old as being out of touch with technological and societal changes. Old people thus treated remain in a state of confusion and retire into themselves. They are frequently regarded with pity and ridicule, rather than with veneration.

Low income determines that the living conditions and the diet of old people will be inferior to that enjoyed by the rest of the community. Old people who remain in old, damp houses are likely to be afflicted by hypothermia and a high incidence of bronchitis.

> Every social worker is aware that far too many elderly people are isolated from their families and their fellow citizens, that their lives are too often characterised by quite inadequate diets, medical provision, heating and domestic comfort and social contact. Facts and figures are not always available to show the magnitude of this problem, but it comes as a shock to learn from the 1961 Census that there are in England and Wales no fewer than 1 084 000 people over pensionable age living alone (that is, forming one-person households). As would be expected from the sex differential in life-expectancy *and* from the lower pensionable age for women, some 921 000 of these are women. The proportion this particular type of one-person household forms of all households is nearly $7\frac{1}{2}$ per cent, which by any standard seems far too high.
>
> (Kelsall, R.K. *Population*)

• Studies of old people

One study which gives an insight into the lives of very old people was conducted by Isaacs, a Glasgow geriatrician who made a survey of 612 patients. The term geriatric became common just after the Second World War and in 1949 the first geriatric unit was set up in Glasgow. Isaacs visited the homes of all cases referred to him by Glasgow Infirmary. His description of the homes are not for the squeamish. One household resembled a Chinese laundry. The occupant was a woman of only sixty-three years; she had refused hospital treatment, but complained of the indifference of her GP. The woman's daughter was so busy looking after her own family that it was 4 a.m. before she finished the washing. The chapter on incontinence indicates the personal distress of a woman who gingerly places soiled sheets in a suitcase which she takes on a bus in order to wash the bedding in her own washing machine. Isaacs's accounts indicate how the family life of the next generation can be ruined by having to care for a geriatric relation. Isaacs described geriatrics as old, old people.... Geriatric patients form the hard core of ill, old people. Older than old and more ill than ill....

    (Isaacs, B. *et al. Survival of the Unfittest*)

Isaacs found that many geriatrics suffer from:

  (a) confusional state of dementia;

  (b) gross disturbances of behaviour;

  (c) incontinence (the stereotype staff attitude to this problem was to deny them liquid refreshment).

The present state of medical science does not offer sufficient care for geriatrics. As the proportion of geriatrics in the population increases, extra measures other than institutional care will be necessary. Cheaper aids which are not capital projects include:

  (a) community care (i.e. services available outside hospitals such as home helps and district nursing);

  (b) expansion of health centres;

  (c) good neighbourhood schemes.

Jack Shaw's account (*On Our Conscience*, 1970) is equally moving. His description of an old woman living in squalor typifies the state of hopelessness in which the neglected old await the relief of death. Perhaps her case was untypical as she had a son who could have helped, but like so many middle-aged sons and daughters, he did not wish to know of his mother in her urine-saturated armchair. In this case she was rescued from her plight (in the bitterly cold weather with neither fuel nor food) by Shaw's newspaper which found her a place in an old people's home.

J.H. Sheldon (*The Social Medicine of Old Age*) found, from his fieldwork in Wolverhampton, that an adjacent relative was the best way of keeping the elderly out of old people's homes. He was the first researcher to draw attention to health variations between elderly males and females. Sheldon found that generally women occupied the middle ground, whereas men were at the ends of the spectrum, i.e. they were in either very good or very poor physical condition. A higher proportion of elderly women were found to be in poor health but they revealed a more tenacious hold on life. Although a large proportion considered a bungalow to be the best type of housing for old people, few were interested in moving. The recent bereavement of a spouse and the loss of physical movement were the two most influential factors in loneliness. Generally bereavement transcends the loss of physical movement. Loneliness has a multiplicity of causes; it is not subject to social analysis as it depends on an individual's response to a particular situation.

> Loneliness cannot be regarded as the simple direct result of social circumstances, but is rather an individual response to an external situation to which other old people may react quite differently.
>
> (Sheldon, J.H. *The Social Medicine of Old Age*)

Peter Townsend (*The Family Life of Old People*) interviewed 203 families in Bethnal Green. Townsend appears to have been a most sympathetic interviewer, and met with only ten refusals. Few social researchers could aspire to Townsend's standard of fieldwork. He found that old people who had had children were rarely in a bad condition but those without relatives were more likely to be neglected and isolated. It is wrong to believe that old people must, of necessity, be subject to loneliness. Substitution and compensation took place on the death of a spouse; it was then that social interaction with other relatives increased. Townsend coined the term 'desolation' to describe the sudden loss of a loved one; he confirmed Seldon's findings that those suffering bereavement suffered most from loneliness. Old people who are secluded from family and society, Townsend describes as isolates.

> A major conclusion of the present analysis is that, though the two are connected, the underlying reason for loneliness in old age is desolation rather than isolation.
> (Townsend, P. *The Family Life of Old People*)

Jeremy Tunstall (*Old and Alone*) reaffirmed that loneliness was less acute when an old person's spouse or close relatives were alive. Tunstall found that old people's clubs helped those who, throughout their lives, had been willing to join in social interaction; life-time non-joiners still refused to participate.

● *Disengagement*

Disengagement is an inevitable process whereby social relations are severed with the advent of old age. Even old people who are in good health tend to withdraw into themselves. Factors attributing to disengagement include:
1 the universal expectation and acceptance of death;
2 diminishing faculties, resulting in communication difficulties and the consequent cutting of social relationships;

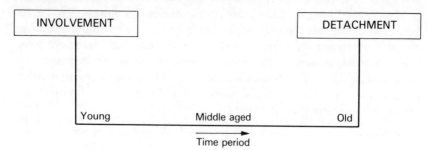

Fig. 7.3 Involvement and detachment continuum of social interaction

3 development of anomie (normative disorder resulting in a state of confusion);

4 the separation of old people from the rest of society by special housing arrangements or because of lack of family links.

Norbert Elias, ('Problems of Involvement and Detachment', *British Journal of Sociology*, Vol. 7, 1956) has pointed out that only small babies and the insane become completely involved in whatever they experience. The normal pattern of behaviour lies somewhere between the extremes of involvement and detachment. Young people naturally become involved in social interaction whereas old people move towards the detachment end of the continuum until they disengage themselves almost entirely (see Fig. 7.3).

Society will not allow old people to totally disengage themselves. The community insists upon caring about them and for them. Only in a Robinson Crusoe situation is it possible for a human being to disengage himself entirely.

Elias relates the terms involvement and detachment to subjectivity and objectivity. These are important tools of thinking associated with how far sociologists are able to be value-free in their study of society and its problems (see section 7.1). The continuum, however, can be usefully transferred to the study of disengagement with the approach of old age.

Males and females have different attitudes to disengagement. For the male, life tends to be instrumental; his work is but a means to an end. His date of retirement is known to him, e.g. at the age of sixty-five. For many males it is the end of the main life-purpose and from that time they begin to disengage.

> Those who had retired gave a little more emphasis to loss of income as a reason for a reluctance to retire than did men remaining at work but they gave as much emphasis to boredom and the related sense of uselessness.... The inescapable conclusion was that after retirement most men in Bethnal Green could not occupy their time satisfactorily. Their life became a rather desperate search for pastimes or a gloomy contemplation of their own helplessness, which, at its worst, was little better than waiting to die. They found no substitute for the companionship, absorption and fulfilment of work.
> (Townsend, P. *The Family Life of Old People*)

Females are more affected by socio-emotional influences which help them to ease tensions. For the majority of women there is no fixed time of retirement. When their own children become adults, they can continue to play the mother-role by 'mothering' their husbands or their grandchildren. There is a convergence of male and female attitudes in old age when both sexes tend to disengage from mainstream society.

The increased tempo of social change has brought changing attitudes.

Earlier retirement and the increase in redundancies have encouraged more people to prepare for retirement. Considered from the symbolic inter-actionist perspective, man perceives of himself as having a hierarchy of roles: the retired man may adopt new roles or indulge in role-taking (whereby he copies others) and build for himself a new self-image. So although he may disengage from his past work-orientation, he engages in new social pursuits. A larger proportion of women follow work-careers from which they retire. They also will have to seek fresh roles as they face the same vacuum which has caused men to disengage.

If we live long enough age will catch up with us all and disengagement will eventually overtake us. The most effective postponement of the process of disengagement is by maintaining a high level of social inter-action and integration with others in the community. Integration can be maintained by contacts with relatives and neighbours. Disintegration may be speeded up by well-intentioned plans for old people's activities such as Over Sixties Clubs, Old People's Clubs and special holidays with their contemporaries. All these activities designate people as 'old'. The old associate together only to disengage from society as a whole. The grouping of the elderly in old people's homes results in the old living in a separate world.

Roscow's study of old people in Cleveland, USA (*Social Integration of the Aged*) contributes to the Concentration versus Dispersal debate. He found that if old people are concentrated together they are more likely to interact than if they are dispersed. However, it is beneficial for old people to mix with other age groups. Young people are often surprised that the old have so much to offer. An acceptance of the worth of old people to society is the most effective way of postponing the onset of disengagement.

● *Institutional care*

Institutional care is historically one of the earliest methods of dealing with such social problems as old age, poverty and crime. There has always been a close association between old age and poverty. Today institutional care is

Table 7.9 Features of an old people's home

1 Inmates are very old men and/or women who enter voluntarily and stay permanently (usually until death).

2 Homes are owned by local councils or voluntary bodies usually on a non-profit basis.

3 The staff ensures a supervised and protected environment.

one of the costliest items in the social service budget although it caters for a small proportion of old people.

The dreadful workhouses, described so vividly in Townsend's *The Last Refuge*, have virtually disappeared but many of the questions which they posed still remain. To what extent are old people stigmatised when they enter a residential home? Does it cause greater confusion and disruption if old people are kept together rather than cared for separately? How far is it possible to mitigate institutional neurosis? To what extent are residential homes for old people the result of humane concern or instruments of social control (i.e. to keep undesirable people out of the way)?

It is useful to consider old people's homes in relation to Goffman's ideal-type of total institution.

> The central feature of total institutions can be described as a breakdown of the barriers ordinarily separating these three spheres of life. First, all aspects of life are conducted in the same place and under the same single authority. Second, each phase of the member's daily activity is carried on in the immediate company of a large batch of others, all of whom are treated alike and required to do the same thing together. Third, all phases of the day's activities are tightly scheduled, with one activity leading at a prearranged time into the next, the whole sequence of activities being imposed from above by a system of explicit formal rulings and a body of officials. Finally, the various enforced activities are brought together into a single rational plan purportedly designed to fulfil the official aims of the institution.
>
> (Goffman, E. *Asylums*)

Goffman thought, on an interactionist perspective, that if people stay for a long duration in a total institution, *disculturation* may occur, i.e. complete isolation from society. Eventually the inmate becomes incapable of dealing with life outside. Disculturation results in role-dispossession, a break from previous roles. The process begins with admission techniques which lead to the curtailment of self. In the older institutions these techniques include:

1 *stripping* people of their identity and their self-repair kits, e.g. teeth, spectacles, combs and nail-files. These might be taken away for reasons of so-called personal security and often by two people, suggesting compulsion, but on the grounds that there should be an independent witness;
2 *segregation* according to sexes and age-groups;
3 *sequestration*, i.e. they give up their furniture, their GP and many individual choices, e.g. room colours and furnishings. Decisions are made for them.

Institutional neurosis may eventually occur. This is a state characterised by apathy, submissiveness, lack of initiative and loss of individuality. Causes of institutional neurosis include the end of contacts with old friends and the outside world, dominance of the institutional staff, enforced idleness and lack of plans. Those suffering from institutional neurosis are excessively present-orientated. Their symptoms of the disease might include the act of sitting in the same chair, doing nothing, for most of the waking day (see Fig. 7.4). The fact that people become institutionalised makes the work of the staff easier: an old person is assigned to a chair according to a custodial seating pattern.

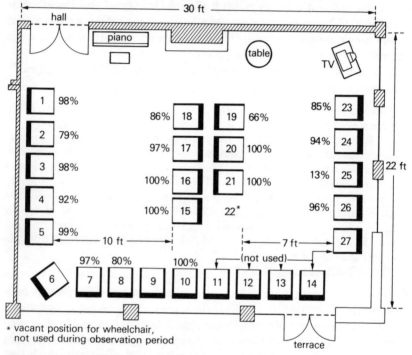

(Lipman, A. 'Chairs as Territory', *New Society*, 20 April 1967)

Fig. 7.4 Chairs as territory
(*New Society*, 20 April 1967)

Old people who enter residential homes are usually older than the average person of pensionable age. They may have outlived their children or are without marital status (i.e. single, divorced or widowed).

Very old people who are childless or have no children in the locality, may well finish up in an institution for the old. Traumatic experiences (such as strokes and falls) force old people into an institution. Neighbours may help out for a brief interlude but are usually unwilling to offer long-term dependency.

We have moved a long way from the Victorian workhouses which housed the old and poor. Gone are the high walls, the great gates, the prison atmosphere and the enclosed environment. Although large institutions allow economies of scale the modern tendency is to have small residential homes or to care for old people in their own homes where possible. Rosow's research (*Social Integration of the Aged*) indicated that grouped housing-arrangements facilitate more social interaction than institutional organisation. Sheltered housing consists of grouped residences for old people, with each person having his or her separate accommodation unit, but with all the residents being able to share in the communal facilities such as a common room, laundry, telephone and the services of the warden.

Table 7.10 Advantages of sheltered housing

1 Independence and privacy.
2 Use of personal territory plus common territory.
3 Status congruity with others in the group.
4 Maintenance of normal appearance and lifestyle.
5 Free access to kin, neighbours and general public.
6 Unplanned encounters.
7 Independent decision-making.
8 Shared interests and contribution to the community.

Some old people prefer to disengage and not enter into social interaction. They find social relationships tiresome and tiring. It is dangerous to generalise and classify old people as 'the institutionalised' or 'the lonely'. Some old people are convinced that institutions and grouped housing units encroach on their personal privacy. It is important to allow them the right to remain independent if they wish, however good the grouped housing arrangements or institutional care provided in old people's homes.

7.4 Racial prejudice

- *Race*

Interactionists would want to argue that the problem of race relations arises from prejudice shown by peoples of one race towards those of another, and in particular the prejudice of whites against coloured people. Marxists argue that these prejudices arise not so much because of the colour of a person's skin, but because the ruling classes of imperialist countries considered that colonial peoples belonged to a lower class which they ruthlessly exploited.

Race hostility, in short, is only a by-product of class hostility, and the white proletariat, in order to bolster up the whole hierarchical class system, have been brought to look on coloured people as a class lower than themselves.
(Mason, P. *Race Relations*)

From the conflict perspective, Marxists contend that colour is merely an accident of birth, so 'race consciousness' is a form of 'false consciousness'. This argument accords with the exclusiveness of the West and exploitation by multi-national companies of coloured peoples in the Third World (see Baran, P.A. and Sweezy, P.M. *Monopoly Capital*).

An analysis of race in terms of class alone does not provide satisfactory answers to all the problems of race exploitation since prejudicial attitudes can be traced back to the Roman slave system before capitalism ever showed any part of its 'unacceptable face'. Race is a sub-category of the human species. There are three main categories of *homo sapiens*: Caucasian, Mongolian and Negroid. However, such divisions are ambivalent: some Caucasians are more white than others, while the term Negro is used to include the 'true' Negroes of Western Africa together with many coloured peoples in America whose ancestry is not African. Race differences are by no means clear-cut, although it is futile to pretend that differences do not exist. The Black Power Movement is but one indication that the race problem is a very real one and constitutes a worldwide public issue.

Racial differences have been highlighted in recent years by Professor Arthur Jensen whose research appeared to indicate that blacks, on average do not perform as well as whites at IQ tests. Jensen attributed intelligence differences to genetic factors. If Jensen's conclusions were accepted, positive discrimination in favour of blacks would compensate for their alleged genetic inferiority. One weakness of the hypothesis of Jensen is that IQ tests reflect the background of testers as much as tested; it is likely that *social* factors are more relevant than genetic factors. IQ tests given to US army recruits indicated that although Negroes proved inferior to whites in every state, the whites in the southern states performed less well on the average than the Negroes of the north (Barnett, A. *The Human Species*). This suggests that environmental factors may be more significant than genetic factors.

One wonders whether those who are so ready to settle for the genetic factor as the principal cause of the differences in IQ between blacks and whites, would also hold that the enormous overall differences, at every age level, in morbidity and mortality rates between these two groups are also due to genetic factors?
(Montagu, A. *Statement on Race*)

Even if Jensen's reports were valid, the individuals concerned would not be less worthy as individuals. A society consists of all manner of people who differ in intelligence, background, class, status and the colour of their skins. The sociologist is concerned with the whole of society, with the old and young, male and female, intelligent and less intelligent, black and white.

● *The coloured population of Britain*

Race problems in Britain have been given too much salience. The size of the non-white population is relatively small compared with the total population. Thirty years ago Britain was almost exclusively a white society. According to the 1951 Census only about 2 per cent of the population were born overseas and of those only 2 per cent were black (i.e. 0.2 per cent of the total population). By 1978 less than 7 per cent had been born overseas of whom 3.3 per cent were coloured.

The first large immigrant contingent was of West Indians many of whom had wartime experiences of a better lifestyle in Britain. The McCarran-Walter Act of 1952 checked the immigration of West Indians to the USA so the people of the Caribbean looked to 'the Mother Country' to give them a better life. At first they were welcomed as Britain needed unskilled labour and the economy was booming. When the British government talked of putting up the shutters, there was a rush to migrate before the 1962 Commonwealth Immigration Act, with its voucher system, took effect. So an Act which was intended to curb immigration succeeded in increasing it in the short term.

Periods	West Indian immigrants
Jan.–July 1962	31 810
Aug.–Dec. 1962	3241
Jan.–July 1963	3641

Despite the internal contradictions of applying the Act, the immediate apparent effect was a dramatic increase in net immigration.

(Peach, C. *West Indian Migration to Britain, a Social Geography*)

Most Asian immigrants came to Britain in the early 1960s before their numbers were checked by the tighter controls of the 1965 Act. In order to analyse the immigration issue realistically, it is important to remember that Britain remains a net exporter of population (see Fig. 3.15).

Statistics published by the Office of Censuses and Population Surveys in 1977 revealed that non-whites originating from the New Commonwealth and Pakistan numbered 1.8 million out of a population of nearly 57 million. Only about one person in thirty is non-white. Coloured immigrants to Britain come mainly from:

	%
West Indies	43
India	26
Pakistan/Bangladesh	16
Others (mostly E. African Asians)	15

• Prejudice

There are many mythical and conflicting stereotypes relating to minority groups in Britain.

> One of these, which fits in with old-fashioned prejudices about the working class, is that the minorities are lazy, feckless or work-shy, and that they take out through social security more than they put in through work.
>
> (PEP report on *Racial Disadvantage in Britain*, 1977)

The PEP research project carried out between 1972–5, and financed by the Gulbenkian Foundation and the Home Office, found that within the age group 16 to 54:

93 per cent of minority men were working

91 per cent of white men were working

Considering that coloured immigrants generally have inferior jobs with lower wages, and that they have larger families to support, it may come as a surprise to find them more independent in the matter of housing than indigenous whites. More than three-quarters of Asians live in owner-occupied houses: 85 per cent of Asian unskilled manual workers own their houses, compared with 20 per cent home-ownership by unskilled workers in the population at large.

	Asians	*West Indians*	*General population*
	%	%	%
Owner-occupied	76	50	52
Council houses	4	26	28
Other sources (mostly privately rented)	20	24	20

Pakistani immigrants help each other in accordance with village-kin ties established in their country of origin: this enables them to retain useful social links even though they are scattered over many parts of Britain. They are less reliant than the white indigenous population upon welfare services and other agencies, such as building societies because:

> the immigrant is indirectly linked by the ethnic entrepreneurs to his fellows all over the country and given access to information relevant to his interests.
>
> (Badr Dahya, 'The Nature of Pakistani Ethnicity in Industrial Cities in Britain' in Cohen, A., ed., *Urban Ethnicity*)

In spite of all the legislation, racial prejudice continues. One of the best-documented accounts of the incidence of race prejudice in Britain is included in *Colour and Citizenship* (Rose, E.J.B., ed.), Section 28, contributed by Dr Mark Abrams. It records the results of a survey of attitudes conducted in Lambeth, Ealing, Wolverhampton, Nottingham and Bradford. Key questions were asked relating to whether white people:

(a) would have coloured people as neighbours;
(b) regarded coloured people as inferior;
(c) thought coloured people should have council houses;
(d) would let property to coloured people.

On the basis of their answers respondents were divided into four groups.

1 *Tolerant:* those respondents who gave non-hostile answers on all four key questions.

2 *Tolerant-inclined:* those who gave only one hostile reply on the four key questions.

3 *Prejudiced-inclined:* those who gave two hostile replies on the four key questions.

4 *Prejudiced:* those who gave three or four hostile replies to the four key questions.

Figure 7.5 indicates the incidence of prejudice.

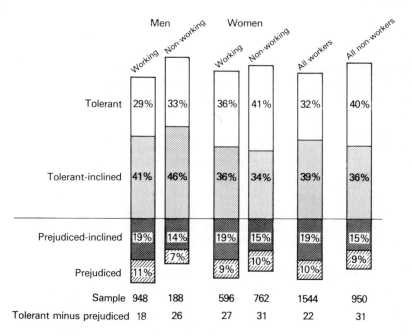

Fig. 7.5 Incidence of prejudice and tolerance
(Rose, E.J.B., ed., *Colour and Citizenship*)

Although it may be considered over-simplistic, the following table gives an indication of trends revealed by the survey.

Table 7.11 Prejudice and tolerance

1 White women are slightly more tolerant than white men towards coloured people.

2 The incidence of prejudice is highest amongst the 45 to 54 age group and falls away on both sides of that line.

3 The highest incidence of extreme prejudice is found among skilled manual workers and their wives in the lower middle class.

4 People whose full-time education goes beyond the minimum school-leaving age are less prejudiced.

(Rose, E.J., ed., *Colour and Citizenship*)

A model of a least prejudiced person would be a middle-class woman under 35 with some full-time education beyond the minimum school-leaving age. The most prejudiced tend to be men aged between 35 and 54 who left school at 15.

- *Race legislation*

Two types of race legislation have been passed by the British government. Negative acts to curb immigration have resulted in a limited number of annual vouchers. Positive race relations acts have been aimed at outlawing racial discrimination.

Immigration Acts
(a) 1962, Commonwealth Immigrants Act – only Commonwealth citizens who had been issued with employment vouchers were given the right of entry.
(b) 1965, *Immigration from the Commonwealth* (White Paper) – abolished vouchers for unskilled workers and reduced the number of vouchers.
(c) 1968, Commonwealth Immigrants Act – restricted the entry of East African Asians (although they were British passport-holders) by making them subject to the voucher scheme.
(d) 1971, Immigration Act – the right to settle was restricted to patrials with a 'substantial connection', e.g. one grandparent born in Britain.
Race Relations Acts
(a) 1965 Act – discrimination on racial grounds illegal in public places such as dance halls, hotels, public houses, restaurants, public transport, etc.

(b) 1968 Act – set up the Community Relations Commission (CRC) and the Race Relations Board (RRB). The CRC attempted to promote the integration of minorities and an atmosphere of mutual tolerance. The RRB was empowered to investigate complaints relating to racial discrimination. The CRC and the RRB had only limited success and were criticised as mere 'buffers' or 'talking shops'.

(c) 1976 Act – established the Commission for Racial Equality (CRE) with greater powers to enforce provisions against discrimination. Emphasis was shifted from individual complaints to measures against institutional discrimination.

> Its predecessors, the Race Relations Acts of 1965 and 1968, managed to get rid of some kinds of crude, overt discrimination but left more subtle forms of prejudice untouched, especially in the field of housing, education and employment.
>> ('A Guide to the Race Act', Melanie Phillips, *New Society*, 3 February 1977)

The CRE has a discretionary power to help an individual complainant who brings a case to court. Most important is the distinction made in the 1976 Act between direct and indirect discrimination. *Direct* discrimination is concerned with people who are treated less favourably on grounds of colour, race, nationality, or ethnic or national origins. *Indirect* unjustifiable discrimination is far-reaching: it covers less obvious things such as clothing requirements (e.g. prohibiting wearing turbans at work), job application forms which deter people with a low standard of English, or job advertisements requiring a minimum of five 'O' levels when such attainments are not necessary in order to do the work. If the 1976 Act was enforced to its maximum possible extent it would be a far stronger measure than any previous Race Relations Act. The Act makes it a criminal offence to use threatening or insulting words to stir up racial hatred, and strengthens existing legislation intended to prevent discrimination in the vital fields of employment, education and housing.

- *A multi-racial society*

A multi-racial society cannot be established simply by passing laws and administrative decrees, but:

> An Act of Parliament is an unequivocal declaration of public policy; as such it helps to establish norms to which the law-abiding citizen will conform.
>> (Daniel, W.W. *Racial Discrimination in England*, Introduction by Mark Abrams)

Since the 1964 General Election, race relations have been an important political issue. The general consensus of the political parties (except for the National Front) is to accept that the immigrants are here and that it is essential that we aim at a multi-racial society with the fullest possible integration of the minority population. Race problems have been mitigated in the following ways:

(a) fewer immigrants arrive annually than in the 1950s and early 1960s;
(b) there is little sympathy for a policy of repatriation;
(c) emigration has exceeded immigration since 1967;
(d) immigration is to be further limited in the future.

The sociology of race relations is of great significance. Studies of ethnicity tend to provide ammunition for those who argue that sociology is rarely a detached objective study, however much sociologists would like to make it so. We must ask ourselves whether a study of race relations is different in any important particulars from other stratification studies. A multi-racial society cannot be brought about by individual action. It concerns what C. Wright Mills, in *The Sociological Imagination*, termed 'public issues' rather than 'private troubles', and:

> ... unless action is based on knowledge of the structure and processes of inter-group relations, it is likely to be self-defeating.
> (Allen, S. *New Minorities, Old Conflicts*)

This is a similar conclusion to that reached by Rex and Moore in their excellent Sparkbrook study. They found that it was only possible to explain why people who had not previously shown racial prejudice began to do so in a new situation,

> not in terms of the personality system, but in terms of the social system, that is in the terms of a structure of social relations.
> (Rex, J. and Moore, R. *Race, Community and Conflict*)

The establishment of a multi-racial society is dependent upon attacking the very roots of racial disadvantages whether they be found in sociolinguistics, school situations, allocation of council houses, membership of trade unions and opportunities for promotion to positions of the highest social esteem.

Brazil provides an example of a country which has accepted a high degree of racial integration. Working-class blacks and whites are not segregated residentially as they are in the zones of transition and the ghettoes of decaying inner-city areas of Britain, the USA and other advanced capitalist societies. In Brazil the antecedents of slavery, imperialism and colonialism obviously affect attitudes about which race is dominant and which is subordinate. Stratification in Brazil is therefore less concerned with colour and more concerned with the social relations of production and the social relations of the market-place. The old Brazilian

Table 7.12 Job level analysed by academic qualifications – white and minority men

Men in job market who have worked:	Men having stated qualifications as highest							
	Degree/prof. qual. to degree level*		'A' level/Asian BA/BSc		'O' level and equivalents			
Job level	white %	minority %	white %	minority %	white %	minority %		
Professional/management	79	31	38	23	33	8		
White-collar	22	48	45	32	37	33		
Skilled manual	0	14	11	27	21	37		
Semi-skilled/unskilled manual	0	7	6	18	9	22		

*excluding Asian first degrees

(*Urban Deprivation, Racial Inequality and Social Policy*, HMSO, 1977) adage that 'a rich Negro is a white man' indicates that although whites may still be regarded as of high social class, nevertheless it is not uncommon for blacks to experience upward social mobility in a way rarely found in Britain. If Britain is to follow the Brazilian example, ethnic minorities must be allowed the same prospects as whites. Table 7.12 shows how far Britain fell short of this situation in 1977.

An analysis of jobs of white and minority men with the same education qualifications indicates how racial discrimination affects the employment prospects of ethnic minorities.

7.5 Problems associated with urbanisation

● *City life*

Structural-functionalists would claim that the urban way of life provides numerous benefits for its citizens by way of work, housing and social facilities, but conflict theorists in contrast argue that city life brings its own peculiar problems. There are vast differences between rural and town communities; the size and density of towns create problems of particular interest to the sociologist, e.g. in social control and social relationships. The great density of population and the heterogeneity of life make the problems of industrial cities far more complex than those of pre-industrial cities. Urban community life is based upon intense division of labour with consequent wide variations in social class, occupations, status, lifestyles and beliefs. These variations lead to a conflict of general interests combined with individual anonymity. Those engaged in busy urban life, experience numerous brief encounters and the people they meet are but passing acquaintances rather than lasting friends, relatives or neighbours. Social relationships are likely to be fragmented and based upon the pursuit of self-interest. Urban life has brought a continuous erosion of both community life and primary face-to-face relationships. Urban society is impersonal and competitive. People have become rootless in the city. The German sociologist, Ferdinand Tonnies, regarded urban life as an association (*gesellschaft*) rather than a community (*gemeinschaft*).

The sociologist has an important role to play in town planning and in attempts to raise the quality of life in urban areas. He collects data, collates opinions and conducts social surveys.

> Town planning, *together with other instruments of social policy*, plays a crucial role in a mixed economy in redistributing spatial resources.
>   (Pahl, R.E. *Whose City?*)

The greatest problem of urban planning is to reconcile demands for *accessibility* and *amenity*. By accessibility is meant the close proximity of home, workplace, school, hospital, offices, shops and places of entertainment. By amenity is meant environmental factors such as open spaces, the countryside, recreational parks, wildlife, peace and quiet, fresh air and water. It is likely that accessibility and amenity will vary in inverse proportion, i.e. the greater the accessibility the less the amenity and vice-versa. S.E. Rasmussen (*London, the Unique City*) has described how the lateral development of London has allowed Londoners to enjoy more amenities than the inhabitants of most modern cities. The people of London have far more space per person than citizens of New York or Tokyo or Paris. However, the price of greater amenity is less accessibility. In Manhattan 80,000 people, on average, are crowded into each square mile: in easy reach of their homes there is an abundance of workplaces, shops and entertainment facilities. The New Yorker enjoys a high degree of accessibility, whereas the typical Londoner spends many hours on buses, tubes or trains.

In some cases, modern improvements in transportation have made possible the combination of both accessibility and amenity. Ebenezer Howard (*Garden Cities of Tomorrow*), envisaged a group of garden cities which would grow into a Social City combining maximum accessibility with maximum amenity. New towns established in Britain since the 1946 New Towns Act have not been planned in groups as Ebenezer Howard recommended, and may appear as social vacuums lacking a nucleus of community life.

> Industrialisation did not necessarily imply urbanisation. Many industrialists preferred to have their workpeople close to the works, not only to ensure punctuality but also as a means of social control. T. Chalmers was urging in the 1820s in a three-volume work on *The Christian and Civic Economy of Large Towns* that cities should be split into smaller localities in order to prevent the people 'forming into a combined array of hostile feeling and prejudice'.
> (Pahl, R.E. *Patterns of Urban Life*)

New towns may provide accessibility and amenity but their citizens struggle to establish the meaningful social relationships associated with a sense of social identity and belonging. The shift of population to new towns and overspill areas has been partly responsible for the inner areas of metropolitan districts becoming places of hopelessness, desolation, loneliness and vandalism.

The ownership of motor cars by the masses has been a major source of change in urban life. Towns should be designed for the citizens as a whole and not for the convenience of vehicle owners. Traffic congestion, road accidents, ugly multi-storey car parks and one-way systems dominate the motor-vehicle-orientated city of today. Victorian cities grew up around the

SOCIOLOGY IN CONTEXT

Table 7.13 Major problems of urban life

1 Those dwelling in twilight zones suffer from inadequacies in the sphere of housing, education, medical care and employment opportunities.

2 About one million urban slum dwellings still exist in the UK despite schemes of slum clearance and urban renewal.

3 18 million people, in the UK, are crowded into seven gigantic conurbations. (About 33 per cent of people live on 4 per cent of the land area.)

4 Overcrowding means increased pollution of earth, water and air, and by noise.

5 Urban life is associated with high rates of crime, suicide and unemployment.

6 The increase in motorised transport is a source of congestion and frustration.

railway station. New urban growth tends to develop as dormitory suburbs. Car ownership has encouraged the 'slurb' of Los Angeles, where slum/suburbs sprawl across the landscape. There is no easy answer to such problems, but there is clearly a pressing need for comprehensive environmental policies made after adequate research by town planners, economists, sociologists and others. They must consider:

> . . . the major problem not only of town-planners and applied sociologists, but of 'successful' capitalist society. Must life become poorer as it becomes richer?
> (Frankenberg, R. *Communities in Britain*)

● *The zone of transition*

The transition zone is a twilight area of a large town or city typified as the area lying between the central business area and the area where working-class dwellings were originally concentrated. In the 1920s, Burgess, Parke and others of the Chicago School of sociologists put forward an ecological account of the growth of industrial towns. The process of expansion was illustrated by a series of concentric circles. Figure 7.6 represents a theoretical model showing five zones.

Burgess argued that cities tended to expand radially from the central business area (I). Encircling this area would be the zone of transition (II) followed by an area (III) inhabited by workers desirous of living within easy access of their work. Beyond this zone, there would be a residential

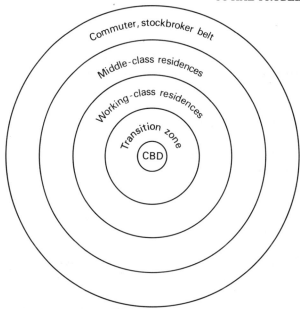

CBD = Central Business District

Fig. 7.6 Burgess's diagram of city ecology
(Pahl, R.E. *Patterns of Urban Life*)

zone (IV) of middle-class dwellings, while beyond the city limit would lie the commuters' zone (V).

Although the term 'zone of transition' has been most commonly used to describe an area of deterioration situated between the business centre (I) and the workers' dwellings (III), in a sense *all* the zones are in a state of transition. This is because there is a tendency for each zone to extend its area by the 'invasion' of the next outer zone. This aspect of 'invasion' may be called 'succession', a term used by ecologists to describe the continuous processes of plant ecology. Burgess made reference to the changing nature of *all* the zones.

> If this chart is applied to Chicago, all four of these zones were in its early history included in the circumference of the inner zone, the present business district. The present boundaries of the area of deterioration were not many years ago those of the zone now inhabited by independent wage-earners, and within the memories of thousands of Chicagoans contained the residences of the 'best families'.
> (Burgess, E.W. 'The Growth of the City' in Parke, E., ed., *The City*)

The functionalist Parke used conceptions developed by plant and animal ecologists in order to study the transition of city areas or zones; he argued that there is a 'web of life' in which all living organisms are bound together by a system of interdependence. Darwin had been well aware of this idea when he illustrated interdependence by relating how next year's crop of clover depended on the number of bees, while the number of bees depended on the number of field mice, while the number of field mice depended in their turn on the number of cats kept by cat-lovers dwelling in the neighbourhood. Thus the ecological concept of interdependence was closely related to the principle of 'competitive cooperation'. Other ecological concepts included mutual adaptation, dominance and succession. The mutual adaptation of competing systems means that the inhabitants assume the character of the environment. The area of dominance is the area of highest land values. The fact that a city moves through a series of more or less clearly-defined stages gives this development the character suggested by the term 'succession'.

Burgess and Parke's ideas are too simplistic; other factors, apart from ecological ones, must be included in a sociological account of the development of the 'zones of transition'. Conflict theorists argue that a realistic sociological study of the city must take account of the class-struggle over housing, for this conflict is at the heart of the transitional nature of the evolution of the city. It follows Weberian ideas that the class-struggle emerges wherever people in a market situation have different access to property. Life cycles determine the demographic content of 'zones of transition'. People live in different places at different times during their life cycles largely because of economic circumstances: single unmarried people tend to gravitate to twilight zones to join old people who are compelled to remain there, because of dire economic straits, until they die.

The Chicago School's transitional zone theories have been criticised on three important grounds:
1 a pattern of transitional zones does not correlate with the growth of every city;
2 the ecological analogies have been exaggerated;
3 the research has been limited to American cities.
However, eminent modern sociologists, such as Rex and Moore, have accepted that the zone of transition is a recurrent urban phenomenon. They adopted the zonal approach in their study of the Sparkbrook area of Birmingham. Rex and Moore reduced the invasion, succession and dominance conflicts to a study of competition for land use.

> We see it as threefold: (1) as continuing competition for the use of sites; (2) as competition for the use of buildings which have now been abandoned by their original users; and (3) a more general competition for the use of available material resources.
>
> (Rex, J. and Moore, R. *Race, Community and Conflict*)

• *Housing and urban residents*

Rex and Moore argue from a conflict perspective that it is not possible to understand the problems of the zone of transition without distinguishing the different types of housing existing in a modern city. They classify types and housing situations as:

1 outright owner of a whole house;
2 owner of a mortgaged whole house;
3 the council tenant –
   (a) in a house with a long life;
   (b) in a house awaiting demolition;
4 tenant of a whole house owned by a private landlord;
5 owner of a house bought with short-term loans who is compelled to let rooms to meet his repayment obligations;
6 the tenant of rooms in a lodging house.

By assuming that their model of the city is composed of four concentric rings around the central business area, and the city itself is surrounded by relatively small towns and villages, then prior to slum clearance, the types of housing and housing class will be as follows:

1 The outright owners will be found especially in the third and fourth zones from the centre and outside the city in nearby small towns and villages.
2 The owners repaying mortgage loans will be found predominantly in the fourth zone.
3 The council tenants of houses with a long expectation of life will also be found in this fourth zone, but after slum clearance they may also be found in higher-density council estates in the first and second zones.
4 Property scheduled for slum clearance will be situated in the first and second zones.
5 Private tenancies will be found in all zones, but especially in zones one, two and three.
6 The lodging houses, occupied by their owners and tenants, will be in zones one and two, but predominantly in zone two.

It can be argued that Rex and Moore do not offer sufficient empirical validation for the exactitude of their zonal housing, but nevertheless their analysis is an improvement on that of the Chicago School because they attempt to investigate the relationship between the culture of the different sub-communities. Although initially the different groups (of upper middle class, lower middle class and working class) become segregated and wish to work out their own lifestyle, in a later stage of development the lower middle classes (including white-collar workers) migrate outwards so that they can ape the life of the upper middle classes. This leaves the twilight zone or 'zone of transition' consisting of deserted houses which pass to a population of social rejects

> The discharged prisoner, the deserted wife, the coloured immigrant and the prostitute have little in common except their housing conditions.
> (Rex, J. and Moore, R. *Race, Community and Conflict*)

The problems of inner cities have been heightened by the enormous size of modern conurbations and the density of population within these conurbations. In some inner-city areas there are no-go areas where vandalism and mugging are rife, and where the state cannot guarantee the safety of its citizens. The inhabitants are often social isolates who seek anonymity and have few kinship ties. When people are detached from their kin, social norms are not transmitted and a sense of anomie (lack of moral regulation) develops. Anonymity contributes to delinquency: 'they can get away with it'. The inner city becomes the area of commercialised vice.

The desertion of inner city areas, by those who have sufficient economic resources to get away, has been accentuated in Britain since the Second World War by the government's 'carrot' policy of offering relatively attractive accommodation in new towns and overspill areas. This policy has resulted in an exodus from conurbations and other large cities which cannot be explained adequately by ecological processes working within the city itself. The plight of the inner cities, including many twilight zones, has been the subject of government commitments to regenerate these areas. In *Policy for the Inner Cities* (White Paper, Cmnd 6845, 1977) it was indicated that between 1966 and 1976 Glasgow lost 205 000 people (21 per cent), Liverpool 150 000 (22 per cent), Manchester 110 000 (18 per cent), inner London 500 000 (16 per cent) and Birmingham 85 000 (8 per cent). Among smaller cities, only Newcastle-upon-Tyne with more than 40 000 loss (12 per cent) and Nottingham (8 per cent) experienced such a fall in population. The flight from the cities has been encouraged by the trend to increased home-ownership, the location of new factories and the supersession of public/collective transport by private/individual transport. Although the above figures mostly represent losses from the total area of the city, it is the twilight zones which give most cause for concern.

Five types of inner-city residents have been classified by Gans, in 'Urbanism and Suburbanism as Ways of Life', in Rose, A.M., ed., *Human Behaviour and Social Processes*.

1 The *'cosmopolites'* include students, artists, writers, musicians and entertainers, as well as other intellectuals and professionals;

2 *the unmarried or childless* can be divided into two sub-types, depending on the permanence or transience of their status;

(a) The temporarily unmarried or childless live in the inner city for only a limited time. (b) The permanently unmarried may stay in the inner city for the remainder of their lives, their housing depending on their income; 3 *ethnic groups* are found in such neighbourhoods as New York's Lower East Side, or Birmingham's Sparkbrook; 4 *the 'deprived'* population consists of the very poor; the emotionally disturbed or otherwise handicapped; broken families; and, most important, the non-white population; 5 *the 'trapped'* are the people who stay behind when a neighbourhood is invaded by those of lower status; they cannot afford to move, or are otherwise bound to their present location.

Rex's study of the way in which housing class situations affect ethnic immigrant groups provides a more analytical insight into the social problems of twilight zones. He noted that people who live in such areas occupy an inferior position in society. The zone of transition includes a relatively high proportion of social misfits, criminals and deviants such as drug addicts and prostitutes. Rex has concluded that the social behaviour of the inhabitants of the twilight zones is the product of numerous interwoven social patterns so

> relations within and between communities will be affected by the fact that there exists in the society a specific pattern of social relations of production and a resulting pattern of class conflict and stratification.
>
> (Rex, J. *Race, Colonialism and the City*)

The inadequacy of housing is closely associated with the worst social problems associated with the 'zone of transition'. Burney (*Housing on Trial*) found that the old, decaying *private* housing of twilight areas provide the main accommodation for newcomers. Immigrants are usually unable to rent council houses because local councils reflect the interests of long-established residents who make up the majority of the electorate. Immigrants, isolates and deviants will be compelled to live in lodging houses. The association of coloured immigrants in certain districts within the 'zones of transition' has given rise to what Burney considers to be a misleading bit of jargon: the use of the term 'ghetto'. This is yet another example of a labelling device where a

> mere metaphor is now taken seriously as a sociological description, in a classic instance of the game of first deciding what you think a word ought to mean, and then describing a situation in terms which fit the meaning.
>
> (Burney, E. *Housing on Trial*)

Burney considers that 'ghetto' is a misleading term because in these districts coloured inhabitants are in the minority and there is not the rigid system confining certain ethnic groups to specific areas as exists for Jews in Warsaw or for Negroes in Chicago. Although there are many coloured immigrants in the 'zones of transition' in the UK, there is not the degree of concentration to justify the use of the term 'ghetto'. The 1961 Census showed that 55 per cent of coloured people were dispersed in districts where they formed under 8 per cent of the population, while the largest concentration in one census enumeration unit, of people born in Commonwealth countries in Asia, Africa and the Caribbean, was only 37 per cent. Nevertheless it would be false to deny that coloured immigrants are attracted to 'zones of transition', but it is not so much the immigrants who bring problems to the zones, but rather:

> they are received there because the problems already exist.
> (Glass, R. and Westergaard, J. *London's Housing Needs*)

Both central and local government have been indicted for the bad housing conditions which exist in many urban areas. It is easy enough to castigate government but this is to neglect the causal significance of zones of transition. More than half a century after the work of Burgess and Parke, it is clear that zones of transition and the consequent poor housing still produce undesirable social consequences seemingly as insoluble as ever.

> In our experience it would seem that there is a majority for whom this is not a zone of transition, but a zone of stagnation. Their problems are never likely to be resolved and for them the zone of transition provides a niche in an otherwise hostile society.
> (Rex, J. and Moore, R. *Race, Community and Conflict*)

• Social work in urban areas

Around the turn of the century there was a close correlation between sociology and social work in urban areas. (See section 7.2 for an account of the work of Booth and Rowntree.) Sociology and social work drifted apart as sociology concentrated upon social theory and scientific methods in an attempt to prove that sociologists were not just woolly do-gooders. A fresh awareness of the sociological importance of social work has increased in recent years with the writings of Goffman, Cicourel, Young and Willmott, Townsend and others.

There may be a case for sociologists not being involved in social work but there is not a case for social workers not having a basis of sociological knowledge. The study of social problems by the sociologists is fraught with difficulties: the political left is likely to be suspicious of those who study the lot of the underprivileged without doing anything about it, while the political right condemns sociologists who are considered to be lobbying for the have-nots.

The sociologist is likely to face role-confusion should he become involved in social work. He is faced with the dilemma of acting as the poor man's therapist who fights the case of the deprived, or of taking the view that his first loyalty is to those in authority who appoint and pay him. He must decide whether his work is part of the effective organisation of present society (crude functionalism) or with the betterment of society (crude social actionism). Sociologists acting as social workers are likely to gain more recognition and credibility if they apply scientific methods and adopt the medical model of diagnosis followed by the prescribing of treatment.

In spite of the efforts of voluntary workers, most social work is government-sponsored. Local authorities carry out their legislative duties to care for orphans, the homeless, the handicapped and others in need. Following the 1968 Seebohm Report, local authorities were required to create a Social Services department. These departments are generic rather than specialised and fragmented. The Director of Social Services attempts to coordinate all types of social work and provide a unified social service.

It is difficult to define the role of the social worker; 'social work is what social workers do'. Burdened with very heavy case-loads, especially in urban areas, social workers are often left to determine their own roles either as agents of social control (e.g. in relation to care orders which deprive people of liberty) or as social actionists fighting on behalf of their clients. Social work is probably best regarded as a form of social intervention which augments the means by which people both individually and collectively try to find a solution to private troubles and public issues.

Table 7.14 Some examples of social work

Function	Example
Care-giving	Welfare of mentally sick and the disturbed, by psychiatric social workers
Innovatory	Mental patients discharged from hospital and rehabilitated into the community
Social Control	Supervision of offenders by probation officers
Information of rights	Right of adopted children to have knowledge of natural parents
Resource Allocation	Vehicles for the disabled, and discretionary powers to make money-gifts in hardship cases
Decision-making	Social inquiry reports, abortions, adoptions, paroles, etc.

- ## Community work in urban areas

A community usually involves *social interaction* by people living in a geographical area. The mark of a community is that the inhabitants share a common identification because they live most of their lives within the community. A community relates to shared interests so it is usual for groups to aim at mutual support and social participation.

> Community work typically consists of work with groups of local people who have come into existence because they want to change something or do something which concerns them. Community work also embraces attempts to relate the activities of social agencies more closely to the needs of the people they serve.
>
> (Gulbenkian Report, *Community Work and Social Change*, 1969)

Community workers aim at achieving social change by encouraging group participation within the local community. The influence of community workers in building up closer social networks within urban areas has become increasingly significant in recent years because of the tendency for decisions to be removed from the local community. Impersonal multinational companies have replaced local firms. National policies control the organisation of education, health and housing. Urbanisation has given rise to extensive social change whereby small traditional communities are replaced by large associations.

Tonnies's terms *gemeinschaft* and *gesellschaft* have already been used to differentiate between these two different types of society.

> A *gemeinschaft* is a communal society in which people feel they belong together because they are of the same kind; ties of kinship are permanent . . . .
>
> A *gesellschaft*, by contrast, is an associated society in which the major social bonds are voluntary, based on the national pursuit of self-interest and defined by contract.
>
> (Scott, W.R. *Social Processes and Social Structures*)

The growth of towns has meant that *gesellschaft* has increased at the expense of *gemeinschaft*. Larger urban areas have *gesellschaft*-like features, yet within these towns there is community life or *gemeinschaft*. It is the job of the community worker's to urge groups of local people to tackle the problems of their area. The transitional nature of town life makes this task difficult. Urban areas tend to display a lack of community spirit which is apparent in attitudes of non-participation, lack of neighbourliness, local isolation and the erosion of informal social controls (e.g. vandalism occurs when parents cannot control their children).

Community workers may identify themselves with *consensus strategies* or with *conflict strategies*, but these strategies are not necessarily alternatives

Table 7.15 Aims of community workers

1 Encourage local groups to play an active part in community life.
2 Inculcate a feeling of belonging to the community.
3 Satisfy needs of the whole community rather than focusing upon individual casework.
4 Improve the relationship between planners and planned (government and governed).
5 Stimulate voluntary participation to counter bureaucratic control.

in every case. Consensus strategies are intended to encourage local people to participate in the existing political machinery and to work with traditional authorities in decision-making. By consensus strategies the initiative of local groups compels the local authority to see the real needs of the community. The agents of the authority may be unaware of local needs until they are expressed by participatory local residents. The authorities may be persuaded to change their ways and cater realistically for community needs.

Conflict strategies are opposed to those who exert power in the community. Resistance to power represents the fundamental dynamic of social change. Conflict strategies include such protest techniques as marches, demonstrations, sit-ins, squatting, rent-strikes, boycotts, petitions, traffic obstructions, etc.

The community worker's role is an enabling role in so far as he stimulates participation by others. He must be able to communicate with the local people and establish good relationships with them. He has to mobilise the resources of the local people to the best advantage; this includes their time, money and skills. Some would argue that little can be done by community workers to solve urban problems unless there are changes in the environment. Others argue that in the face of existing problems, community workers have to encourage local participation now and press for institutional changes later.

The term *community action* refers to locally-based action whereby ordinary people try to bring improvements to community life. Such action may be inspired by a professional community worker but it might well arise from the initiative of the people themselves. Broadly speaking any work done on behalf of the community is community work.

The term *community development* is used to refer to a government project set up to aid a specific area. It is a coordinated government-financed development, aimed at involving the people in the improvement of social conditions. It therefore involves the consensus model. Community developments originated in the United States. The failure of schemes of urban renewal provided the seedbed for the founding of community development projects. Urban dwellers were persuaded to participate in helping to meet their own needs rather than rely upon the theoretical ideas of town-planners who had no experience of living in areas of social deprivation.

Following the American experience, the Home Office decided to set up twelve community development projects in Britain. These projects were begun in the early 1970s and were sited in urban areas with certain common factors.

Table 7.16 Locations of community development projects

1 Urban areas of declining population caused by declining industry and unemployment.

2 Urban areas with a large proportion of old people, unskilled workers, immigrants, etc.

3 Urban areas of poor housing, much of it privately owned.

4 Areas associated with important reports which identified social needs, e.g.
   (a) Milner-Holland Report (on housing)
   (b) Plowden Report (on education)
   (c) Seebohm Report (on social development).

British community development projects were wound up after only a few years of existence. Compared with US experiments in this field, too little power of participation was given to those who lived in the area. The Home Office and the local authorities were not prepared to plough sufficient funds into the projects, and in spite of the fact that social research was one of the main aims, little information came out of these projects. Community development projects could offer a solution to many urban problems providing that they are adequately financed and staffed by competent professional community workers able to involve local people in improving the quality of their lives.

7.6 Some other social problems

Many social problems are closely linked to the extent of urbanisation in society. Although it would obviously be fallacious to argue that in rural communities there is no experience of such problems as juvenile delinquency or suicide or drug addiction, or mass unemployment, nevertheless statistics indicate that these problems are more prevalent in large towns and cities. Desmond Morris (*The Human Zoo*) has argued that man is little removed biologically from the simple tribal animal who existed in pre-civilised times and he is thus ill-fitted to face up to the social hazards presented by overcrowded impersonal urban communities.

> When the pressures of modern living become heavy, the harassed city-dweller often refers to his teeming world as a concrete jungle. This is a colourful way of describing the pattern of life in a dense urban community, but it is also grossly inaccurate, as anyone who has studied a real jungle will confirm.
>
> Under normal conditions, in their natural habitats, wild animals do not mutilate themselves, masturbate, attack their offspring, develop stomach ulcers, become fetishists, suffer from obesity, form homosexual pair-bonds, or commit murder. Among human city-dwellers, needless to say, all of these things occur....
>
> The comparison we must make is not between the city dweller and the wild animal, but between the city-dweller and the captive animal. The modern human animal is no longer living in conditions natural for his species. Trapped, not by a zoo collector, but by his own brainy brilliance, he has set himself up in a huge, restless menagerie where he is in constant danger of cracking under the strain.

Sociologists have long drawn attention to the social disorders of industrial towns. Max Weber argued that these disorders arise from the bureaucratic and dehumanised nature of modern society. Emile Durkheim argued that a feeling of anomie exists in industrial towns and that the inhabitants have lost their moral values.

• *Juvenile delinquency*

Juvenile delinquency provides an example of a social problem which has increased with urbanisation. The most common criminal offender is a young male, living in an *urban* area, and coming from a working-class background (see Table 7.17). The urban crime rate is about twice that for rural areas.

One possible reason is that urban social relationships are often secondary and impersonal (*gesellschaft*). In a small rural community (*gemeinschaft*) everybody knows everybody else. Clandestine acts, which offend accepted moral codes, are likely to attract the hostility of 'the locals'. A stranger is soon spotted, whereas in a town a person may successfully hide behind the cloak of anonymity and escape into the crowd.

Some American sociologists have argued that industrial and post-industrial society is crimogenic. Large towns induce an endemic discontent among young males, especially where capitalism generates excessive materialism encouraged by mass advertising, supermarkets and rapid social changes. Table 6.14 (Section 6.4) indicates that 68 per 1000 young males aged 14–16 offended against the criminal law in 1979, compared with only 12 per 1000 males aged 21 and over.

The growth of large urban areas has witnessed a marked decrease in the exercise of *informal* social control. A group of youngsters caught stealing apples, in a close-knit rural community, are likely to be warned by a local inhabitant that they will be reported to their parents or headmaster, but in an urban area the police are more likely to be called to the scene. In rural areas intended crimes may be prevented by informal social control, while crimes committed are less likely to be included in official criminal statistics. In large towns, where young people are unknown to passers-by, informal social control rarely operates. David Matza (*Delinquency and Drift*) has argued that some juveniles become delinquents through a feeling of helplessness and as a protest at being pushed around by authority. They subconsciously regard the middle class as the law-makers and the working class as the law-breakers.

Table 7.17 Social class and delinquency

| | | Court appearance or caution | | | |
| | | Aged 8–14 | | Aged 15–21 | |
	No delinquency %	One offence %	More than one %	One offence %	More than one %
Entire group	82.1	3.6	5.6	6.8	1.9
Upper middle class	96.4	1.4	–	1.8	0.4
Lower middle class	87.6	3.3	1.8	5.4	1.8
Upper manual class	87.6	2.0	3.2	6.0	1.1
Lower manual class	76.3	4.5	8.6	8.1	2.4

(Wadsworth, M.E.J. 'Delinquency – a National Sample of Children', *British Journal of Criminology*, Vol. 15, No. 2)

The findings of other sociologists support David Matza's arguments.

Stealing is part of the 'normal' behaviour of boys in Bethnal Green, as it apparently is in other working-class areas.

(Willmott, P. *Adolescent Boys of East London*)

... delinquency flourishes in working-class neighbourhoods because of the support it finds in working-class culture.

(Morris, T. *The Criminal Area*)

E.A. Cohen (*Delinquent Boys*) has described a delinquent subculture of young working-class males who fail to gain the rewards offered by the dominant middle-class culture. They gain status from their fellows by confrontation with such middle-class moral values as respect for private property, acceptance of adult authority, good manners and politeness. D.M. Downes (*The Delinquent Solution*) found that young East-Enders used their leisure time for rebellion against middle-class values. J.B. Mays's study of Liverpool's dockland (*Growing up in the City*) indicates that some forms of delinquency are regarded as the norm. The city youngster leaves his overcrowded home to form street gangs which indulge in petty pilfering or vandalism. This type of delinquency is far less serious than the acts of the few 'conscienceless' delinquents who indulge in crimes such as mugging.

Help for the juvenile delinquent is to be found in better housing, with less over-crowding and extended amenities. Improved cultural surroundings could contribute towards a decreasing crime rate among the young. There are more opportunities for delinquent acts in the streets of dilapidated urban areas (see T. Morris, *The Criminal Area*). When faced with urban slum conditions of dereliction and decay delinquent sub-cultures provide a functional solution for young urban males.

The first act of Mrs Thatcher's Conservative Government in 1979 was to increase the pay of the police with the avowed intention of improving police recruitment and securing a more efficient police force. The maintenance of law and order is seen as a primary objective of government, but it must be realised that the larger and more efficient the police force, the greater the number of offences detected and the higher the recorded crime rate.

In urban areas, the experiences of the police lead them to have a different attitude towards crime and potential offenders from their rural counterparts. A rural policeman is more likely to be concerned with preventing crime (by befriending those on his beat) than with apprehending offenders after crimes have taken place.

Media reports of urban crimes tend to exaggerate the extent and seriousness of juvenile delinquency. An extension of the recent Cornish experiment whereby the goal of the policeman is 'to keep a peaceful patch' could well redress the balance.

Most of the offences of juveniles lack the gravity and substance, or the scheming and planning, which the public associates with crime. Even when one examines the crimes of boys from approved schools, many of whom are confirmed recidivists, it appears that their range is mostly limited to minor thefts and traffic offences, and that serious violence, sexual assaults and professionally organized crimes are most uncommon. A somewhat older age group, the late teens and early twenties, includes some of the most dangerously violent offenders in existence, but fortunately they are very rare, and have little in common with the general run of young thieves or sporadic hooligans. The over-all impression left behind from a cursory examination of the statistical trends is that though the numbers are enormous they mostly stand for minor offences. Like an attack of measles, a first conviction in a school boy, though it can be serious, does not usually portend a blighted future.

(West, D.J. *The Young Offender*)

• *Suicide*

Explanations of suicide are an important field of sociological study; the sociologist is naturally interested in why a person deliberately opts out of society by committing an act of self-destruction. An analysis of social factors likely to lead to suicide provides an insight into societal pressures exerted upon individuals.

Many factors have been linked with suicide. Urban living and a high density of population both statistically correlate with an above-average incidence of suicide.

> ... the social causes of suicide are ... closely related to urban civilisation and are most intense in these great centres.
> (Durkheim, E. *Suicide*)

Many familiar aspects of town life are linked with suicide: these include such diverse situations as a high standard of living or economic hardships accompanying unemployment. Other factors, not confined to urban dwellers, such as old age, widowhood and childlessness, are also associated with higher than average rates of suicide.

A 1979 report commissioned by the World Health Organisation (in an attempt to discover reasons why England and Wales had the only sharply-declining suicide rate in Europe between 1963 and 1974) linked different rates of social change with movements in the suicide rate. The report produced an index of the rate of social change for 18 countries based upon 15 factors, giving special weight to those involving women, in view of the fundamental changes which have taken place in the roles of women in society. The implication of the report is that social changes which are increasing the rate of suicide throughout most of Europe either have not yet occurred in Britain or have already occurred. It is not without significance that Britain was the first industrialised nation and that its industrial towns have reached greater maturity than towns elsewhere. In spite of earlier beliefs that the Samaritan Movement contributed greatly to the decline in Britain's suicide rate from 1963 (it was 12 per 100 000 in the 1950s and 7 per 100 000 by 1974), studies on towns with and without Samaritan branches show little difference in the suicide rate. A trained sociologist views statistics with suspicion.

> The term 'potential suicide rate' is used here rather than the more normal term 'real suicide rate', simply because it is a fundamental part of the argument throughout this work that there does not exist such a thing as a 'real suicide rate'. Suicides are not something of a set nature waiting to be correctly or incorrectly categorised by officials.
> (Douglas, J. *The Social Meanings of Suicide*)

Suicides may go undetected (or may be recorded as natural deaths or even murders), while attempted suicide may be more apparent than real, i.e. an individual may feign suicide in order to draw attention to inner conflicts arising from a lack of integration with a social group with which he or she closely identifies.

The findings of Emile Durkheim provide the most satisfactory explanations of suicide. His studies suggested that suicide rates correlated with an individual's degree of integration into various groups in society. The groups might include a relatively small number of relations, friends or workmates: they might be large groups associated with a church, or a local or national community. It is dangerous to make simplistic generalisations but it is logical to assume that in a *gemeinschaft* (as typified by a rural community) people would feel a greater sense of belonging than in a *gesellschaft* (as typified by an urban industrial area) where the inhabitants are anonymous, isolated and less closely bound together.

Durkheim distinguished between three 'ideal' types of suicide.

1 *Anomic suicide*

Anomic suicide occurs when an individual experiences social or personal disorientations accompanied by a loss of familiar norms. Anomic suicide is

> ... caused by the sudden dislocation of normative systems, the breakdown of values by which one may have lived for a lifetime....
> (Nisbet, R.A. *The Sociological Tradition*)

Monotonous jobs accompanying intense division of labour and economic crises caused by redundancies and rapidly changing circumstances result in a vacuum of moral standards. When an individual is uncertain about his fate, disintegration from the social group occurs and he may, as a last resort, take his own life.

2 *Altruistic suicide*

On the other hand, an extremely high level of integration may drive a person to suicide. An individual may commit suicide if he judges that he has dishonoured a social group to which he feels a deep commitment. A Japanese soldier may commit *hara-kiri* because he feels he has disgraced his nation. Durkheim used the term *obligatory* altruistic suicide to describe acts where individuals feel that it is their duty to commit suicide.

> In Polynesia, a slight offence often decides a man to commit suicide. It is the same among the North American Indians; a conjugal quarrel or jealous impulse suffices to cause a man or woman to commit suicide. Among the Dacotas and Creeks the least disappointment often leads to desperate steps. The readiness of the Japanese to disembowel·themselves for the slightest reason is well known. A strange sort of duel is even reported there, in which the effort is not to attack one another but to excel in dexterity in opening one's own stomach. Similar facts are recorded in China, Cochin China, Thibet and the Kingdom of Siam.
> In all such cases a man kills himself without being explicitly forced to do so.
> (Durkheim, E. *Suicide*)

3 *Egoistic suicide*

Egoistic suicide occurs when an individual's feelings of intense responsibility for his actions is not shared by a social group with which he is closely associated. Durkheim found that, in the nineteenth century, suicide was more prevalent amongst Protestants than Roman Catholics because Protestants were left to work out their own salvation. A spirit of free inquiry animated the practising Protestant, but if he was unsuccessful in shaping his own faith, he could be left with doubts and disintegration leading to egoistic suicide. Roman Catholics were willing to accept the authority of their church and had clear-cut conceptions of needs and goals. Durkheim thus found that suicide rates depended on the degree of social cohesion. Groups with *high* integration had lower suicide rates than groups with *low* integration – and vice-versa. The high integration of Roman Catholics and Jews meant that their suicide rates were low compared with Protestants who were less prone to accept authority and put greater emphasis upon the importance of free-will and individual choice. Durkheim's law of social integration allowed him to make empirical generalisations. Thus:
Sociological law: social groups with high integration have lower suicide rates;
Empirical generalisation: Catholics are more likely to have lower suicide rates than Protestants.

A prediction based on Durkheim's law is likely to be true but there may be exceptions. According to Durkheim, large cities generally have a higher rate than country districts, but cities have no monopoly of suicide.

● *Drug-dependency*

The use of drugs is common to all human societies. Drugs have been used from time immemorial in an attempt to relieve human suffering, but they only become a social problem when taken compulsively for non-medical reasons. The drug-taker may seek escape from conflicts and problems of the world. A 'trip' may provide a temporary sensation of happiness.

It can be argued that drugs have a social purpose as they assist group interaction. The offering of a cigarette is a gesture of friendship: alcoholic drinks enable people to cast aside their inhibitions. A socially acceptable drug may become one of the main props of the principal religious ceremony of a society: alcoholic wine is central to the Christian communion service for most denominations.

The term 'drug-dependency', in common parlance, is usually associated with the smoking of soft drugs such as cannabis (marijuana or 'pot') or of hard drugs such as heroin or methadone. The consumption of these drugs is illegal and regarded as deviant behaviour by society. The partaking of other drugs, such as alcohol and nicotine (in tobacco) is not regarded as deviant because these drugs are accepted by society and are legally consumed.

It is arguable which of the many drugs constitutes the most serious social problem in modern society. Some drugs, such as caffein (in tea or coffee) and acetylsalicylic acid (in aspirin), are regarded as relatively harmless although there are those who would wish to argue the point.

Other socially acceptable drugs have incontrovertibly dangerous consequences. In 1975 over 13 000 people were admitted to hospital for alcoholism. In line with their changing roles in society the number of women admitted for alcoholism more than doubled between 1964 and

Table 7.18 Dangerous drugs: registered addicts in the UK, 1971–6

	1971	1972	1973	1974	1975	1976
Number registered as taking drugs on 31 December	1549	1615	1815	1971	1953	1881
Males	1133	1194	1269	1459	1438	1389
Females	416	421	446	512	515	492
Age distribution						
Under 20 years	118	96	84	64	39	18
20 and under 25	722	727	750	692	562	411
25 and under 30	288	376	530	684	754	810
30 and under 35	112	117	134	163	219	247
35 and under 50	112	118	136	163	169	189
50 and over	177	165	180	197	193	188
Age not stated	20	16	1	8	17	18

(*Social Trends* No. 8, 1977)

1975. There is no certain way of knowing the number of road accidents caused through drinking alcohol or the number of crimes committed through drunkenness. Smokers make up well over 90 per cent of the 30 000 men and 8000 women who die annually of lung cancer, while it has been estimated that at least another 50 000 die from respiratory or heart diseases directly contributable to heavy smoking.

Considering the publicity given by the media to so-called dangerous drug addiction, in the form of hard drugs such as heroin, it may come as a surprise to find there are fewer than 2000 registered addicts in the UK.

Of course not all drug addicts are state-registered and some consumption of hard drugs, such as heroin and methadone, is not included in official statistics. In Britain, drug addicts are able to secure their supplies through NHS treatment centres. In 1976, there were 88 treatment centres of which 58 had specialised addiction units. It is recognised that one cure for drug addiction is a gradually controlled withdrawal of the drug. In the USA there is no system of legalised help, so 'junkies' resort to crime to replenish their supplies from drug 'pushers'. In Britain, under the 1971 Misuse of Drugs Act, drug-pushing is regarded as a far more serious criminal offence than the possession of drugs.

It is usually accepted that cannabis is not a drug which leads to addiction, but it has to be recognised that it is extremely difficult to make a clear distinction between an addictive and a non-addictive drug. The likelihood of a cannabis smoker becoming physically dependent upon the drug is negligible, i.e. there is little or no evidence of danger of withdrawal symptoms; but there are those who argue that there is a possibility of psychological dependence on cannabis, i.e. the person who smokes a 'joint' feels that he needs it if he is to function adequately. A WHO Committee on Addiction-Producing Drugs declared that it is preferable to use the term *drug-dependency*, rather than drug-addiction, to include all types of drug-taking.

The Wootton Committee Report (1968) by the Government Advisory Committee on Drug Dependence recommended a softening of the drug laws especially in relation to cannabis, but the recommendations were dismissed after the Wootton Committee was abused by the media.

The model which the mass media used to analyse the Report was in a classic absolutist mould: a permissive and powerful minority had pressurized a misguided committee into an unwise decision. A motley collection of experts were interviewed and quoted as opposing the report; dubious figures about escalation, derived from numerous and inapplicable social situations, were generalised to Britain as a whole, and worse, to a Britain where hashish was freely available. Correlation does not, as any first-year sociology student well knows, mean causation. That correlation between the rise of marihuana smoking and heroin addiction might be the result of complicated relationships directly affected by the illegal status of marihuana was largely ignored.

(Young, J. *The Drugtakers*)

It may be true that the majority of so-called addicts, now dependent upon hard drugs, began by experimenting with soft drugs; Jock Young considers that consumers of soft and hard drugs feel affinity because both groups are hounded by the police. In accordance with Becker's interactionist labelling theory, as all drug-takers are seen as deviants by the rest of society they react by considering themselves as deviants and act the part. A young American policeman expressed his reaction,

I tell you there's something about users that bugs me. I don't know what it is exactly. You want me to be frank? OK. Well, I can't stand them; I mean I really can't stand them. Why? Because they bother me personally. They're *dirty*, that's what they are, filthy. They make my skin crawl.

It's funny, but I don't get that reaction to ordinary criminals. You pinch a burglar or a pickpocket and you understand each other; you know how it is, you stand around yacking, maybe even crack a few jokes. But Jesus, these guys, they're a danger, you know what I mean, they're like Commies or some of those CORE people.

There are some people you can feel sorry for. You know, you go out and pick up some poor chump of a paper hanger (bad cheque writer) and he's just a drunk and life's got him all bugged. You can understand a poor guy like that. It's different with anybody who'd use drugs.

(Blum, R. *Utopiates*)

Jock Young believed that the young drug-takers whom he studied in Notting Hill gathered mainly for social purposes which were heightened by drug-taking.

Drug-taking is – at least to start with – essentially a peripheral activity of hippie groups. That is, it does not occupy a central place in the culture; the central activities are concerned with the values outlined above (for example, dancing, clothes, aesthetic expression). Drug-taking is merely a vehicle for the realization of hedonistic, expressive goals.

Drugs hold a great fascination for the non-drug-taker and in the stereotype drugs are held to be the primary concern of such groups. That is, a peripheral activity is misperceived as a central group activity.

(Young, J. 'The Role of the Police as Amplifiers of Deviancy' in Cohen, S. *Images of Deviance*)

It is understandable that the middle-aged regard tobacco, beer and spirits as different from other drugs; they have been socialised in the social acceptance of nicotine and alcohol. Although alcohol is undoubtedly a dangerous sedative drug it is consumed legally. Is this because the middle class (which makes the laws) refuses to accept that alcohol can lead to addiction largely because many of its number are themselves addicted? The WHO Committee on Addiction-Producing Drugs concluded that alcohol is a drug which may lead to physical addiction. Alcoholism is a social problem viewed in the light of the two yardsticks of:

(a) *costing* society substantial sums of money by way of crime, absenteeism, road accidents, illness (liver cirrhosis) and hospital treatment;

(b) *involving* large numbers of people (possibly 400 000, according to *Alcohol House*, Office of Health Economics). The drug finds acceptance, in spite of its being a serious social problem, because the consumption of alcohol is a cultural norm. It promotes social intercourse and a sense of *bonhomie*, but it is no less dangerous for that. Giant financial interests reap profits from mass consumption of nicotine and alcohol. The media in general, and extravagant advertising in particular, promote the image of time-honoured social customs, both legal and acceptable. Yet drug-dependency is a problem whatever form it takes.

- *Unemployment*

There is a danger of reducing social problems to mere statistics, so it is refreshing to find that the analysis by Mervyn Jones (*Life on the Dole*) takes an interactionist approach and concentrates upon the effects of unemployment in one particular town. That town is Merthyr Tydfil in South Wales where unemployment is undermining life and morale.

> Unemployment in itself – the rejection of a man's energies and skills, the growing sense of disappointment as one unsuccessful application follows another, the sheer stupid waste – is bad enough without any need for me to paint a picture of despair or hunger.... Ultimately, a town is only as big as the opportunities that it offers, and the basic opportunities are those which provide a wide variety of work.

Merthyr Tydfil has experienced the agonies of unemployment since the great depression and the hunger marches of the 1930s. Mervyn Jones begins his analysis in October 1971 when a demonstration was organised under the slogan 'The Right to Work'.

In an individual society based upon the division of labour, the right to employment has long been considered to be a basic human right. Employment results in wages which in their turn result in goods and services. Employment is regarded as a functional prerequisite of an industrial society, while unemployment is considered to be a scourge. In a future technological society dependent upon silicon chips and micro-electronics it may well be otherwise, and a government may be judged to have succeeded if its policies result in increasing the number of leisure hours rather than decreasing the number of those unemployed.

However, it is still the ideology of work which dominates. It is still the case that people without work are profoundly unhappy. This may well turn out to be the wrong approach. But in the meantime, the total sum of those people's personal unhappiness is likely to produce enormous strains in society as the new technology begins to bite into employment and to disrupt the accepted patterns of work.

('Technology', in *Society Today*, 12 May 1979)

Unemployment, in an industrial society, is considered to exist when people who register for employment are unable to find work. In Britain, the highest rate of unemployment exists in the towns of the industrial north and especially in the conurbations of Newcastle (Tyneside) and Liverpool (Merseyside). Unemployment persists for the following reasons:

1 Unemployment has long been associated with unplanned capitalist economies. Karl Marx argued that capitalism flourished while an army of unemployed existed. The Soviet Union has claimed that unemployment does not exist in Russia: unemployment benefits are not paid by the Soviet state but work is offered to those who are unemployed. This policy accords with the belief of early communist thinkers, that 'only those who work should eat'.

2 Advances in industrial processes can destroy jobs. Crude mechanisation brought about the Luddite revolts of 1811. Modern technology is even more menacing as a creator of unemployment: in the last decade, thousands of Swiss workers have lost their jobs with the development of the electronic quartz watch, while Dunlop has closed many factories in Britain since long-lasting radials have replaced the cross-ply tyres.

3 Structural unemployment is a term economists use to describe changes in industry caused by switches in demand. The decline of old staple industries in Britain (such as shipbuilding, railways, cotton and woollen manufacture, etc.) has been brought about by a decline in demand for the products of these industries.

4 Frictional unemployment occurs when there are job opportunities in certain areas, but because of the immobility of labour, unemployed workers from other areas do not move in to fill the vacancies.

5 The interdependence of different countries brought about by increases in international trade, make all countries vulnerable to world recessions. The first example of the importation of unemployment on a vast scale occurred with the world slump of 1929–33 when 12 million were unemployed in the USA.

In Britain the unemployment rate remained above 10 per cent during the 1930s.

Unemployment fell a little from the 1932 rate of 22 per cent, but only to 20 per

cent in 1933, 17 per cent in 1934, and 16 per cent in 1935. Even in 1939 it was
still 12 per cent.
    (Stewart, M. *Keynes and After*)

Keynes's economic policies of using the unemployed upon public works
helped to alleviate the spectre of unemployment, but in the pre-Keynesian
period, unemployment was not considered to be a problem which could be
alleviated by social and economic planning.

> Finally, when the misfortune had struck, the attitudes of the time kept anything
> from being done about it. This, perhaps, was the most disconcerting feature of
> all. Some people were hungry in 1930 and 1931 and 1932. Others were tortured
> by the fear that they might go hungry. Yet others suffered the agony of the
> descent from the honour and respectability that go with income into poverty.
> And still others feared that they might be next. Meanwhile everyone suffered
> from a fear of utter hopelessness. And given the ideas which controlled policy,
> nothing could be done.
>   (Galbraith, J.K. *The Great Crash*)

6 Seasonal and casual unemployment occurs because of the nature of the
work involved.

'Full employment' (in the sense that no individual is unemployed if he
desires to work) is not possible within the framework of an unplanned
capitalist society. 'Full employment' (even in a mixed economy with a
public sector and government controls over the private sector) is a
situation when employment exists for over 97 per cent of those registered
for work. Since the Beveridge Report of 1944 (*Full Employment in a Free
Society*) the aim of British governments has been to keep unemployment
below 3 per cent of the available workforce.

> Three per cent appears as a conservative, rather than an unduly hopeful, aim to
> set for the average unemployment rate of the future under conditions of full
> employment.
>   (Lord Beveridge, *Full Employment in a Free Society*)

For a quarter of a century, from 1945 to 1970, 'full employment' (in
Beveridge's meaning: less than 3 per cent unemployed) was maintained.
In 1970, unemployment in Britain exceeded one million for the first time
since the Second World War. In October 1981 over three million were
unemployed in the UK, representing about 11 per cent of the work force.
Right-wing thinkers have argued that much higher levels of unemployment are tolerable in contemporary society in the interests of controlling
inflation.

> People should keep unemployment figures in perspective.... There is an

enormous obsession with unemployment. It is all too easy to talk oneself into a position of gloom and despondency

(Sir John Eden, Minister for Industry, 27 September 1971)

The interactionist perspective of unemployment, as seen by many unemployed persons, is that unemployment comes as a personal tragedy. In 1933, W.W. Daniel conducted for PEP (Political and Economic Planning) the first national survey of the unemployed in Britain. He found that the level of social security benefits did not compensate the unemployed for the feeling of uselessness associated with the loss of a job nor did they reduce the incentive to work. Although the unemployed are often portrayed as an enormous army of social security scroungers, Daniel found that malingering was most prevalent among managerial and professional workers and least common amongst unskilled workers. Twenty-three per cent of unemployed managerial and professional workers had no intention of finding work compared with only 8 per cent of unskilled workers.

Older managerial and professional workers enjoy advantages which enable them to avoid the sufferings inflicted upon older manual workers. Advantages enjoyed by older workers in the higher socio-economic groups include:

(a) little likelihood of being downgraded if unable to cope with the job;

(b) opportunity for early retirement;

(c) lump-sum payments;

(d) occupational pension schemes.

On approaching retirement age, managerial and professional workers are more likely to be willing to live on unemployment benefits and other personal resources. Daniel's research exposed the fallacy of the stereotype of work-shy manual workers, who are popularly supposed to make up the largest proportion of the feckless unemployed.

Unemployment is a serious *social problem* largely in relation to urban, male manual workers. The degree of hardship experienced by the unemployed is closely associated with social class; the scales are tipped heavily against manual workers. Older manual workers may be downgraded or even sacked when they become less able to perform the worktask. Their status declines from skilled to semi-skilled, and finally to unskilled. At this point they may find the job intolerable and leave of their own accord. They then join the army of unemployed and are castigated for opting out of work. For them there are no golden handshakes, no redundancy pay, no lump sums and no generous pensions. At employment exchanges they may be pressurised by civil servants intent on denying them benefits.

... when questions are asked, about 15 per cent of beneficiaries stop claiming at

Table 7.19 Proportion of unemployed having little interest in finding a job or quickly finding a new one

	un-skilled %	semi-skilled %	skilled %	supervisory %	clerical/technical %	managerial/professional %	total %
did not intend to find a job	8	11	11	21	17	23	12
thought it not important to find a job	9	8	10	10	10	19	10
job found within one month	4	8	8	4	5	3	5
total	21	27	29	35	32	45	27
(base)	(674)	(270)	(204)	(58)	(159)	(114)	(1,479)

(Daniel, W. W. *A National Survey of the Unemployed*, PEP Broadsheet, No. 546)

once. When people are asked to come in for an interview, a further 15 per cent to 20 per cent stop claiming after the first interview.

(Mr Patrick Jenkin, The Secretary of State for Social Services, answering a question in the House of Commons, 13 June 1979)

In 1977, W.W. Daniel and Elizabeth Stilgoe published a follow-up report based upon interviews with two-thirds of those who were the subject of the earlier study and whom they had been able to trace. The 1977 report analyses the situation faced by young people. Although there has been an increase in the number of young people out of work, they have been the subject of considerable aid. The government is concerned that the discontent of the young jobless should not be expressed in the form of violence and crime. The Manpower Services Commission and Job Creation Programmes have concentrated upon helping the 16-to-24 year-olds.

It is still older manual workers who suffer more from unemployment. Family men, in their thirties or forties suffer most; they fight continually to make ends meet in the face of a high rate of inflation. Their leisure activities are curtailed as their main aim is to provide the family with the basic needs of food, clothing and housing.

Further Reading

Abel-Smith, B. & Townsend, P. *The Poor and the Poorest* (G. Bell & Sons)

Allen, S. *New Minorities, Old Conflicts* (Random House)

Atkinson, A.B. *Poverty in Britain and the Reform of Social Security* (Cambridge University Press)

Becker, H. *Outsiders: Studies in the Sociology of Deviance* (Free Press)

Burney, E. *Housing on Trial* (Oxford University Press)

Butterworth, E. & Weir, D. (eds) *Social Welfare in Modern Britain* (Fontana)

Coates, K. & Silburn, R. *Poverty: The Forgotten Englishmen* (Penguin)

Cohen, A. (ed.) *Urban Ethnicity* (Tavistock)

Cohen, S. (ed.) *Images of Deviance* (Penguin)

Daniel, W.W. *Racial Discrimination in England* (Penguin)

Frankenberg, R. *Communities in Britain* (Penguin)

Goffman, E. *Asylums* (Penguin)

Goffman, E. *Stigma* (Penguin)

Jones, M. *Life on the Dole* (Davis-Poynter)

Marris, P. & Rein, M. *Dilemmas of Social Reform* (Penguin)

Marsden, D. *Mothers Alone* (Penguin)

Marsden, D. & Duff, E. *Workless* (Penguin)

Mason, P. *Race Relations* (OUP)

Merton, R.K. & Nisbet, R.A. *Contemporary Social Problems* (Harcourt Brace)

Montagu, A. *Statement on Race* (OUP)

Pahl, R.E. *Whose City?* (Penguin)

Pahl, R.E. *Patterns of Urban Life* (Longman)

Rex, J. & Moore, R. *Race, Community and Conflict* (OUP)

Rose, A.M. (ed.) *Human Behaviour and Social Processes* (Routledge & Kegan Paul)

Runciman, W.G. *Relative Deprivation and Social Justice* (Penguin)

Rutter, M. & Madge, N. *Cycles of Disadvantage* (Heinemann)

Stengel, E. *Suicide and Attempted Suicide* (Penguin)

Townsend, P. *The Concept of Poverty* (Heinemann)

Townsend, P. *Sociology and Social Policy* (Penguin)

Tunstall, J. *Old and Alone* (Routledge & Kegan Paul)

West, D.J. *The Young Offender* (Penguin)

Willmott, P. *Adolescent Boys of East London* (Penguin)

Worsley, P. (ed.) *Problems of Modern Society* (Penguin)

Young, J. *The Drugtakers* (Paladin)

Index

reality: classroom, 194–7; definition of, 34–5, 195, 196, 390; social, 23–4, 195, 196
Registrar-General's social class scale, 90, 91–2, 96, 103, 270
Reimer, Everett, 239, 241
religion: as control, 376–7; decline, 377–83; functions, 376; and politics, 364; strength, 383–5; and suicide, 17–18, 440
residential care, 407, 410–13
Resler, Henrietta, 112–13
restrictive practices, 309
retirement, 409, 410
revolution, 53
Rex, John, 28, 420, 426–30
Robbins Report (1963), 233
role, 13–15; ascribed, 261; conflicts, 14; and definition, 34–5; inequality, 316; pairs, 14; performance, 14–15; selection, 81–2; taking, 14
Rose, Arnold M., 345
Rosenfeld, Eva, 83
Rosser, C., 137
roughs, the, 99–100
Rowntree, Seebohm, 8, 392, 393, 396–9
rules, social, 366, 371, 372
Rutter, Michael, 236, 399

Sacks, Harvey, 37
salariat, 97–8
sampling, 66–7
savings, 112
Schofield, M., 60
schools: alternatives to, 239–43; community, 215–19; organisation, 197–209; private, 189, 191–2, 215, 342, 354–5; see also education
Schumpeter, J.A., 347–8
science, criteria of, 16
Scott, C.P., 251
secondary data sources, 67–8, 69
secondary school achievement, 230–6
sects, religious, 381, 384
secularisation, 377–83, 384
Seebohm Committee, 218, 431

self, components, 34
self-fulfilling prophecies, 1, 6, 99
service class, 123
service economy, 273, 275
sex ratio, 171–3
shareholders, power, 288, 290–1, 341
Sharpe, R., 207, 208
Shaw, George Bernard, 137–8
Shaw, Jack, 407
Sheldon, J.H., 407
sheltered housing, 413
shop-stewards, 307, 311–12
Simon, B., 214, 233
Simon, Herbert, A., 292
single-parent families, 166–7
situation, definition, 34–5, 195, 196, 390
slavery, 74–5
slums: and crime, 437; culture of, 400–2; and education, 221–4, 233
Smelser, Neil, 81
Smith, Dennis, 208–9
smoking, 398, 442
social class, see class
Social Democratic Party, 356, 359, 360
socialisation, 9–10, 46, 366; and the family, 142, 143, 151–2, 188; political, 353–5
social mobility, see mobility, social
social order, see order, social
Social Trends, 62–3
social workers, 431
society: as social system, 148–9, 189; whole, 4, 5, 27
sociology: controversy in, 1–2; related subjects, 39–55; as science, 16–23; and social worker, 430–1
solidarity, 266–8
sources, data, 67–8, 69
Spencer, Herbert, 4, 27, 189
Spens Report (1938), 211
Stacey, Margaret, 67, 99
Stalker, G., 352
statistics, 62–6, 68, 439; population, 167–86
status, 13, 15, 76, 82, 90; groups, 191